DEMOCRACY
IN INDONESIA

The **ANU Indonesia Project**, a leading international centre of research and graduate training on the Indonesian economy and society, is housed in the **Arndt-Corden Department of Economics, Crawford School of Public Policy, ANU College of Asia and the Pacific** at the **Australian National University (ANU)**. Established in 1965 in response to profound changes in the Indonesian economic and political landscapes, the ANU Indonesia Project has grown from a small group of Indonesia-focused economists into an interdisciplinary research centre well known and respected across the world. Funded by ANU and the Australian Government Department of Foreign Affairs and Trade, the ANU Indonesia Project monitors and analyses recent developments in Indonesia; informs the Australian and Indonesian governments, business and the wider community about those developments and about future prospects; stimulates research on the Indonesian economy; and publishes the respected *Bulletin of Indonesian Economic Studies*.

ANU College of Asia and the Pacific's **Department of Political and Social Change** focuses on domestic politics, social processes and state–society relationships in Asia and the Pacific, and has a long-established interest in Indonesia.

Together with the Department of Political and Social Change, the ANU Indonesia Project holds the annual Indonesia Update conference, which offers an overview of recent economic and political developments and devotes attention to a significant theme in Indonesia's development. The *Bulletin of Indonesian Economic Studies* publishes the conference's economic and political overviews, while the edited papers related to the conference theme are published in the Indonesia Update Series.

The **ISEAS – Yusof Ishak Institute** (formerly Institute of Southeast Asian Studies) is an autonomous organisation established in 1968. It is a regional centre dedicated to the study of sociopolitical, security, and economic trends and developments in Southeast Asia and its wider geostrategic and economic environment. The Institute's research programs are grouped under Regional Economic Studies (RES), Regional Strategic and Political Studies (RSPS), and Regional Social and Cultural Studies (RSCS). The Institute is also home to the ASEAN Studies Centre (ASC), the Singapore APEC Study Centre, and the Temasek History Research Centre (THRC).

ISEAS Publishing, an established academic press, has issued more than 2,000 books and journals. It is the largest scholarly publisher of research about Southeast Asia from within the region. ISEAS Publishing works with many other academic and trade publishers and distributors to disseminate important research and analyses from and about Southeast Asia to the rest of the world.

Indonesia Update Series

DEMOCRACY IN INDONESIA

FROM STAGNATION TO REGRESSION?

EDITED BY

THOMAS POWER
EVE WARBURTON

ISEAS YUSOF ISHAK
INSTITUTE

First published in Singapore in 2020 by
ISEAS Publishing
30 Heng Mui Keng Terrace
Singapore 119614

E-mail: publish@iseas.edu.sg
Website: http://bookshop.iseas.edu.sg

ISEAS Library Cataloguing-in-Publication Data

Names: Power, Thomas, editor. | Warburton, Eve, editor.
Title: Democracy in Indonesia: from stagnation to regression? / edited by
  Thomas Power and Eve Warburton.
Description: Singapore : ISEAS – Yusof Ishak Institute, 2020. | Series: Indonesia
  Update Series | '... an outcome of the Indonesia Update Conference held in
  Canberra on 6–7 September 2019' | Includes bibliographical references.
Identifiers: ISBN 9789814881500 (softcover) | ISBN 9789814881517 (hardcover)
  | ISBN 9789814881524 (PDF) | ISBN 9789814881531 (ePub)
Subjects: LCSH: Democracy—Indonesia. | Indonesia—Politics and government.
Classification: DS644.4 I41 2020

Cover photo: Supporters of presidential candidate Prabowo Subianto protest outside the Constitutional Court during its confirmation of Joko Widodo's election victory, 21 August 2014. Photo by Ray Yen.

Edited and typeset by Tracy Harwood and Beth Thomson, Canberra
Indexed by Angela Grant, Sydney

Contents

PART 3 POPULAR SUPPORT FOR DEMOCRACY

PART 4 DEMOCRATIC INSTITUTIONS

PART 5 LAW, SECURITY AND DISORDER

Tables and figures

Tables

Figures

Contributors

Puspa Delima Amri, Assistant Professor of Economics, Sonoma State University, Rohnert Park, California

Diego Fossati, Assistant Professor of Asian and International Studies, City University of Hong Kong

Liam Gammon, PhD candidate, Department of Political and Social Change, College of Asia and the Pacific, Australian National University, Canberra

S.P. Harish, Assistant Professor of Political Science, William & Mary, Williamsburg, Virginia

Allen Hicken, Professor of Political Science, University of Michigan, Ann Arbor

Sana Jaffrey, Postdoctoral Fellow, Asia Research Institute, National University of Singapore

Dyah Ayu Kartika, Researcher, Center for the Study of Religion and Democracy (Pusat Studi Agama dan Demokrasi, PUSAD), Paramadina, Jakarta

Ferran Martinez i Coma, Senior Lecturer, School of Government and International Relations, Griffith University, Brisbane

Marcus Mietzner, Associate Professor, Department of Political and Social Change, College of Asia and the Pacific, Australian National University, Canberra

Abdil Mughis Mudhoffir, Lecturer, Department of Sociology, State University of Jakarta; and Postdoctoral Visitor, Asia Institute, University of Melbourne

Burhanuddin Muhtadi, Senior Lecturer in Political Science, Faculty of Social and Political Sciences, Syarif Hidayatullah State Islamic University, Jakarta; Executive Director, Indikator Politik Indonesia, Jakarta; and Director of Public Affairs, Lembaga Survei Indonesia

Siswo Mulyartono, Researcher, Center for the Study of Religion and Democracy (Pusat Studi Agama dan Demokrasi, PUSAD), Paramadina, Jakarta

Nava Nuraniyah, Analyst, Institute for Policy Analysis of Conflict, Jakarta

Mochamad Pasha, Economist, The World Bank, Jakarta

Thomas Power, Lecturer, Department of Indonesian Studies, School of Languages and Cultures, University of Sydney

Irsyad Rafsadie, Researcher, Center for the Study of Religion and Democracy (Pusat Studi Agama dan Demokrasi, PUSAD), Paramadina, Jakarta

Ken M.P. Setiawan, Lecturer, Asian and Indonesian Studies, Asia Institute, University of Melbourne; and Associate, Centre for Indonesian Law, Islam and Society, Melbourne Law School

Dan Slater, Director, Weiser Center for Emerging Democracies (WCED), Department of Political Science, University of Michigan, Ann Arbor

Ross Tapsell, Senior Lecturer, Department of Gender, Media and Culture, College of Asia and the Pacific, Australian National University, Canberra

Risa Toha, Assistant Professor of Political Science, Yale-National University of Singapore

Eve Warburton, Postdoctoral Fellow, Asia Research Institute, National University of Singapore

Foreword
Is Indonesian democracy in decline?

Verily, along with every hardship is relief
Qur'an 94:6

There is a growing consensus among scholars that Indonesia's democracy is in decline, although, in fairness, many new and established democracies around the world are suffering the same fate. I am not going to challenge the consensus. Democracy in Indonesia is indeed declining.

The Australian National University appropriately picked democracy as the main theme for its Indonesia Update conference in September 2019. Since Indonesia had just held a general election in April, it was important to reflect on how far the country had come in its march to democracy these past two decades. These were the fifth democratic, free and fair legislative elections in post-Suharto Indonesia, and the fourth direct presidential election, and were widely recognised as remarkable achievements for a nation with a large and diverse population. Indonesia shines when compared to many of its neighbours, including Thailand and the Philippines.

But is Indonesia's democracy following the same path taken by many other democracies in Southeast Asia and beyond? The next few years will tell.

I did have some reservations to the title of the Indonesia Update 2019 'From stagnation to regression? Indonesian democracy after twenty years' and I made my feeling known in an opinion article I wrote for the *Jakarta Post* in July. Based on my own reading, the title suggested there was only one other possible course for Indonesia's democracy, besides stagnation: regression. Although the title is framed as a question, it stills portrays a bleak future and allows little, if any, possibility for democracy in Indonesia to go in the other direction: progression. This may be true and indeed many analyses, some of which were highlighted in this conference, suggest things are likely to get worse.

The optimist in me, however, refuses to believe that this is the case. As a journalist who has reported and written about Indonesia's political development over the past 36 years, I cannot accept that this backsliding of democracy is irreversible. Over the course of time, going back to the last decade of the Suharto years, I have seen many setbacks to democracy; but the overall trajectory has always been to move forward.

Like the one-time popular Indonesian poco-poco dance, democracy has been a case of two steps forward and one step back. Looking at the situation today, someone may have improvised the dance and forced democracy to take five huge steps back. But as long as we keep on dancing, we shall recover. I certainly hope so.

Underlining my optimism is not just my own bias. The majority of Indonesians have strong faith in democracy. They showed this when they thronged the polling stations in April. The turnout surpassed everyone's expectation: more than 81 per cent of the 193 million registered voters cast their ballots for the presidential and legislative elections. Relative to other countries with non-compulsory voting, electoral turnout is remarkably high in Indonesia.

More than reflecting that electoral democracy is functioning, this is testament to the faith that many Indonesians put in their democracy. There are many reasons to explain why the turnout was high, and enthusiasm is one of them. I saw this first hand when I volunteered to run the polling station in my neighbourhood. Voters came in the belief their votes mattered in determining Indonesia's future.

Two huge protests in September 2019 further highlighted this participatory democracy. Demonstrators opposed the House of Representatives decision to rush through a new law that weakens the Corruption Eradication Commission (Komisi Pemberantasan Korupsi, KPK), and its plans to pass a new more draconian Penal Code. People not only vote for their leaders and representatives during elections, but people will also protest from time to time when they feel the need. The protests suggested that people's participation in democracy remains high even between elections.

Indonesia certainly needs to move from being just an electoral democracy to a full-fledged one with stronger guarantees for various freedoms and basic rights. Democracy remains a work in progress, as it has been and will always be.

The problems facing Indonesia's democracy are immense and many of these were thoroughly explored and discussed at the Indonesia Update. The excellent papers from various scholars are published in this volume.

Topics include the growing polarisation of society; the rise of Islamism, vigilantism and violence; and the faith people have in democracy. Some speakers highlighted bright spots as well as solutions, raising hopes that the current decline is not irreversible.

Allow me to comment on some of the topics raised, drawing from my observations as a journalist rather than from studies or surveys.

On polarisation, most elections by definition have that impact and this is even more so in a two-party electoral system, or in the two-horse presidential races Indonesia experienced in 2014 and 2019. In both elections, the former furniture salesman Joko Widodo ran against former army general Prabowo Subianto—polarisation became more pronounced in the last election. Both camps used social media effectively, with their supporters weaponising fake news, to make the divide even deeper. The results of the two elections showed how the nation has become divided almost down the middle, with splits of 53/47 in 2014 and 56/44 in 2019, both times in Widodo's favour.

It remains to be seen whether this polarisation will be a permanent feature of the political landscape. Much depends on who will run in the 2024 presidential race, and how many candidates are contesting. We can take cue that there was little polarisation in 2004 and 2009 when the presidential races involved five and three candidates, respectively.

Much has been said about the inroads Islamism—defined here as the aspirations to turn Indonesia into an Islamic state, and/or to see Indonesia embrace the sharia as the law of the land—is making, but I don't see this moving any further. Indonesia is nowhere near becoming an Islamic state.

I believe election results are still the best indication of how much or how little support Islamism enjoys. The political parties with an Islamic identity—the Prosperous Justice Party (Partai Keadilan Sejahtera, PKS), the United Development Party (Partai Persatuan Pembangunan, PPP) and to a lesser extent the National Mandate Party (Partai Amanat Nasional, PAN) and the Crescent Moon and Star Party (Partai Bulan Bintang, PBB)—together polled just over 20 per cent of the total votes in April. This is a decline from the 22 per cent they won in 2014.

This low figure has been consistent throughout all five post-Suharto elections. There is always a segment of voters, around one-fifth, who cast their ballots for Islamic parties, that in post-Suharto Indonesia are free to contest on this platform. These parties try to capture, in part, the votes of Muslims with Islamist aspirations and win representation in the House and even in the coalition government. But they remain a minority. The majority of Indonesian voters, including the majority of Muslims, give their vote to the pluralist parties, and in 2019 the three top winners were the Indonesian Democratic Party of Struggle (Partai Demokrasi Indonesia-Perjuangan, PDI-P), Gerindra and Golkar.

The fear of Islamism has been compounded by the rise of radicalism (including vigilantism in the name of Islam). But arguably more concerning is the rise of conservatism, which is not the same as radicalism. Following the global trend, Indonesian society has become more conservative. The sharia by-laws now in place in some provinces and districts, and the more strict Islamic codes in the draft Penal Code, are proposed not just by Islamist parties, but by the more conservative politicians within pluralist parties.

There is an ongoing culture war in Indonesia that seems to have escaped the analyses of Indonesianists more focused on Islamism and radicalism. The religious conservatives, present in almost every political party and in Widodo's government, are advancing their agenda with little pushback from the more progressive and liberal segments of society.

While we are concerned about the rise of religious radicalism, our failure to distinguish it from the rise of conservatism could lead to wrong conclusions and wrong policy prescriptions. Framing Indonesia in terms of the emerging conservative/liberal divide could be an alternative to the old *santri-abangan* divide.

Radicalism and vigilantism are issues for the police to deal with, and there is a huge problem in the capability of Indonesia's law enforcement agency, which partly explains the declining quality of democracy. But how do you stop the rise of conservatism, which also undermines democracy? This is something that the liberal and progressive segments of the political spectrum have to answer, not the government or the police.

By international standards, Indonesia today remains an illiberal democracy. The discussions at the Indonesia Update, and the papers presented in this volume, are food for thought, not just for scholars and Indonesianists, but also for decision-makers about how to strengthen, or at least sustain, democracy. The 2019 general election has given Indonesia another five-year lease for democracy. Whether it regresses or progresses ultimately depends on the people, and if they have faith in democracy as they showed in April, they should participate to ensure its continuation and success.

Endy Bayuni
June 2020

Acknowledgments

The majority of contributions to this volume, with the exception of those by Marcus Mietzner, Ross Tapsell and Thomas Power, were developed out of papers presented at the 37th annual Indonesia Update conference, held at the Australian National University (ANU), Canberra, on 6–7 September 2019.

At each of the annual ANU Indonesia Updates since 2014, authors of the political update papers expressed growing concern about the downhill trajectory of Indonesia's democracy. The 2019 Update took stock of this trend by posing a question: had Indonesian democracy shifted from a state of *stagnation*, as proposed at the same venue five years previously, to one of *regression*? The excellent array of papers presented by the contributors to this book revealed an overwhelming, and profoundly troubling, answer.

We wish to express our thanks to each of the authors represented in this volume for being part of this endeavour. Not only did the contributors travel to Canberra to share their expert analyses, but in the months that followed they gave much of their time to our editorial process. The result is, we believe, an important and comprehensive evaluation of Indonesia's democratic decline at the outset of President Joko Widodo's second term.

We are immensely grateful to the organiser and host of the Indonesia Update, the ANU Indonesia Project, and to all the people who made the conference possible in 2019. As director of the Indonesia Project, Blane Lewis was a constant source of support throughout—from the initial planning and preparation of the conference to the subsequent editorial process. We are also thankful to the staff at the Indonesia Project who worked tirelessly to ensure a successful event. Special thanks go to Nurkemala Muliani, Lydia Napitupulu, Olivia Cable and Kate McLinton. As is the case every year, the 2019 Update relied on the effort and dedication of a large team of volunteers, too numerous to list individually, but invaluable in guaranteeing the smooth running of the conference.

We also wish to express our gratitude to the Australian Government Department of Foreign Affairs and Trade, whose ongoing support for the Indonesia Project ensures that the ANU remains a leading centre for independent and cutting-edge research on Indonesia's politics, economy and society. This support made both our conference and this volume possible.

At the ANU we wish to thank the director of the Coral Bell School of Asia Pacific Affairs, Professor Toni Erskine, as well as Professor Michael Wesley, former dean of the College of Asia and the Pacific, who launched the conference with thoughtful and generous opening remarks. We want to also acknowledge the support of the Department of Political and Social Change (PSC), headed by Paul Kenny, for its longstanding and vital contribution to the Update. Within PSC, we extend particular thanks to Edward Aspinall, Marcus Mietzner and Greg Fealy for their support and guidance throughout the conference and editorial process.

The 2019 Update was followed with two additional events ('mini updates'), at the Lowy Institute in Sydney and at the Griffith Asia Institute, Griffith University, Brisbane. Our particular thanks to Ben Bland at the Lowy Institute, and Ian Hall and Carrie Zhang at the Griffith Asia Institute, for putting together these opportunities for cross-institutional collaboration.

Finally, we have had the good fortune to work with two outstanding editors, Tracy Harwood and Beth Thomson. Their fine editorial work and immeasurable patience were critical to the success of the volume, and for that we are profoundly grateful. We also wish to thank the ISEAS – Yusof Ishak Institute in Singapore, which has been publishing the Indonesia Update series since 1994. In particular, we extend our thanks to Ng Kok Kiong and Rahilah Yusuf for ensuring a smooth publication process in the midst of the 2020 COVID-19 lockdown. We also thank Angela Grant for preparing the index.

Thomas Power and Eve Warburton
June 2020

Glossary

212 movement	union of hardline Islamic groups named for the date of an anti-Ahok rally on 2 December 2016
abangan	nominal Javanese Muslim whose syncretic beliefs include mystical animist, Hindu and Buddhist elements (or the outlook of this group)
ABRI	Angkatan Bersenjata Republik Indonesia (Armed Forces of the Republic of Indonesia)
AGO	Kejaksaan Agung (Attorney General's Office)
Ahmadiyah	Islamic sect (seen as unorthodox by some Indonesian Islamic groups) whose members venerate the teachings of Mirza Ghulam Ahmad
Ahok	Basuki Tjahaja Purnama (former governor of Jakarta)
AJI	Aliansi Jurnalis Independen (Alliance of Independent Journalists)
Aksi Bela Islam	Defence of Islam movement
Ansor	the young men's branch of Nahdlatul Ulama
Apindo	Asosiasi Pengusaha Indonesia (Indonesian Employers Association)
Banser	Barisan Ansor Serbaguna (Ansor Multipurpose Front; paramilitary youth wing of Nahdlatul Ulama)
Bappenas	Badan Perencanaan Pembangunan Nasional (National Development Planning Agency)
Bawaslu	Badan Pengawas Pemilu (Elections Supervisory Agency)
Bhinneka Tunggal Ika	'Unity in Diversity', the official national motto of Indonesia
BIN	Badan Intelijen Negara (State Intelligence Agency)
BNPT	Badan Nasional Penanggulangan Terrorisme (National Counterterrorism Agency)
BPIP	Badan Pembinaan Ideologi Pancasila (Pancasila Ideology Development Agency)

BPK	Badan Pemeriksa Keuangan (National Audit Agency)
BPS	Badan Pusat Statistik (Statistics Indonesia)
bupati	head of a *kabupaten* (district)
COVID-19	coronavirus disease 2019
DPRD	Dewan Perwakilan Rakyat Daerah (regional parliament)
fatwa	religious ruling; pronouncement by a recognised Islamic religious authority
FPI	Front Pembela Islam (Islamic Defenders Front)
FUI	Forum Umat Islam (Forum of the Islamic Community)
FUIB	Forum Umat Islam Bersatu (United Muslims Forum)
Gafatar	Gerakan Fajar Nusantara
GDP	gross domestic product
Gerindra	Gerakan Indonesia Raya (Greater Indonesia Movement)
GITA	Gerakan Kita Indonesia (Our Indonesia Movement)
GNPF MUI	Gerakan Nasional Pembela Fatwa MUI (National Movement to Guard the Fatwa of the MUI)
GNPFU	Gerakan Nasional Pengawal Fatwa Ulama (National Movement to Guard the Fatwa of Ulama)
Golkar	Golongan Karya (the state political party under the New Order, and a major post–New Order party)
Hanura	Partai Hati Nurani Rakyat (People's Conscience Party)
haram	forbidden, unclean (to Muslims)
HTI	Hizbut Tahrir Indonesia (Indonesian Liberation Party)
IDI	Indonesia Democracy Index
Indikator	Indikator Politik Indonesia, an independent public opinion research institute
INDO-DAPOER	Indonesia Database for Policy and Economic Research
ISIS	Islamic State in Iraq and Syria
Islam Nusantara	Archipelagic Islam
ISOMIL	International Summit of Moderate Muslim Leaders
ITE Law	Law No. 11/2008 on Electronic Information and Transactions
Jokowi	(President) Joko Widodo
Kadin	Kamar Dagang dan Industri (Chamber of Commerce and Industry)
kafir	infidel
Kemdagri	Kementerian Dalam Negeri (Ministry of Home Affairs)

kemerdekaan	independence
Kemkumham	Kementerian Hukum dan Hak Asasi Manusia (Ministry of Justice and Human Rights)
kiai	religious scholar or leader
KMP	Koalisi Merah Putih (Red and White Coalition)
KPK	Komisi Pemberantasan Korupsi (Corruption Eradication Commission)
KPU	Komisi Pemilihan Umum (General Elections Commission)
LBH	Lembaga Bantuan Hukum (Legal Aid Foundation)
LGBT	lesbian, gay, bisexual and transgender
LKPP	Laporan Keuangan Pemerintah Pusat (Central Government Financial Report)
LSI	Lembaga Survei Indonesia (Indonesian Survey Institute)
MD3 law	Law No. 27/2009 on Legislative Institutions
MK	Mahkamah Konstitusi (Constitutional Court)
MPR	Majelis Permusyawaratan Rakyat (People's Consultative Assembly)
Muhammadiyah	modernist Islamic organisation founded in 1912
MUI	Majelis Ulama Indonesia (Indonesian Council of Islamic Scholars)
muktamar	national congress of Nahdlatul Ulama, held every five years
Muslimat NU	Nahdlatul Ulama women's organisation, founded in 1946
nahdliyin	Nahdlatul Ulama members
NasDem	Partai Nasional Demokrat (National Democratic Party)
New Order	political regime under President Suharto, 1966–1998
NKRI	Negara Kesatuan Republik Indonesia (Unitary Republic of Indonesia)
NU	Nahdlatul Ulama (traditionalist Islamic organisation founded in 1926)
NVMS	National Violence Monitoring System (World Bank dataset of communal violence in Indonesia from 1997 to 2014)
OPEC	Organization of the Petroleum Exporting Countries
ormas	organisasi massa (mass organisation)
PAN	Partai Amanat Nasional (National Mandate Party)
Pancasila	the five guiding principles of the Indonesian state: belief in God, humanitarianism, nationalism, democracy and social justice; or, in another formulation: belief in one supreme God, just and civilised humanity, national unity, democracy led

	by wisdom and prudence through consultation and representation, and social justice
PBB	Partai Bulan Bintang (Crescent Moon and Star Party)
PD	Partai Demokrat (Democratic Party)
PDI	Partai Demokrasi Indonesia (Indonesian Democratic Party)
PDI-P	Partai Demokrasi Indonesia-Perjuangan (Indonesian Democratic Party of Struggle)
penetapan	confirmation
perda	*peraturan daerah* (regional government regulation)
Perindo	Partai Persatuan Indonesia (Indonesian Unity Party)
perjuangan	struggle
Perppu Ormas	Regulation in Lieu of Law (Peraturan Pemerintah Pengganti Undang Undang, Perppu) on Societal Organisations
pesantren	Islamic boarding school
pilkada	local elections
PK	Partai Keadilan (Justice Party)
PKB	Partai Kebangkitan Bangsa (National Awakening Party)
PKI	Partai Komunis Indonesia (Indonesian Communist Party)
PKPI	Partai Keadilan dan Persatuan Indonesia (Indonesian Justice and Unity Party)
PKPNU	Pendidikan Kader Penggerak NU (Nahdlatul Ulama Activist Cadre Training)
PKS	Partai Keadilan Sejahtera (Prosperous Justice Party)
PLN	Perusahaan Listrik Negara (the state electricity company)
PNI	Partai Nasional Indonesia (Indonesian National Party)
Polri	Polisi Republik Indonesia (Indonesian National Police)
PPP	Partai Persatuan Pembangunan (United Development Party)
PSI	Partai Solidaritas Indonesia (Indonesian Solidarity Party)
PTIK	Perguruan Tinggi Ilmu Kepolisian (Police Higher Education Institute)
rakyat	the common people
reformasi	'reform'; name for the post-Suharto period (since 1998)
SAFEnet	Southeast Asia Freedom of Expression Network
santri	devout Muslim students in Javanese society (or the outlook of these students)

Sat Binmas	Satuan Pembinaan Masyarakat (Community Guidance Unit)
Susenas	Survei Sosio-Ekonomi Nasional (National Socioeconomic Survey)
TNI	Tentara Nasional Indonesia (Indonesian National Army)
TVRI	Televisi Republik Indonesia; state-owned, public broadcasting television network
UGM	Universitas Gadjah Mada (Gadjah Mada University)
UKSW	Universitas Kristen Satya Wacana (Satya Wacana Christian University)
ulama	Islamic scholar
ummah	the Islamic community
UNDP	United Nations Development Programme
V-Dem	Varieties of Democracy

© Australian National University
Base map CAP 12-215a

INDONESIA

THAILAND
CAMBODIA
VIETNAM

PHILIPPINES

PACIFIC
OCEAN

South China Sea

MALAYSIA

BRUNEI

SINGAPORE

Riau Is.

Aceh

North
Sumatra

Riau

West
Sumatra

Jambi

South
Sumatra

Bengkulu

Lampung

Banka
Belitung

Banten

West
Java

Jakarta

Central
Java

Yogyakarta

East
Java

Bali

West Kalimantan

Central
Kalimantan

South
Kalimantan

East
Kalimantan

North
Kalimantan

Celebes Sea

North
Sulawesi

Gorontalo

Central
Sulawesi

West
Sulawesi

South
Sulawesi

South East
Sulawesi

North
Sulawesi

North
Maluku

Maluku

West Papua

Papua

West Nusa
Tenggara

East Nusa
Tenggara

TIMOR LESTE

Java Sea

Banda Sea

Arafura Sea

Timor
Sea

INDIAN
OCEAN

AUSTRALIA

International boundary
Province boundary
Jakarta Province name

kilometres

0   1000

10°N
0°
10°S

100°E
120°E
140°E

1   The decline of Indonesian democracy

Thomas Power and Eve Warburton

Indonesia should feature prominently in any global account of democratisation. In a few heady years after the 1998 collapse of Suharto's autocratic New Order, Indonesia was transformed from one of the world's last and largest bulwarks of Cold War authoritarianism into one of Asia's most vibrant democracies. The details of this transition are well known, but bear repeating: the withdrawal of the armed forces from politics; the liberalisation of the party system; free and competitive elections; the proliferation of independent media; legal and judicial reform; expanded space for civil society; and a vast decentralisation program that devolved political power to elected local leaders. These achievements were yet more remarkable given they took place in an ethnically and religiously diverse country struggling to recover from the ravages of the Asian financial crisis. During this time, Indonesia appeared a democratic outlier (Carothers 2009; Diamond 2008; Lussier 2016): a rare case of successful transition and consolidation, not only within Southeast Asia, but globally amid the ebbing of democracy's third wave (Huntington 1991) and the onset of the democratic recession (Diamond 2015; cf. Levitsky and Way 2015).

Yet two decades after the landmark elections of 1999, a different—and far more pessimistic—scholarly consensus is taking shape. Where political analysts once lauded Indonesia as a beacon of democracy in a troubled region, most now agree that its democracy is in decline (Aspinall and Mietzner 2019; Diprose et al. 2019; Hadiz 2017). Recent studies have drawn attention to deterioration across an array of indicators: populist mobilisations, growing intolerance and deepening sectarianism (Mietzner et al. 2018; Warburton and Aspinall 2019); increasingly dysfunctional electoral and representative institutions (Aspinall and Sukmajati 2016; Muhtadi 2019); the deterioration of civil liberties (Marta et al. 2019); and the executive's expansion of an authoritarian toolkit for suppressing opposition and curtailing criticism (Mietzner 2019; Power 2018).

In the early months of 2020, as we finalised this volume for publication, the COVID-19 pandemic was sweeping into Indonesia's population centres. The central government was struggling to contain the virus, the death toll was rising, and the administration's instructions on lockdowns and social distancing were being poorly articulated and unevenly implemented. The government proved far more proactive and capable, however, in clamping down on criticism of its response to the pandemic. In April, the national police issued a regulation instructing officers to arrest and charge citizens who 'insulted' the president or other government officials in relation to COVID-19. Police harassment and arrests of ordinary citizens, activists and opposition figures then became a prominent and disturbing feature of the Jokowi's government's pandemic response.

For example, a prominent government critic, Said Didu, was threatened with criminal charges after criticising the administration for prioritising the economy over public welfare amid the pandemic. This followed the arrest of a university student activist for a Facebook post that made similar criticisms of Jokowi's policy priorities (Nashr 2020). Ravio Patra, an activist and health policy researcher who penned an article detailing the shortcomings of the government's pandemic response, was arrested for attempting to incite riots through dubious private messages sent from one of his social media accounts. It soon emerged that his account had been hijacked, prior to the dissemination of these messages, using a phone number apparently belonging to a police officer. As of early May, more than 100 Indonesians had been arrested for spreading what authorities deemed 'hate speech' or 'misinformation' relating to COVID-19.

These arrests were not just a symptom of crisis politics; rather, they fit a broader trend of growing state intolerance towards dissent. During the first term in office of President Joko Widodo (Jokowi), defamation laws were used with increasing regularity by ordinary citizens, politicians and officials to silence and punish their detractors (see Chapter 13 by Ken Setiawan). At the start of Jokowi's second term, legislators and government elites sought even more restrictions on personal and political rights. Proposed revisions to the Criminal Code, for example, were set to impose hefty penalties for 'insulting' the president, incumbent government and state institutions, while also outlawing extramarital sex, cohabitation and most means of abortion. Although parliamentary deliberations on the controversial laws were delayed following mass demonstrations in September 2019, they were back on the table five months later amid a deepening health crisis and looming economic recession. As in other declining and fragile democracies, COVID-19 provided the Indonesian government with an opportunity to pursue its illiberal policy agenda without fear of renewed opposition mobilisation.

What explains Indonesia's democratic regression? Which areas of democratic life are most affected? Where are the sources of democratic persistence and resilience? And how does Indonesia's experience compare with other countries in the context of a global democratic recession? This volume sets out to address these questions, and to provide a comprehensive and wide-ranging analysis of the health of Indonesian democracy.

In this introductory chapter, we map the contours of Indonesia's democratic decline and introduce the major themes and arguments put forward by each contributing author. We begin with a brief history of political developments since the end of the Suharto era. Here we trace the evolution of scholarly discourse, from cautious praise for Indonesia's dynamic—if imperfect—democratisation in the early and mid-2000s; to a growing emphasis on stalled reform and democratic stagnation in the late Yudhoyono years; to the present focus on democratic deterioration under Jokowi.

Section two revisits longstanding problems that have plagued Indonesian democracy throughout the post–New Order period, including the institutional and social legacies of authoritarian rule, entrenched political and material inequality, and weak rule of law and endemic corruption. All of these structural challenges have made democratic deepening difficult in Indonesia, and left it vulnerable to renewed illiberal threats.

The third and fourth sections of this chapter then turn to identify and assess the most proximate threats to Indonesia's democracy. Here we distinguish between those that emanate 'from above', in the form of anti-democratic actors within the political elite and formal state institutions, and those threats that come from 'from below', manifested in illiberal social movements and grassroots support for chauvinist or authoritarian agendas. Alarmingly, Indonesian democracy is beset from both directions, with few compelling advocates for liberal democracy able to check the current process of decline. We close by outlining the structure of the rest of the book.

FROM STAGNATION TO REGRESSION

Indonesia's sustained period of democratic reform and stability in the decade following the collapse of the New Order was surprising for students of comparative democratisation. As Diamond (2010: 25–7) notes, Indonesia's relatively low-income status, its high levels of corruption, its experiences of ethnic and separatist violence, and the polarisation and political instability around the turn of the century echoed patterns common to many of the 'the troubled and failed democracies of the third wave'. Yet despite these challenges, comparative indices showed substantial progress through Indonesia's first democratic decade across various measures, including political rights and participation, freedom of expression and organisation, and government accountability and effectiveness (Freedom House 2009).

If these comparative analyses tended to emphasise the success of Indonesian democratisation, studies produced by close observers of Indonesian politics were more mixed in tone. Though some praised Indonesia's post-authoritarian reform and forecast continued democratic consolidation through the 2010s (Liddle and Mujani 2013; MacIntyre and Ramage 2008: 53), many emphasised the shortcomings of its new democracy, drawing particular attention to the problems of corruption and 'money politics', a weak rule of law and the retention of patrimonial power structures (Aspinall 2010; Bhakti 2004; Dwipayana 2009; Indrayana 2008; Mietzner 2009; Webber 2006). One influential interpretation of Indonesian democratisation held that post-Suharto power structures remained beholden to an oligarchic class that had emerged under the New Order (Robison and Hadiz 2004; Winters 2011). Yet although these analyses disagreed as to the quality of Indonesia's new democracy, they concurred in one important regard: all conceded that the *direction* of post–New Order change was towards relatively more open and competitive politics.

By the time of Yudhoyono's 2009 re-election, the dominant paradigm in political analysis had started to shift. As reforms stalled through the latter part of the 2000s, a growing number of observers argued that Indonesian democracy had entered a period of stagnation. As one scholar put it, the waning of reform cemented Indonesia's status as a 'reasonably stable yet low-quality democracy' (Tomsa 2010: 309). Then, during Yudhoyono's second term, some leading analysts pointed to warning signs of democratic regression led by a broad coalition of forces within the political elite (Fealy 2011; Mietzner 2012). In one indication of this gathering trend, 2013 saw Indonesia slip from a Freedom House ranking of 'free'—which it had held since 2005—to 'partly free' after the introduction of new restrictions on civil society organisations (Freedom House 2014). Although Yudhoyono preserved Indonesian democracy during his decade in power, his legacy was tarnished by his unwillingness to challenge emerging anti-democratic forces and his failure to consolidate important institutional gains (Aspinall et al. 2015).

The threat posed by these anti-democratic forces was embodied in the 2014 presidential bid of ex-general Prabowo Subianto, Suharto's one-time son-in-law. Prabowo's campaign, built on ultranationalist and neo-authoritarian rhetoric, brought Indonesia dangerously close to the kind of illiberal populist rule that threatens democratic norms and institutions in countries like Brazil, the Philippines and the United States. When Jokowi prevailed in that election—albeit by a relatively narrow margin— it was to the immense relief of Indonesia's reformist constituency and most academic observers. Aspinall and Mietzner (2019: 306), for example, argued that the 'survival of the country's democracy was at stake' in 2014. Though it is not clear that a majority of Indonesian voters viewed their electoral choice in such stark terms (Gammon and Berger 2014), the anti-democratic machinations of Prabowo's supporters in the aftermath of Jokowi's victory reinforced the view that Indonesia had been 'saved' from a would-be autocrat (Aspinall and Mietzner 2014). In addition, the end of Yudhoyono's increasingly aloof, lame-duck second term instilled some hope for renewed democratic reform led by a new president from outside the established political elite. Thus, despite the stagnation of the Yudhoyono years and an electoral flirtation with authoritarian populism, much political analysis in the mid-2010s retained a cautiously optimistic tone about the underlying robustness of Indonesian democracy (Case 2017; Chu et al. 2016; Horowitz 2013).

Yet it is under Jokowi—no doubt the more credible democratic choice in 2014—that the tenor of analysis has shifted, once again, for the worse. Writing on Jokowi's first year in office, Muhtadi (2015) observed a president who displayed an increasingly weak commitment to the promises of clean government that he made in his campaign. The following year, Warburton (2016) presented a more negative assessment of Jokowi's democratic credentials, casting the president as a narrow developmentalist with no deep dedication to the norms and institutions of liberal democracy. Following the Islamist-led mobilisations that swung Jakarta's 2017 gubernatorial election against the Christian, ethnically Chinese incumbent, Basuki Tjahaja Purnama ('Ahok'), Hadiz (2017) argued that Indonesia had entered a new phase of 'deepening illiberalism'. Then, as the 2019 presidential campaign got underway, Power (2018: 307) documented the government's 'increasingly open repression and disempowerment of political opposition' in order to secure re-election for the incumbent president, and argued the Jokowi administration was taking an 'authoritarian turn'.

By 2019, as Jokowi reached the end of his first term in office, Indonesia's democracy had sunk to its lowest point since the end of the New Order. Again, international indices were instructive: during Jokowi's first five years, the ratings produced by Freedom House, the Economist Democracy Index and V-Dem all tracked a deterioration in the quality of Indonesia's democratic institutions and the protection of civil liberties. The Economist Intelligence Unit's 10-point scale, for example, had Indonesia scoring above 7 when Jokowi first came to office. That score sank to 6.39 in 2017–18. A marginal bump to 6.48 in 2019 was surprising, given the unprecedented violent riots that met the announcement of the presidential election results (Chapter 17 by Toha and Harish), the government's hollowing out of the Corruption Eradication Commission (Komisi Pemberantasan Korupsi, KPK), and its subsequent clampdown on mass pro-democracy protests in the final months of 2019 (Chapter 14 by Power). Recent years have, nevertheless, seen a steady downwards trend. Although Indonesia is still considered a 'flawed democracy' (6–8) by the Economist Intelligence Unit, the democratic backsliding of the Jokowi era has moved it closer to the category of 'hybrid regime' (4–6) (EIU 2020).

The two chapters that follow this introduction delve into the comparative dimensions of Indonesia's present democratic decline. As Allen Hicken and Dan Slater emphasise, Indonesia is by no means alone in its democratic shortcomings. Indeed, against the backdrop of a global democratic recession and alarming trends in certain other Southeast Asian countries, Allen Hicken (Chapter 2) re-emphasises some of Indonesia's continuing democratic strengths. Indonesia's democratic decline has (so far) been less dramatic and wide-reaching than those of the Philippines and Thailand, for instance, where incumbents have more openly attacked core democratic institutions, including elections, courts and media freedom. Meanwhile, Dan Slater (Chapter 3) suggests that the source of Indonesia's relative democratic success in the post-Suharto period can be located in its unique historical inheritances—a plural nationalism and strong state institutions—which have helped prevent the kind of authoritarian reversal to which young democracies are often prone.

Yet these assessments also diagnose some of the major challenges to Indonesia's democratic health at the present time. Slater warns that illiberalism remains 'the main lingering threat to Indonesian democracy', and Hicken is especially concerned about deteriorations in the protection of individual freedom and civil society space, as well as the continued weakening of political parties and deepening political polarisation. The persistence of these forces means Indonesia remains vulnerable to renewed autocratisation.

These comparative contributions show that the patterns of backsliding described in this volume are not unique to Indonesia. Indeed, it is Indonesia's democratic successes—not its shortcomings—that have historically confounded the expectations of comparative democratisation scholarship. There can be little doubt, however, that most readers will derive cold comfort from the conclusion that Indonesia is now 'catching up' to a global pattern of democratic regression.

THE STRUCTURAL SHORTCOMINGS OF DEMOCRATIC CONSOLIDATION

Beyond the comparative context, this volume focuses on why Indonesia's democracy has fallen into retreat, and what has brought about the contemporary reversals taking place across multiple democratic indicators. One prominent stream of analysis emphasises structural features of Indonesia's political economy in explaining the deteriorating quality of its democracy. As noted above, Indonesia shares some of the structural conditions that have prevented the process of 'democratic deepening' (Heller 2009) in other countries: stable but low levels of economic growth, high wealth inequality, patronage politics, endemic corruption, and the political and social legacies of authoritarianism (Bourchier 2015; Hadiz 2018; Warburton and Aspinall 2019).

Several contributors examine how economic conditions can profoundly affect the health and depth of democratic consolidation. Abdil Mughis Mudhoffir (Chapter 7) focuses on the ways in which severe material disparities both undermine Indonesia's democratic quality and threaten its democratic institutions. He shows how Indonesia's economic growth has mostly concentrated wealth in the pockets of a narrow elite, leaving a large constituency of lower-middle class Muslims in economic precarity. In a country where formal class politics faces continued repression, he argues, these economic grievances have been more readily framed in religious terms and contributed to the surge of popular mobilisation behind Islamist political causes.

The relationship between economic conditions and democratic quality is also explored by Puspa Delima Amri and Mochamad Pasha (Chapter 12). Drawing on existing measures of democratic performance at the subnational level, they identify a positive association between the health of local democratic institutions and socioeconomic indicators such as urbanisation and literacy. These findings underscore the importance of investing in political institutions and participatory mechanisms in Indonesia's poorer and more rural regions. However, Amri and Pasha also emphasise the need for more rigorous, independent research into regional variations in democratic quality.

In addition to examining economic structures, students of Indonesian democratisation have emphasised how political compromises brokered during the post-Suharto transition wove institutional weaknesses into the fabric of the new democratic regime. For instance, Aspinall (2010) argues that the inclusive character of Indonesia's transition from authoritarianism ensured reactionary elites and potential anti-democratic spoilers were integrated into the new political settlement. On one hand, this incorporation of ancien régime elements made for a relatively smooth and stable transition to electoral democracy; on the other, it allowed entrenched, illiberal powerbrokers to maintain authority over democratic institutions to which they had little commitment. Contemporary politics thus continues to be shaped by the institutional holdovers from authoritarianism, including ambiguous and malleable legal authority, widespread illegality and elite impunity. In this vein, Thomas Power (Chapter 14) draws attention to the ways in which these structural legacies—institutionalised corruption, a weak rule of law and the vulnerability of law enforcement agencies to politicisation—have provided fertile ground for the Jokowi administration's efforts to curtail criticism, tame opposition and dismantle democratic checks and balances.

There is little doubt that the structural conditions imposed by economic distribution and institutional arrangements have hampered Indonesia's democratic consolidation. Nevertheless, these structural shortcomings cannot wholly explain the present pattern of democratic deterioration. An array of political actors—elites, activists, organisations and ordinary citizens—are shaping and contesting Indonesia's present democratic trajectory, both from within the ruling elite and from the grassroots.

DEMOCRATIC REGRESSION FROM ABOVE

Given the extreme imbalances in wealth and power that structure post–New Order politics, it is unsurprising that the role of political elites features prominently in many analyses of Indonesia's post-Suharto shortcomings and stagnation (Ambardi 2008; Aspinall 2010; Mietzner 2012; Robison and Hadiz 2004; Slater 2004). Similarly, anti-democratic elites are central actors in Indonesia's present democratic deterioration (Hadiz 2017; Mietzner 2016; Power 2018; Warburton 2016; Warburton and Aspinall 2019). Political party leaders, elected politicians, state officials and wealthy capitalists have coalesced to erode the sorts of checks, balances and liberal guardrails that are critical to a healthy democracy, including an effective rule of law, diverse and critical media, robust human rights protections, and an open and representative political party system.

One clear indication of elite-led democratic deterioration is the declining quality of Indonesia's political parties. Parties are a crucial barometer of a country's democratic health, and Hicken (Chapter 2) describes them as 'the symbolic face of democracy'. While Indonesian parties were at times excessively criticised in the 2000s—particularly when compared to their counterparts in other young democracies (Mietzner 2013)—the 2010s saw a marked decline across multiple indicators of party performance, including societal representation and internal accountability. As Marcus Mietzner documents in Chapter 10, the Jokowi presidency has seen a 'comprehensive' deterioration in the quality of Indonesia's party system. Prohibitive expense and rising parliamentary thresholds have made it virtually impossible to establish new parties, unless they are funded by powerful tycoons and oligarchs. Mietzner also diagnoses an illiberal turn within party organisations, characterised by the decline or abandonment of internal mechanisms for democracy and accountability.

Parties have also come under external attack from the Jokowi government. Most notably, the president and his allies have reactivated authoritarian-era executive powers in order to coerce opposition parties into supporting their coalition (Mietzner 2016). As Power explains in Chapter 14, this is one manifestation of the incumbent administration's efforts at executive aggrandisement, carried out through a wide-ranging assault on formal and informal mechanisms of democratic accountability. In addition to its suppression of party-based opposition, the Jokowi government has taken unprecedented steps to co-opt subnational administrations, and has defanged Indonesia's only credibly independent law enforcement agency—the KPK. It has simultaneously sought to repress its critics and opponents in civil society—ranging from the anti-democratic forces of intolerant Islamism to the overtly pro-democracy protests that mobilised to defend the KPK in late 2019.

Such efforts to restrict and repress free political expression within civil society are perhaps the most widely cited examples of the elite-led erosion of Indonesian democracy. During the latter part of Yudhoyono's tenure, analysts and activists began voicing concern about new regulations that stifled critical speech and public dissent. Ken Setiawan (Chapter 13) describes how the notoriously malleable Law No. 11/2008 on Electronic Information and Transactions (ITE Law), which criminalises 'defamatory' electronic media communication, has been wielded with growing regularity by powerful elites seeking to silence criticism from political opponents, journalists, activists and ordinary citizens. Drawing on detailed case data, she shows that ITE Law prosecutions have become more frequent and ostensibly more targeted under the Jokowi administration. More than any of its predecessors, the Jokowi government has weaponised online surveillance and intimidation to cow political opponents and stymie popular criticism.[1]

These trends have not been confined to the realm of social media. As Ross Tapsell details in Chapter 11, Indonesia's traditional and corporate media is also struggling to fulfil crucial democratic functions. Indonesia's media landscape, once regarded as among the freest in the region, is now dominated by an oligopoly comprising mostly government-aligned owners—several of whom are party chiefs and ministers within Jokowi's coalition. Building on his previous research (2017), Tapsell suggests that Indonesia's traditional media is under mounting pressure to curb critiques of the incumbent government, and describes how state interventions into media outlets are restricting space for 'diverse political conversations' and critical commentary.

These analyses beg the question of why Indonesia is falling prey to accelerated processes of elite-led democratic deconsolidation. Much recent comparative literature has emphasised the rise of populist politicians who come to power by challenging established power structures, then try to free themselves of institutional constraints in the name of governing for 'the people' (Kenny 2019; Norris and Inglehart 2019: 65–7; Pappas 2019). As Liam Gammon explains in Chapter 6, Jokowi, Prabowo and the Islamist '212 movement' have all been cast as manifestations of populism, and analysts have argued that each actor or group has contributed to Indonesia's current moment of democratic decline (Aspinall 2015; Mietzner 2020; Robison and Hadiz 2017). Yet Gammon shows that Indonesia's democratic deterioration has not followed the path of fragile democracies in Latin America, or in parts of Europe, where a populist outsider seeks to personalise power by dismantling core democratic institutions. Rather, Jokowi's erosion of Indonesian democracy is taking place 'in concert with a diverse coalition of incumbent non-populist political actors' and exhibits 'a broad level of elite buy-in'. In his analysis of Islamic populism, Mudhoffir (Chapter 7) draws attention to the ways in which self-interested elites have sought to manipulate channels of popular dissatisfaction for narrow electoral purposes, arguing that the Muslim populist constituency

---

1   These findings are important for comparative analyses of internet freedom, some of which significantly underestimate the extent of government efforts to control and censor online space. For example, Freedom House's 2019 Freedom on the Net report overlooked pro-government manipulation of online discussion and the expanded weaponisation of ITE Law cases against government critics. *Despite this,* Indonesia suffered a 3-point drop in its internet freedom score from 2018 to 2019—the equal highest in Southeast Asia (Freedom House 2019).

remains 'on the political margins, subordinated by opportunistic but powerful politico-economic elites'.

That the rollback of Indonesian democracy is a product of intra-elite cooperation rather than 'outsider' populism is by no means a reassuring finding. First, it reveals an absence of intra-elite resistance to Indonesia's present democratic regression. Second, it implies that contemporary trends are unlikely to be arrested with the conclusion of Jokowi's presidential tenure: he is, no doubt, a critical actor in this moment of democratic decline—but he has been aided and abetted by an ensemble cast of illiberal elite allies. Third, expansive elite buy-in contributes to the normalisation of deepening democratic deficits, both reflected in and reinforced by a largely uncritical and at times propagandist media.

Elite-led attacks on vital democratic rights and institutions may be the most overt expression of Indonesia's democratic predicament, but they do not wholly explain the shift from stagnant reform to gathering regression. To drill more deeply into the drivers of democratic decline, we now turn to the roles of non-state actors, social groups and ordinary citizens.

DEMOCRATIC REGRESSION FROM BELOW

Comparative scholars have long tied democratic consolidation and stability to particular social conditions, including the spread and depth of popular support for democratic institutions and the liberal norms that underpin them, and to the vibrancy of a liberal civil society (Graham and Svolik 2019; Helmke and Levitsky 2006). In the Indonesian context, scholars have historically contrasted the anti-democratic tendencies of political elites with civil society's role as a bulwark against renewed autocratisation (Mietzner 2012; Mujani and Liddle 2009). As Mietzner (2012: 209) put it, civil society was 'democracy's most important defender' against 'anti-reformist elites' during the Yudhoyono years.

Yet through the latter part of the 2010s, civil society organisations have struggled to live up to this billing, reflected in the rise of new political forces at the grassroots, the aggravation of existing sociopolitical cleavages, and evolving popular attitudes towards key aspects of democracy. Multiple contributions to this volume describe emergent challenges and threats to Indonesian democracy arising from the societal level, often showing how grassroots developments are encouraging or reinforcing the patterns of elite-led regression described in the previous section.

One prominent marker of Indonesia's democratic decline is a now well-documented deterioration in the protection of minorities. As Fealy and Ricci (2019: 2) point out, Indonesia's ethnic, religious and sexual minorities have over the past decade faced growing 'condemnation or denigration'—not just by political leaders, but also 'by other sections of society'. Increasingly bold expressions of intolerance and majoritarianism were widely diagnosed during the Yudhoyono era (Bush 2015), but drew global attention with the 2016–17 Islamist mobilisations that swung Jakarta's gubernatorial race. The anti-Ahok campaign—which consigned the incumbent to electoral defeat and imprisonment for blasphemy—was a watershed moment for Indonesian democracy. Not only did the 2017 Jakarta election reveal the reach and influence of intolerant, sectarian ideas and groups; it further exacerbated the religio-ideological polarisation that had riven national politics during a bitter presidential contest in 2014.

Many of the Jokowi administration's repressive tactics have been framed as essential measures to contain the Islamist threat to Indonesia's religiously pluralist foundations. As Eve Warburton emphasises in Chapter 4, the president's supporters have proven willing to accept such illiberal measures when they are directed against ideological opponents. Popular support for key democratic values and norms is therefore rendered 'contingent' by polarisation, with partisans on both sides of Indonesia's contemporary ideological divide willing to trade off the erosion of crucial institutions for the repression and coercion of their political enemies. As Warburton notes, there has been meagre pushback from traditionally pro-democracy civil society against the government's efforts to silence and purge its ideological opponents.

The problem of polarisation is also taken up by Nava Nuraniyah (Chapter 5), who explores how the fractious political contests of recent years have been animated by a longstanding religious conflict between the traditionalist Muslim constituency exemplified by Indonesia's largest Islamic organisation, Nahdlatul Ulama (NU), and the rising forces of puritanical Islamism embodied in groups like the Prosperous Justice Party (Partai Keadilan Sejahtera, PKS) and the now-banned Hizbut Tahrir Indonesia (HTI). Nuraniyah's analysis is a refreshing departure from much of the previous commentary on this issue, as she focuses her attention not on the threat of reactionary Islamism, but rather on how the illiberal and repressive tactics adopted by NU are exacerbating polarisation and hastening democratic regression. She thus argues that both Islamists and religious pluralists are 'subordinating the preservation of democratic principles' to a bitter rivalry between 'competing visions of Indonesian Islam'.

As well as highlighting the increasingly polarised character of Indonesia's popular politics, the 2017 Jakarta campaign revealed the expanding clout of intolerant organisations like the Islamic Defenders Front (Front Pembela Islam, FPI) and its leader, Habib Rizieq Shihab.

FPI's evolution from a relatively peripheral vigilante organisation into a vehicle for Islamic populism has provoked concern among many observers (Mietzner et al. 2018). Gammon (Chapter 6) notes that the types of populism associated with social organisations like FPI present a more proximate threat to Indonesia's democratic fabric than 'populism from above'.

In Chapter 15, Sana Jaffrey explores how the forces of religious vigilantism have been able to effectively expand their social legitimacy through the democratic era. Benefiting from close ties to state officials and law enforcement agencies, religious militias and vigilante groups now police a 'widening range of moral and religious offences', allowing these organisations—from FPI to the NU-affiliated Banser—to accrue deep reserves of social and political capital. Jaffrey argues that vigilantism is 'dismantling liberal rights' and 'basic democratic freedoms from the bottom up'. In this way, civil and political rights are beset on multiple fronts—threatened by the increasingly authoritarian exercise of power at both the apex of the political system and at the community level.

Despite the growth of violent vigilantism as a means to punish social and moral transgressions, Indonesia's post-Suharto elections have been overwhelmingly peaceful at both the national and local levels. As Risa J. Toha and S.P. Harish (Chapter 17) point out, the relative absence of violence in Indonesian elections sits in stark contrast to many young democracies of comparable size, diversity and development. However, their analysis of data from the National Violence Monitoring System—which tracked reporting of violent incidents until its unfortunate closure in 2014—suggests an uptick in some types of election-related violence during the latter part of the Yudhoyono presidency. They supplement this finding by tracing the post-2016 rise of mass opposition mobilisations as an electoral strategy, drawing attention to a steady increase in incidents of violence that culminated in the deadly Jakarta riots of May 2019. Toha and Harish note that the manipulation of religious sentiment, strategic mobilisation of protesters and aggressive deployment of security personnel threaten the traditionally peaceful character of elections—potentially eroding a longstanding strength of Indonesian democracy.

Many analyses of the 2019 post-election riots drew attention to the role of rumour and disinformation in inciting and spreading violence (Temby 2019). These patterns, while new at the level of national elections, are a longstanding problem in subnational regions shaped by ethnoreligious cleavages and historical cycles of conflict. As Irsyad Rafsadie, Dyah Ayu Kartika and Siswo Mulyartono detail in Chapter 16, the 2018 West Kalimantan gubernatorial election saw ethnically and religiously divisive rumours disseminated within an electorate already polarised by the aftershocks of the 2017 Jakarta race and local legacies of ethnic violence. Following the defeat of the incumbent Christian Dayak coalition by a Muslim Malay ticket, supporters of the losing candidates mounted a campaign of intimidation that drove Muslim residents from their homes and threatened to spark renewed bloodshed. In a troubling echo of Toha and Harish's conclusions, Rafsadie, Kartika and Mulyartono argue that the increasingly widespread deployment of polarising political rumours for electoral advantage heightens the chances of violent outbreaks, especially in post-conflict areas.

These accounts present a relatively pessimistic view of the evolving role of civil society organisations and grassroots polarisation in Indonesia's democratic downturn. However, any analysis of 'bottom-up' drivers of democratic regression must also take account of popular support for democracy (Linz and Stepan 1996). Over almost two decades, national surveys of Indonesians have shown reliably high levels of satisfaction with, and support for, democratic government. From 2005 to 2019, the Indonesian Survey Institute (Lembaga Survei Indonesia, LSI) published 63 national surveys of satisfaction with the functioning of democracy; only one of these polls—published in mid-2012—found that more Indonesians were dissatisfied than satisfied with democracy (LSI 2019). While numbers have fluctuated, an overall picture since 2005 shows around two in three Indonesians are satisfied with democracy, with one-fifth to one-third indicating dissatisfaction. The number of Indonesians who endorse democratic government is higher again; according to a survey published in June 2019, 82 per cent of voters believed democracy to be the best system of government, compared to just 3 per cent who believed authoritarianism was acceptable 'under certain circumstances' (SMRC 2019: 57). Nevertheless, some analyses have questioned the robustness of these democratic commitments, both among civil society groups (Menchik 2019) and the broader voting public (Aspinall et al. 2020; Mujani et al. 2018). Indeed, support for and satisfaction with democracy can be contingent upon incumbent performance, perceptions of economic inequality, or ideological and partisan commitments.

Burhanuddin Muhtadi (Chapter 8) explores the contingency of democratic support in more detail. Noting the importance of buy-in from democratic losers for the maintenance of democratic legitimacy and stability, he investigates whether voters whose preferred candidate suffers electoral defeat express reduced satisfaction with democratic performance, or reduced enthusiasm for democracy as a regime. Using pre- and post-election survey data for each presidential election, Muhtadi finds that electoral losers are indeed more likely to show dissatisfaction with democracy. Notably, this effect grew significantly in the wake of the divisive 2019 election, when Prabowo voters were also more likely to feel their civil liberties were under attack. Nevertheless, Muhtadi emphasises that a strong majority of Indonesians continue to prefer democracy over other forms of government—whether or not their candidates lose.

But this finding raises another important question: what does it mean when Indonesians say they support and prefer democratic government? How do citizens conceive of democracy and judge its quality? Diego Fossati and Ferran Martinez i Coma address these questions in Chapter 9. They find that Indonesians understand democracy in a variety of ways, with some seeing it in more liberal and egalitarian terms, and others understanding it in terms of participation. Echoing Muhtadi, they emphasise the need to scrutinise the diverse ways in which Indonesians perceive and judge democratic government. However, both chapters offer much-needed cause for optimism about the breadth and depth of popular support for democracy in contemporary Indonesia.

CONCLUSION AND OUTLINE OF THE BOOK

This volume argues that Indonesian democracy is at its lowest point since the fall of the New Order. Despite 20 years of democratic government, Indonesia's democracy is not continuing to consolidate; rather, it is sliding into deepening illiberalism. Many of the achievements listed at the start of this chapter are under threat. Law enforcement and security agencies are undergoing a process of repoliticisation. The party system is compromised by illiberal state interventions and declining popular legitimacy, and its constituent parties are increasingly elite-dominated and unaccountable. Elections remain competitive, but the incumbent administration has sought to unbalance the playing field during campaigns and is stepping up efforts to wind back direct elections at the subnational level. The traditional media landscape is dominated by politico-business elites with close ties to government, while to publish critical comment in independent and social media means risk of state harassment and arrest. Longstanding shortcomings in the rule of law have been exacerbated with the politicisation of criminal cases and the government's dismantling of the KPK.

Expressive and associative freedoms are under attack from social forces as well. Civil society is increasingly polarised, to the extent that Indonesia's largest community organisations have actively endorsed the state's deployment of authoritarian tactics against their ideological rivals. Recent years have seen the hardening of old social cleavages and new manifestations of political violence.

Even Indonesia's regional autonomy program, long seen as the strongest institutional bulwark against a renewal of centralised authoritarian rule, is facing new threats. Recent months have seen proposals to phase out local elections and strengthen central government authority to replace local leaders, as well as the introduction of regulations investing the national executive with ultimate power to appoint, remove and relocate bureaucrats at all levels of state administration.

There are, still, some bright spots in this otherwise gloomy picture. Most obviously, public support for democracy remains high. Although the 2019 student protests against the dismantling of the KPK and proposed Criminal Code revisions were effectively quashed by forces in government, they did reveal that hundreds of thousands of young Indonesians were willing to stand up for their democracy. Meanwhile, some distinguished Indonesian commentators—people like television host Najwa Shihab, documentary filmmaker Dandhy Laksono, lawyers Haris Azhar and Bhivitri Susanti, and Amnesty International's Usman Hamid, as well as the journalists working for publications like *Tempo* and *Tirto*—have used their platforms to discuss and critique many features of the present democratic regression. Ensuring such independent and critical voices escape suppression or co-option will be essential if Indonesian democracy is to arrest its present decline. Additionally, elections remain competitive, and while these institutions remain robust there is some hope that more committed democrats may one day come to power. That said, the barriers to nomination for truly reformist candidates look harder and harder to overcome.

The rest of this book is organised into five parts. Each is anchored in a specific aspect of democratic theory, and is designed to identify and assess core features of Indonesia's trajectory of decline. The volume begins with a look at Indonesia's democratic health through a historical and comparative lens. Part Two examines two interrelated threats to Indonesia's democratic stability—deepening political polarisation and the rise of populist mobilisation. Part Three turns to a critical dimension of democratic success—the depth and nature of public support for democratic institutions. Part Four sheds light on the state of core democratic institutions, and demonstrates how elected politicians and state officials have colluded to erode the sorts of checks, balances and liberal guardrails that are critical to a healthy democracy—like political parties, the media and human rights protections. Finally, Part Five reflects on issues relating to law, security and state power in contemporary Indonesia.

REFERENCES

Ambardi, K. 2008. 'The making of the Indonesian multiparty system: a cartelized party system and its origin'. PhD thesis. Columbus, OH: Ohio State University.

Aspinall, E. 2010. 'The irony of success'. *Journal of Democracy* 21(2): 20–34.

Aspinall, E. 2015. 'Oligarchic populism: Prabowo Subianto's challenge to Indonesian democracy'. *Indonesia* 99(April): 1–28.

Aspinall, E. and M. Mietzner. 2014. 'Indonesian politics in 2014: democracy's close call'. *Bulletin of Indonesian Economic Studies* 50(3): 347–69.

Aspinall, E. and M. Mietzner. 2019. 'Indonesia's democratic paradox: competitive elections amidst rising illiberalism'. *Bulletin of Indonesian Economic Studies* 55(3): 295–317.

Aspinall, E. and M. Sukmajati, eds. 2016. *Electoral Dynamics in Indonesia: Money Politics, Patronage and Clientelism at the Grassroots*. Singapore: NUS Press.

Aspinall, E., M. Mietzner and D. Tomsa, eds. 2015. *The Yudhoyono Presidency: Indonesia's Decade of Stability and Stagnation*. Singapore: Institute of Southeast Asian Studies (ISEAS).

Aspinall, E., D. Fossati, B. Muhtadi and E. Warburton. 2020. 'Elites, masses, and democratic decline in Indonesia'. *Democratization* 27(4): 505–26.

Bhakti, I.N. 2004. 'The transition to democracy in Indonesia: some outstanding problems'. In *The Asia-Pacific: A Region in Transition*, edited by J. Rolfe, 195–206. Honolulu: Asia-Pacific Center for Security Studies.

Bourchier, D. 2015. *Illiberal Democracy in Indonesia: The Ideology of the Family State*. Abingdon: Routledge.

Bush, R. 2015. 'Religious politics and minority rights during the Yudhoyono presidency'. In *The Yudhoyono Presidency: Indonesia's Decade of Stability and Stagnation*, edited by E. Aspinall, M. Mietzner and D. Tomsa, 239–57. Singapore: Institute of Southeast Asian Studies (ISEAS).

Carothers, T. 2009. 'Stepping back from democratic pessimism'. *Carnegie Paper* No. 99. Washington, DC: Carnegie Endowment for International Peace.

Case, W. 2017. *Populist Threats and Democracy's Fate in Southeast Asia: Thailand, the Philippines, and Indonesia*. Abingdon: Routledge.

Chu, Y.-H., Y.-T. Chang, M.-H. Huang and M. Weatherall. 2016. 'Re-assessing the popular foundation of Asian democracies: findings from four waves of the Asian Barometer Survey'. *Asian Barometer Working Paper Series* No. 120. http://www.asianbarometer.org/publications//b15620cf8549caa8a6cc4da5d481c42f.pdf

Diamond, L. 2008. 'The democratic rollback: the resurgence of the predatory state'. *Foreign Affairs* 87(2): 36–48.

Diamond, L. 2010. 'Indonesia's place in global democracy'. In *Problems of Democratisation in Indonesia: Elections, Institutions and Society*, edited by E. Aspinall and M. Mietzner, 21–49. Singapore: Institute of Southeast Asian Studies (ISEAS).

Diamond, L. 2015. 'Facing up to the democratic recession'. *Journal of Democracy* 26(1): 141–55.

Diprose, R., D. McRae and V.R. Hadiz. 2019. 'Two decades of *reformasi* in Indonesia: its illiberal turn'. *Journal of Contemporary Asia* 49(5): 691–712.

Dwipayana, A.A.G.N. 2009. 'Demokrasi biaya tinggi: dimensi ekonomi dalam proses demokrasi elektoral di Indonesia pasca orde baru'. *Jurnal Ilmu Sosial dan Ilmu Politik* 12(3): 257–79.

EIU (Economist Intelligence Unit). 2020. 'Democracy Index 2019'. EIU. https://www.eiu.com/topic/democracy-index

Fealy, G. 2011. 'Indonesian politics in 2011: democratic regression and Yudhoyono's regal incumbency'. *Bulletin of Indonesian Economic Studies* 47(3): 333–53.

Fealy, G. and R. Ricci, eds. 2019. *Contentious Belonging: The Place of Minorities in Indonesia*. Singapore: ISEAS – Yusof Ishak Institute.

Freedom House. 2009. *Freedom in the World 2009*. Washington, DC: Freedom House.

Freedom House. 2014. *Freedom in the World 2014: The Democratic Leadership Gap*. Washington, DC: Freedom House.

Freedom House. 2019. *Freedom on the Net 2018: The Rise of Digital Authoritarianism*. Washington, DC: Freedom House.

Gammon, L. and D. Berger. 2014. 'Did Indonesians fluke it?'. *New Mandala*, 12 August. https://www.newmandala.org/did-indonesians-fluke-it/

Graham, M.H. and M.W. Svolik. 2019. 'Democracy in America? Partisanship, polarization and the robustness of support for democracy in the United States'. *American Political Science Review* 114(2): 392–409.

Hadiz, V.R. 2017. 'Indonesia's year of democratic setbacks: towards a new phase of deepening illiberalism?'. *Bulletin of Indonesian Economic Studies* 53(3): 261–78.

Hadiz, V.R. 2018. 'Imagine all the people? Mobilising Islamic populism for right-wing politics in Indonesia'. *Journal of Contemporary Asia* 48(4): 566–83.

Heller, P. 2009. 'Democratic deepening in India and South Africa'. *Journal of Asian and African Studies* 44(1): 123–49.

Helmke, G. and S. Levitsky, eds. 2006. *Informal Institutions and Democracy: Lessons from Latin America*. Baltimore, MD: Johns Hopkins University Press.

Horowitz, D.L. 2013. *Constitutional Change and Democracy in Indonesia*. Cambridge: Cambridge University Press.

Huntington, S.P. 1991. *The Third Wave: Democratization in the Late Twentieth Century*. Norman, OK: University of Oklahoma Press.

Indrayana, D. 2008. *Indonesian Constitutional Reform 1999–2002: An Evaluation of Constitution-Making in Transition*. Jakarta: Kompas.

Kenny, P.D. 2019. *Populism in Southeast Asia*. Cambridge: Cambridge University Press.

Levitsky, S. and L.A. Way. 2015. 'The myth of democratic recession'. *Journal of Democracy* 26(1): 45–58.

Liddle, R.W. and S. Mujani. 2013. 'Indonesian democracy: from transition to consolidation'. In *Democracy and Islam in Indonesia*, edited by M. Künkler and A. Stepan, 24–50. New York: Columbia University Press.

Linz, J.J. and A. Stepan. 1996. *Problems of Democratic Transition and Consolidation: Southern Europe, South America and Post-Communist Europe*. Baltimore and London: Johns Hopkins University Press.

LSI (Lembaga Survei Indonesia). 2019. 'Tantangan intoleransi dan kebebasan sipil serta modal kerja pada periode kedua pemerintahan Joko Widodo: temuan survei nasional 8–17 September 2019'. Jakarta: LSI. http://www.lsi.or.id/file_download/175

Lussier, D.N. 2016. *Constraining Elites in Russia and Indonesia: Political Participation and Regime Survival*. Cambridge: Cambridge University Press.

MacIntyre, A. and D. Ramage. 2008. *Seeing Indonesia as a Normal Country: Implications for Australia*. Canberra: Australian Strategic Policy Institute.

Marta, A., L. Agustino and B. Wicaksono. 2019. 'Democracy in crisis: civic freedom in contemporary Indonesia'. In *Proceedings of the International Conference of Democratisation in Southeast Asia*, Advances in Social Science, Education and Humanities Research Vol. 367, 255–7. Atlantis Press.

Menchik, J. 2019. 'Moderate Muslims and democratic breakdown in Indonesia'. *Asian Studies Review* 43(3): 415–33.

Mietzner, M. 2009. 'Indonesia and the pitfalls of low-quality democracy: a case study of the gubernatorial elections in North Sulawesi'. In *Democratization in Post-Suharto Indonesia*, edited by M. Bunte and A. Ufen, 124–49. London and New York: Routledge.

Mietzner, M. 2012. 'Indonesia's democratic stagnation: anti-reformist elites and resilient civil society'. *Democratization* 19(2): 209–29.

Mietzner, M. 2013. *Money, Power, and Ideology: Political Parties in Post-authoritarian Indonesia*. Singapore: NUS Press.

Mietzner, M. 2016. 'Coercing loyalty: coalitional presidentialism and party politics in Jokowi's Indonesia'. *Contemporary Southeast Asia* 38(2): 209–32.

Mietzner, M. 2019. 'Authoritarian innovations in Indonesia: electoral narrowing, identity politics and executive illiberalism'. *Democratization*. doi: 10.1080/13510347.2019.1704266

Mietzner, M. 2020. 'Rival populisms and the democratic crisis in Indonesia: chauvinists, Islamists and technocrats'. *Australian Journal of International Affairs*. doi: 10.1080/10357718.2020.1725426

Mietzner, M., B. Muhtadi and R. Halida. 2018. 'Entrepreneurs of grievance: drivers and effects of Indonesia's Islamist mobilization'. *Bijdragen tot de Taal-, Land- en Volkenkunde* 174(2–3): 159–87. doi: 10.1163/22134379-17402026

Muhtadi, B. 2015. 'Jokowi's first year: a weak president caught between reform and oligarchic politics'. *Bulletin of Indonesian Economic Studies* 51(3): 349–68.

Muhtadi, B. 2019. *Vote Buying in Indonesia: The Mechanics of Electoral Bribery*. Singapore: Palgrave Macmillan. https://link.springer.com/book/10.1007/978-981-13-6779-3

Mujani, S. and R.W. Liddle. 2009. 'Muslim Indonesia's secular democracy'. *Asian Survey* 49(4): 575–90.

Mujani, S., R.W. Liddle and K. Ambardi. 2018. *Voting Behavior in Indonesia since Democratization: Critical Democrats*. Cambridge: Cambridge University Press.

Nashr, J.A. 2020. 'Diduga sebar ujaran kebencian kepada Jokowi, mahasiswa ditangkap'. *Tempo*, 17 March. https://nasional.tempo.co/read/1320651/diduga-sebar-ujaran-kebencian-kepada-jokowi-mahasiswa-ditangkap

Norris, P. and R. Inglehart. 2019. *Cultural Backlash: Trump, Brexit and Authoritarian Populism*. Cambridge: Cambridge University Press.

Pappas, T.S. 2019. *Populism and Liberal Democracy: A Comparative and Theoretical Analysis*. Oxford: Oxford University Press.

Power, T.P. 2018. 'Jokowi's authoritarian turn and Indonesia's democratic decline'. *Bulletin of Indonesian Economic Studies* 54(3): 307–38.

Robison, R. and V.R. Hadiz. 2004. *Reorganising Power in Indonesia: The Politics of Oligarchy in an Age of Markets*. London and New York: RoutledgeCurzon.

Robison, R. and V.R. Hadiz. 2017. 'Indonesia: a tale of misplaced expectations'. *Pacific Review* 30(6): 895–909.

Slater, D. 2004. 'Indonesia's accountability trap: party cartels and presidential power after democratic transition'. *Indonesia* 78(October): 61–92.

SMRC (Saiful Mujani Research & Consulting). 2019. 'Kondisi demokrasi dan ekonomi politik nasional pasca-peristiwa 21–22 Mei 2019: sebuah evaluasi publik'. SMRC, 16 June. https://twitter.com/saifulmujani/status/1140136674451546114

Tapsell, R. 2017. *Media Power in Indonesia: Oligarchs, Citizens and the Digital Revolution*. London: Rowman and Littlefield.

Temby, Q. 2019. 'Disinformation, violence, and anti-Chinese sentiment in Indonesia's 2019 elections'. *Perspective* No. 67, 2 September. Singapore: ISEAS – Yusof Ishak Institute. https://www.iseas.edu.sg/images/pdf/ISEAS_Perspective_2019_67.pdf

Tomsa, D. 2010. 'Indonesian politics in 2010: the perils of stagnation'. *Bulletin of Indonesian Economic Studies* 46(3): 309–28.

Warburton, E. 2016. 'Jokowi and the new developmentalism'. *Bulletin of Indonesian Economic Studies* 52(3): 297–320.

Warburton, E. and E. Aspinall. 2019. 'Explaining Indonesia's democratic regression: structure, agency and popular opinion'. *Contemporary Southeast Asia: A Journal of International and Strategic Affairs* 41(2): 255–85. https://www.muse.jhu.edu/article/732138

Webber, D. 2006. 'A consolidated patrimonial democracy? Democratization in post-Suharto Indonesia'. *Democratization* 13(3): 396–420.

Winters, J.A. 2011. *Oligarchy*. Cambridge: Cambridge University Press.

PART 1

Historical and Comparative Perspectives

2 Indonesia's democracy in a comparative perspective

Allen Hicken

About 10 years ago I sat in the audience at an international conference as a group of panelists argued about the state of Indonesian democracy 10 years after the fall of Suharto. The conversation was very much glass half-empty/half-full in character. The participants were largely in agreement about the bright spots and the worrying aspects of Indonesia's democracy. On the positive side of the ledger: 10 years of political stability; elections that were relatively free, fair and peaceful; a lack of electoral success for ethnic, regional or extremist parties; independent checks on state power in the form of the Constitutional Court and the Corruption Eradication Commission (Komisi Pemberantasan Korupsi, KPK); and three peaceful transitions of power. Concerns included continued high levels of corruption; new threats to the power and independence of supervisory agencies; illiberal responses to Islamic extremist groups; and the diminution of accountability in the face of party cartels.[1] Where the panelists disagreed was on the weight they assigned to each of these indicators. Some, looking backward and outward (comparing Indonesia with countries like Russia or Thailand), could not help but be impressed at Indonesia's ability to successfully navigate the difficult seas of a democratic transition. Others, looking forward and inward, could not take their eyes off the storm clouds they saw on the horizon.

Ten years later we sit at another natural assessment point. Despite its many challenges and weaknesses, Indonesian democracy has survived

---

1 For examples of these arguments in print form, see Aspinall (2011), Davidson (2009), Kimura (2012), Lussier and Fish (2012), Mietzner (2009), Scarpello (2008), Slater (2009) and Zaman (2008).

another decade. Twenty years of stable, functioning democracy is no mean achievement, and should be recognised and praised for the accomplishment it is. And yet, the global and regional trend towards autocratisation, even among some longstanding democracies, should give us pause. The erosion of democratic norms and practices in countries as diverse as the Philippines, Hungary, Venezuela and the United States suggests that democracy should not be taken for granted—even as we acknowledge Indonesia's impressive accomplishments to date.

In this chapter I examine the state of democracy in Indonesia through an explicitly comparative lens. I begin with a brief overview of the state of democracy in the world, before taking a closer look at Southeast Asia. I find that, in a comparative light, Indonesian democracy looks fairly good. Next, I review some of the theories and data related to autocratisation, focusing on what the comparative literature teaches us about early warning indicators and sources of concern. Finally, I re-examine the health of Indonesian democracy in light of this literature and discuss areas of potential vulnerability. I argue that while Indonesian democracy is generally healthy, weak parties, high levels of vote buying, the erosion of liberal freedoms and institutions, and serious polarisation present significant threats to the stability of democracy in Indonesia.

THE GLOBAL AND REGIONAL PICTURE

To assess the state of Indonesian democracy it is helpful to begin with how Indonesia looks from a comparative perspective. To sketch this comparative picture I rely on data from the Varieties of Democracy (V-Dem) Project (http://www.v-dem.net). V-Dem contains data on more than 450 indicators related to democracy for 200 countries from 1789 to 2018. I will rely primarily on V-Dem's measure of liberal democracy, though V-Dem also provides measures of other conceptions of democracy.[2] Liberal democracy is defined as the combination of the degree of electoral democracy (essentially, Dahl's concept of polyarchy) and three indexes that capture the strength of civil liberties and the extent of institutional constraints on the executive (Coppedge et al. 2019). The resulting Liberal Democracy Index ranges from 0 (lowest level of liberal democracy) to 1 (highest level).

---

2   These include electoral, participatory, deliberative and egalitarian. The basic patterns discussed below do not change if we replace liberal democracy with one of these alternative conceptions.

The first thing to note is that the international and regional context today is one of the decline of democracy, both globally and regionally. This decline goes by a variety of names, including autocratisation, democratic backsliding, democratic decline and democratic erosion, but regardless of the label it is clear that the global advance of democracy that was the norm for almost 40 years has not only come to a halt, but actually reversed. We have entered what some have called a 'third wave' of autocratisation (Lührmann and Lindberg 2019).

Lührmann and Lindberg (2019) have identified two global trends. First, the rate of democratic improvement has fallen dramatically over the past 20 years. Part of this reflects the fact that there is less room for improvement as more and more countries have become democracies during the course of the third wave of democratisation, but this is not the full story. This brings us to the second trend. Over the past 20 years democracy has been on the decline in many countries, with a noticeable acceleration over the last five. In fact, in the last few years autocratisers have outnumbered democratisers.

Let's take a closer look at what is happening globally. There is obviously a continuum from autocracy to democracy, but it can be helpful to break things into four regime types: (1) closed autocracies, which do not hold multiparty elections; (2) electoral autocracies, which hold multiparty elections, but which in practice are neither free nor fair; (3) electoral democracies, which hold free and fair, multiparty elections in a pluralistic media and associational environment; and (4) liberal democracies, which also include protections for civil liberties and constraints on the executive (Lührmann and Lindberg 2019).

For most of the past 40 years we've seen a process of global democratisation. This long third wave of democratisation was largely about the death of closed autocracies. Closed autocracies have almost vanished from the world, making up only 14 per cent (N = 25) of all countries today. Some of those closed autocracies became liberal democracies (22 per cent of all countries today), but most became electoral autocracies (31 per cent) or electoral democracies (34 per cent) (Coppedge et al. 2019). The recent turn towards autocratisation has not included a resurgence in the number of closed autocracies. Instead, what we see are liberal democracies eroding and becoming electoral democracies, electoral democracies breaking down to become electoral autocracies and, within each category, a deterioration or decline in the level of democracy, even if we don't cross categorical thresholds (Lührmann and Lindberg 2019).

That is the picture globally, but how has democracy been faring in Southeast Asia? In Figures 2.1–2.4 I draw on V-Dem data to plot the past

Figure 2.1   Democracy in Southeast Asia: Liberal Democracy Index

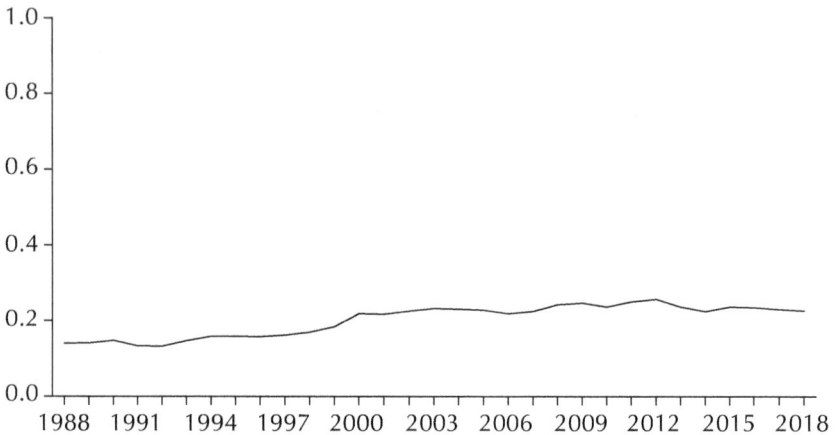

Source: Coppedge et al. (2019).

30 years of democracy scores, which allows us to get a sense of the changes over time at the regional and country levels.

Figure 2.1 displays the average score on the Liberal Democracy Index for Southeast Asia as a whole. Overall, democracy has improved in Southeast Asia over the past 30 years. Only two countries in the region are less democratic today than they were in 1988: the Philippines and Thailand. But overall, consistent with global trends, the pace of democratisation has stalled in the region, despite significant progress in countries such as Malaysia and Myanmar in recent years.

Figures 2.2–2.4 present a closer look at the region, country by country. In all three figures I use Japan, which sits near the top of the democracy scale, as a reference point. Figure 2.2 shows the level of democracy for the set of countries in which we see very little change over the past 30 years. From top to bottom according to their 2018 ratings, these are Singapore, Malaysia, Vietnam and Cambodia, each of which is either an electoral or closed autocracy.

In contrast to these steady-state polities, we see huge changes over the past 30 years in other parts of Southeast Asia. Figure 2.3 displays the ratings for the big democratisers in the region: Indonesia, Timor-Leste and Myanmar. In the case of Indonesia, we can see dramatic improvement in the score from the depths of the Suharto years to a peak in 2006. Between 2006 and the beginning of the Jokowi presidency there is a modest decline. Under Jokowi we see an initial improvement followed by a small decline.

Figure 2.2   Countries in Southeast Asia with stable democracy scores: Liberal Democracy Index

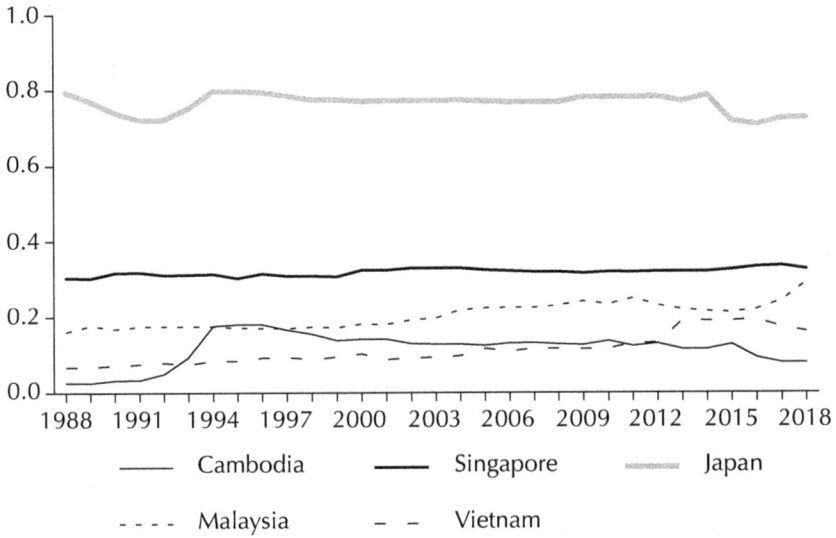

Source: Coppedge et al. (2019).

Figure 2.3   Significant democratisers in Southeast Asia: Liberal Democracy Index

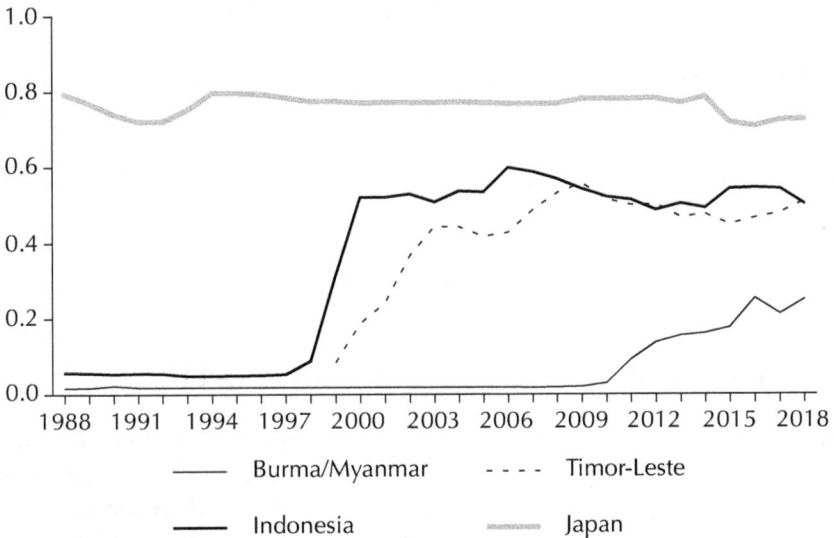

Source: Coppedge et al. (2019).

We see an equally dramatic democratic opening in Timor-Leste. Today Indonesia and Timor-Leste are the most democratic states in the region by a fair margin, both earning the designation of electoral democracies. We see more modest, but still substantial, democratic improvement in Myanmar as the country has gone from a closed autocracy to an electoral autocracy over the past eight years.

Finally, Figure 2.4 contains data on the only two countries in the region whose liberal democracy ratings are lower today than they were 30 years ago. In the Philippines there is democratic decline during the Estrada and Arroyo years, a recovery during the Aquino administration, followed by a sharp decline since Duterte came to power, though the country was still considered an electoral democracy in 2018. Thailand's score reflects the volatility of Thai politics since 1988 and the reality of life under a military government since 2014. Thailand was considered a closed autocracy in 2018.

If we consider Indonesia in this comparative light there is much to be positive about. Compared with the rest of the world it is in the top 30–40 per cent of countries in terms of its liberal democracy rating, putting it in the company of countries like Timor-Leste, Bulgaria, Colombia, Burkina Faso and Mexico. Indonesia is now the most democratic country in the region and has had stable electoral democracy for two decades, without suffering a dramatic democratic collapse in the manner of Thailand, or the sharp erosion of democratic norms that has characterised the Philippines. So, whether we compare contemporary Indonesia with the rest of the region, with the rest of the world or with the Indonesia of the past, its democratic accomplishments are impressive.

As impressive as these accomplishments may be, if the recent past has taught us anything, it is that we cannot take democracy for granted. The long-held idea that democracies can become consolidated—that is, no longer at serious risk of breakdown—is withering away as democracies across the globe come under increasing strain. So, what can we learn from recent comparative work about the patterns, warning signs and causes of autocratisation? I consider this question in the next section.

OLD AND NEW PATHS TO AUTOCRATISATION

There is a large and growing literature in comparative politics focused on describing and explaining how democratic breakdowns occur, and how the paths towards autocratisation have changed in recent years (e.g. Bermeo 2016; Gandhi 2019; Levitsky and Ziblatt 2018; Svolik 2019). Bermeo (2016) observes that the ways in which democracies die have

Figure 2.4   Significant autocratisers in Southeast Asia: Liberal Democracy Index

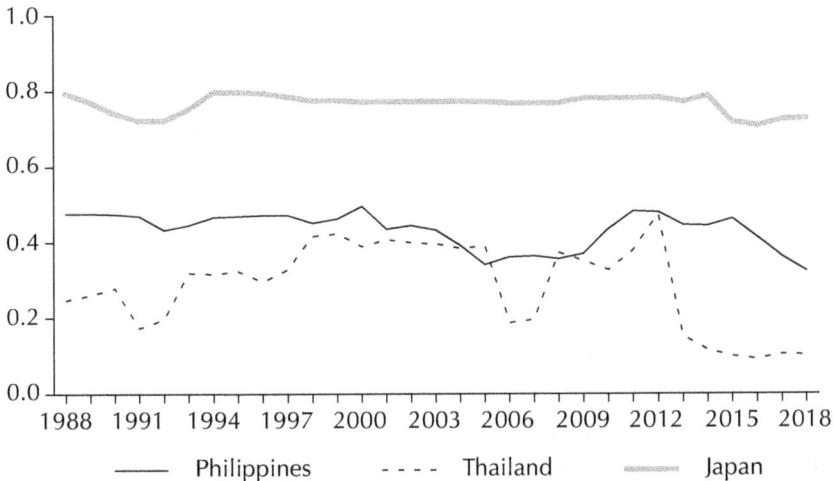

Source: Coppedge et al. (2019).

changed since the end of the Cold War. Before the end of the Cold War, democracies tended to end in one of three ways: classic open-ended coups, executive coups and electoral fraud (Bermeo 2016). The most common way was an open-ended coup d'état, where the tanks rolled in, civilian democrats were ousted from power and the coup-makers intended to rule in perpetuity. In Southeast Asia, Thailand, Burma/Myanmar and 1965 Indonesia are the most prominent examples of open-ended coups. But these kinds of coups against democracy have become increasingly rare since the end of the Cold War (Powell and Thyne 2011). This is no longer how most democracies die.

Also common in earlier eras were executive coups. These 'self-coups' or autogolpes involved a freely elected chief executive suspending elections in order to amass power in one fell swoop (examples being Marcos or Sukarno). However, executive coups have also become increasingly rare. They were a common path to dictatorship during the Cold War but their frequency has declined dramatically since then. According to Bermeo (2016: 7), between 2000 and 2013, Niger was the only example of an executive coup against democracy.

Finally, some democratic regimes came to an end when incumbents decided to remain in power by manipulating election results, that is, through electoral fraud. But in the past few decades we see that states are actually getting better at organising nominally clean elections

(Coppedge et al. 2019). Blatant electoral fraud, such as stuffing ballot boxes, manipulating voter rolls or the count, or relying on violence and intimidation, is increasingly rare. Where we see such strategies in use today, they tend to be the mark of desperate amateurs. Sophisticated and capable regimes generally don't have to resort to such crude measures. This is evident in Figure 2.5, which displays data on the cleanliness of elections using V-Dem's Clean Elections Index.[3] Even as we are experiencing a third wave of autocratisation, electoral administration has continued to improve globally. In most countries, elections are technically 'cleaner' than they have ever been. This is largely the case in Indonesia too, where estimates of the cleanliness of elections place Indonesia well above the global average (but below the high of the mid-2000s).

If most democracies no longer die as a result of open-ended coups, executive coups and electoral fraud, what is driving the current wave of autocratisation? While coups are now rare, when they do occur, open-ended coups have been replaced by what Bermeo calls 'promissory coups' (2016: 8). In a promissory coup, the coup leaders launching the putsch come to power promising their time in power has an expiry date. They pledge to restore democracy and elections, and emphasise that their intervention is only temporary. They frame their intervention as necessary to restore order, or to undertake the reforms required to produce a better democracy. Coup leaders may claim they have to temporarily put democracy in a coma in order to save it. Promissory coups now make up 85 per cent of all coups, compared with just 35 per cent before 1990 (Bermeo 2016: 9).

In practice, these promissory coup leaders usually fail to keep their promises. The temporary suspension of democracy often turns out to be not so temporary, and once elections are finally held, the military often continues to play a role and democracy almost never returns to its pre-coup level (Bermeo 2016: 10). Thailand is the poster child for the pitfalls associated with the promissory coup. When the military launched its coup in 2014, it initially promised a quick return to democracy after it had restored stability and reformed the system. Instead, the military ruled unchecked for nearly five years, and then managed to ensure that it remained at the helm even after elections returned in March 2019.

While promissory coups have largely replaced open-ended coups, remember that they are still relatively rare. Since the end of the Cold War,

3 The Clean Elections Index is constructed from the following indicators: the autonomy and capacity of the electoral management body, the quality of the voter registry, the prevalence of vote buying, voting irregularities, government intimidation and electoral violence, and the degree to which elections are free and fair.

Figure 2.5   *Electoral management in Indonesia versus the rest of the world: Clean Elections Index*

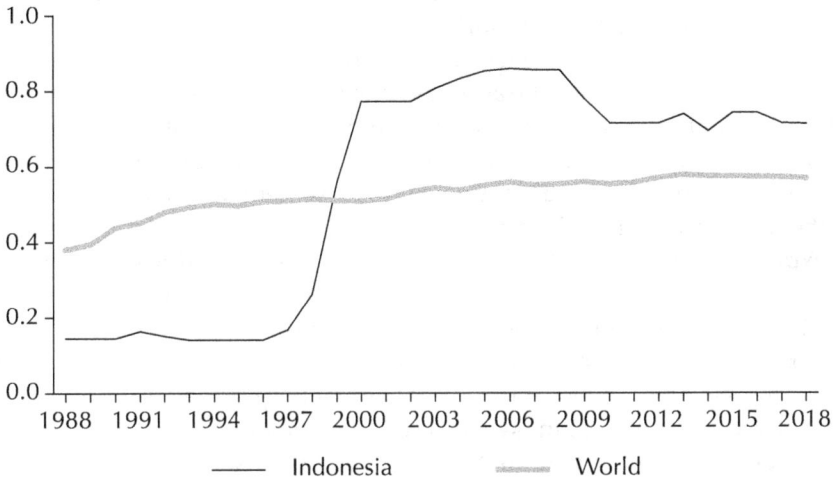

Source: Coppedge et al. (2019).

most democratic breakdowns have not, in fact, been caused by generals, but by elected politicians in what scholars term 'executive aggrandisement' or 'executive takeovers' (Bermeo 2016; Svolik 2019). According to Svolik, 70–90 per cent of breakdowns in the 2000s were caused by executive takeovers (2019: 22). So, what does executive aggrandisement look like? As in the past, the leaders of executive takeovers come to power through elections, but unlike in past eras, when the Marcoses of the world seized power via autoglope, the new autocratisers leave the trappings of democracy in place, but hollow it out from the inside. They don't abrogate the constitution. They don't suspend elections. They don't shutter parliament. Indeed, a defining feature of executive aggrandisement is that the aggrandisers can claim to be operating under the charge of an electoral mandate and within constitutional limits (Bermeo 2016: 11; Levitsky and Ziblatt 2018).

Instead, these elected executives undertake a series of institutional changes designed to weaken the checks on executive power. The menu of reforms includes things like doing away with term limits, weakening the judiciary or packing it with loyalists, weakening or co-opting the legislature, and increasing the power of the executive to act unilaterally. At the same time, these elected executives work to hamper the power of opposition forces to challenge executive power. They do this by working to undermine freedom of association, freedom of expression and media freedom in an effort to criminalise opposition, and by politicising the distribution of government resources to reward their allies and starve their opponents. Again, it is important to emphasise that most of these actions are presented as taking place within the bounds of the constitution and the rule of law. Nascent authoritarians use the very institutions of democracy to weaken and eventually destroy it.

Finally, blatant electoral fraud has now been replaced by more subtle efforts to manipulate the electoral environment in ways that give an unfair advantage to the incumbent (Bermeo 2019: 13). Such manipulation often goes hand-in-hand with executive aggrandisement, and employs many of the same tactics, including harassing the opposition, attacking freedom of expression, placing restrictions on the media and turning government resources towards partisan ends. Other examples of manipulation of the electoral environment include 'keeping opposition candidates off the ballot, hampering voter registration, packing electoral commissions, [and] changing electoral rules to favour incumbents' (Bermeo 2019: 13). The goal of such actions is to make electoral outcomes a foregone conclusion, but to do so in such a way that the elections themselves do not appear fraudulent. Singapore and Malaysia represent the global gold standard for these types of strategies.

In summary, the main drivers of the most recent turn towards autocratisation are executive aggrandisement and the manipulation of the electoral environment. What makes this wave of autocratisation so insidious is that it occurs gradually, often over several electoral cycles, and is carried out under the cover of constitutionalism by leaders who claim an electoral mandate. Each reform—especially when considered in isolation—is minor and does not seem to cross a red line. By itself, no single change amounts to an outright violation of core democratic principles (Levitsky and Ziblatt 2018). But as these changes compound over time, the foundations of democracy begin to crumble. In the end, executive aggrandisement and the manipulation of the electoral environment combine to gradually undermine the ability of any actors to hold incumbents accountable. This is the story unfolding in a significant number of democracies around the world. But where does Indonesia sit in all this?

THE STATE OF DEMOCRACY IN INDONESIA: RISKS AND WARNING SIGNS

We already saw that Indonesian democracy has been impressively stable since 1998. But what risk is there, if any, of autocratisation? Where is Indonesian democracy vulnerable? A team of scholars have used V-Dem

Figure 2.6   Risk of an adverse regime transition in 2019–20 (%)

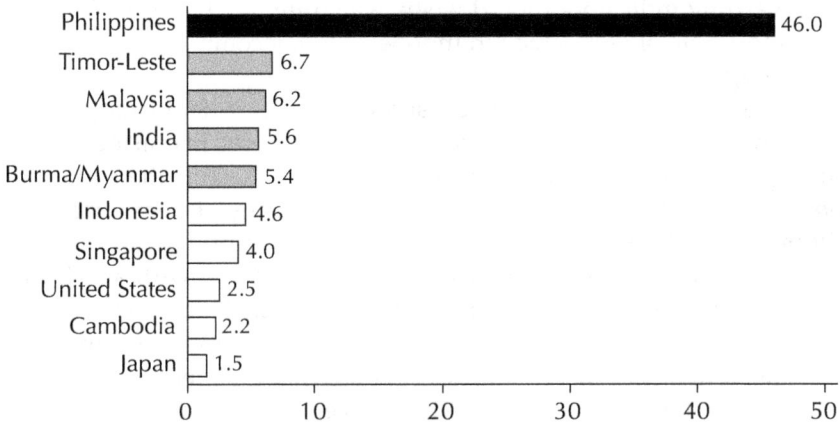

Source: V-Forecast: Predicting Adverse Regime Transitions (PART). https://www.v-dem.net/en/
analysis/Forecast/

data on past episodes of democratic breakdown to build a forecasting tool that tries to predict the risk of autocratisation.[4] Specifically, the forecasting tool calculates each country's risk of experiencing a shift in an autocratic direction—that is, an 'adverse regime transition'—within a two-year window (Morgan et al. 2019). I use this tool to compare the risk of an adverse regime transition in Indonesia relative to some of its neighbours, with the results displayed in Figure 2.6.

Among this set of countries, Japan has the lowest risk of an adverse regime transition, with only a 1.5 per cent chance of an adverse transition in the next two years. Indonesia has a slightly higher risk, at 4.6 per cent, but it is still considered to be in the low-risk category, alongside Singapore, the United States and Cambodia.[5] Burma/Myanmar, India, Malaysia and Timor-Leste are estimated to be at somewhat higher risk of an adverse transition. Finally, the Philippines has the dubious honour of being the regime judged most at risk of an adverse transition in 2019–20 (not just in this sample, but among all the countries for which data are available), with odds of an adverse transition that are just under 50:50.

---

4 The tool is available at https://www.v-dem.net/en/analysis/Forecast/.
5 Note that for Singapore and Cambodia the forecasting tool is estimating the risk of a move from electoral autocracy to a closed autocracy with no elections at all.

So, in terms of these numbers, Indonesia's situation again looks pretty good. But what are the trouble spots in Indonesia's democracy? What early warning indicators should we be watching for? Let us look first at the overall state of democracy in Indonesia today compared with 10 and 20 years ago.

The top two panels of Figure 2.7 show Indonesia's democracy ratings across five different measures of democracy—electoral, liberal (our focus), participatory, deliberative and egalitarian. The chart in the upper left compares 1998 with 2008. We know that the status of democracy was still pretty bleak in 1998, as Indonesia was just beginning its transition. Ten years later we see a dramatically different story, with significant improvements in all five democratic indexes. By 2008–09 Indonesia was one of the world's democratic success stories—a solid electoral democracy.

We would hope, and perhaps even expect, that Indonesian democracy would continue to deepen and expand over the next decade. Instead, what we see is a contraction across all five indexes between 2008 and 2018 (upper right panel in Figure 2.7). Of course, we should keep this relatively small contraction in perspective. Indonesia is still far from the precipice of democratic breakdown. For context, the bottom two panels show the democracy ratings for Hungary and the United States over the past 10 years. Hungary is a clear case of autocratisation and democratic breakdown, and this is reflected in the dramatic contraction across all five measures of democracy. The pattern for the United States looks very similar to Indonesia, with small declines across the board, and the biggest decline in the area of deliberative democracy.

The V-Dem data also allow us to drill down and see what specific indicators are driving this perceived decline in Indonesia's democracy. Keeping in mind the patterns of modern autocratisation discussed above, I focus on the quality of elections, the strength of Indonesia's political parties and the degree of polarisation.

QUALITY OF ELECTIONS

In terms of the quality of elections, there are things Indonesia is doing well and areas where there is reason for concern. One area of strength is electoral administration, specifically the capacity and autonomy of the General Elections Commission (Komisi Pemilihan Umum, KPU), which competently organises one of the most complex sets of elections in the world. The fact that Indonesian elections continue to occur with little in the way of election-related violence is also a strength, although the May 2019 post-election violence was a disturbing departure from this norm, as Toha and Harish explain in this volume. In aggregate, freedom of expression has held steady, and freedom of association is robust, particularly as it pertains to the rights of political parties. Overall, the V-Dem data suggest that Indonesian elections are free and fair, as one would expect.

But there are some areas of concern. While freedom of association is holding steady and parties are free to organise and compete, the environment for civil society has deteriorated. Civil society organisations face more restrictions and repression than they did 10 years ago, and this is particularly true of certain religious groups. Contributions to this volume document a worrying rise in government interventions that erode rather than protect citizens' freedoms, including the freedoms to express one's political beliefs, criticise state agencies and political figures, and practise one's faith.

Another area of concern is that, while elections are generally well run, free and fair, there has been an increase in perceived electoral irregularities since 2008, including an increase in the prevalence of vote buying. Every election since 1999 has been accompanied by an increase in vote buying in Indonesia, according to V-Dem data.[6] The fact that vote buying is ubiquitous in Indonesian elections is widely accepted (Aspinall and Sukmajati 2016; Muhtadi 2019). The question is, is this a concern for democratic stability? There is actually some debate about this in the comparative literature. On one hand, clientelism, including vote buying, provides material benefits to citizens that otherwise might be underserved by the state. On the other hand, vote buying and other forms of clientelism can skew the incentives and behaviour of elected officials and voters. Specifically, vote buying and other forms of money politics drive up the cost of elections, and politicians must somehow recoup those costs once in office. This in turn drives corruption and a morselisation or particularisation of public policy. It also corresponds to an undersupply of much-needed public goods and public policies (Aspinall and Berenschot 2019: 167–8). This increase in corruption and the undersupply of essential public goods can feed public discontent and disillusionment with democracy.

---

6 Data are not yet available for the 2019 election.

Figure 2.7   Changes in Indonesian democracy over time

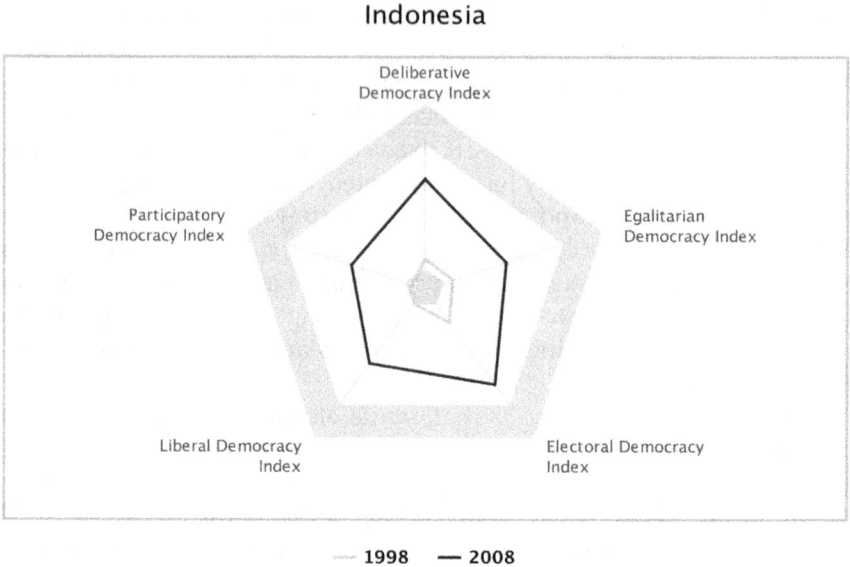

Indonesia

Deliberative Democracy Index

Participatory Democracy Index

Egalitarian Democracy Index

Liberal Democracy Index

Electoral Democracy Index

1998   2008

Highcharts.com | V-Dem data version 9.0

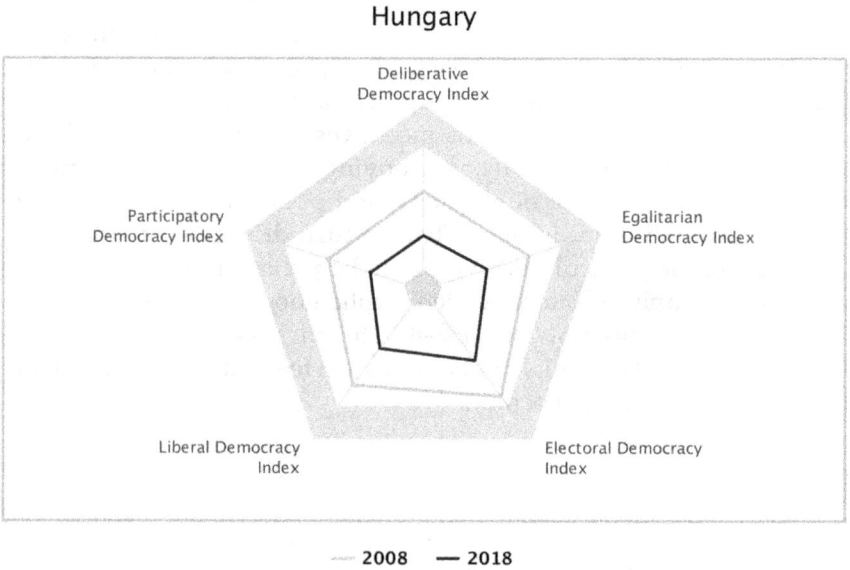

Hungary

Deliberative Democracy Index

Participatory Democracy Index

Egalitarian Democracy Index

Liberal Democracy Index

Electoral Democracy Index

2008   2018

Highcharts.com | V-Dem data version 9.0

Figure 2.7 (continued)

Indonesia

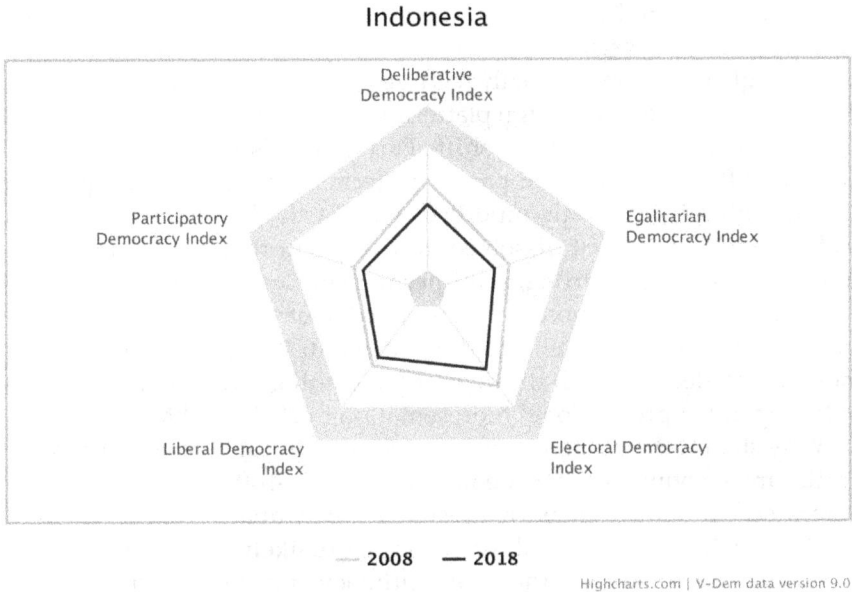

--- 2008 — 2018

Highcharts.com | V–Dem data version 9.0

United States of America

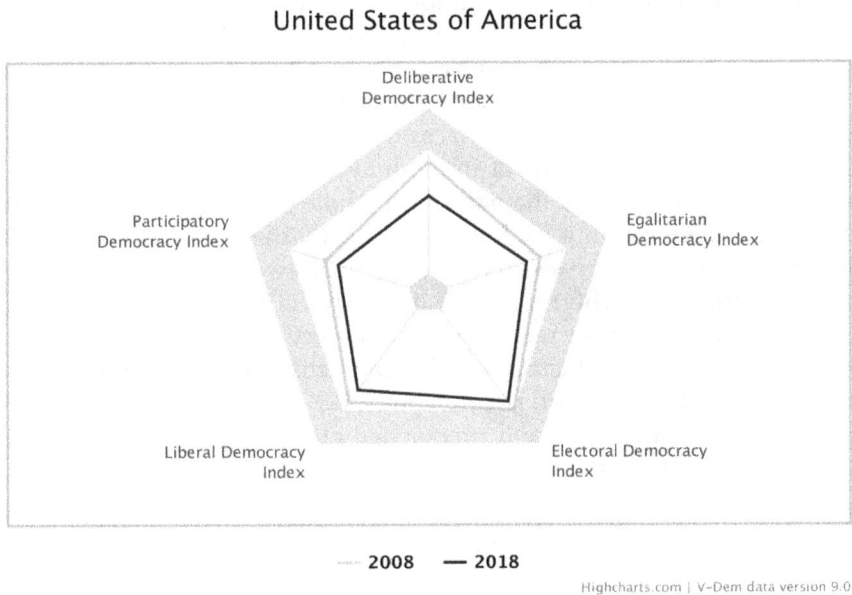

--- 2008 — 2018

Highcharts.com | V–Dem data version 9.0

Source: Coppedge et al. (2019).

STRENGTH OF POLITICAL PARTIES

A second area of concern is the weakening of Indonesian political parties, which has occurred along several dimensions over the past 10 years. Parties are weaker organisationally than they were in the past—they are increasingly reliant on externally recruited candidates and they are failing to maintain coherent campaign platforms (see Mietzner, this volume, for a comprehensive analysis of this shift). Parties are also less programmatic, and the differences between parties in terms of programs and policies are becoming increasingly muddled. Finally, the links between voters and parties have all but dissolved, to the extent that we see an almost complete severing of strong, semi-permanent ties between parties and well-defined groups of voters. The proportion of voters who say they are close to a political party fell from 86 per cent in 1999 to 10 per cent in the most recent election, with the biggest fall coming after the introduction of full open-list proportional representation in 2009 (Muhtadi 2019).

Why should the weakness of Indonesian political parties concern us? Parties are the symbolic face of democracy. These are often the organisations voters see and interact with most regularly, apart from individual candidates. If they work well, voters are more likely to be satisfied with democracy. If they do not, then the legitimacy of democracy itself can be a casualty. They are also the workhorses of democracy. They aggregate and articulate interests, they help lower the costs of campaigning and mobilisation, they facilitate collective action within the legislature, and they enable voters to hold governments accountable (Hicken 2009). Parties also typically have longer time horizons and broader constituencies than individual politicians, and this places them in a position to balance the short-term, narrow interests of individual politicians against the long-term, broader interests of the party as a whole (Hicken 2018). There are exceptions, of course, but we know empirically that autocratisation and democratic reversals are less likely in countries with strong parties and a strong civil society (Bernard et al. 2015). This is because strong parties and a robust civil society raise the cost of defecting from the democratic bargain for would-be autocrats. We also know that populists are less likely to emerge and be successful in countries where parties are strong, while weak party organisations and unattached electorates provide an open door for populists (Self and Hicken 2018).

POLARISATION

Toxic polarisation in the public sphere—the division of society into distrustful, antagonistic camps—is an increasing threat to democracy worldwide. In a recent review of significant cases of autocratisation in liberal and electoral democracies, researchers found that polarisation had increased significantly in all but one case (Coppedge et al. 2019). In autocratising countries, political elites' respect for opponents, use of factual reasoning and engagement with society decline, while the use of hate speech increases. Digitisation and the growth of social media can help to amplify and enflame this polarisation. The reason polarisation (and its bedfellow, populism) is so dangerous is that it eats away at the two fundamental pillars of stable democracy: loser's consent and winner's restraint. Let me briefly discuss each in turn.

Loser's consent. A crucial test for democratic consolidation is how individuals and groups respond when they are on the losing end of elections. Do they agree to submit to and be governed by the winners? Do they abide by the rules of the game and accept the other side as legitimate? Or do they refuse to accept the results of the election as accurately representing the views of the citizens, and seek to undermine or oust the elected government? One mark of polarisation is the rhetoric coming from these groups after the election. Fierce criticism and disappointment are fine—this is the language of a loyal opposition. But rhetoric of illegitimacy is worrying—this is the language of insurgency.

Winner's restraint. Democracy cannot survive if, once in power, the winner is perceived to be actively trying to punish or eliminate their opponents. We are not talking here about the usual 'winner gets the spoils' approach to politics. It is normal that the winner will seek to reward their supporters, at some cost to their opponents. But if the rhetoric coming out of the winning camp is about the illegitimacy of the opposition, if the winner works to permanently bend the institutions of government to their advantage, criminalise opposition or permanently exile their opponents, then we begin to worry about the stability of democracy.

A number of factors affect the probability that losers will give their consent and that winners will show restraint. Both are more likely if elections are viewed as free and fair. Loser's consent and winner's restraint are also more likely if power is shared among several parties, and if there are constraints, checks and balances on the winner. Both winners and losers are more likely to abide by the democratic rules of the game if they believe there is a good chance that the next election could produce a different winner/loser. Finally, political opponents are less likely to feel threatened by the other side when they are closer ideologically than when they perceive the other side to have preferences that are very different from their own. To summarise, free and fair elections, power sharing, alternation in power, checks and balances, and lack of polarisation are the main factors contributing to loser's consent and winner's restraint, while the absence of these factors undermines these two pillars of democracy.

How does Indonesia stack up in terms of these five factors? We have already seen that—despite some problems with the electoral environment and the health of civil society organisations and parties—Indonesian elections, in general, continue to be free and fair. When it comes to power sharing, Indonesia is an innovator. Slater and Simmons (2013) have described what we typically see in Indonesia as 'promiscuous powersharing'—with large, oversized coalition governments and no parties permanently shut out of access to resources (see also Slater 2004). While there are certainly costs to this high degree of power sharing, it has helped to lower the stakes for both winners and losers and to keep most sides committed to democratic norms. The fact that no single party has managed to dominate presidential and legislative elections also means that most actors remain invested in democracy. And in terms of checks and balances, institutions such as the legislature and judiciary, while far from perfect, have not yet been completely captured or sidelined by the executive in the ways seen in many autocratising contexts.

That said, the introduction in late 2019 of a law that stripped the Corruption Eradication Commission of important powers and undermined its independence is extremely concerning (see Power, this volume). The new law constitutes an unprecedented attack on one of Indonesia's most important institutional checks on political corruption.

Finally, we turn to the question of polarisation. Here the data are much less sanguine. Polarisation, in my view, is the looming Achilles' heel of Indonesian democracy. According to several major indicators, the degree of polarisation in Indonesia has increased in recent years and the civility of discourse has deteriorated. This is often discussed in the popular media and by scholars and pundits (see Nuraniyah; Warburton, this volume) and is evident in laws aimed at criminalising criticism of government institutions and officials (see Setiawan, this volume). It is also picked up in the V-Dem data.

Let us consider a few different indicators of how deliberative or divided Indonesian democracy is.

Over the past 10 years, there has been a small increase in the use of hate speech by major political parties, a reduction in the extent to which there is widespread public deliberation about important policy issues,

Figure 2.8   The rise of polarisation in Indonesia

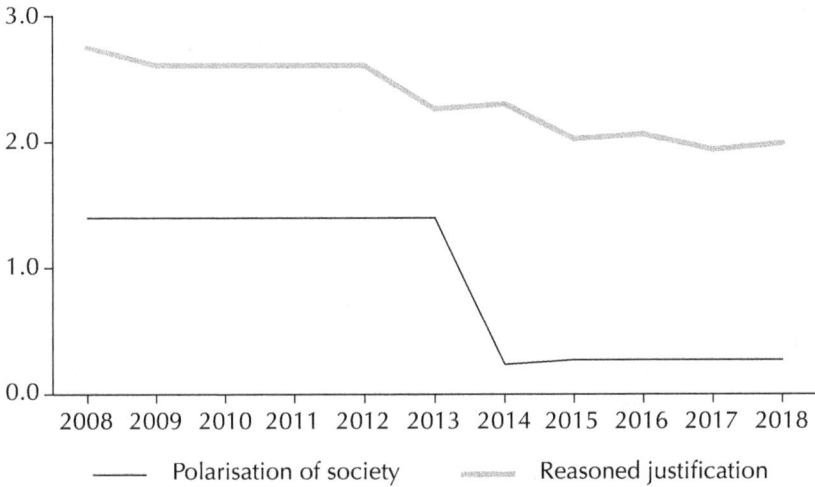

Note: Lower scores denote greater polarisation or less willingness to engage in reasoned debate.
Source: Coppedge et al. (2019).

and a mild decline in the extent to which political elites acknowledge and respect counterarguments. More alarmingly, we see a sharp decline in the perceived willingness of political elites to engage in meaningful, reasoned policy debate by offering up public and considered justifications for their positions (Figure 2.8). The latter is typically an indicator of the degree of polarisation, and indeed V-Dem has documented a disturbing increase in polarisation in the past few years. In Figure 2.8, lower scores correspond to greater polarisation. On a scale that runs from serious polarisation to no polarisation, the level of polarisation in Indonesia is now coded as serious. One might argue that the increase in polarisation is temporary: perhaps it is just an artefact of the past two presidential elections, which were fought between only two candidates, and the same two each time. Nevertheless, polarisation is a warning indicator for Indonesian democracy.

Why is polarisation potentially so problematic? One of the puzzles of the third wave of autocratisation is how autocratisers are able to get away with undermining democracy. Why do voters and parties who routinely profess a commitment to democracy, as they do in Indonesia, simultaneously support leaders who subvert it? It is useful to remember that institutions on their own cannot constrain autocratic behaviour. To be effective, they must be backed by parties, citizens and norms of acceptable behaviour. In other words, parties and citizens must be willing to hold leaders accountable for deviations from democratic norms and attacks on democratic institutions. However, polarisation tends to short-circuit this accountability mechanism. Polarisation is associated with a rhetoric and attitude of intolerance, involving the separation of society into two homogeneous and antagonistic groups. Where polarisation is high, one group not only opposes but also despises the other side, and seeks to defeat it by any means possible.[7] Where such attitudes take root and grow, democracy is at risk.

Svolik (2019: 23) details how the type of polarisation that seems to be growing in Indonesia can eat away at the foundations of democracy. He notes that, in a democracy, voters are often confronted with a choice between two potentially conflicting concerns: their support of democratic principles, and their political or partisan interests. In effect, aggrandisers 'ask their supporters to trade off democratic principles for partisan interests' (ibid.). In polarised societies citizens become contingent democrats, in favour of democracy as long as their side wins. But if punishing a leader's authoritarian tendencies requires supporting or defending the opposing side, many will balk (Svolik 2019: 24). In short, in sharply polarised electorates, loser's consent and winner's restraint begin to crumble, as even the voters who value democracy become willing to sacrifice democratic norms and institutions for the sake of supporting politicians who champion their interests, or punish their opponents (ibid.).

These new would-be autocrats do not directly threaten democratic elections, at least at first. In fact, they draw their legitimacy from their electoral victory. But once elections are over, they view checks on their power as obstacles to be overcome, or even to be swept away. They treat disagreement with their policies and priorities as irrelevant, illegitimate and immoral. 'Polarization thus presents aspiring authoritarians with a structural opportunity: they can undermine democracy and get away with it' (Svolik 2019: 24; see also Gandhi 2019). In short, polarisation is an important weapon in the arsenal of would-be aggrandisers and autocratisers, and we are already beginning to see the deployment and consequences of this weapon in Indonesia.

---

7   This is also the core division that populists seek to create and exploit (Mudde 2017).

CONCLUSION

To sum up, Indonesian democracy is imperfect, as all democracies are, but generally healthy when compared with its neighbours, and with many other democracies around the world. Indonesia's two-decade history of democratic stability is laudable, as is its record of holding elections that are, for the most part, peaceful, free and fair. A focus on the vulnerabilities within Indonesia's democracy should not detract from these successes, but rather provide hope for Indonesia's continued resilience in the face of new challenges.

However, there are areas of concern—warning indicators that deserve attention if Indonesia is to avoid or arrest movement down the path towards autocratisation. Weak political parties and high levels of electoral clientelism continue to encumber Indonesia's democratic progress. But most concerning is the increasingly polarised political and social environment, which is contributing to a worsening environment for civil society groups, undermining trust in electoral results among some groups, and helping to fuel efforts to criminalise dissent. These are the areas supporters of democracy must attend to if Indonesia is to remain the leading democracy in Southeast Asia.

REFERENCES

Aspinall, E. 2011. 'Democratization and ethnic politics in Indonesia: nine theses'. *Journal of East Asian Studies* 11(2): 289–319.

Aspinall, E. and W. Berenschot. 2019. *Democracy for Sale: Elections, Clientelism, and the State in Indonesia*. Ithaca, NY: Cornell University Press.

Aspinall, E. and M. Sukmajati, eds. 2016. *Electoral Dynamics in Indonesia: Money Politics, Patronage and Clientelism at the Grassroots*. Singapore: NUS Press.

Bermeo, N. 2016. 'On democratic backsliding'. *Journal of Democracy* 27(1): 5–19.

Bernard, M., A. Hicken, C. Reenock and S.I. Lindberg. 2015. 'Institutional sub-systems and the survival of democracy: do political and civil society matter?'. V-Dem Working Paper 4. Gothenburg: Varieties of Democracy Institute. https://www.v-dem.net/media/filer_public/62/8e/628e4e08-ffb4-45ee-84c5-a25032d1b0dc/v-dem_working_paper_2015_4.pdf

Coppedge, M., J. Gerring, C.H. Knutsen, S.I. Lindberg, J. Teorell, D. Altman, M. Bernhard, et al. 2019. 'V-Dem dataset—version 9'. Gothenburg: Varieties of Democracy Institute. https://doi.org/10.23696/vdemcy19

Davidson, J.S. 2009. 'Dilemmas of democratic consolidation in Indonesia'. *Pacific Review* 22(3): 293–310.

Gandhi, J. 2019. 'The institutional roots of democratic backsliding'. *Journal of Politics* 81(1): e11–e16.

Hicken, A. 2009. *Building Party Systems in Developing Democracies.* New York: Cambridge University Press.

Hicken, A. 2018. 'Party systems and the politics of development'. In *Handbook on the Politics of Development,* edited by C. Lancaster and N. van de Walle, 499–516. Oxford: Oxford University Press.

Kimura, E. 2012. 'Indonesia in 2011: a glass half-empty'. *Asian Survey* 52(1): 186–94.

Levitsky, S. and D. Ziblatt. 2018. *How Democracies Die.* New York: Broadway Books.

Lührmann, A. and S.I. Lindberg. 2019. 'A third wave of autocratization is here: what is new about it?'. *Democratization* 26(7): 1,095–113.

Lussier, D.N. and M.S. Fish. 2012. 'Indonesia: the benefits of civic engagement'. *Journal of Democracy* 23(1): 70–84.

Mietzner, M. 2009. 'Indonesia's 2009 elections: populism, dynasties and the consolidation of the party system'. *Analysis.* Sydney: Lowy Institute for International Policy. May. https://www.files.ethz.ch/isn/100187/Mietzner_0509LowyAnalysis.pdf

Morgan, R.K., A. Beger and A. Glynn. 2019. 'Varieties of forecasts: predicting adverse regime transitions'. V-Dem Working Paper 89. Gothenburg: Varieties of Democracy Institute. https://www.v-dem.net/media/filer_public/b9/b2/b9b2c233-ec45-425d-a397-1cd80dadb63a/v-dem_working_paper_2019_89.pdf

Mudde, C. 2017. 'Populism: an ideational approach'. In *The Oxford Handbook of Populism,* edited by C.R. Kaltwasser, P. Taggart, P.O. Espejo and P. Ostiguy. New York: Oxford University Press.

Muhtadi, B. 2019. *Vote Buying in Indonesia: The Mechanics of Electoral Bribery.* Singapore: Palgrave Macmillan. https://link.springer.com/book/10.1007/978-981-13-6779-3

Powell, J.M. and C.L. Thyne. 2011. 'Global instances of coups from 1950 to 2010: a new dataset'. *Journal of Peace Research* 48(2): 249–59.

Scarpello, F. 2008. 'Ten years after Suharto, Indonesia is a glass half full'. *World Politics Review,* 21 May. https://www.worldpoliticsreview.com/articles/2163/ten-years-after-suharto-indonesia-is-a-glass-half-full

Self, D. and A. Hicken. 2018. 'Why populism? How parties shape the electoral fortune of populists'. V-Dem Working Paper 76. Gothenburg: Varieties of Democracy Institute. https://www.v-dem.net/media/filer_public/d8/eb/d8ebc26f-733e-4fa9-b48a-e50a4833c9a7/v-dem_working_paper_2018_76.pdf

Slater, D. 2004. 'Indonesia's accountability trap: party cartels and presidential power after democratic transition'. *Indonesia* 78(October): 61–92.

Slater, D. 2009. 'Democracy yes, accountability no?'. *Inside Indonesia* 95(Jan–Mar). https://www.insideindonesia.org/democracy-yes-accountability-no

Slater, D. and E. Simmons. 2013. 'Coping by colluding: political uncertainty and promiscuous powersharing in Indonesia and Bolivia'. *Comparative Political Studies* 46(11): 1,366–93.

Svolik, M.W. 2019. 'Polarization versus democracy'. *Journal of Democracy* 30(3): 20–32.

Zaman, A.N. 2008. '10 years after Suharto'. Common Ground News Service, 16 July. https://www.worldpress.org/Asia/3200.cfm

3   Indonesia's tenuous democratic success and survival

Dan Slater

Democracy is receding and authoritarianism is rising across the globe. Against this ominous backdrop, Indonesia has long stood out as a relative success story—albeit an increasingly tenuous one. This essay offers a historically grounded explanation for why Indonesia has achieved the relative democratic success that it has over the past two decades. It also aims to clarify the exact ways in which Indonesian democracy has faltered and remains most vulnerable to further backsliding. My point of departure is a conviction that explaining democratic success requires thorough attention to the variety of ways that democracies can fail.

My argument for why Indonesian democracy has surprisingly succeeded centres on the historical inheritances the country enjoyed when transitioning to democracy in 1998–99: specifically, (1) *egalitarian nationalism* inherited from before the authoritarian period, and (2) *institutional developments* inherited from the authoritarian period itself. I argue that these historical inheritances best explain why Indonesia has managed to avoid the four major pitfalls that new democracies so often confront: state failure, military takeover, electoral authoritarianism and illiberal democracy.[1]

However, I also argue that Indonesia has not fully escaped, and can never fully escape, the fourth danger: illiberal democracy. Whether

---

1   A fifth pitfall in Indonesia that I have discussed elsewhere at length (perhaps for some readers, ad nauseam), what we might call elite collusion, is better considered a threat to democratic quality than survival. If elite collusion is to lead to outright democratic breakdown, it would need to do so through one of the other pitfalls discussed here.

Indonesia will avoid succumbing to an illiberal democratic fate depends largely on whether its deep but increasingly distant inheritance of egalitarian nationalism can withstand the challenges of those who would undermine and undo it. Indeed, it has been Indonesia's lingering vulnerability to illiberal democracy that explains the softness in the country's democracy rating. But it is vital to appreciate that the three other main threats to democracy—state failure, military takeover and electoral authoritarianism—have all been successfully evaded. I expect those critical escapes to continue, and these are no small accomplishments.

In the following section I explain why the egalitarian nationalism that arose during Indonesia's fierce independence struggle and the institutional development that occurred under Suharto's authoritarian New Order regime (1966–98) have given Indonesia a set of historical inheritances that have helped its democracy take root. The subsequent section distinguishes the four common pitfalls that democracies face and details how Indonesia's historical inheritances have served as resources for avoiding each of those pitfalls. The conclusion remarks on the enduring and even endemic danger of illiberal democracy, not just in Indonesia but across the democratic world.

HISTORICAL INHERITANCES

Egalitarian nationalism

Nationalism has a bad rap in liberal circles, and not without reason. Treating the nation as a higher priority than more universal values can lead to harmfully prideful behaviours abroad and dangerously prejudicial actions at home. For present purposes, the critical point is that nationalism is often deployed against ethnic and religious minorities, defining them as second-class citizens undeserving of the full liberal protections that are supposed to accompany democracy as it is substantively understood. For democracy to thrive, it may seem, nationalism needs to be tamed.

Yet nationalism comes in many different varieties, and not all of them work at cross-purposes to democratic development. Two main distinctions are important.[2] First, the national political community can be defined in more inclusive terms or exclusive terms when it comes to ascriptive identities such as ethnicity and religion. As scholars have long argued, nationalism can be more civic or more ethnic in character, and

---

2   This paragraph and broader argument draws on my collaborative work with Maya Tudor of Oxford University (see, for example, Tudor and Slater 2016).

this matters greatly for democratic development. Second, some nations are built through the mobilisation and lionisation of ordinary people, whereas others are born without removing traditional, hereditary and feudalistic elites from their comfortable perches as fathers (and never seemingly mothers) of the nation. One might call this the distinction between elitist nationalism and popular nationalism (Vom Hau 2008). When nationalism is both civic and popular in character, it can be considered *egalitarian*, whereas nationalisms that combine ethnic and elitist features might be called *hierarchical*. The first main argument I make here is that Indonesian nationalism is far more egalitarian than hierarchical, especially in comparison to most of its South Asian and Southeast Asian neighbours, and this has served as one of the most significant historical contributors to Indonesia's surprising democratic success.

Indonesia's egalitarian nationalism was a product of its revolutionary path to independence in 1949. As by far the most significant and valuable colony in the Dutch empire, Indonesia was not going to gain its freedom without a fight. If India was the jewel in Britain's crown, Indonesia was Holland's diamond-encrusted tiara. So when World War II ended and Japan surrendered to the Allies after its four-year reign over Indonesia, the Dutch returned to the scene with every intention of staying for good. What followed was a bloody and brutal battle for independence, known simply in Indonesian nationalist lore as *perjuangan*: struggle (Reid 1974; see also Kahin 1952). The most prominent figure in this struggle was Sukarno, a charismatic and polyglot orator who had been inspiring popular mobilisation against the Dutch, across every imaginable social divide, for decades. Sukarno's consistent message was that Marxists, Muslims and nationalists could all unite, and indeed must unite, for Indonesia to expel the Dutch. All good things would follow from ending colonialism. Sukarno spent much of the prewar period in a colonial prison for expressing these ideas and mobilising them as the leading founder of the Indonesian National Party (Partai Nasional Indonesia, PNI). Japan's conquest of Indonesia was a godsend for Sukarno and the nationalist movement he led, since Japan aimed to rule with the collaboration of radical popular anti-Dutch nationalists rather than traditional pro-Dutch collaborators. They even went so far as to mobilise an entirely new Indonesian army dedicated to national self-defence. Under Japanese rule, egalitarian nationalists like Sukarno shared power, not prison cells. That left them in an ideal position after Japan's defeat and departure to lead the violent popular struggle for independence against the returning Dutch, and to make their ideals the founding principles of the newborn republic.

These nationalist ideals were neither exclusionary nor elitist. In both its civilian and military wings, Indonesia's nationalist movement was led by figures lacking hereditary status or any other kind of formal hierarchical standing. They did not valorise old feudalistic or dynastic elites, but the common people, or *rakyat*, a word that gained mythic nationalist power rivalling both *perjuangan* (struggle) and *kemerdekaan* (independence). Perhaps even more significantly, Indonesia's leading nationalists fended off efforts to define the nation in religious terms, either by making the majority religion of Islam the only recognised national religion, or by mandating that Muslims must follow Islamic law. Although Indonesia would not be defined as a secular nation like India, the state would maintain a formal equidistance from all of the country's major religions. According to the official national philosophy of Pancasila, belief in God is mandatory, and citizens must adhere to one of six officially sanctioned religions: Islam, Buddhism, Protestantism, Catholicism, Hinduism or Confucianism.

Egalitarian nationalism does not ensure democracy—no single causal factor does, including economic development—but it does help secure and sustain it. When a dictator becomes too corrupt, popular nationalism helps instil the sense of popular sovereignty that draws crowds into the streets to topple him. When forces of ethnic or religious intolerance attack minorities in ways incompatible with substantive democracy, civic nationalism provides a set of narratives, laws and practices that can help defend disfavoured groups.

To be sure, types of nationalism are ideal types, and no nation is defined in entirely egalitarian or hierarchical fashion. Equally importantly, the triumph of egalitarian nationalism at the moment of independence does not eliminate those favouring more hierarchical visions of the nation from the political scene. Initial battles to define the nation in egalitarian terms evolve into ongoing battles to defend the nation from those who refuse to accept that all citizens—regardless of ethnicity or religion—should have the same rights and equal political status. Indonesia's egalitarian nationalism is far from pristine, and it is even further from unchallenged. Yet it provides an enduring resource for democratic development and defence that many of Indonesia's neighbours lack.

Institutional development

Every democracy in the world relies, to some degree, on features that developed before that country became a democracy. Perhaps a vibrant urban middle class emerged during authoritarian times. Maybe a smoothly functioning legal system was built by a coloniser with nothing but authoritarian intentions. Sometimes a sense of national self-consciousness, solidarity and social capital emerges in the very process of collectively defying a tyrant, whether homegrown or foreign in origin. Widespread literacy might have first emerged through religious instruction when a country was still ruled by a precolonial dynasty. Of most importance for the discussion here, sometimes authoritarian regimes build institutions that a democracy can inherit and turn to purposes of democratic stability, even if that was not the original intent of those institutions' creators.

Institutional development under Suharto's authoritarian regime was especially impressive in two domains, both of which ultimately paid surprising and unintended dividends for democratic stability. The first was state capacity. The Dutch colonial state had been world-renowned for its governing effectiveness—albeit mostly for repressive and extractive purposes—but this institutional inheritance was largely squandered during Indonesia's first two decades of independence. Once the authoritative executor of commands across the vast archipelago, Indonesia's postcolonial bureaucracy found itself starved of resources and bereft of operational autonomy during the hypermobilised years of revolution, parliamentary democracy and Sukarno's 'Guided Democracy' (Feith 1962). Sukarno profoundly mistrusted political parties, but he respected bureaucrats even less. By the time Sukarno was toppled in the confusion of conspiracy, communism and coup d'état that ripped the country apart in 1965–66, the Indonesian state was in no position to govern, and there was scarcely a functioning private economy to govern in any event.

The tide turned dramatically with Suharto's takeover. In the transition's first phase, anti-communist elements in the Indonesian military, led by Suharto and allied closely with Islamic civil society, unleashed a horrific bloodbath against the Indonesian Communist Party (Partai Komunis Indonesia, PKI) and its alleged sympathisers. Hundreds of thousands died. It was upon this mountain of corpses—and it would be a disservice to those lost souls to call it anything less—that Suharto's 'New Order' would be built. Yet with the truly enormous and epically tragic exceptions of the PKI and, after the mid-1970s, East Timor, the Suharto regime governed not so much through deadly repression as through smothering coercion and sweeping co-option. The anti-communist mass killings were not the exception that proved the rule; they were the exception that established New Order rule.

It was only through the wholesale reconstruction and revamping of the Indonesian state that the Suharto regime achieved such stability and longevity. The military was the political heart of the New Order, but it was by no means its organisational entirety. For starters, Suharto invested massive new resources in the bureaucracy, at first thanks to the revenue floods of Western foreign aid and the OPEC oil boom, and later by virtue of the booming revenues that restored economic growth and foreign direct investment made possible. Military officers were typically given a variety of leading positions in government ministries, but this was more to ensure the political loyalty of the bureaucracy than to install military governance. Bureaucrats were entrusted and empowered to govern, in areas ranging from family planning to rice self-sufficiency to managing price volatility in vital basic commodities. Considering that bureaucrats overwhelmingly supported the New Order as a bulwark against communism and as a welcome source of developmental and technocratic energy—in addition to the obvious risks of openly associating either with communist or Sukarnoist ideology—Suharto need not have worried that bureaucrats needed military oversight to do the regime's bidding.

The upshot of the state-building that unfolded during the three decades of the New Order was a highly impressive track record of economic growth and a remarkable run of relative political stability (Hill 1994). To be sure, both growth and stability were fuelled by colossal corruption that ultimately helped bring the Suharto regime down in the 1997–98 Asian financial crisis (Aspinall 2005). Yet the fact remains that a leviathan quite capable of governing was one of the Suharto regime's most important by-products. As we will see in the next section, this has especially helped Indonesian democracy avoid the pitfalls of state failure and military takeover.

The second critical domain for institutional development under Suharto's New Order was in political parties. Since the regime had such widespread support across the political spectrum, it did not fear a return to highly controlled electoral and party politics within the first decade of its founding. Although the New Order was a military regime, it commanded tremendous civilian support. Party development and electoral politics provided these supportive civilians with routes to influence and largesse, even under the suffocating coercive blanket of New Order rule. Most significantly, Suharto quickly supported the building of a regime-supporting political party called Golkar. The party's name reveals both its origins and its governing purpose. Short for *golongan karya* (functional groups), Golkar was a political vehicle constructed from the wide variety of conservative political organisations that arose to counter the radical leftist mass mobilisation of Sukarno and the PKI during the early- to mid-1960s. In formal terms, Golkar was not a political party but an umbrella organisation—symbolically, a hovering banyan tree— under which all these political organisations could shelter and coalesce. This made it easier for Suharto to mandate that all Indonesian civil servants become Golkar members, since the organisation was more like a bureaucratic super-ministry than a partisan vehicle in legal terms. Yet in practice, Golkar would compete in national elections every five years against the two parties that the regime permitted to form—the Islamic United Development Party (Partai Persatuan Pembangunan, PPP) and the nationalist Indonesian Democratic Party (Partai Demokrasi Indonesia, PDI)—and crush them. In essence, the state apparatus itself assumed the electoral role of a political party, without surrendering any of the powers or resources it held by virtue of being Indonesia's ultimate sovereign authority.

By both hook and crook, Golkar commanded overwhelming electoral support from the New Order's founding election of 1971 until its final election of 1997. Unlike the many pure military regimes and single-party regimes that transitioned to democracy after the Cold War with no recent electoral experience, Indonesia became a democracy in 1999 with a firmly established electoral system already in place (see, for example, Antlöv and Cederroth 2004). Party competition had been tightly governed, but it had not been absent. Moderate and conservative politicians knew that elections were something they could continue to win, at impressive levels if not at the landslide levels of the authoritarian era, even after full democratic competition was installed. Golkar was the only political party with an established presence at the local level across the entire Indonesian archipelago (Tomsa 2008). The economic crisis and surrounding corruption that felled Suharto in the mass protests of 1998 left Golkar weakened but not destroyed. For all the uncertainty that surrounded Indonesia's democratic transition in 1998–99, regularised democratic procedures quickly served more as a source of stability than of instability amid the general tumult. The stoutness of both the state apparatus and the Golkar-led party system built under the Suharto regime was critical to the surprising democratic stability that followed it.

FOUR PITFALLS

I have argued thus far that Indonesia's nationalist movement and revolution built a relatively egalitarian nationalism, both in class and ethnoreligious terms, and that Indonesia's authoritarian New Order built relatively effective party and state organisations. In this section I clarify how these two key inheritances have helped Indonesia avoid four distinctive pitfalls.

A new democracy can experience (1) *state failure*, if governance fails and either the country falls apart in civil war or separatism, or ruling elites take extreme authoritarian measures to prevent such outcomes from arising. It can also fall through (2) *military takeover*, if men in fatigues refuse to accept the hindrances that democratic politics presents. In less extreme scenarios, democracy can backslide into (3) *electoral authoritarianism*, if politicians start doing whatever they want to win elections, or (4) *illiberal democracy*, if they start doing whatever they want after winning elections.[3] Put otherwise, electoral authoritarians target their coercion against opposition parties through the ballot box; illiberal democrats take coercive aim at minorities, critics and protesters who challenge their majoritarian mandate.

In light of the arguments offered in this chapter, how have Indonesia's inheritances of egalitarian nationalism and institutional development helped the country avoid wrecking on these multiple sharp shoals? And why does illiberal democracy continue to loom as the deepest pitfall into which Indonesian democracy remains likely to plunge?

State failure

State failure loomed especially large as a potential outcome during Indonesia's tumultuous transition years. The provinces of East Timor, Aceh and West Papua all presented credible separatist claims. Ethnic and religious violence erupted in various parts of the archipelago, most notably in the eastern Indonesian districts of Ambon, Maluku and Poso. Riots against Indonesia's ethnic Chinese minority hit as close to home as Jakarta itself. Islamist terrorism delivered repeated blows, most infamously in Bali. Leading country experts quite seriously asked whether the republic could endure without the military holding it all together by force. Less than a decade removed from the collapse of the Soviet Union and Yugoslavia, the notion that powerholders in Jakarta would fail to keep the country intact and minimally governable was far from far-fetched.

Inheritances of strong nationalism and a strong state proved up to these challenges, however. Remarkably, in hindsight—and even in real time—East Timor was permitted to exit Indonesia by popular referendum, though pro-integration militias long backed by the Indonesian military inflicted a horrible price on East Timor's people for so choosing. Not only was it remarkable that East Timor was allowed to secede: equally remarkable was the lack of separatist sentiment in other parts of the archipelago that, like East Timor, had sizeable Christian majorities. Even as Christian communities feared eradication in the deadly religious conflicts that erupted in demographically divided regions like Ambon and Maluku, no wider push for Christian separation and self-determination

---

3 I develop this distinction between electoral authoritarianism and illiberal
   democracy in Slater (2018).

gathered steam. In part this was because national politicians invoked the pluralistic version of nationalism, embodied by the concept of Pancasila, in their condemnations of religious violence. Christians might not have been made to feel at home in certain areas, but their rightful place in the Indonesian nation was never seriously questioned.

The Indonesian state also came decisively to the rescue of the country's founding 'Unity in Diversity' ideal. Steeled by over three decades of military rule, the Indonesian military and security services were quickly deployed to conflict zones across the archipelago and restored peace in surprisingly short order. A national policy of decentralisation also allowed divided provinces and districts to split, making local ethnoreligious conflicts less intractable. Islamist terrorism was also effectively contained by relatively expert and well-equipped intelligence services. In sum, state failure was avoided because the Indonesian nation was inclusive enough and the Indonesian state was capable enough to prevent the republic from violently unravelling.

Military takeover

While the Indonesian military was strong enough to help keep the country together, it did not use this strength to reassume direct control of the political system. Herein lay perhaps the biggest surprise of Indonesian democratisation. During the years preceding Suharto's fall, the overwhelming consensus among Indonesia-watchers was that his New Order would be followed by some variety of collective military rule.

Yet this did not come to pass. The first reason was because Suharto had increasingly personalised, factionalised and to some extent Islamicised the military during his final years in power. This left the Indonesian military as the country's most powerful actor, but not a highly cohesive one, as Suharto exited the scene in the face of cascading mass protests and elite defections. Of particular importance was the intense factional rivalry between Suharto's son-in-law, Prabowo Subianto, who commanded the military's strategic units in and around Jakarta, and the national head of the military, Wiranto. Prabowo proved ready and willing to unleash violence as a way of justifying martial law and his own assumption of dictatorial powers—much as his father-in-law had done in 1965. Wiranto and other professional soldiers saw Prabowo as an up-jumped opportunist who was a scourge on the military rather than a saviour of national stability. It was more important to Wiranto and his ilk to restrain Prabowo and restore military unity during a time of crisis than it was either to keep Suharto in power or to salvage the military's leading governance role.

This is not to say the military simply stepped aside. For the first five years of Indonesian democracy, the military retained a sizeable proportion of appointed parliamentary seats, and prominent military officers played a major role in electoral politics (Mietzner 2009). Indeed, Indonesia's first directly elected president, Susilo Bambang Yudhoyono (2004–14), was one of the top military officials of the late Suharto era. Yet the military surrendered its parliamentary seats with nary a fuss in the constitutional revisions that followed democratisation in plenty of time for the 2004 national elections.

The best explanation for why the military did so lies in Indonesia's party–state institutional inheritance. Electoral support in 1999 and 2004 did not flow to former radical opponents of the New Order or to proponents of root-and-branch military reform, but to conservative and moderate parties and politicians with deep experience in Indonesia's military-led political system. Of particular importance was the continued leading role played by Golkar, which has remained one of Indonesia's top electoral performers and has consistently secured substantial representation in governing coalitions and cabinets. With the military able to rely on Golkar and the bureaucracy as pillars of political stability, there was little manifest reason for military men to dominate the civilian arena.

Electoral authoritarianism

Besides avoiding the fates of state failure and military takeover, Indonesian democracy has, over two decades, avoided backsliding into electoral authoritarianism. This arises when one party or political leader gains majoritarian control through elections, then uses that control to stifle opposition and competition for the country's top political posts. The main reason Indonesia has been at least relatively immune from electoral authoritarianism is its sheer scale and diversity, combined with the role of egalitarian nationalism in ensuring that Indonesia's vast array of ethnic and religious communities enjoy an active role in national political life. Golkar was unable to maintain the kind of majority support that could have allowed it to rebuild the electoral authoritarianism of the New Order era. Electoral support in 1999 flowed to the party vehicles of egalitarian nationalism: the Indonesian Democratic Party of Struggle (Partai Demokrasi Indonesia-Perjuangan, PDI-P), representing Indonesia's Sukarnoist, pluralist, Pancasila ideological stream; the National Awakening Party (Partai Kebangkitan Bangsa, PKB), channelling the world's largest Islamic social organisation, Nahdlatul Ulama (NU); and the National Mandate Party (Partai Amanat Nasional, PAN), the main vehicle for another massive Islamic group, Muhammadiyah. All of these parties had roots in the ideological developments of the nationalist struggle and had maintained much of their vibrancy during the New Order. If any party had prospects of capturing majority electoral support and imposing electoral authoritarianism from that perch, it was almost certainly PDI-P, which, led by Sukarno's daughter, Megawati Sukarnoputri, secured over 33 per cent of the 1999 parliamentary vote. Yet the robustness of Islamic parties as well as the continued kingmaking role of Golkar ensured that Megawati was brought into sweeping power-sharing arrangements rather than being allowed to rule alone after she was elevated to the presidency in 2001.

If any politician and party have posed a threat of re-establishing electoral authoritarianism in Indonesia, it has been via the re-emergence of Prabowo Subianto and his populist party vehicle, Gerindra (Gerakan Indonesia Raya; Greater Indonesia Movement). After being dishonourably discharged from the military and spending a spell overseas burnishing his economic fortunes if not his political reputation, Prabowo returned to the scene for the 2009 elections and garnered a spot as Megawati's running mate for the vice presidency. The Megawati–Prabowo team was trounced in President Yudhoyono's landslide re-election. Prabowo then rose to the top of the ticket in both 2014 and 2019, standing as one of the two presidential candidates in both contests. Both times Prabowo was defeated by former Jakarta governor Joko Widodo (Jokowi), a member of PDI-P and a stalwart of Indonesia's religiously pluralist Pancasila tradition. It is impossible to say with confidence whether Prabowo would have either attempted to undermine Indonesian democracy to the point that it would be better considered electorally authoritarian, or would have succeeded at doing so. What is certain is that he has simply lacked the numbers to give it a try. Indonesian democracy has thus passed its sternest test by defeating a likely aspiring authoritarian at the ballot box, rather than desperately trying to restrain him after he has gained presidential powers.

Illiberal democracy

This leaves illiberal democracy as the main lingering threat to Indonesian democracy. Whereas electoral authoritarianism would see an elected leader stifling political opposition, illiberal democracy in Indonesia would most likely see him attacking religious minorities as second-class citizens. The very diversity that tempers the threat of electoral authoritarianism, as just discussed, simultaneously and permanently tempts opportunistic politicians to become illiberal democrats.

It is here where egalitarian nationalism has mattered most, and must continue to hold the line against those who would undermine it. In both the 2014 and 2019 presidential campaigns, Prabowo began assembling an alliance of conservative Muslim forces for his battles against PDI-P and Jokowi. This cleavage had remained salient throughout the post–New Order period: indeed, during the 2004 and 2009 campaigns, Yudhoyono curried favour with conservative Islamists in his successful efforts to trounce Megawati and her more pluralist electoral coalitions. Yet the 2014 election—and particularly Prabowo's campaign—raised religious sectarianism to another level. This increasing religious polarisation showed its greatest effect in 2017 when ethnic Chinese Jakarta governor Basuki Tjahaja Purnama, popularly known as Ahok—the plain-spoken running mate for Jokowi in his 2012 gubernatorial campaign—was defeated in his re-election campaign and subsequently imprisoned for insulting Islam in the wake of massive protests to bring him to justice for doing so. The defeat and imprisonment of Ahok sent chills down the spine of every believer in Indonesia's ethnic and religious pluralism. The looming question in the wake of Ahok's jailing was whether the Islamic mass movement that arose to bring him down would then succeed in 2019 by doing the same to Jokowi, removing from power a president who hews to pluralist nationalism rather than Islamism.

Jokowi prevailed in that contest, but only by tilting further in the direction of illiberal democracy than his pluralist backers preferred (Aspinall and Mietzner 2019; Power 2018). Most importantly, Jokowi replaced Golkar leader Jusuf Kalla as his running mate, instead selecting a deeply conservative Islamic leader from NU, Ma'ruf Amin, to become his new vice president. The clear goal was to inoculate himself from religious attacks without squandering his overwhelming support among pluralist nationalists. Although the Islamist rhetoric was even stronger in 2019 than in 2014, it was surely more muted than it would have been had Jokowi not protected his Islamic flank as he did with his controversial choice of running mate. In fact, the main difference between the 2019 and 2014 votes was that Jokowi gained overwhelming support from followers of NU, especially in Central Java and East Java, after basically splitting the NU vote with Prabowo in the 2014 campaign (Shofia and Pepinsky 2019). Additionally, Jokowi's stupendous advantage over Prabowo among non-Muslims became even more pronounced in 2019 than in 2014. In regions such as Bali, where the population is predominantly Hindu, Jokowi secured over 90 per cent of the vote. It is thus clear that Jokowi was able to tap into Indonesia's deep reservoirs of egalitarian nationalism—a nationalism in which Islam plays a major role, but never a solitary leading role—to save both his own presidency and, arguably, Indonesian democracy from its most dramatic avatar of illiberalism, Prabowo.

CONCLUSION

Indonesia's democratic success is as fragile as it is impressive. Its success at avoiding state failure, military takeover and electoral authoritarianism by no means ensures it will continue to succeed at staving off the nastiest features of illiberal democracy. If Indonesia's pluralists cannot continue to defend the egalitarian version of the nation that the country's revolutionary generation first defined, Indonesia will surely follow further in the footsteps of so many other democracies that have turned sharply illiberal in recent years.

Egalitarian nationalism takes a long time to build. Unfortunately, illiberal democracy can be imposed in a matter of moments. All it really takes is for an elected chief executive, backed by a sufficient segment of the ruling political elite, to start strong-arming and even silencing his critics. In this sense it is not just Prabowo, but anyone elected to the presidency who has the power to turn Indonesian democracy in a decisively illiberal direction.

With so many illiberal allies backing his presidency, Jokowi himself has been increasingly tempted, especially since his re-election, to deepen his own illiberal practices in turn. When protests erupted before Jokowi's second inauguration over bills passed by parliament that would gut Indonesia's independent anti-corruption commission, remove environmental regulations on the mining industry, and restrict certain forms of political dissent, the newly re-elected president unleashed police repression and internet controls not seen since Indonesia democratised. This is not an electoral authoritarian gaining a stranglehold on national power for himself and his ruling party by restricting his electoral opponents. This is an increasingly illiberal democrat, backed by the legitimacy of an emphatic double-electoral mandate, using the full force of the state apparatus against society at large when it challenges and speaks out against the political designs he shares with the broad swathe of Indonesia's political elite. By subsequently inviting Prabowo to serve as his defence minister, Jokowi signalled with abundant clarity that his second term would be defined by the pursuit of economic development and political stability, not the continued defence of democracy. That job is once again being left to Indonesia's civil society, armed with an egalitarian nationalist spirit that provides a strong defence, but not an unbreakable guardrail, against the ravages of illiberal democracy. However, as other contributions to this volume show, growing restrictions on civil liberties, critical discourse and democratic activism are reducing the capacity for civil society to act as a bulwark against this illiberal push.

The spectre this now casts upon the Indonesian body politic is a haunting one. As multiple chapters in this volume detail, Jokowi was not above using strong-arm tactics during his first term to get his way. The fact that he is an ethnic and religious pluralist lent confidence in the 2019 campaign that he would never be the kind of illiberal democratic president who assaults vulnerable minorities. Yet this does not mean he would never use the vast powers at his disposal to keep society at large from criticising him or constraining his developmental agenda. As in the New Order period, a unified state obsessed with development and stability could be pitted in the next five years against every segment of society that fights to defend its rights and make its voice heard. In Indonesia, as in so much of the world, democratic success and survival are tenuous—and only becoming more so.

REFERENCES

Antlöv, H. and S. Cederroth, eds. 2004. *Elections in Indonesia: The New Order and Beyond*. London: RoutledgeCurzon.

Aspinall, E. 2005. *Opposing Suharto: Compromise, Resistance and Regime Change in Indonesia*. Stanford, CA: Stanford University Press.

Aspinall, E. and M. Mietzner. 2019. 'Indonesia's democratic paradox: competitive elections amidst rising illiberalism'. *Bulletin of Indonesian Economic Studies* 55(3): 295–317.

Feith, H. 1962. *The Decline of Constitutional Democracy in Indonesia*. Ithaca, NY: Cornell University Press.

Hill, H., ed. 1994. *Indonesia's New Order: The Dynamics of Socio-economic Transformation*. St Leonards: Allen & Unwin.

Kahin, G.M. 1952. *Nationalism and Revolution in Indonesia*. Ithaca, NY: Cornell University Press.

Mietzner, M. 2009. *Military Politics, Islam, and the State in Indonesia: From Turbulent Transition to Democratic Consolidation*. Leiden: KITLV Press.

Power, T.P. 2018. 'Jokowi's authoritarian turn and Indonesia's democratic decline'. *Bulletin of Indonesian Economic Studies* 54(3): 307–38.

Reid, A. 1974. *The Indonesian National Revolution, 1945–1950*. Hawthorn: Longman.

Shofia, N. and T. Pepinsky. 2019. 'Measuring the "NU effect" in Indonesia's election'. *New Mandala*, 1 July. https://www.newmandala.org/measuring-the-nu-effect-in-indonesias-election/

Slater, D. 2018. 'After democracy: what happens when freedom erodes?'. Foreign Affairs, 6 November. https://www.foreignaffairs.com/articles/2018-11-06/after-democracy

Tomsa, D. 2008. *Party Politics and Democratization in Indonesia: Golkar in the Post-Suharto Era*. London: Routledge.

Tudor, M. and D. Slater. 2016. 'The content of democracy: nationalist parties and inclusive ideologies in India and Indonesia'. In *Parties, Movements and Democracy in the Developing World*, edited by N. Bermeo and D.J. Yashar, 28–60. New York: Cambridge University Press. https://www.bsg.ox.ac.uk/sites/default/files/inline-files/Bermeo%20%26%20Yashar_Chapter%20two.pdf

Vom Hau, M. 2008. 'State infrastructural power and nationalism: comparative lessons from Mexico and Argentina'. *Studies in Comparative International Development* 43(3–4): 334–54.

PART 2

Polarisation and Populism

4   How polarised is Indonesia and why does it matter?[1]

Eve Warburton

Global events have reignited scholarly interest in the relationship between polarisation and democratic quality. Populist victories in Europe, Donald Trump's electoral success in America, and the sustained popularity of figures like Recep Tayyip Erdoğan in Turkey and Narendra Modi in India, have all depended upon the mobilisation of social and political division. In these parts of the world, the intensification of political conflict along ideological and identity-based lines has occurred in tandem with a decline in democratic quality.

More and more, analysts see polarisation as a critical factor in processes of democratic regression. Carothers and O'Donohue (2019: 2), for example, compare a range of countries from Latin America, Asia and Europe, and find that polarisation undermines democracy because it 'routinely weakens respect for democratic norms, corrodes basic legislative process … exacerbates intolerance and discrimination, diminishes societal trust, and increases violence throughout the society'. Intense partisanship and polarisation create the conditions under which elite and mass support for liberal aspects of democracy—protection of freedoms and liberties for everyone—becomes increasingly 'contingent' or 'conditional'.

---

1 This chapter is based in part on a previous publication: 'Polarization and democratic decline in Indonesia', in *Democracies Divided: The Global Challenge of Political Polarization*, edited by Thomas Carothers and Andrew O'Donohue (2019). My research for this chapter was conducted as part of a comparative project on polarisation sponsored by the Carnegie Endowment for International Peace.

Until recently, analysts viewed Indonesia as immune to such severe political polarisation and its pernicious effects. A divide between Islamic and pluralist parties has long structured Indonesia's party system: Islamic parties and their supporters promote a larger role for Islamic precepts in public life and politics, while pluralist parties have a more secular orientation. But patronage-driven politics has largely papered over ideological divisions in the democratic era. Indeed, when surveyed, a vast majority of politicians said they and the party to which they belong are willing to form coalitions with any of the other political parties (Aspinall et al. 2020). High levels of ethnic and religious fragmentation have also worked against the development of a divisive identity-based politics of the sort found in Malaysia—at least at the national level. In particular, complex doctrinal divisions and conflicts among proponents of political Islam made it difficult to categorise organisations or voters neatly into either a pluralist or Islamic camp.

The absence of polarisation for much of the democratic period can also be attributed in part to President Yudhoyono's (2004–2014) style of leadership. In his approach to governing, Yudhoyono valued compromise and stability over competition and conflict. As Aspinall, Mietzner and Tomsa wrote back in 2015 (p. 3), 'Yudhoyono viewed himself as leading a polity and a society characterised by deep divisions, and he believed that his most important role was to moderate these divisions'. Yudhoyono also attracted votes from diverse constituencies, including, for example, supporters of the conservative Islamic Prosperous Justice Party (Partai Keadilan Sejahtera, PKS), as well as non-Muslim minorities and more secular Muslims that make up the traditional base of the Indonesian Democratic Party of Struggle (Partai Demokrasi Indonesia-Perjuangan, PDI-P). Yudhoyono's preference for compromise made him reluctant to engage in tough or disruptive reform, and so Indonesia's democratic progress stagnated; but these were also years of political stability and a notable absence of divisive political conflict.

In 2014, however, Indonesia entered a new phase of political polarisation. In three major elections—the 2014 presidential election, the 2017 gubernatorial election in Jakarta, and the 2019 presidential election—the contest between President Joko Widodo (Jokowi) and then opposition figure, Prabowo Subianto, and their coalitions reignited an otherwise latent Islamic–pluralist cleavage. Prabowo allied with conservative Islamic parties and Islamist groups, and came to represent this stream of Indonesia's sociopolitical life. Jokowi and his coalition represented the pluralist stream. By 2019, this cleavage was the major determinant of voters' presidential choice, and the election results revealed an electorate deeply divided along socioreligious lines. Whereas Indonesia was once described as the least polarised country in Southeast Asia (Slater and Arugay 2018), analysts now agree that politics are much more polarised under Jokowi than under Yudhoyono (Aspinall and Mietzner 2019; Davidson 2018; see also Nuraniyah, this volume).

Yet there continues to be uncertainty about the *depth* of polarisation, and about the role that a more divided politics is playing in the incremental decline of Indonesia's democratic quality. This chapter, therefore, examines the severity of political polarisation in contemporary Indonesia. In a functioning democracy, it is normal for parties and candidates to present voters with distinct choices and to attract distinct sorts of identity-based constituencies. Some scholars even warn against imputing deep societal divisions from electoral results, which may simply reflect the nature of the different choices on offer to voters in a given election (Fiorina et al. 2008). So how do we know when 'normal' political divisions have evolved into something more pernicious? When does polarisation threaten a country's democratic institutions and its social fabric?

To answer these questions, this chapter takes lessons from the comparative literature to identify the signs of severe polarisation. First, in cases of severe polarisation, politics is described by political actors in terms of 'us versus them', and each side frames the other not just as a competitor or opponent with different views and goals, but as an 'illegitimate' outsider and an existential threat (Somer and McCoy 2018). Second, where politics is severely polarised, incumbents frame political opponents as 'enemies of the state', and in doing so create a pretext for intimidating and repressing opposition forces (Somer and McCoy 2018; Svolik 2019). Third, signs of worsening 'affective' polarisation emerge, in which animosity between partisans at the societal level intensifies (McCoy et al. 2018). Finally, pernicious outcomes emerge: government stops functioning, violence between groups increases, and democracy begins to erode as each side abandons liberal norms and institutions for the sake of containing and defeating their political enemy (Carothers and O'Donohue 2019; Svolik 2019).

I argue that Indonesia fulfils some, but not all, of the criteria for a highly polarised country. During moments of intense electoral competition, both the Jokowi and Prabowo teams used divisive rhetoric, and both sides cast their opponents as existential threats. And yet, between elections, elite politics has fallen back into a predictable pattern: most parties and politicians on both sides continue to work together in broad coalitions at both national and regional levels. The most illustrative example is Prabowo's entry into Jokowi's governing coalition after the 2019 election, and his appointment as Jokowi's minister for defence. Indonesia's patronage-soaked politics makes elite polarisation less sharp and pernicious than in countries such as Thailand, Turkey and America, and government here continues to function.

However, Prabowo's peace with Jokowi has done little to ease tensions between the Jokowi government and proponents of political Islam, either at elite or societal levels. The incumbent administration has taken a range of illiberal measures to contain alleged Islamist 'threats', and in doing so maintained a mood of existential crisis both within the state and at the grassroots. In this chapter I present anecdotal evidence and survey results that suggest levels of affective polarisation within society that are, along some measures, comparable with deeply divided countries such as America.

The rest of this chapter is structured around several indicators of severe polarisation gleaned from the comparative literature: increasingly divisive political rhetoric, the casting of opponents as 'enemies of the state', intensifying affective polarisation at the societal level, and the breakdown of governance and security. The concluding section argues that polarisation is a process, not a static state, and while Indonesia has not descended into a severely polarised polity, its democracy is already suffering as a result of the more divided political and social landscape.

ILLEGITIMATE OPPONENTS AND EXISTENTIAL THREATS

Severe polarisation collapses the complex of identities and group loyalties that characterise a political community into just two warring sides (McCoy et al. 2018). Even though there may be internal rifts, fragmentation and intragroup competition within each camp, those divisions mostly dissolve and politics is transformed into a binary conflict in which actors on each side become unified by their animosity towards a common enemy (Carothers and O'Donohue 2019). Partisans on each side begin to describe politics and society in terms of 'us versus them', and two competing forces treat the 'other' not just as a political competitor but as an illegitimate outsider and an existential threat to their own group's political survival. In doing so, each side raises the stakes of electoral competition.

Since 2014, analysts have documented precisely this trend in several Indonesian elections. Candidates running for political office at both the national and regional levels have increasingly cast their rival as a category of person that does not have a legitimate claim to run for high political office, based on some feature of their socioreligious or ethnic identity. Pluralist and secular-oriented candidates were the initial target of campaigns executed by coalitions of mainstream politicians and Islamist groups.

Prabowo, most notably, aggravated polarisation by pioneering a sectarian, populist campaign strategy in 2014 (Aspinall 2015). His rival, Jokowi, a member of the most pluralist party, PDI-P, ran for president with a coalition of mostly non-Islamic parties. Prabowo saw that Jokowi's secular political orientation made him vulnerable to a religiously themed campaign. He exploited that vulnerability and, together with allies from conservative Islamic parties, Islamist figures and hardline Muslim groups, spread the message that Jokowi was not a pious Muslim, that he was even perhaps a closet Christian with communist links, and that his politics were too secular to govern a Muslim-majority nation. Prabowo's strategic alliance with fringe Islamist groups and willingness to engage in sectarian-themed smear campaigns were unprecedented in Indonesia's presidential elections, and his political style has played a major role in producing a more polarised electorate.

Jokowi, on the other hand, initially contributed indirectly to polarisation. Unlike many Indonesian politicians, Jokowi did not—during the early stages of his political career—make Islam a prominent part of his political identity, and he was unable to appeal across the Islamic–pluralist divide in the way that Yudhoyono had done as a candidate and as a president. Indeed, Jokowi's rise caused anxiety among a class of conservative Muslim elites who had enjoyed generous state funding, ministerial positions and other patronage opportunities under President Yudhoyono (Bush 2015). Jokowi was a secular politician from outside the predominant political class and a member of PDI-P, Indonesia's most pluralist party, and conservative Islamic groups feared that Jokowi would marginalise them and cut off their access to patronage. Prabowo allied strategically with this political faction, enflamed their fears and framed Jokowi (and Ahok too, see below) as an existential threat to the prominent place that Islam enjoyed during the Yudhoyono era (Mietzner 2015). The 2014 election was, therefore, a competition between a politician willing to enflame divisions and another who was unable to bridge them.

A more explicitly sectarian campaign was then used to defeat Jakarta's popular governor, Basuki Tjahaja Purnama (known as Ahok), in the 2017 gubernatorial election. Ahok, a Christian, ethnically Chinese Indonesian and a Jokowi ally, attracted vehement opposition from Islamist groups that claimed a non-Muslim had no right to hold high political office in a Muslim-majority country. Ahok's opponent, Prabowo-aligned Anies Baswedan, joined forces with the hardline Islamist groups opposed to Ahok, and these groups spread a sectarian campaign message through online networks, prayer groups and mosques. That campaign gained broad public traction after Ahok made clumsy remarks about the Qur'an's position on non-Muslim leaders. Both hardline and more mainstream

Muslim groups and organisations called for Ahok's arrest on charges of blasphemy and rallied hundreds of thousands of Indonesians onto the streets of Jakarta in a powerful display of opposition to the Christian Chinese politician.

This sectarian campaign delivered Anies a resounding victory. Ahok, who had been the favourite leading into the election, not only lost decisively but also was prosecuted for blasphemy and sentenced to two and a half years in prison. Quick-count results indicated that religious identity was indeed a central driver of voting behaviour. There was a striking divide between Muslim and non-Muslim voters, whereby Muslims were uniformly more likely to vote for Anies, whatever their other characteristics, such as income or education (Warburton and Gammon 2017). Non-Muslims, on the other hand, overwhelmingly voted for Ahok. That election had an enduring effect on Indonesia's political landscape. In other regional elections around the country where rival candidates lined up along the Islamic–pluralist cleavage, the more pluralist candidates feared being '*di-Ahok-kan*', or defeated by an Islamist-inspired campaign.

The polarising 'us versus them' rhetoric reached its zenith in the 2019 presidential elections, because this time *both* sides cast the other as an illegitimate outsider and an existential threat. On the Prabowo side, Jokowi was again depicted as an enemy of the *ummah*, and his victory was framed as a threat to pious Muslims and Islamist organisations. However, Jokowi and his coalition went on the offensive and leveraged an equally polarising narrative about the rival camp: Prabowo's victory would lead to an Islamic caliphate, and his coalition threatened the essence of Indonesia's national identity and way of life. The traditionalist Islamic organisation Nahdlatul Ulama (NU) was crucial to this campaign. Long viewed as the guardian of Indonesia's more tolerant and pluralist form of Islamic practice, NU had struggled for two decades to maintain its constituency against competition from the kinds of puritanical organisations and figures that allied with Prabowo (see Nuraniyah, this volume). Together with Jokowi and PDI-P, NU and its nominal political arm, the National Awakening Party (Partai Kebangkitan Bangsa, PKB), launched a major offensive across Java's vote-rich heartland to convince their followers that Prabowo's Islamist coalition represented an existential threat, and that once in office Islamist hardliners associated with the Islamic Defenders Front (Front Pembela Islam, FPI), Hizbut Tahrir Indonesia (HTI) and even the political party PKS would force Islamic law upon Indonesia's diverse Muslims and religious minorities.

These campaigns resonated across the country and produced a deeply divided electorate: minorities voted en masse for Jokowi, as did the traditionalist Islamic constituencies in NU's heartland of Central

Java and East Java; regions where people practise a more conservative and puritanical brand of Islam, such as Aceh and West Sumatra, voted overwhelmingly for Prabowo. As Aspinall and Mietzner (2019) point out in their review of the election, the results bore a striking resemblance to regional voting patterns of the 1955 election, a time when Indonesia's politics were deeply divided along socioreligious and geographic lines.

ENEMIES OF THE STATE

A second indicator of severe polarisation is that incumbents frame their opponents as a threat to the regime and an ideological enemy of the state. Oftentimes, the side that holds office will leverage the advantages of incumbency and use the state's coercive apparatus to contain or repress the opposition. Supporters of the incumbent accept such illiberal tactics as a necessary strategy for containing their enemy. At the same time, those affiliated with the opposition become increasingly isolated and embittered and the divide between each side deepens further (Somer and McCoy 2018; Svolik 2019).

Again, this scenario has played out in Indonesia over the past five years. Human rights organisations including Amnesty International, SAFEnet and Human Rights Watch, as well as political analysts such as Aspinall and Mietzner (2019), Hadiz (2017) and Power (2018), have documented in compelling detail the Jokowi government's increasing embrace of illiberal tools to co-opt and contain critical voices and sources of opposition. Controversial laws on treason and defamation, for example, have been used far more by this administration in five years than by President Yudhoyono's government during his decade in office (see Setiawan; Power, this volume).

More important for understanding polarisation, however, is the way Jokowi and his government have revived Pancasila as an ideological tool to justify the harassment of opponents and new constraints on dissent. New laws and institutions make use of Pancasila as a means of rendering people, groups and ideas unnationalistic, or as a threat to the ideological foundations of Indonesia's unitary state—an approach that draws heavily on New Order–era discourses of control (Warburton and Aspinall 2019: 261). Three cases stand out as emblematic of the way in which Jokowi's administration has recast opponents as enemies of the state and of the Indonesian nation more broadly.

First, in 2017 Jokowi introduced a decree, the Regulation in Lieu of Law (Peraturan Pemerintah Pengganti Undang Undang, Perppu) on Societal Organisations (Perppu Ormas), giving the government broad powers to disband any organisation deemed anti-Pancasila, a concept that is only vaguely defined and therefore ripe for political manipulation. The purpose of the decree was to ban HTI, the radical but non-violent Islamist organisation that had received legal recognition from the Yudhoyono administration just a decade earlier. The Jokowi government argued HTI's loyalty to a transnational Islamic caliphate made it an ideological enemy of the republic; but HTI was also a political threat to the pluralist coalition in power—its members were active in the anti-Ahok protests, and the organisation's expansion over the preceding decade into NU constituencies made it a direct threat to Jokowi's major ally. In effect, the Jokowi administration did NU's bidding and made intra-Islamic tensions a mainstream political and policy issue (Nuraniyah, this volume). While the decree had a very specific organisational target, observers pointed out that, with this decree, the government had 'forged a tool of repression' that could be used against a range of organisations rendered dangerous by the state, whether in the near or distant future (Hamid and Gammon 2017).

Then, during the 2019 election campaign, the Jokowi team cast Prabowo and his coalition as an ally of HTI—a now banned organisation. In particular, members of NU and its nominal political arm, PKB, told voters that a Prabowo victory was a victory for HTI and would lead to HTI's political expansion and, eventually, to the establishment of an Islamic caliphate. Speaking at a public event in Singapore in February 2019, Yenny Wahid of NU even described the election as a matter of 'life or death' for religious pluralism in Indonesia. This campaign narrative was deployed systematically around the country. From the NU strongholds of East Java and Central Java (Aspinall 2019; Fachrudin 2019) to the more Islamist regions and Prabowo strongholds like West Nusa Tenggara (Warburton 2019), religious leaders told their followers that this year's presidential election would determine the ideological foundations of the Indonesian nation, and that what was at stake was nothing less than Indonesia's pluralist identity and way of life.

This narrative permeated non-religious institutions too. Many in Jakarta's business elite, including senior members of the Chamber of Commerce and Industry (Kamar Dagang dan Industri, Kadin) and the Indonesian Employers Association (Asosiasi Pengusaha Indonesia, Apindo), had formed an alliance with Jokowi and campaigned actively on his behalf. In an interview, one businessperson explained that not only was he mobilising his staff to attend pro-Jokowi rallies, he also planned to purge his company of people with Islamist beliefs or, as he put it, '*orang HTI-PKS*' (HTI-PKS people) (personal communication, 15 April 2019). In a different interview, a senior member of the State Secretariat (Sekretariat Negara) spoke in similar terms of an urgent need to weed out problematic bureaucrats from the ministries, people he also described as '*orang* HTI-PKS' (personal communication, 15 April 2019). Jokowi's political coalition, allies in the influential business community and senior members of the government were, in the lead-up to the election, spreading a narrative that conflated two very different organisations: one was a hardline, and now illegal, Islamist organisation and alleged enemy of the state (HTI), and the other was an Islamic-based political party and legitimate member of the democratic opposition (PKS).

Even after securing re-election in 2019, the Jokowi government sustained the mood of ideological war by encouraging a purge of Islamist elements from state agencies. A joint ministerial decree issued in November 2019, for example, forbids civil servants from engaging in 'hate speech' against Pancasila, or even against the government. It also forbids state employees from liking, retweeting or commenting on online material deemed to be hate speech, or being a member of any organisation deemed anti-Pancasila. All of these terms are again vaguely defined, and the presidential decree—just like that used against HTI—is ripe for political manipulation.

The Jokowi administration's targeting of its enemies is not yet as systematic, explicit or widespread as what we see taking place in other deeply polarised places, such as Erdoğan's Turkey, Madura's Venezuela or Thailand under the military junta, where dissidents are routinely threatened, intimidated, fired from their jobs, bankrupted, imprisoned or disappeared. Opposition actors in Indonesia, and those critical of the government more generally, can speak and organise relatively freely. But the space for particular types of dissent is narrowing at an alarming pace. The Jokowi government has framed parts of the democratic opposition—those more ideologically Islamist—as threats to and enemies of the state, and in doing so has created a pretext for the erosion of Indonesia's fragile democratic freedoms.

AFFECTIVE POLARISATION WORSENS

A third indicator of severe polarisation is that tensions and hostilities at the community level worsen. This trend is termed 'affective polarisation', and it describes a situation where people express immense animus and dislike towards people associated with the political 'out-group' (Iyengar et al. 2019). Political divisions infect relationships at workplaces, within friendship networks and even within family circles. Severe polarisation means partisans express hostility towards those who side with the political 'other', such that it becomes difficult to find common ground, and personal relationships begin to break down (Carothers and O'Donohue 2019). Importantly, in deeply divided societies, the signs of affective polarisation are visible long after an election ends.

This indicator of polarisation in Indonesia is the most difficult to study, and one for which data are limited. However, there is growing anecdotal evidence that many Indonesians feel they are living in a more divided political landscape, and that those divisions permeate social relations outside election season. In an important study from 2018, Sandra Hamid documents the experience of people living in Jakarta in the wake of the 2017 gubernatorial election, many of whom feel marginalised from community and family events because of their support for either Ahok or Anies. She tells stories of Muslims living in mixed neighbourhoods who now socialise less and less with their non-Muslim neighbours for fear of engaging in *haram* (forbidden, unclean) activities. Her research suggests that the political preference people held in that election came to be seen as an indicator of their religious persuasion or their Muslim credentials. The Islamists' message that Muslims should not elect non-Muslim candidates also resonated beyond the election. Mietzner et al. (2018) tracked public attitudes using national surveys between 2016 and 2017, and their data indicated a rise in the number of people who expressed intolerance towards non-Muslims holding high political office after the anti-Ahok campaign.

Similar stories emerged around the country during the lead-up to the 2019 presidential elections. During my own fieldwork in Mataram, Lombok, in the weeks before election day, residents spoke of neighbourhoods that were 'solid' Prabowo or 'solid' Jokowi, and individuals or families that supported the rival candidate in such areas were well known to everyone. In a primary school in one such Prabowo neighbourhood, parents disapproved of and singled out the sole Jokowi supporter in their WhatsApp groups. Children understood their parents' partisan loyalties too, and one child of pro-Jokowi parents was teased on the playground for her parents' presidential choice. Still in Lombok, members of Nahdlatul Wathan, a local Islamic organisation that formally declared support for Jokowi, were told they must cancel their membership if they wished to vote for Prabowo.

Workplaces became more divided too. In companies owned by Jokowi allies, staff were banned from participating in the Prabowo campaign, but not the Jokowi campaign. One businessperson emphasised in an interview that companies were not forcing staff to vote a particular way, but instead discouraging public expressions of support for the opposition candidate (personal communication, 15 April 2019). Such rules politicised private sector workplaces and encouraged people to see their colleagues' political preferences as right or wrong.

These sorts of experiences reveal worsening affective polarisation in the lead-up to and wake of divisive electoral campaigns. But such data paint, at best, a fragmented and partial picture of the process of polarisation at the societal level. In the comparative literature, analysts usually use polling data to test partisans' desire for social distance from the out-group, and to gauge levels of intergroup animus. Surveys of this nature have rarely been done in the Indonesian context, because for most of the democratic era few analysts viewed political polarisation as a phenomenon worthy of analytical attention.

So, with the assistance of Burhanuddin Muhtadi, director of Indikator Politik Indonesia (Indikator), one of Indonesia's major polling organisations, we conducted a nationally representative survey in May 2019, several weeks after the election. We adopted a set of questions that have been asked before in deeply polarised countries in order to draw some tentative cross-country comparisons and get a sense of the severity of affective polarisation in Indonesia. The questions ask people about how they feel towards those they associate with political 'in-groups' and 'out-groups'. As such questions have not been asked before, the results do not give a sense of change over time; instead, the intention is to provide a snapshot of affective polarisation along the pluralist–Islamist cleavage, and among Prabowo and Jokowi supporters specifically.

First, we told respondents to imagine they are moving house to a new neighbourhood, and asked them how important it is for them to consider a specified range of factors when deciding where to live. More than 80 per cent stated that living near family, good schools and good health facilities were very important or important factors to consider. But as Figure 4.1 demonstrates, a strong majority of Indonesians also expressed a preference for living among co-ethnics and people of the same religion.

Importantly, a significant minority of 30–40 per cent expressed a preference for political homogeneity—they would prefer to live in an area where most people vote for the same party or presidential candidate. These numbers climb slightly when we look at the responses of partisans— people who say they feel close or very close to either political figure. We found that 34 per cent of Indonesians express feelings of closeness to Jokowi, and of these partisans 44 per cent stated they would prefer to live in areas with people who vote the same way in presidential elections. When it came to Prabowo, 22 per cent of Indonesians interviewed felt close to him, of which 41 per cent expressed a desire to live near other Prabowo voters. In sum, a large minority of 39 per cent of Indonesians would prefer

Figure 4.1   How important are the following when deciding where to live? (%)

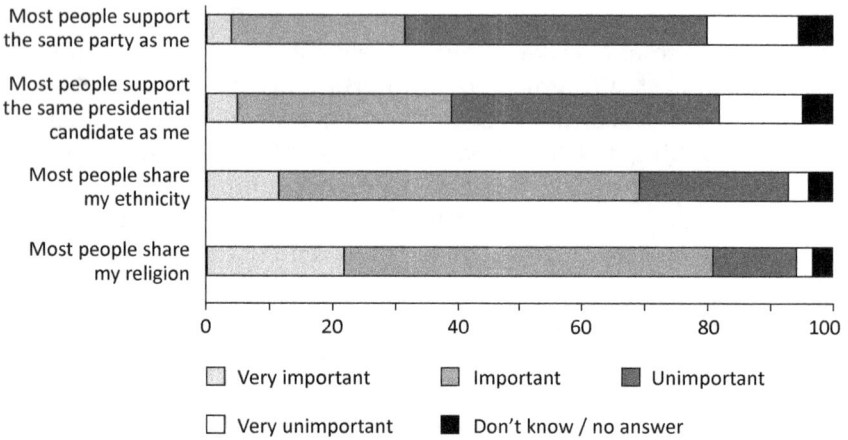

to live around people who share their electoral preferences; that number is higher among partisans on both sides.

These results are comparable to studies conducted in other countries considered highly polarised. For example, back in 2014 a Pew Research Center survey found that 28 per cent of Americans feel it is important to live in a place where most people share their political views—fewer than the percentage of Indonesians who prefer to live in areas where people vote the same way. That number rose to 50 per cent for Americans that Pew categorised as consistently conservative, and 35 per cent for consistent liberals.[2]

Questions about personal relationships are also used in surveys to gauge levels of affective polarisation. In America, for example, a 2018 survey by PRRI (Public Religion Research Institute) found that 35 per cent of Republicans would be unhappy if their child married a Democrat. Conversely, 45 per cent of Democrats felt this way about their son or daughter marrying a Republican (Jones and Najle 2019: 20). In Turkey, where there is deep division between supporters of Erdoğan's Islamic AK Parti (Justice and Development Party) and those who support secular political parties, a survey found that over 80 per cent of respondents did

---

2 https://www.people-press.org/2014/06/12/political-polarization-in-the-american-public/

Figure 4.2   How would you feel if a member of your family married a ... (%)

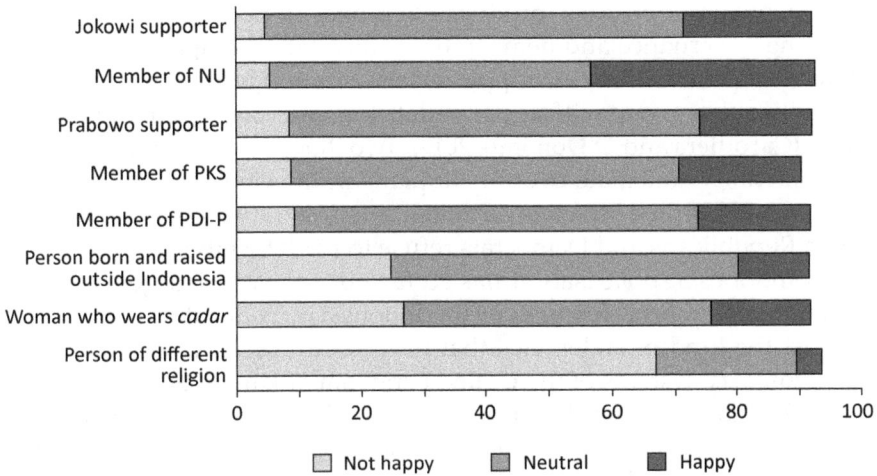

not want their daughter to marry a person from a party they felt the most 'distant' from (Erdoğan 2018).

When we asked a similar question in Indonesia, we found far less extreme responses. Overall, Indonesians are not concerned about the political persuasion of a person marrying into their family. Only between 5 and 9 per cent of Indonesians would be unhappy about someone in their family marrying a supporter of a particular presidential candidate, or a supporter of PKS (the most Islamic party) or PDI-P (the most pluralist party). Instead, people care most strongly about their family member marrying someone of the same religion—67 per cent would be unhappy about an inter-religious marriage (Figure 4.2).

Once we zoom in on partisans, the numbers look quite different—but still not as extreme as in other deeply polarised countries. For example, among people who feel close to Prabowo, 22 per cent would be unhappy if their family member married someone from PDI-P, the party to which Jokowi belongs; while 15 per cent of Jokowi partisans would be upset if a family member married a PKS supporter.

These data thus paint a complex picture of affective polarisation in Indonesia. We find evidence that a large minority of Indonesians prefer social distance from supporters of the political 'out-group'; but when it comes to important personal relations, such as a family member's choice of husband or wife, Indonesians—including partisans—are far less likely to express animus towards the political 'other'.

PERNICIOUS OUTCOMES

Severe polarisation also produces a range of pernicious outcomes affecting governance and democratic quality. First, comparative studies show how polarisation can cripple legislatures and bring government to a halt if neither group will accommodate the interests or demands of the other (Carothers and O'Donohue 2019). Two illustrative examples are the parliamentary stalemate over Brexit plans in the United Kingdom, and the extended United States government shutdowns that have taken place when Republicans and Democrats refuse to work together.

In Indonesia, polarisation has so far not undermined government functions. Structural features of the Indonesian political system guard against the kind of stalemates that have encumbered governments in the two-party systems of the United Kingdom or United States in recent years. In Indonesia's multiparty, patronage democracy, there continues to be a willingness to work across both ideological divides. Even parties that have remained outside big governing coalitions—such as PDI-P during the Yudhoyono years and PKS under the Jokowi presidency—are often willing to side with the government in parliamentary processes if achieving consensus means access to patronage, pork or other political inducements.

Second, in deeply polarised societies intergroup violence increases. Zero-sum political games between partisans raise tensions, which can boil over into sporadic or widespread violence (Carothers and O'Donohue 2019). As Toha and Harish show in their contribution to this volume, contemporary Indonesia overall suffers comparatively little electoral or broader political violence. But they also argue that the Jokowi era has been marked by an increase in street protests and riots. In May 2019, when the Electoral Commission formally announced Jokowi's victory, Prabowo encouraged his supporters to take to the streets in protest against what he claimed was a fraudulent result. What started as a peaceful act of opposition descended into violent riots in which ten people lost their lives. These were Jakarta's worst political riots since 1998, and must be viewed in the context of rising political tensions and of an election campaign in which each side raised the stakes and delegitimised their opponent.

The third and final pernicious outcome concerns the quality of democratic institutions. The comparative literature suggests that in deeply polarised polities, elites and masses become increasingly willing to erode democratic norms and institutions in order to defeat, contain and exclude the political 'outgroup' (Somer and McCoy 2018). As explained above, and as the many chapters in this volume demonstrate, the Jokowi government has indeed introduced a range of illiberal tools to harass and contain an ideologically defined threat. But *public responses* matter immensely in processes of democratic decline. As Svolik (2019: 24) explains, 'in sharply polarised electorates, even voters who value democracy will be willing to sacrifice fair democratic competition for the sake of supporting politicians who champion their interests' or with whom they identify.

Studies have shown that many Indonesians do not conceive of democracy primarily in liberal terms, that is, as a system for protecting individual rights and freedoms. Rather, they associate democracy with economic rights, public welfare and clean government (Mujani et al. 2018; Warburton and Aspinall 2019). This alone might help explain why, despite a now well-documented erosion in the protection of minority rights and individual liberties over the past five years (McGregor and Setiawan 2019), Jokowi continues to enjoy strong public support and high levels of satisfaction with his government (Warburton and Aspinall 2019).

But in polarised settings, partisan loyalties can shift people's preferences even further from liberal democratic norms. One way to test this effect is with survey experiments that expose people to cues from their preferred party or leader. In a nationally representative survey conducted in collaboration with Indikator in late 2019, we asked Indonesians how they felt about religious by-laws. Specifically, they were asked whether they agreed with either of the following two statements:

1. Some believe that Indonesian law should not be based on any particular religion, and regional religious by-laws violate the constitution and have the potential to undermine the rights of minorities and women.

2. Others believe that religious by-laws are legitimate in Indonesia, as a Muslim-majority country, and so such laws do not violate the constitution or undermine minority or women's rights.

Respondents were divided into a control group that received just the statements above, and a treatment group that was told that Jokowi supports statement one, and Prabowo supports statement two. The results of this experiment are displayed in Figure 4.3, organised according to respondents' preferred presidential candidate.

Indonesians' views about religious laws and human rights are immensely influenced by their partisan loyalties. Without cues (the control group), each side is divided on the issue. But when prompted by a cue from their preferred leader, a majority of partisans on both sides follow their leaders' position. Support for liberal democracy is not absolute in Indonesia; instead, in a highly polarised political atmosphere, support for liberal principles appears contingent and highly vulnerable to partisan politics.

Figure 4.3   Support for religious by-laws (%)

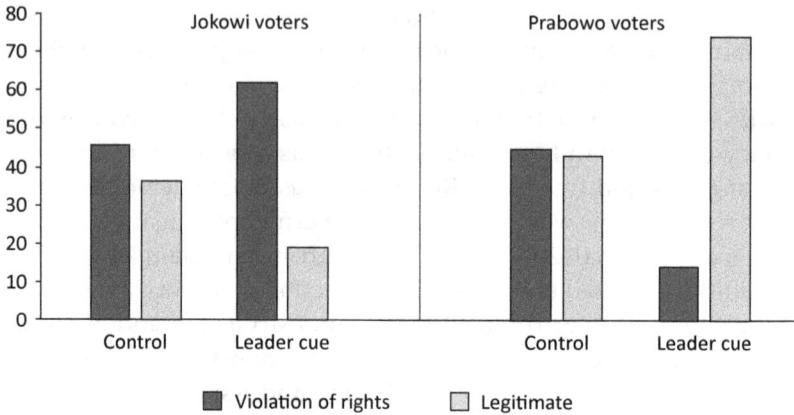

CONCLUSION

Competition along the Islamist–pluralist cleavage has animated Indonesian politics since independence. Yet, despite the enduring importance of this socioreligious divide, most of Indonesia's elections over the past two decades have been remarkably free of ideological or identity-based conflict. Patronage has served as a powerful incentive for compromise and cooperation across ideological lines.

But Indonesia's political landscape has changed over the past five years as leaders on both sides have turned latent ideological divisions into an axis of political conflict. In each major election since 2014, candidates running for office have allied with competing religious organisations outside the parties and claimed to be defending the 'right' version of Indonesian Islam and the 'right' ideological position. Political figures have designed campaigns to delegitimise opponents, and they have raised the stakes of electoral competition, claiming the victors will determine the moral foundation of the Indonesian nation.

The Jokowi administration in particular has deepened polarisation by tapping into and inflaming simmering fears at the community level about a creeping Islamist influence in the halls of power and at the grassroots. In doing so, the government has engineered an atmosphere of existential crisis among pluralist constituencies, which in turn gives the incumbent just cause to introduce illiberal interventions for containing groups deemed threatening. Indonesia's democratic institutions are under increasing pressure, but the more polarised atmosphere means public opposition has been remarkably weak.

To be sure, polarisation in Indonesia has not reached the debilitating levels found in places like Turkey, Thailand or America. But it is critical that analysts continue to monitor and measure the trajectory of polarisation along the indicators laid out in this chapter, because polarisation is a process, not a static state, and it is a process that is already playing a critical role in Indonesia's current moment of democratic decline.

REFERENCES

Aspinall, E. 2015. 'Oligarchic populism: Prabowo Subianto's challenge to Indonesian democracy'. *Indonesia* 99(April): 1–28.

Aspinall, E. 2019. 'Indonesia's election and the return of ideological competition'. *New Mandala*, 22 April. https://www.newmandala.org/indonesias-election-and-the-return-of-ideological-competition/

Aspinall, E. and M. Mietzner. 2019. 'Indonesia's democratic paradox: competitive elections amidst rising illiberalism'. *Bulletin of Indonesian Economic Studies* 55(3): 295–317.

Aspinall, E., M. Mietzner and D. Tomsa. 2015. 'The moderating president: Yudhoyono's decade in power'. In *The Yudhoyono Presidency: Indonesia's Decade of Stability and Stagnation*, edited by E. Aspinall, M. Mietzner and D. Tomsa, 1–22. Singapore: Institute of Southeast Asian Studies (ISEAS).

Aspinall, E., D. Fossati, B. Muhtadi and E. Warburton. 2020. 'Elites, masses, and democratic decline in Indonesia'. *Democratization* 27(4): 505–26.

Bush, R. 2015. 'Religious politics and minority rights during the Yudhoyono presidency'. In *The Yudhoyono Presidency: Indonesia's Decade of Stability and Stagnation*, edited by E. Aspinall, M. Mietzner and D. Tomsa, 239–57. Singapore: Institute of Southeast Asian Studies (ISEAS).

Carothers, T. and A. O'Donohue. 2019. 'Introduction'. In *Democracies Divided: The Global Challenge of Political Polarization*, edited by T. Carothers and A. O'Donohue, 1–16. Washington, DC: Brooking Institution Press.

Davidson, J.S. 2018. *Indonesia: Twenty Years of Democracy*, Elements in Politics and Society in Southeast Asia. Cambridge: Cambridge University Press.

Erdoğan, E. 2018. 'Dimensions of polarization in Turkey: summary of key findings'. Istanbul: Istanbul Bilgi University Center for Migration Research. https://goc.bilgi.edu.tr/media/uploads/2018/02/06/dimensions-of-polarizationshortfindings_DNzdZml.pdf

Fachrudin, A.A. 2019. 'Jokowi and NU: the view from the pesantren'. *New Mandala*, 11 April. https://www.newmandala.org/jokowi-and-nu-the-view-from-the-pesantren/

Fiorina, M.P., S.A. Abrams and J.C. Pope. 2008. 'Polarization in the American public: misconceptions and misreadings'. *Journal of Politics* 70(2): 556–60. https://doi.org/10.1017/s002238160808050x

Hadiz, V.R. 2017. 'Indonesia's year of democratic setbacks: towards a new phase of deepening illiberalism?'. *Bulletin of Indonesian Economic Studies* 53(3): 261–78.

Hamid, S. 2018. 'Normalising intolerance: elections, religion and everyday life in Indonesia'. CILIS Policy Paper. Melbourne: Centre for Indonesian Law, Islam and Society. https://law.unimelb.edu.au/centres/cilis/research/publications/ cilis-policy-papers/normalising-intolerance-elections,-religion-and-everyday-life-in-indonesia

Hamid, U. and L. Gammon. 2017. 'Jokowi forges a tool of repression'. *New Mandala*, 13 July. https://www.newmandala.org/jokowi-forges-tool-repression/

Iyengar, S., Y. Lelkes, M. Levendusky, N. Malhotra and S.J. Westwood. 2019. 'The origins and consequences of affective polarization in the United States'. *Annual Review of Political Science* 22(1): 129–46.

Jones, R.P. and M. Najle. 2019. *American Democracy in Crisis: The Fate of Pluralism in a Divided Nation*. Washington, DC: PRRI. https://www.prri.org/wp-content/ uploads/2019/02/Democracy-in-Crisis-3-Pluralism-1.pdf

McCoy, J., T. Rahman and M. Somer. 2018. 'Polarization and the global crisis of democracy: common patterns, dynamics, and pernicious consequences for democratic polities'. *American Behavioral Scientist* 62(1): 16–42.

McGregor, K. and K. Setiawan. 2019. 'Shifting from international to "Indonesian" justice measures: two decades of addressing past human rights violations'. *Journal of Contemporary Asia* 49(5): 837–61.

Mietzner, M. 2015. 'Indonesia in 2014: Jokowi and the repolarization of post-Soeharto politics'. In *Southeast Asian Affairs 2015*, edited by D. Singh, 119–38. Singapore: Institute of Southeast Asian Studies (ISEAS).

Mietzner, M., B. Muhtadi and R. Halida. 2018. 'Entrepreneurs of grievance: drivers and effects of Indonesia's Islamist mobilization'. *Bijdragen tot de Taal-, Land- en Volkenkunde* 174(2–3): 159–87. https://doi.org/10.1163/22134379-17402026

Mujani, S., R.W. Liddle and K. Ambardi. 2018. *Voting Behavior in Indonesia since Democratization: Critical Democrats*. Cambridge: Cambridge University Press.

Power, T.P. 2018. 'Jokowi's authoritarian turn and Indonesia's democratic decline'. *Bulletin of Indonesian Economic Studies* 54(3): 307–38.

Slater, D. and A.A. Arugay. 2018. 'Polarizing figures: executive power and institutional conflict in Asian democracies'. *American Behavioral Scientist* 62(1): 92–106.

Somer, M. and J. McCoy. 2018. 'Déjà vu? Polarization and endangered democracies in the 21st century'. *American Behavioral Scientist* 62(1): 3–15.

Svolik, M.W. 2019. 'Polarization versus democracy'. *Journal of Democracy* 30(3): 20–32.

Warburton, E. 2019. 'Polarisation in Indonesia: what if perception is reality?'. *New Mandala*, 16 April. https://www.newmandala.org/how-polarised-is-indonesia/

Warburton, E. and E. Aspinall. 2019. 'Explaining Indonesia's democratic regression: structure, agency and popular opinion'. *Contemporary Southeast Asia: A Journal of International and Strategic Affairs* 41(2): 255–85. https://www. muse.jhu.edu/article/732138

Warburton, E. and L. Gammon. 2017. 'Class dismissed? Economic fairness and identity politics in Indonesia'. *New Mandala*, 5 May. https://www.newmandala. org/economic-injustice-identity-politics-indonesia/

5   Divided Muslims: militant pluralism, polarisation and democratic backsliding

Nava Nuraniyah

Indonesia's most recent elections have been dubbed the most polarising in over 50 years. In 2017, the Christian Chinese governor of Jakarta, Basuki Tjahaja Purnama (better known as Ahok), was ousted following a series of Islamist-led protests that resulted in his conviction on blasphemy charges. The 2019 presidential election between Joko Widodo (Jokowi) and Prabowo Subianto was no less divisive: many in the Prabowo camp claimed that Jokowi was anti-Islamic or even a communist, and many on Jokowi's side asserted that Prabowo's 'radical' Islamist supporters were seeking to turn Indonesia into an Islamic theocracy. Muslim voters were divided along ethnic and ideological lines: Javanese traditionalist Muslims overwhelmingly voted for Jokowi, while more puritan, modernist Muslims in the outer islands largely backed Prabowo (Shofia and Pepinski 2019).[1] An unprecedented 97 per cent of non-Muslims voted for the 'pluralist' Jokowi, even though his running mate, Ma'ruf Amin, was widely known for his deeply conservative politics (Indikator Politik Indonesia 2019).

---

1   Indonesian Muslims are almost exclusively Sunni. The majority are 'traditionalist' Sunni Muslims, as represented by Nahdlatul Ulama, who follow the Shafi'i school of law and Ash'arite school of theology. Traditionalist Muslims are known for being accommodative towards Sufism and longstanding cultural practices such as praying for the dead and visiting Muslim shrines. 'Modernist' Sunni Muslims, as represented by Muhammadiyah, are committed to purifying Islam of what they perceive to be unwarranted innovations (*bid'ah*) and superstitions.

This kind of identity-based polarisation has serious consequences for democratic quality. Comparative studies emphasise that political polarisation makes normal democratic competition seem an existential battle between two sides with mutually exclusive identities. This in turn prompts voters to view elections as a zero-sum game, and both sides become willing to accept less democratic strategies and rules if it means ensuring their candidate wins office (García-Guadilla and Mallen 2018; McCoy et al. 2018). As other contributions to this volume explain, political polarisation in the Jokowi era has already begun to erode liberal democratic norms and institutions in this way (see Hicken, this volume). The Jokowi administration's constraints on opposition actors and Prabowo's initial refusal to accept the 2019 election results are two powerful examples of the anti-democratic implications of a more polarised electoral atmosphere (see Warburton, this volume).

In this chapter, I examine the role of Islamic organisations and leaders in producing a more polarised political climate and, in turn, a less democratic Indonesia. Much recent literature focuses on one part of the equation: the increasing political significance of hardline Islamist organisations (e.g. Arifianto 2019; IPAC 2018; Mietzner and Muhtadi 2018). I look instead at the 'militant pluralist' counter-mobilisation spearheaded by Indonesia's largest traditionalist organisation, Nahdlatul Ulama (NU). While NU's militant pluralism has emerged as a major bulwark against the agents of puritanical Islamism, I argue that the organisation's increasing willingness to embrace illiberal ideas and tactics is exacerbating polarisation and contributing to Indonesia's democratic decline. Competition between Islamist activists and traditionalist Muslims is nothing new. But its contemporary political manifestation has seen both sides become more 'militant' and more committed to their respective causes, even if it means promoting such causes through illiberal means. In this way, both Islamist *and* pluralist forces are subordinating the preservation of democratic principles to the ideological struggle between competing visions of Indonesian Islam.

This chapter is structured as follows: I begin by sketching the ideological and political cleavage within Indonesian Islam. This discussion focuses primarily on NU as the leading representative of pluralist Islam, rather than on Indonesia's second-largest Islamic organisation, Muhammadiyah. This is because NU is more decisively pluralist and enjoys far greater political influence than its modernist counterpart. I demonstrate how, in response to the encroachment of new Islamist organisations and leaders into its traditional base, NU has undergone an ideological revival focused on the construction of a highly differentiated and antagonistic collective identity, making it more militantly pluralist than ever.

I then explain how the NU–Islamist conflict entered mainstream politics. While President Bambang Susilo Yudhoyono (2009–14) accommodated Islamist groups and their political agendas, the Jokowi administration views such groups with immense suspicion. NU became a natural ally for the government in its efforts to contain Islamist forces, and as a result its political clout and material strength have grown immensely.

In the final section, I examine the Jokowi government's authoritarian turn, and the complicity of NU in that turn. I argue that NU's new and more militant brand of pluralism has helped the organisation to mobilise and invigorate its base, and enabled a close and materially fruitful relationship with the government. But it has also been a critical resource for the Jokowi government in justifying, both ideologically and rhetorically, an increasingly illiberal approach towards its enemies, and an increasingly illiberal democratic order.

THE RECENT ORIGINS OF POLARISATION

The rivalry between NU and Islamist groups has been growing since the mid-2000s as the Islamists have gained greater political influence and encroached on traditionalist Muslim constituencies. New-found freedoms in the post-1998 reform era enabled the flourishing of previously suppressed Islamist groups such as Hizbut Tahrir Indonesia (HTI), Salafi activists and the Muslim Brotherhood–linked Justice Party (Partai Keadilan, later renamed the Prosperous Justice Party—Partai Keadilan Sejahtera, PKS), as well as the emergence of new ones such as the Islamic Defenders Front (Front Pembela Islam, FPI). In this section, I outline how NU has responded to this changing social context by crafting more systematic indoctrination programs that emphasise the irreconcilable differences between NU and the so-called 'transnational' Islamic groups.[2]

Islamist encroachment on NU's base

While cultural Islamisation had been a long-term trend in Indonesia, the 'conservative turn' in the post-*reformasi* era was given impetus by President Yudhoyono's accommodationist approach to Islamist aspirations (Bush 2015; van Bruinessen 2013). Yudhoyono had assigned several ministerial portfolios to PKS and given substantial political weight

---

2 'Transnational' Islam is typically associated with puritanism, and is thus distinguished from the more syncretic and localised doctrines and practices associated with NU and other traditionalist groups.

to the otherwise non–legally binding fatwa of the Indonesian Council of Islamic Scholars (Majelis Ulama Indonesia, MUI). The other major beneficiary of Yudhoyono's accommodation was HTI, an extension of the transnational Hizbut Tahrir network that seeks to restore the caliphate through non-violent means. It first spread in Indonesia through campus-based proselytisation networks (*dakwah kampus*) in the 1980s (Mohamed Osman 2010). In the 1990s, HTI quietly made inroads into the urban professional class in private companies and government agencies.[3] The political openness that accompanied *reformasi* enabled HTI to emerge from its cocoon. It applied for a mass organisation (*ormas*) permit in 2001, although this was not granted until Yudhoyono came to power. In 2005, two HTI figures joined MUI: Ismail Yusanto and Muhammad Al Khaththath. In 2006, HTI obtained the long-awaited recognition of its status as a legal *ormas* from the Ministry of Home Affairs.

NU was particularly anxious about HTI's growing influence. A turning point came in 2007, when the International Caliphate Conference was held at Jakarta International Stadium. It was the first of its kind: some 100,000 HTI sympathisers from other parts of Java converged on the capital, parading black flags and listening eagerly to celebrity preachers such as Aa Gym. To NU's dismay, HTI held similar rallies in the NU heartlands of East Java and Central Java, displaying banners that read '*Nahdliyin* [that is, NU members] long for a caliphate' (*Liputan Islam* 2014). HTI had long distributed its *Al-Waie* magazine and *Al-Islam* Friday bulletin throughout NU mosques. It even opened a booth at the 2006 meeting of NU clerics in Surabaya to expose traditionalist clerics to HTI publications.[4] By 2007, NU officials in East Java were reporting that their mosques in Banyuwangi, Sidoarjo and Pasuruan had been taken over by Islamist groups, particularly HTI (NU Online 2007b).

Yudhoyono's accommodation of such Islamist political groups, and their growing popularity at the grassroots, threatened NU's organisational interests. In April 2007, NU's chair, Hasyim Muzadi, released an official warning against the spread of 'transnational Islamic ideologies ...

---

3   HTI had founded a number of religious study groups with neutral-sounding names such as Majelis Taklim Wisma Dharmala Sakti and Forum Kajian Sosial Kemasyarakatan. Its economics school in Yogyakarta is called Sekolah Tinggi Ekonomi Islam Hamfara ('Hamfara' being an abbreviation of the Qur'anic verse *hadza min fadli rabbi*) and its school network is called Sekolah Islam Terpadu Insantama. Its early publications—for example, *Al-Islam* bulletin (since 1994) and *Al-Waie* magazine (since 2000)—did not bear the HTI name either. HTI's first official website, www.hizbut-tahrir.or.id, was launched in 2004 (Ilhamdi 2015).

4   I wish to thank Martin van Bruinessen for raising this point.

that are threatening the Unitary Republic of Indonesia [and] Pancasila ideology' (NU Online 2007a). The first major clash between pluralist and Islamist blocs took place on 1 June 2008 when an FPI–HTI mob attacked a religious freedom march at the National Monument (Monas) in Jakarta. Islamists accused the marchers of defending Ahmadiyah, a minority Islamic sect that had been declared deviant by MUI. Those injured included prominent figures of NU and its affiliated party, the National Awakening Party (Partai Kebangkitan Bangsa, PKB) (Suaedy et al. 2009: 181). Police subsequently arrested the leader of FPI, Habib Rizieq Shihab, but Yudhoyono's accommodationist impulse nevertheless saw him capitulate to Islamist demands by issuing a decree that effectively repressed Ahmadiyah (ICG 2008: 1).

The Monas incident, coupled with blatant Islamist infiltration of NU's traditional political domains and organisational infrastructure, raised the stakes in the burgeoning contestation between NU and these Islamist groups. During NU's 32nd national congress (*muktamar*), held in Makassar in 2010, several delegates expressed concern about transnational Islam, blaming NU's preoccupation with electoral politics for the organisation's declining influence over traditionalist society (Feillard and Madinier 2011). In the ensuing leadership race, Hasyim Muzadi lost to the more pluralist Said Aqil Siraj—a protégé of former NU heavyweight Abdurrahman Wahid (Gus Dur)—who promised to renew NU's sociocultural focus.

NU responds

Said Aqil and other pluralists felt that NU urgently needed to reaffirm its religiously tolerant identity in order to counter Islamist influence. He picked a deputy who was considered perfect for the job: As'ad Said Ali, a prominent NU figure and former deputy director of the State Intelligence Agency (Badan Intelijen Negara, BIN). The duo formed a taskforce to analyse NU's organisational weaknesses and formulate strategies to make the organisation more organised, militant and disciplined. While outsiders may have seen As'ad's rise in NU as a form of government intervention, most *nahdliyin* were proud to claim him as an NU representative of a prestigious government agency.

As'ad and other BIN officials had long been claiming that non-violent Islamists were more dangerous than violent jihadists because their peaceful methods rendered them more acceptable to local society—a view he imparted to NU leaders. A document attributed to BIN mentioned five transnational Islamic groups: Salafis, HTI, PKS, Shi'a and Jamaah Tabligh (Ali 2012; Universitas Hasanudin 2008). PKS and HTI were declared the most dangerous because they had supposedly infiltrated the state structure—the former by contesting elections and securing control over political offices, and the latter by recruiting bureaucrats and military officers. Interestingly, the traditionalist FPI was not considered a threat despite its long list of violent offences.

In 2010 the As'ad-led team conducted an assessment of NU's strength in East Java and Central Java, concluding that NU was strong culturally but not organisationally. Adnan Anwar, one of As'ad's team members, added a lack of zeal (*ghirrah*) to the list of problems:

> According to research conducted [in 2010] by the National Police and the Psychology Faculty of the University of Indonesia, our cadres' level [of commitment] is much lower than that of HTI. The average score of HTI members was 10, [whereas] NU's average was below 5. (Anwar 2017)

NU responded to the observed shortage of zeal among its members by introducing various programs designed to enhance ideological and organisational commitment at the grassroots. In 2012, As'ad's team launched a new identity-building project that tied nationalism to NU identity. Called the NU Activist Cadre Training (Pendidikan Kader Penggerak NU, PKPNU), it not only taught organisational skills but also imparted in-depth knowledge to prepare for the 'war of faith' (*perang aqidah*) between NU and the 'others'—apparently referring to its Islamist rivals (Majalah Madani 2018). The main goal, often referred to as 're-ideologisation', was to inoculate cadres against NU's ideological opponents by transforming them from being 'culturally NU' (that is, merely born into NU families) to being conscious members committed to implementing the organisation's political, social and doctrinal agenda (NU Online 2018b; Thoyib 2017).

While the PKPNU program staunchly defends the principle of religious tolerance, this concept is defined in ultra-nationalist terms and incorporates hostility towards a range of 'foreign' ideological forces. It maintains particular animosity towards three ideological enemies: Western liberalism, Eastern communism and Middle Eastern Islamism, all of which are constructed as part of a non-military 'proxy war' being waged against Indonesia (interview with PKPNU alumni, 27 August 2019; *Bangkit Media* 2017).

As'ad's team first tested the PKPNU module in 2012 on members of Ansor and its paramilitary unit, the Ansor Multipurpose Front (Barisan Ansor Serbaguna, Banser), with additional militaristic features. Military and police officers were invited to provide physical training to the participants, a practice that has been adopted in subsequent PKPNU programs (Setiono 2018; *Suara Merdeka* 2019). Ansor also introduced patriotic marches, including the song 'Ya lal Wathon' (O Youth of the

Nation), which went viral on social media and became a favourite among NU children.[5] By 2019, there were around 750,000 PKPNU alumni, with many even paying to join the program (Anwar 2019).

Above all, PKPNU introduced a pledge of loyalty (*bai'at*) to NU and Indonesia. Such a political pledge was common in extremist groups but not in NU.[6] It includes:

> With all my body and soul, I am prepared to fight the enemies of and traitors to traditionalist Sunni Islam (*Ahlus sunnah wal jamaah*), NU and the Unitary Republic of Indonesia, which is based on Pancasila and the 1945 Constitution. (Mukri 2017)

This essentially declared NU's Islamist rivals to be enemies of the state inasmuch as they embraced the concept of transnational Islam. Simultaneously, it reinforced NU's status as the primary ideological and organisational bulwark against Indonesia's transnational Islamist enemies. Follow-up programs by and for PKPNU alumni were held regularly to strengthen fraternity and expand NU's outreach activities. PKPNU alumni in Central Java, for instance, built new NU hospitals and expanded charity programs (NU Online 2018a; NU Pringsewu 2019). In the outer islands, PKPNU revived inactive branches and created new ones.

Other NU bodies and members have also launched numerous traditionalist cultural-revivalism initiatives, some of which are not as hypernationalistic or militant. Young entrepreneurs infuse pop culture into NU's identity-building project, commodifying it and making it 'cool' for young people through Android apps, short films, children's story books and so on. Gus Dur's daughter Alissa Wahid has since 2010 been developing 'Gusdurian', an interfaith cultural network with branches all over Indonesia. In 2013, NU's media team launched several high-quality, one-stop Islamic websites that offer everything from religious instruction to political news and motivational videos. These sites have been very successful in countering the hardliners' previous hegemony over online Islamic discourse.[7]

---

5 The catchy song lyrics warn children to be vigilant against the enemies of Indonesia and NU:
   O Indonesia my country, my love for you is in my faith … O Indonesia my country, you are the symbol of my dignity; whoever comes to threaten you will be crushed under your thorns.

6 Traditionalists were more familiar with *bai'at* in the context of formal initiation into a Sufi order (*tarekat*), but not as a declaration of political loyalty.

7 The new NU websites cunningly use neutral names or names resembling those of existing jihadist/Islamist sites. In addition to the official NU Online, the NU-affiliated websites include Islami.co, Arrahmah.co.id and Muslim-medianews.com. In late September 2019, Alexa.com's web traffic analysis

NU's identity-building project carried on even as its leaders took opposing sides during the 2014 presidential election campaign. Hasyim Muzadi and PKB declared support for Jokowi, while Said Aqil—despite being very close to the pro-Jokowi PKB—publicly endorsed Prabowo. NU as an organisation refrained from all-out campaigning for either candidate, though individual NU elites played active and important roles in the election. When Jokowi emerged as the victor, NU bided its time while awaiting an extension of government support and state largesse, rather than making immediate overtures to the new administration. But in the years to come, NU would emerge as a major beneficiary of the Jokowi government, and the president's need for Islamic allies.

THE POLITICAL ACTIVATION OF ISLAMIC INFIGHTING

The brewing religio-political schism between NU and Islamist groups did not come to the forefront of national politics until NU forged an alliance with Jokowi and his secular-nationalist camp. Alliances between moderate traditionalist Muslims and non-Muslims/secular-nationalists are not a new phenomenon in Indonesia, but their success and intensity has fluctuated greatly depending on broader political dynamics. Even though Gus Dur had long cultivated good relations with non-Muslims and secular-nationalists, his successors saw the relationship as imbalanced, with *nahdliyin* supposedly bearing a disproportionate burden in the struggle against intolerant and puritanical Islam. This meant that Jokowi, as a member of the secular-nationalist Indonesian Democratic Party of Struggle (Partai Demokrasi Indonesia-Perjuangan, PDI-P), needed to prove his value to NU clerics in order to win their trust.

NU and Jokowi: the early days

Some academics have noted that NU did not fully fall into line behind Jokowi until he showered them with material assistance in the aftermath of the anti-Ahok protests (Mietzner 2018; Power 2018). In fact, the story behind NU's endorsement of Jokowi is slightly more nuanced. First, although NU may not have welcomed Jokowi with any fanfare, the popularity of his vice president, Jusuf Kalla, with the *nahdliyin* ensured

---

ranked Islami.co as the 134th most visited site in Indonesia and NU Online as the 326th, whereas Eramuslim.com, one of the longest-established Islamist news sites, took 725th place.

the president's acceptance among NU members. Second, the relations between NU and Jokowi had started to strengthen, albeit slowly, even before the Ahok debacle. This process, partly facilitated by PKB, reflected a confluence of interests—material and ideological—between NU and the Jokowi government.

On one hand, NU was seeking state support for its ambitious Archipelagic Islam (Islam Nusantara) project—NU's version of local, tolerant Islam—which it was trying to promote as a panacea for global jihadism. On the other hand, Jokowi was facing security challenges associated with radical Islam—such as the domestic rise of pro-ISIS terrorist groups—as well as his own political insecurities. Jokowi's opponents had often framed him as a mere puppet of PDI-P leader Megawati Sukarnoputri, while Islamist groups had spread false rumours that he was ethnically Chinese, a communist or a closet non-Muslim. These insecurities led Jokowi to go out of his way to consolidate support from an expansive coalition of political parties and organisations (Mietzner 2016; Tomsa 2017). When he belatedly tried to cultivate closer relations with Muslim groups, NU as the largest, Java-centric Islamic organisation seemed a natural ally.

Wearing a sarong and *peci*, the trademark outfit of traditionalist students (*santri*), Jokowi addressed the NU *muktamar* in August 2015, praising Islam Nusantara as the antidote to sectarianism and extremism. In the same year, he declared 22 October as 'National Santri Day' to honour NU's contribution to the national independence struggle; he also declared NU's founding father a national hero. However, many in NU still viewed these as mere symbolic gestures, given that there was no commensurate increase in material support (Power 2018).

NU found other allies in the government beyond the president himself. It received significant funding from the National Counterterrorism Agency (Badan Nasional Penanggulangan Terrorisme, BNPT) to hold an International Summit of Moderate Muslim Leaders (ISOMIL) in May 2016. Around the same time, as part of Indonesia's (unavailing) efforts to play a role as a peacemaker in the Middle East, foreign minister Retno Marsudi engaged NU to establish an Islamic centre in Afghanistan to promote peace and moderatism (Kwok 2016). Religious affairs minister Lukman Hakim Saifuddin—an NU politician from the United Development Party (Partai Persatuan Pembangunan, PPP)—channelled funds to NU, including by commissioning research projects to strengthen the Islam Nusantara concept (Safitri 2018).

Despite the steady development of collaborative relations between NU and the Jokowi administration, the first two years of Jokowi's presidency saw the perpetuation of underlying internal tensions and differences within the pluralist bloc. Some in NU complained that PKB took most of the patronage that was meant for NU, and others felt that NU was doing all the work in the war against Islamists while secular groups and nationalist parties enjoyed the benefits. For these differences to be set aside, there needed to be a common enemy. The Islamist mobilisation against Ahok provided this unifying force.

2016 Islamist mobilisation as the tipping point

The Defence of Islam movement (Aksi Bela Islam) was the tipping point in Jokowi's relationship with NU. This movement, orchestrated by an alliance of FPI, HTI, Salafis and other hardline groups, severely exacerbated the schism between pluralist Muslims and non-Muslims on one hand, and Islamists on the other. The first protest took place in October 2016, two weeks after Ahok's allegedly blasphemous speech went viral on social media. In the speech, Ahok decried his political opponents' use of a Qur'anic verse (Al-Maidah 51) to claim that Muslims were prohibited from accepting non-Muslim political leaders. The largest of the protests, which took place on 2 December 2016, drew as many as a million participants. It inspired the 212 movement (Aksi 212), named for the date of this demonstration.

The Defence of Islam movement intensified the trend towards intra-Islamic polarisation in three ways: by driving Jokowi closer to NU and pushing his main rival Prabowo into the arms of the Islamists; by unifying NU elites and the grassroots membership; and by steering non-Muslim communities into the NU-dominated pluralist camp. It is important to note that NU was initially split over the Ahok blasphemy issue. Ma'ruf Amin, the supreme leader of NU and the chair of MUI, was responsible for the MUI fatwa that had declared Ahok's speech blasphemous. Later, his court testimony would help send Ahok to prison. Members of NU's conservative faction, the self-labelled NU Straight Path (Garis Lurus), especially those in Jakarta and Madura, took an active part in the anti-Ahok mobilisation (IPAC 2018: 11–16). Said Aqil, on the other hand, urged the public to accept Ahok's apology. Ansor leaders publicly supported Ahok too.

Although NU's central leadership and social base were initially divided, the ever-growing popularity of Islamist groups after 2016 contributed to the reunification of NU's elites and the grassroots membership as competing factions recognised a common organisational adversary. NU's reconsolidation was an important prerequisite for its subsequent large-scale mobilisation behind Jokowi. Anecdotal examples from East Java show that rank-and-file members who initially sympathised with the

212 cause subsequently expressed regret, feeling they had been 'used' by HTI to advance its 'treacherous caliphate agenda' (interview with NU women in Jombang, 28 October 2018). Material incentives also played a role in NU's reunification, as the anti-Ahok mobilisation forced Jokowi to make far greater concessions to NU than he had previously. In July 2017, he recruited Ma'ruf Amin and other senior NU religious leaders (*kiai*) for a new presidential religious council (Majelis Zikir Hubbul Wathon); Ma'ruf was also given a prestigious position in the newly formed Pancasila Ideology Development Agency (Badan Pembinaan Ideologi Pancasila, BPIP). To win over the grassroots, Jokowi visited NU boarding schools (*pesantren*) much more frequently from 2017 onward, providing soft-loan and entrepreneurship training programs and occasionally funding new buildings (Fachrudin 2019; Fealy 2018).

The massive Islamist show of force not only changed Jokowi's strategy towards NU, but also compelled non-Muslims and secularists to do more to fight intolerance, including by giving more resources to NU. For instance, in May 2017 a group of non-Muslim and secularist activists, artists and businesspeople established the Our Indonesia Movement (Gerakan Kita Indonesia, GITA), which aimed to promote tolerance through cultural and educational outreach in schools, universities and villages (discussions with GITA activists, 27 July 2019). Chinese-Indonesian tycoons who had been longstanding Gus Dur supporters reportedly increased their donations to support the NU-led tolerance campaign. In early 2017, a group of non-Muslim businesspeople held a discussion series on Islamist extremism, during which some Chinese-Indonesian participants proposed giving more funds to Banser, which they saw as a proven vanguard of Indonesian pluralism (discussion with a Jakarta-based researcher, 19 September 2019).

Indeed, the 212 movement proved to be a blessing in disguise for Ansor and Banser. According to Ansor's secretary-general:

> Ansor and Banser membership increased [from 1.7 million people in 2016] to 4.7 million members in 2018. [It increased] especially after the 212 groups threatened and harassed our clerics. The harassment reached its peak during the 2017 Jakarta election, because Ansor held a consultation of religious scholars (*bahtsul masail*) that resulted in a ruling permitting non-Muslims to be political leaders. But the more they mocked and harassed our clerics, the more militant [*nahdliyin* at the grassroots] became. People came in droves to join Ansor [...] and we welcomed them with intensive cadre-training programs. (Interview, 31 July 2019)

While the number of new members was probably exaggerated, Banser did indeed mount a successful recruitment drive that obtained political momentum and financial sponsorship from late 2016 as an upshot of sharpening polarisation.

NU paramilitary: the tolerant vigilantes?

Banser's expansion is an important manifestation of the growing militancy of Indonesia's pluralist camp. Despite criticising FPI's 'anti-vice' vigilantism, NU has shown a willingness to adopt vigilante tactics of its own in service of its organisational and ideological objectives.

Ansor first formed a counterterrorism unit within Banser in 2011, named Densus 99 (resembling the name of the Indonesian counterterrorism police, Densus 88). However, the unit's activities were limited to guarding churches during Christmas and New Year, which Banser members had already been doing since the Christmas bombings by Jemaah Islamiyah in 2000. In 2015, PKB parliamentarian Yaqut Cholil Qoumas took over the leadership of Ansor and adopted more proactive tactics to halt the expansion of intolerant and extremist groups, including through the use of force and intimidation.

Beginning in 2015, local Densus 99 teams were specifically instructed to map out the types and modus operandi of Islamist groups—particularly HTI and Salafis—in their respective areas (interview with Densus 99 chief, 26 August 2019). They were to report this information to Ansor's regional and central leaderships, usually through WhatsApp groups, and discuss an appropriate response. The first tactic would be to lobby local governments to deny permits for radical Islamist activities. If this failed, they would mobilise mobs of Banser members to forcefully halt the activities, for example by intimidating the participants or by blocking access to or raiding the venues.

In April and May 2016, Banser launched its first systematic attempt to disrupt HTI meetings in eight East Java cities. In NU's birthplace of Jombang, the local government was cooperative, officially prohibiting an HTI meeting scheduled to be held near Pesantren Tebuireng (*Tempo* 2016). In Jember, however, Banser mobilised a large mob, leading to a violent clash with HTI members. Police and military officers mediated by facilitating Banser's demand to have HTI leaders sign an agreement stating that they would refrain from spreading their ideology (Solichah 2016). Banser's tactics echoed those commonly used by Islamist vigilante groups to target so-called deviant Islamic sects and moral offenders.

Ansor members argue they are not engaged in 'vigilantism' as long as they 'help and work together with' state security forces in containing the Islamist challenge to the Pancasila-based state (interview with Densus 99 chief, 26 August 2019). Close cooperation with the state apparatus has been a feature of Ansor's anti-Islamist campaign. Yaqut has taken pride in the fact that Banser's cadre development courses have involved physical training provided by instructors from the army's territorial commands (Prabowo 2018; TNI AD 2017). Banser has also made sure to involve local police and army officers in its anti-'radical' raids.

In 2018 and 2019, Banser mobilisations and clashes played into partisan divisions. In August 2018, some Ansor members joined a mob that was trying to disrupt the '2019 Change the President' (2019 Ganti Presiden) rally in Surabaya, causing a brawl between Ansor and FPI youth. Tensions escalated again in October, when a group of Islamists infiltrated NU's National Santri Day parades and waved the black flags commonly associated with HTI.[8] In Garut, Banser members confiscated and burned the black flags, causing a massive outcry on social media because the flags had the name of God written on them. When Islamists mobilised to protest the flag burning, Ansor and NU responded by holding a Grand Prayer Rally (Istighotsah Kubro) in Sidoarjo, East Java, which attracted over 100,000 participants. The Jokowi campaign drew on NU's shows of strength in much the same way as Prabowo had sought to benefit from the 212 movement. Ansor organised a series of pluralist rallies called 'One Nation Marches' (Kirab Satu Negeri) in the second half of 2018, which Jokowi endorsed and attended. The president also gave a speech at the Jakarta stadium in January 2019 to commemorate the anniversary of the NU women's organisation, Muslimat; the event resembled a Defence of Islam rally in its mass mobilisation of people from outside the capital, its designation as a 'mass prayer' event (despite having an obvious political agenda) and its commencement with a congregational dawn prayer.

NU played a major role in the Jokowi campaign in 2019, believing that the president would reward it with the material largesse and political legitimacy it needed to crush its religio-ideological rivals once and for all. These hopes were only partially fulfilled in the early months of Jokowi's second term.

AUTHORITARIAN PLURALISM?

By November 2019, the relationship between Jokowi's second-term government and NU had developed in two important ways. On one hand, the president's relationship with NU became stressed when the formation of his second-term cabinet did not deliver to NU the handsome

---

8 Since the advent of the 212 movement, this flag has also been used by other Muslim groups as a generic symbol of resistance.

rewards its elites had expected. On the other hand, however, this by no means distracted the pluralist bloc from its common enemy. Even as NU leaders were denied substantial material gains, the president continued to co-opt NU's anti-radicalism agenda and strengthen its use as a tool for repression.

NU was riding high in the immediate aftermath of Jokowi's re-election, even supporting his administration's controversial move to emasculate the Corruption Eradication Commission (Komisi Pemberantasan Korupsi, KPK), which triggered a wave of student-led protests in September 2019. Some Jokowi supporters, including those from NU, justified the policy on the grounds that KPK had been infiltrated by an Islamist faction they derisively referred to as the 'Taliban'. According to some NU *kiai*, KPK prosecutors from the 'Taliban' faction had tried to damage NU's reputation by selectively targeting prominent NU politicians for investigation and arrest (interview, 27 September 2019).[9]

NU's honeymoon with Jokowi was somewhat disrupted, however, when he announced his new cabinet. Jokowi denied NU all the strategic positions it had hoped for, even as he expanded his party coalition (and strengthened a pattern of party 'cartelisation') by assigning the defence portfolio to his former nemesis, Prabowo. This was a kick in the teeth for NU's leaders, who believed that Jokowi owed his victory to their staunch support during the campaign and had expected several ministerial positions in return. In addition, NU elites were frustrated by the president's continued refusal to ensure that NU's channels of patronage were separated from those directed to PKB: PKB was assigned three ministerial seats in the October 2019 cabinet, with Mahfud MD being the only non-PKB *nahdliyin* to receive a ministerial portfolio (as coordinating minister for politics, law and security).

Nahdliyin were particularly angry that Jokowi picked retired military general Fachrul Razi as his minister of religious affairs, a position that had long been reserved for NU-linked politicians. As a consolation prize, the president appointed Ma'ruf Amin as the chief coordinator of an anti-radicalism taskforce that involved 11 ministries, and NU was given a handful of less strategic positions, such as deputy ministerial posts and positions on the vice president's special staff. Some officials of the NU Central Board openly expressed their disappointment with Jokowi, and many activists shared in this disillusionment. One NU activist who had assisted Jokowi throughout the whole campaign compared him to a baby:

---

9   KPK arrested two prominent NU politicians in 2019: Romahurmuziy (former chair of PPP) and Imam Nahrawi (former minister of youth and sports).

'We've held him and now he pees on us' (WhatsApp group discussion, 21 October 2019).

Yet, despite being snubbed in cabinet appointments, NU remains strongly committed to the Jokowi government's ideological agenda and continues to share its goal of weeding out Islamists from the civil service, state-owned enterprises and academic institutions. Government officials and NU elites alike assert there is an 'emergency of civil servant radicalism' (*darurat radikalisme ASN*), citing survey data that indicate that 20 per cent of civil servants have an 'anti-Pancasila' ideology (Friana 2018). The term 'radicalism', which used to be reserved for people associated with violent extremism, has been redefined to include intolerant or unpatriotic individuals who have not necessarily committed any criminal act—a perspective very much influenced by BIN. The civil service 'emergency' came to wider public attention with the leak of a classified document that contained the names of civil servants, military officers and academics who purportedly sympathised with HTI. However, accusations of radicalism have extended to those who sympathise with the opposition party PKS, or with other legal organisations that participated in the 212 movement. Pro-Jokowi internet activists have targeted 'radicals' within the bureaucracy by spreading photographs of government employees who joined the 212 movement.

Many analyses have concluded—correctly—that the rise of overt religious intolerance and fundamentalism presents a problem for Indonesian democracy. However, the Jokowi government's response to Islamism has entailed a range of draconian policies and tactics that have similarly undermined democracy. In 2018, at least four university lecturers were sacked for expressing sympathy for HTI or the 212 movement through social media. Several pro-Prabowo public schoolteachers were arrested for allegedly spreading 'hoaxes'. At the same time, the government has done very little to address the messages of intolerance spread by firebrand preachers (including some former terrorist detainees) at university and government mosques. Since 2018, six ministries have introduced carefully crafted screening tests for new recruits designed to prevent the recruitment of 'radicals' (NU Online 2019). While similar policies could justifiably be directed against anti-state extremists, their merits are far more dubious when directed against civil servants, given the broad criteria used to diagnose 'radicalism' and the opaque, unaccountable nature of these screening processes.

One recent and particularly powerful demonstration of the detrimental impact that this pluralist backlash has had upon Indonesian democracy is the Joint Ministerial Decree on Managing Radicalism and Strengthening Nationalism in the Civil Service, issued in November 2019. Once again, it adopts an excessively broad definition of 'radicalism', ensuring that its implementation is highly malleable and prone to partisan and personal biases. It details 11 types of radicalism, including 'hate speech' against Pancasila, the constitution, the principle of Unity in Diversity (Bhinneka Tunggal Ika) and the government; ethnoreligious hate speech; liking, retweeting or commenting on the above types of hate speech on social media; spreading hoaxes; defaming Pancasila or other state symbols and the government; and holding membership of, or possessing attributes associated with, organisations considered hostile to Pancasila and the government. There is no mention of violent extremism or discrimination in the definition of radicalism, thus exempting groups like FPI that publicly endorse Pancasila but nevertheless use violent methods. Notably, the decree effectively proscribes civil servants from voicing criticisms not only of state symbols and institutions, but also of the incumbent *government*.

Given the government's strong ideological endorsement of NU, some civil servants are concerned that non-NU forms of Islamic piety may arbitrarily be stigmatised as extremist or unorthodox. These concerns have been magnified by the government's introduction of an online portal where citizens can lodge complaints against civil servants who breach the rules on 'radicalism'. There can be little doubt that the societal policing of religious expression and political discourse is prone to abuse. With such broadly defined offences and a lack of precautionary review mechanisms, the decree could seriously harm freedom of speech and expression.

The anti-Ahok mobilisations of late 2016 sparked alarm about rising Islamism, but the draconian responses adopted by the Jokowi administration and its NU allies now raise the spectre of a revived pluralist authoritarianism. Islamist–pluralist polarisation is tearing at Indonesia's democratic foundations, and the preservation of democratic institutions has been subordinated to a struggle over the country's religio-ideological orientation.

CONCLUSION

In this chapter I have argued that polarisation between Indonesia's Islamist and pluralist factions is contributing to an ongoing process of democratic decline. Rather than focusing on the role of intolerant Islamist groups, however, I have argued that the greater problem for contemporary democratic quality is an illiberal—and increasingly authoritarian—backlash from agents of militant pluralism.

The cleavage between Muslims who endorse religious pluralism and those with a more puritanical agenda is nothing new in Indonesia, but it has become more pronounced with the success and growing popularity of Islamist and ultra-conservative groups since 1998. Liberalisation and democratisation, among other factors, enabled Islamist inroads into both NU's traditional base and the state bureaucracy. Groups like HTI, PKS and Salafis attracted middle-class Muslim recruits in particular, making them better resourced and politically savvier. As Islamist parties and organisations benefited immensely from President Yudhoyono's highly accommodationist approach in the mid-2000s, NU began to push back against the Islamist challenge. It developed new indoctrination programs that focused on instilling an NU identity and cultivating a deep animosity towards NU's doctrinal enemies.

The unprecedented street protests mobilised by Islamist groups against Ahok in 2016 were the watershed event that exacerbated these intra-Islamic rivalries. The sheer magnitude of the movement shocked the Jokowi government and alarmed pluralist and religious-minority groups. It forced the president to pay more attention and devote more resources to NU as the bastion of moderate Islam. It also encouraged secular-nationalists and religious minorities to renew their alliance with NU. From 2017, an increasingly empowered NU emerged as the fulcrum of a government-sponsored backlash against 'radicalism', as it strengthened its paramilitary force and employed increasingly aggressive tactics against its Islamist opponents.

By the time the presidential election campaign started in late 2018, Prabowo had successfully courted Islamist groups while pluralist organisations had gathered around Jokowi. By early 2019, some elements of the Prabowo and Jokowi coalitions were so far apart that they saw each other as existential threats rather than as democratic rivals. Polarisation evidently diminished the norms of 'loser's consent' and 'winner's restraint' that are critical to a functioning democratic government (see Hicken, this volume). As soon as Jokowi was declared victor in May 2019, Prabowo's angry supporters took to the streets to resist what they claimed was a rigged election result, while Jokowi supporters encouraged a harsh police response to the protests.

Even after Jokowi reconciled with Prabowo and made him defence minister, polarisation remained rampant. Elite-level reconciliation did not prevent the government from continuing its crackdown on the grassroots Islamist movement that had endorsed Prabowo's candidacy. This was evidenced by the provisions introduced in November 2019 to curb 'radicalism' in the public service. The government's use of 'anti-Pancasila' discourse as a primary indicator of radicalisation echoes Suharto-era measures to curtail political dissent and regulate political expression in the civil service.

In short, the case of the Jokowi–NU alliance demonstrates that religious pluralists are not necessarily democrats. Indeed, despite its tolerance towards Indonesia's non-Muslim minorities, the pluralist coalition has shown little tolerance for ideological or religious expression that contravenes its own doctrinal orientation, and NU's support has been used by the Jokowi government to facilitate its own anti-democratic policy measures, on the pretext of combating 'intolerance' and 'radicalism'. In the years to come, the continued rise of militant pluralists may turn out to be the most significant factor in Indonesia's present democratic regression.

REFERENCES

Ali, A.S. 2012. *Ideologi Gerakan Pasca Reformasi: Gerakan-gerakan Sosial Politik dalam Tinjauan Ideologis*. Jakarta: LP3ES.

Anwar, A. 2017. 'Ngurusi NU harus berani mati KH'. YouTube video, 22 September. https://www.youtube.com/watch?v=gqdbRFL1NxU

Anwar, A. 2019. 'Pidato kebangsaan bersama KH. Adnan Komandan PKPNU, di reuni ke 3 penggerak NU Kab Brebes'. Facebook video, 9 April. https://www.facebook.com/watch/?v=1067108623486955

Arifianto, A.R. 2019. 'Is Islam an increasingly polarizing political cleavage in Indonesia?' *Order from Chaos*, 25 April. Washington, DC: Brookings Institution. https://www.brookings.edu/blog/order-from-chaos/2019/04/25/is-islam-an-increasingly-polarizing-political-cleavage-in-indonesia/

Bangkit Media. 2017. 'Kader NU harus waspada terhadap musuh agama dan negara'. *Bangkit Media*, 16 April. https://bangkitmedia.com/kader-nu-harus-waspada-terhadap-musuh-agama-dan-negara/

Bush, R. 2015. 'Religious politics and minority rights during the Yudhoyono presidency'. In *The Yudhoyono Presidency: Indonesia's Decade of Stability and Stagnation*, edited by E. Aspinall, M. Mietzner and D. Tomsa, 239–57. Singapore: Institute of Southeast Asian Studies (ISEAS).

Fachrudin, A.A. 2019. 'Jokowi and NU: the view from the pesantren'. *New Mandala*, 11 April. https://www.newmandala.org/jokowi-and-nu-the-view-from-the-pesantren/

Fealy, G. 2018. 'Nahdlatul Ulama and the politics trap'. *New Mandala*, 11 July. https://www.newmandala.org/nahdlatul-ulama-politics-trap/

Feillard, A. and R. Madinier. 2011. *The End of Innocence? Indonesian Islam and the Temptations of Radicalism*. Singapore: NUS Press.

Friana, H. 2018. 'Sebanyak 19,4 persen PNS tak setuju ideologi Pancasila'. *Tirto*, 17 November. https://tirto.id/kemendagri-sebut-194-persen-pns-tak-setuju-ideologi-pancasila-daef

García-Guadilla, M. and A. Mallen. 2018. 'Polarization, participatory democracy, and democratic erosion in Venezuela's twenty-first century socialism'. *ANNALS of the American Academy of Political and Social Science* 681(1): 62–77.

ICG (International Crisis Group). 2008. 'Indonesia: implications of the Ahmadiyah decree'. *Asia Briefing* No. 78. Jakarta/Brussels: ICG. 7 July.

Ilhamdi, A. 2015. 'Gerakan politik Islam Hizbut Tahrir Indonesia (HTI): transformasi menuju pengakuan resmi pemerintah (2000–2006)'. Undergraduate thesis. Jakarta: University of Indonesia.

Indikator Politik Indonesia. 2019. 'Exit poll pemilu 2019'. Jakarta: Indikator Politik Indonesia. 17 April. http://indikator.co.id/agenda/details/64/Rilis-Exit-Poll-Pemilu-2019

IPAC (Institute for Policy Analysis of Conflict). 2018. 'After Ahok: the Islamist agenda in Indonesia'. *IPAC Report* No. 44. Jakarta: IPAC. 6 April.

Kwok, Y. 2016. 'Could Indonesia's president become the Middle East's new mediator?'. *Time*, 20 January.

Liputan Islam. 2014. 'HTI catut logo NU'. *Liputan Islam*, 21 February. https://liputanislam.com/tabayun/hti-catut-logo-nu/

Majalah Madani. 2018. 'Setrategi mutakhir dengan PKPNU'. Majalah Madani, 2 January. https://www.majalahmadani.com/2018/01/setrategi-mutakhir-dengan-pkpnu.html

McCoy, J., T. Rahman and M. Somer. 2018. 'Polarization and the global crisis of democracy: common patterns, dynamics, and pernicious consequences for democratic polities'. *American Behavioral Scientist* 62(1): 16–42.

Mietzner, M. 2016. 'Coercing loyalty: coalitional presidentialism and party politics in Jokowi's Indonesia'. *Contemporary Southeast Asia* 38(2): 209–32.

Mietzner, M. 2018. 'Fighting illiberalism with illiberalism: Islamist populism and democratic deconsolidation in Indonesia'. *Pacific Affairs* 91(2): 261–82.

Mietzner, M. and B. Muhtadi. 2018. 'Explaining the 2016 Islamist mobilisation in Indonesia: religious intolerance, militant groups and the politics of accommodation'. *Asian Studies Review* 42(3): 479–97.

Mohamed Osman, M.N. 2010. 'Reviving the caliphate in the Nusantara: Hizbut Tahrir Indonesia's mobilization strategy and its impact in Indonesia'. *Terrorism and Political Violence* 22(4): 601–22.

Mukri, K. 2017. 'Ikrar kesetiaan kader penggerak NU'. YouTube video, 17 April. https://www.youtube.com/watch?v=z4buKCOStFM

NU Online. 2007a. 'Himbauan ketua umum PBNU soal gejala konflik internal umat Islam'. NU Online, 25 April. https://www.nu.or.id/post/read/8825/himbauan-ketua-umum-pbnu-soal-gejala-konflik-internal-umat-islam

NU Online. 2007b. 'PBNU peringatkan kelompok Islam yang merebut masjid NU'. NU Online, 4 June. https://www.nu.or.id/post/read/9124/pbnu-peringatkan-kelompok-islam-yang-merebut-masjid-nu

NU Online. 2018a. 'Keberhasilan program NU karena kaderisasi PKPNU'. NU Online, 21 April. https://www.nu.or.id/post/read/89188/keberhasilan-program-nu-karena-kaderisasi-pkpnu

NU Online. 2018b. 'Perkuat gerakan, pimpinan pusat Pergunu gelar PKPNU'. NU Online, 24 July. https://www.nu.or.id/post/read/93337/perkuat-gerakan-pimpinan-pusat-pergunu-gelar-pkpnu

NU Online. 2019. 'Lakpesdam PBNU kembangkan alat ukur kecenderungan radikalisme CPNS'. NU Online, 21 November. https://www.nu.or.id/post/read/113765/lakpesdam-pbnu-kembangkan-alat-ukur-kecenderungan-radikalisme-cpns

NU Pringsewu. 2019. 'Keinginan warga NU ikut pendidikan karakter tak terbendung'. NU Pringsewu, 7 August.

Power, T.P. 2018. 'Jokowi's authoritarian turn and Indonesia's democratic decline'. *Bulletin of Indonesian Economic Studies* 54(3): 307–38.

Prabowo, M.P. 2018. '150 calon Banser Jatim peroleh materi dari TNI dan Polri, soal militer hingga religius'. *TribunJatim*, 19 August. https://jatim.tribunnews.com/2018/08/19/150-calon-banser-jatim-peroleh-materi-dari-tni-dan-polri-soal-militer-hingga-religius

Safitri, D. 2018. 'Rhetoric debate on Islam Nusantara discourse'. *KnE Social Sciences* 3(10): 151–73.

Setiono, R. 2018. 'Pendidikan wasbang bagi anggota PKPNU Kec. Turen'. *Kodim0818*, 7 October. https://kodim-0818.id/pendidikan-wasbang-bagi-anggota-pkpnu-kec-turen/

Shofia, N. and T. Pepinsky. 2019. 'Measuring the "NU effect" in Indonesia's election'. *New Mandala*, 1 July. https://www.newmandala.org/measuring-the-nu-effect-in-indonesias-election/

Solichah, Z. 2016. 'Kegiatan muktamar tokoh umat HTI Jember dihentikan'. *Antaranews*, 1 May. https://jatim.antaranews.com/berita/176993/kegiatan-muktamar-tokoh-umat-hti-jember-dihentikan

Suaedy, A., Rumadi, M.S. Azhari and B.S. Fata. 2009. *Islam, the Constitution, and Human Rights: The Problematics of Religious Freedom in Indonesia.* Jakarta: Wahid Institute. http://wahidinstitute.org/wi-id/images/upload/buku/islam_constitution_human_rights_wahid_institute.pdf

Suara Merdeka. 2019. 'Kader PKPNU Tanjung digembleng semangat nasionalisme'. *Suara Merdeka*, 20 January. https://www.suaramerdeka.com/news/baca/161582/kader-pkpnu-tanjung-digembleng-semangat-nasionalisme

Tempo. 2016. 'Batalkan muktamar, Hizbut Tahrir Jombang hindari konflik'. *Tempo*, 1 May. https://nasional.tempo.co/read/767562/batalkan-muktamar-hizbut-tahrir-jombang-hindari-konflik/full&view=ok

Thoyib, A.S. 2017. 'Masyhuri Malik: PKPNU, jawaban kegelisahan Kiai Hasyim Muzadi tentang lunturnya militansi ber-NU'. Jagatngopi.com, 29 October. https://www.jagatngopi.com/masyhuri-malik-pkpnu-jawaban-kegelisahan-kiai-hasyim-muzadi-tentang-lunturnya-militansi-ber-nu/

TNI AD (Tentara Nasional Indonesia Angkatan Darat). 2017. 'Pupuk jiwa nasionalime generasi muda dengan Diklatsar'. TNI AD, 29 January. https://tniad.mil.id/2017/01/pupuk-jiwa-nasionalime-generasi-muda-dengan-diklatsar/

Tomsa, D. 2017. 'Indonesia in 2016: Jokowi consolidates power'. In *Southeast Asian Affairs 2017*, edited by D. Singh and M. Cook, 149–62. Singapore: ISEAS – Yusof Isak Institute.

Universitas Hasanudin. 2008. 'Gerakan Islam transnasional dan pengaruhnya di Indonesia (di-release dan diedarkan oleh BIN)'. Universitas Hasanudin. https://adoc.tips/gerakan-islam-transnasional-dan-pengaruhnya-di-indonesia-di-.html

van Bruinessen, M., ed. 2013. *Contemporary Developments in Indonesian Islam: Explaining the 'Conservative Turn'.* Singapore: Institute of Southeast Asian Studies (ISEAS).

6 Is populism a threat to Indonesian democracy?

Liam Gammon

Populism looms large as a contributing factor in the global democratic recession. The hazards to liberal democracy posed by populism, which I define here as 'a *political strategy* [emphasis added] through which a personalistic leader seeks or exercises government power based on direct, unmediated, uninstitutionalized support from large numbers of mostly unorganized followers' (Weyland 2001: 14), are manifold. Foremost among the concerns is what might, for simplicity's sake, be referred to as the process of 'populist autocratisation'. In this scenario, a political outsider is elected as head of government on an anti-establishment platform and falls into conflict with old elites and the institutions they control. Thereafter, the new leader moves to erode horizontal checks on presidential power, buoyed by the support of 'the people' in whose name they claim to govern (Levitsky and Loxton 2013). Evidence from Latin America shows that populist rule, on average, serves to lower countries' quality-of-democracy scores (Huber and Schimpf 2016) and is particularly associated with the erosion of checks on executive power (Houle and Kenny 2018) and attacks on press freedom and freedom of expression (Kenny 2019a). Similar studies using global databases have found that populist rule is correlated with the erosion of civil liberties and checks and balances (Kyle and Mounk 2018).

With this global context in mind, scholars have long speculated that Indonesia was 'structurally vulnerable' (Slater 2014: 312) to a populist reaction to the manifest failings of the post–New Order democracy. So prominent were some of the social and institutional correlates of populism in the Indonesian case that, by the end of the presidency of Susilo Bambang Yudhoyono (2004–14), the emergence of a populist threat to democracy was 'almost over-determined' (Aspinall 2015: 3). Now, midway through the tenure of President Joko Widodo (Jokowi)—who emerged not only as a populist, but also as an outsider to the national political elite—it is worth reassessing what role, if any, populism is playing in the democratic regression that is the subject of this volume.

In this chapter, I first emphasise how, in spite of the ample 'raw material' for populism found in the post-Suharto political system, key features of Indonesia's institutional framework have put barriers in the way of individuals and groups seeking to launch populist parties, movements and candidacies. These barriers, I argue, have insulated Indonesia from the emergence of a true *populist outsider* presidency of the sort that has so often imperilled democracy in Latin America. Jokowi is typically categorised as a populist politician by Indonesianists and comparativists alike. Yet, when describing his brand of populism, scholars have emphasised its 'polite' (Mietzner 2014), 'inclusive' (Gammon 2014) or 'partial' (Kenny 2019b: 8) nature. His reliance on populist governing strategies as president has been negligible, having quickly accommodated himself to Indonesia's conventions of coalitional presidentialism after winning office in 2014 (Muhtadi 2015; Warburton 2016). In fact, Jokowi's political strategy has come to be based on mutually expedient alliances with the sorts of oligarchic actors and intermediary organisations— political parties, civil society organisations and bureaucracies—that populists typically seek to subvert and undermine.[1]

On one hand, the weakness of Indonesian parties, and widespread disaffection with the political elite, creates structural opportunities for mobilising voters along populist lines. At the same time, key features of the electoral system reinforce the power of political parties at the apex of the political system, by positioning their leaders as both the gatekeepers to executive office and the main building blocks of a president's governing coalition. The result for outsider populists like Jokowi is that populism has to be channelled through established parties and power structures. In doing so, outsider populism loses a great deal of its disruptive character on its way to office. By implication, the democratic regression under way is not an effect of a populist outsider president's attempts to personalise power at the expense of checking institutions controlled by established elites. Instead, it is clear that Jokowi's erosion of democratic norms has been enacted in concert with a diverse coalition of incumbent non-populist political actors, and has occurred with a broad level of elite buy-in precisely because it is *not* occurring along populist lines.

---

1 See, in particular, Nuraniyah, this volume; and Aspinall and Mietzner (2019).

Second, I argue that while Indonesia's institutional design has succeeded in protecting the country's democracy from *some* of the hazards posed to it by populist rule, it remains vulnerable to populism in other areas. The first of these is the as-yet-unproven potential threat of non-outsider populist challenges to democracy, that is, those that emerge from the heart of the oligarchy. In contemporary Indonesia, such a challenge is effectively synonymous with the political ambitions of Jokowi's electoral opponent in 2014 and 2019, Prabowo Subianto. Any comments about the viability of such an attempt at populist autocratisation from a member of the oligarchy are speculative, yet the capacity of Indonesia's democratic foundations to weather a populist challenge remains in serious question.

The second way in which populism is harming Indonesian democracy, meanwhile, is not hypothetical. The side effects of the divisive rhetoric that is frequently a part of populist political strategies pose less tangible but nevertheless real problems at the societal level. Many, but not all, populists make strident rhetorical attacks on 'elites' or minorities, who are often framed as benefiting from an unjust political order at the expense of the majority 'people'. Such ideas, once implanted in society and legitimised, can undermine social cohesion and contribute to sociopolitical polarisation between social groups on the basis of political affiliation or cultural identity. In Indonesia today, we are witnessing illiberal challenges to pluralist values on the part of religious organisations that embrace populist ideological and rhetorical constructs to delegitimise the participation of religious and ethnic minorities in politics. Increasingly, attempts to mobilise religious voters through divisive nationalist and Islamic populist strategies have had harmful side effects for the pluralist foundations of Indonesian democracy that go beyond the well-documented repression that has come to mark the government's response to its Islamist opponents (IPAC 2019b; Mietzner 2018). In short, while populism 'from above' has not been a factor in the present democratic decline, Indonesia may well be an example of a country where the side effects of civil society–led populist mobilisation are corroding the quality of democracy from the grassroots upward.

POPULISM'S POTENTIAL IN INDONESIA

At first glance, recent political contests would seem to vindicate concerns about Indonesia's vulnerability to populism and its harms. In 2014, two populist candidates competed to become Indonesia's second directly elected president. Whereas Prabowo Subianto certainly seemed to fit the template of the authoritarian strongman menace, it was Jokowi and what was at the time seen as his more benign form of populism that won out in the brutal 2014 campaign. That Jokowi's presidency has nonetheless been marked by an acceleration of the democratic regression that began under his predecessor is clear from the contributions elsewhere in this volume. Moreover, under Jokowi's presidency, conservative Islamic forces hostile to the president and his coalition have reinvigorated an 'Islamic populism', which has been used by political elites to unite and politically mobilise disparate elements of the Muslim community through appeals to identity-based grievances.

Use of the term 'populism' in studies of Indonesian politics reflects how the concept itself is both 'widely used and widely contested' (Gidron and Bonikowski 2013: 1). Scholars have implicitly conceived of populism in *policy* or *distributional* terms. The re-election of Yudhoyono in 2009 was attributed to his deployment of 'populist' cash transfer policies (Mietzner 2009). At the local level, 'electoral populism'—defined as 'contestants for political office [offering] redistributive policies and other concessions to their lower class constituents' (Aspinall 2013: 103)—is now commonplace in local electoral contests. More recently, renewed interest in the tradition of 'Islamic populism'—defined as 'a variant of populist politics' where 'the concept of the *ummah* substitutes for the notion of "the people" ' (Hadiz 2016: 28)—and its contemporary manifestations has seen the application of *ideational* definitions of populism gain popularity.

For the purposes of my analysis here, I conceive of populism as a political strategy based on the mobilisation of mass constituencies through charismatic appeals, and which emphasises the disintermediation of linkages between elites and grassroots constituencies. In populist modes of organisation and mobilisation, the use of redistributive policies and appeals to identity politics, while not necessarily present in every case, is still frequently instrumental in the construction and maintenance of that direct linkage which is the essence of populist politics. For instance, Islamic populism promotes the idea of an authentically Muslim 'people' collectively beset by marginalisation and exploitation at the hands of secular or non-Muslim elites. In doing so, Islamic populism collapses the heterogeneity of contemporary Muslim society, which remains divided on organisational, theological and class lines, and renders it available for mobilisation by political elites on the basis of a shared sense of Muslim grievance (Hadiz 2016). The constituencies that populism aims to mobilise, and the policy and rhetoric used in that mobilisation, are varied and can come from any point along Indonesia's religious–nationalist ideological spectrum. For example, Prabowo Subianto's demonisation of 'foreign' forces and their purported domestic proxies (Aspinall 2015) is part and parcel of a political strategy aimed at uniting an otherwise diverse and divided electorate through a shared disdain for vaguely defined elites and outsiders.

Why are such populist political strategies attractive to Indonesian politicians? A key factor in the creation of large electoral constituencies available for populist mobilisation is the weakness of political parties as vehicles for the mobilisation of voters and as arbiters of patronage distribution at the grassroots. Comparative research has identified that where programmatic or patronage-based parties are poorly institutionalised, and their connections with social constituencies are weak, opportunities open up for the entry of populist parties and candidates to attract support (Self and Hicken 2018). Indonesia's political parties are by and large poorly institutionalised (see Mietzner, this volume), with the electorate displaying 'extraordinarily low' levels of party identification (Muhtadi 2019: 17). Cross-national studies have highlighted how the incoherence of party-based patronage networks creates opportunities for populists (Kenny 2017), and in this context Indonesia stands out as a case where vertical coherence of patronage networks is largely absent (Kenny 2017: 142–50).

As a result of the structural weaknesses of parties and party-based mobilisation, Indonesian politics has turned to a range of populist electoral strategies. In the 2004 elections, when Yudhoyono ran for the presidency with his new Democratic Party (Partai Demokrat, PD), it became clear that parties could not rely on their organisational infrastructure in the regions to get out the vote (Aspinall 2005). Instead, Yudhoyono showed how candidates with negligible party infrastructure, but with high popularity and media exposure, could engage with voters through populist appeals, connecting with an electorate that was rapidly ditching its emotional attachments to parties (Muhtadi 2019: 140; Mujani and Liddle 2010: 45–7).

During the Yudhoyono years, Prabowo Subianto came to epitomise an emergent 'oligarchic populism' (Aspinall 2015). He followed Yudhoyono's template of personalist party-building, establishing his Gerindra Party in 2006, while embracing a classically populist form of rhetorical appeal that was distinctive in the Indonesian context. Prabowo, despite his origins in the heart of the New Order power elite, framed himself rhetorically as an outsider who challenged the irretrievably corrupt democratic establishment, and who would lead Indonesia back to national greatness through 'firm' (*tegas*) leadership in the face of foreign threats. As he appeared to inch closer to the presidency in 2014, the anti-democratic elements of Prabowo's rhetoric came to the fore when he criticised the concept of direct elections as being alien to Indonesian culture and expressed the need to return to a less liberal form of democracy that was purportedly more attuned to the national character (Aspinall and Mietzner 2014).

But despite the presence of this 'oligarchic populism' in the Yudhoyono years, Indonesia had yet to see an outsider use populist political tactics to gain national prominence and contest the presidency. The emergence of an outsider populist in the form of Jokowi, therefore, was a noteworthy development. A major preoccupation of scholars of populism is the potential threat that an outsider presidency poses to the stability of democracy. The scenario for populist autocratisation is already well characterised in the political science literature, most famously by Guillermo O'Donnell (1994), who highlighted the vulnerability of multiparty presidentialism in weakly consolidated democracies to what he famously termed 'delegative democracy'. The experience in Latin America has substantiated many of O'Donnell's concerns, it would seem, with populism being identified as the proximate cause of transitions from electoral democracy to competitive authoritarianism in a number of Latin American presidential systems (Levitsky and Loxton 2013).

Jokowi's candidacy in 2014 was merely the zenith of a political strategy that had been used by Indonesia's oligarchic figures in the years beforehand. But more significantly, 2014 was the first time that an outsider to the national political elite had emerged as a viable presidential candidate, and had done so through a populist political strategy. Whereas Yudhoyono and Prabowo were populist candidates who had emerged from the heart of the national oligarchy—indeed, they were prominent legatees of the New Order—Jokowi was far more alienated from the Jakarta political establishment than any presidential contender before him.[2] As mayor of Surakarta city and then as governor of Jakarta, he made the most of the structural opportunities now available to political entrepreneurs from the regions to satisfy a growing public hunger for new candidates who could provide alternatives to the Jakarta-based oligarchy. He also leveraged electronic media as a conduit for building a national profile in the absence of a well-developed personal political infrastructure (Tapsell 2015). Jokowi rose from the margins of national politics to become the most popular politician in the country in the space of less than two years, and did so without building any political infrastructure—until the formal start of the 2014 election campaign was imminent. His transition from mayor

---

2   Barr (2009: 33) defines an outsider as 'someone who gains political prominence not through or in association with an established, competitive party, but as a political independent or in association with new or newly competitive parties'. Given that Jokowi maintained only the most nominal affiliation with his own party during his years as mayor of Surakarta and governor of Jakarta, and remained alienated from much of its national leadership during this time, it is appropriate to consider him as having risen in the Indonesian context as an outsider.

to governor to national figure followed not so much the template set by Yudhoyono as that of the Latin American 'neopopulists' of the 1980s and 1990s. These figures made up for their relative lack of organisational and financial resources by taking strategic advantage of the electronic media to connect with voters they could not easily reach through traditional means of campaigning or patronage provision (Boas 2005).

POPULISM IN CIVIL SOCIETY

Religious leaders would also come to embrace populist political strategies in their efforts to mobilise on behalf of political candidates who were hostile to the Jokowi administration. Unlike Yudhoyono, who had indulged Islamist leaders throughout his presidency, Jokowi moved early on in his first term to cut them off from channels of state patronage (Mietzner 2018: 269–70). Already predisposed to oppose Jokowi on ideological grounds because of his links to the secular-nationalist Indonesian Democratic Party of Struggle (Partai Demokrasi Indonesia-Perjuangan, PDI-P), Islamist preachers intensified their propagation of the idea that Jokowi was not a 'good' Muslim leader, and that his government was complicit in the economic exploitation of ordinary Muslims by Indonesia's ethnic Chinese business elite. This narrative was spread primarily through social media.

Then, a loose coalition of Islamist organisations came together in late 2016 to organise the enormous protests against Jokowi's ally, Jakarta governor Basuki Tjahaja Purnama ('Ahok'), ahead of the 2017 Jakarta gubernatorial election. The *populist* nature of the mobilisation was not lost on scholars, who highlighted how the power of narratives of Muslim grievance and marginalisation, and the importance of reclaiming Islamic unity, was able at least momentarily to unify diverse sections of the Muslim community that would normally be divided along theological, organisational and socioeconomic lines (Fachrudin 2018; Fealy 2016; Setijadi 2017).

The viability of populist mobilisation for presidential candidates and civil society–centred coalitions like the 212 movement—a union of hardline Islamic groups named for the date of a huge anti-Ahok rally on 2 December 2016—is rooted in a common set of structural causes. Among them are the weakness of parties and class-based forms of mobilisation, and the resulting atomisation of a heterogeneous electorate; in this context, appeals based on the charismatic qualities of individual leaders (such as Jokowi or Prabowo) or a shared sense of identity and grievance towards a purported antagonist (in the case of contemporary Islamic populism) hold ample utility for elites in political contestations. But, as I discuss in the next section of this chapter, the structural conditions that encourage the emergence of populist candidacies and modes of campaigning are counterbalanced by institutional factors that artificially enhance the power of parties at the apex of the political system, notwithstanding their weakness in society.

THE LIMITS TO POPULISM AS A GOVERNING STRATEGY

While populist modes of political mobilisation are increasingly commonplace, Indonesia has come no closer to the sort of full-blown populist government that has precipitated major shifts in democratic quality. In many other presidential systems, outsider candidates who trod a similar path to national popularity either built a party 'on the fly' in time for a presidential election, or gained the nomination of a minor or dormant party to similarly act as a nominating vehicle for a presidential campaign. In Brazil's 1989 presidential election, for example, regional governor Fernando Collor de Mello won an upset victory after mounting a populist campaign on the ticket of a small right-wing party cobbled together quickly for the purpose of nominating him (Weyland 1993: 3–13). In Peru, Alberto Fujimori likewise captured the presidency in the 1990 election with a shell party established for the purpose; so stunning was Fujimori's populist, poorly organised campaign that copycat attempts by other elites laid waste to the Peruvian party system over the course of his government (Levitsky and Cameron 2003: 2). In the Philippines, where political parties are notoriously weak across the board, Rodrigo Duterte followed in the footsteps of previous populists like Joseph Estrada. Duterte campaigned from his regional base in Mindanao for the presidency, on the back of the nomination of a tiny, regionally based party that controlled only one legislative seat at the time of his nomination for the 2016 presidential election.

While the probabilistic relationship between rule by a populist and democratic regression is clear, it is obvious that not all populists radically undermine democratic quality by eroding formal checks and sidelining accountability actors such as party leaders. A close look at the comparative evidence from Latin America suggests that the danger that populism poses to a particular country's democratic system is very much shaped by the circumstances in which a populist president rises. Saskia Ruth (2018: 360) identified a combination of political and institutional conditions that interact to create 'the political opportunity structure [that] condition[s] either the incentive or the capability of populist presidents to erode [horizontal accountability]'. Her analysis shows that the populists who moved to substantially weaken checks on their power did so in a particular set of emboldening circumstances: hostile legislatures, weakness of established elites and a president's personal popularity. As far as this specific model of populist autocratisation 'from above' is concerned, Indonesia clearly was not a soft target for the autocratising impulses of a newly elected populist when Jokowi became president.

The opportunity for Jokowi to convert his own mass popularity into a presidential candidacy in 2014 rested on his ability to gain the support of the political parties to whom his popularity was in no small part a rebuke. Whereas in 2004 Yudhoyono had nominated himself using a shell party founded by supporters the previous year, that option was not available to Jokowi. Changes to the electoral system made after 2004 foreclosed the ability to form a personal vehicle party and have it nominate an outsider candidate in its own right. Since 1999, Indonesian electoral laws had gradually raised the requirements for a new party to be eligible to participate in national elections. By the time Jokowi ran for the presidency, a new party had to demonstrate that it maintained branches in 100 per cent of provinces and in 75 per cent of the districts in those provinces. To achieve such a level of national reach implies an immense outlay of cash and recruitment of loyal personal networks in the regions; it is no coincidence that since the founding of the first personal vehicle party, PD, in 2003, all of Indonesia's personalist parties have been founded by oligarchs who have the financial and organisational wherewithal to engage in the expensive, years-long process of establishing such a network of branches in order to become eligible to contest national elections.

Even if Jokowi had possessed the financial and organisational resources to build a personal vehicle party and have it approved for the 2014 election, it would have been of little benefit to him. By 2014, the presidential threshold in Indonesia's electoral law, which had also been steadily raised since 2004, required that a presidential candidate be nominated by a party or coalition of parties that had won 20 per cent of seats or 25 per cent of votes in the preceding legislative elections. At the same time, the party system had become progressively more fragmented—making single-party nominations even less viable given the rising nomination threshold. The presidential threshold almost guaranteed that such a personal vehicle party would, on its first outing, be ineligible to nominate a presidential candidate on its own, and would be forced into doing a deal with other incumbent parties in order to nominate a presidential candidate. Nominating coalitions are of course common in other similar systems, where party representation in presidents' cabinets is a key feature of patterns of coalitional presidentialism (Raile et al. 2011). But Indonesia is unique in *forcing* aspirants for the presidency, including would-be populists, to form these large pre-election nominating coalitions with established parties.

Jokowi's adaptation to the institutional realities saw him pose as a party loyalist in a way he had not done in the lead-up to his nomination, damaging the credibility of his anti-establishment appeal. As soon as Jokowi committed to trying to gain the endorsement of an ambivalent PDI-P to run for president in 2014, he began to attend the party's events, embrace its rhetoric and symbols, and make ostentatious displays of fealty to Megawati Sukarnoputri, its chairperson. Having been bound so closely into quid pro quo deals with parties in exchange for their support in 2014, Jokowi would begin his presidency with a series of political blunders, largely to do with making unpopular appointments under pressure from his party allies (Muhtadi 2015: 362–3). Having had enough trouble dealing with his own party coalition, Jokowi responded to an initially hostile legislature by legally intervening in the leaderships of wavering opposition parties and by extending patronage to key opposition players (Mietzner 2016). While Jokowi initially harboured hopes of using his personal popularity as a weapon in intra-elite conflicts, he quickly came to see his outsider status as a liability rather than an asset, and instead reinforced the conventions of coalitional presidentialism that had been nurtured by his predecessors (Mietzner 2019).

The institutional strictures on extra-oligarchic populist candidacies and movements also prevented the civil society coalition driving much of the new Islamic populism from emerging as an electoral vehicle in its own right. The 212 coalition or a similar Islamic movement might plausibly have given rise to a religiously tinged version of 'movement populism'.[3] Yet this Islamic populism failed to produce an Islamic populist candidacy, in the form of either an individual or a party, despite the undeniable charisma of some of its most popular figures—particularly the leader of the Islamic Defenders Front (Front Pembela Islam, FPI), Habib Rizieq Shihab. The gamut of organisations seeking to represent the *ummah* and make appeals along identity lines is extraordinarily diverse, and once the unifying cause of the campaign against Ahok in Jakarta faded, the organisational coherence of the 212 movement was eventually 'weakened more from its own internal contradictions than from government intervention' (IPAC 2018: 17). Tensions within the movement also emerged when it came time to choose its stance in the 2019 presidential elections; despite the enthusiasm of some for a 212-linked *ulama* to run for president

---

3   This term is used to categorise cases of populist leadership that emerge from social movements, the most notable example being former Bolivian president Evo Morales (Levitsky and Loxton 2013: 110).

in his own right, in the end the 212 leaders' options were dictated by the reality that parties had a lock on nominations, and would always privilege their own. The best the 212 coalition was able to do was to encourage its best option, Prabowo, to nominate one of its own *ulama* as his running mate, and even then they were left disappointed when Prabowo instead chose his former business partner, Sandiaga Uno, for the vice-presidential slot (IPAC 2019a: 6–9). Social or religious movements that might become the basis of populist candidacies are just as inhibited by the barriers to entry created by the electoral system as political entrepreneurs, forced to channel their political aspirations through established political vehicles.

WHAT ROLE FOR POPULISM IN INDONESIA'S DEMOCRATIC DECLINE?

If Jokowi has failed to govern as a populist—or is only a 'partial populist' (Kenny 2019b)—then it follows that the sources of the contemporary democratic regression in Indonesia lie elsewhere. Certainly, the populist autocratisation that has been behind the dramatic declines in democratic quality in Latin America and the Philippines is not being mirrored in Indonesia under Jokowi. In the analysis of the 'executive illiberalism' that emerged during Jokowi's first term, it is difficult to detect much motive towards the personalisation of power in Jokowi's hands at the expense of parties and other accountability institutions. Regressive laws such as the controversial 2019 revisions to the Criminal Code, the efforts to bring the military back into some aspects of civilian governance and the targeted repression of government opponents using broadly drafted provisions of the country's electronic transactions law (Law No. 19/2016 on Electronic Information and Transactions) have been done with the support, tacit or explicit, of Jokowi's party allies. A number of the illiberal responses to perceived Islamist enemies of the Jokowi administration have been enacted at the urging of such organisations' theological and organisational rivals, most notably Nahdlatul Ulama (NU). Jokowi's issuance in 2017 of a highly problematic decree on mass organisations[4] was done at the urging of NU, and Jokowi had every incentive to join in the crackdown on Hizbut Tahrir Indonesia (HTI) and other Islamic organisations because of his desire to position NU as a key ally in mobilising the votes of traditionalist Muslims in Java for the 2019 election (see Nuraniyah, this volume). When the Indonesian parliament was deliberating on the design of the electoral

---

4   Government Regulation in Lieu of Law No. 2/2017 Amending Law No. 17/2013.

law that would govern the 2019 elections, Jokowi intervened on the side of preserving, not relaxing, the 25 per cent of votes/20 per cent of seats formula for the presidential nomination threshold. In numerous public comments, he embraced the justification for the presidential threshold that had long been advanced by Indonesian elites, namely that presidential candidates must enjoy the support of a broad coalition of parties in the name of ensuring harmonious executive–legislative relations (Daud and Bayu 2017).

Nevertheless, where populism is taking its toll on Indonesian democracy is in the manifestations of populism, as it were, 'from below'. The attempts to mobilise Muslim constituencies on identity lines have had side effects that have damaged the pluralist values that remain so indispensable to the substantive quality of Indonesian democracy—first, by popularising majoritarian notions of Muslim political supremacy among many Indonesian Muslims; second, by contributing to a polarisation within society along both sides of the Islamist–nationalist divide that structures Indonesian politics; and third, by providing a rationale for the collective efforts of the Jokowi administration and its civil society allies to embrace illiberal responses to Islamic populist mobilisations.

A critical question for researchers after the mass Islamic mobilisations of 2016 and 2017 in Jakarta was whether, and how, the 212 movement was reflecting or generating an increase in ethnic and religious intolerance and polarisation. Survey data collected in the periods before and after the protests by Mietzner et al. (2018) demonstrate that the messages propagated by the anti-Ahok campaign—specifically, that Muslims were not permitted to elect non-Muslim political leaders—had 'significantly hardened during and after the mobilization, [even] while other attitudes of intolerance unrelated to the mobilization continued to soften' (p. 161). To an extent, the partisan polarisation between Jokowi and Prabowo supporters—which has only sharpened since the election of 2014—has overlapped with a growing cultural divide within Indonesian society about the role Islam ought to play in daily life and in politics.

So disconcerted was the Jokowi administration by the mobilisational power of Islamic populism that it responded with targeted repression of the 212 movement's leaders (Power 2018: 314–15). In a polarised cultural and political climate (see Warburton, this volume), much of the repression under way against purported 'Islamist' opponents of pluralist politics has occurred with the tacit or explicit support of pluralist civil society, which sees the protection of the pluralist tradition as a more important priority than the protection of freedom of association and conscience. The showcasing of Islamic populism's mobilisational potential in the 2016–17 mass protests undoubtedly accelerated the 'decoupling' of support for democratic norms and socioreligious pluralism among many sectors of Indonesia's progressive civil society and political elite (Aspinall and Mietzner 2019). Thus, even if Islamic populism remains, as I argue, inchoate as a case of populist mobilisation for electoral ends, the side effects of attempts to capture the support of this populist constituency have had clearly damaging effects on the substantial quality of democracy.

CONCLUSION

This chapter has focused on the role of electoral rules and institutional frameworks in blunting the force of populism in Indonesia, despite the (in some senses) hospitable environment Indonesia provides for the emergence of populist politics. What I have sought to emphasise is how Indonesia's electoral rules have succeeded in insulating Indonesia from some, but by no means all, of the hazards posed by populism to democracy. This question has been touched upon elsewhere and, in particular reference to Indonesia, Kenny (2019b: 3) has argued that electoral rules play little role in influencing whether populists are able to gain power. Certainly, the electoral threshold and barriers to party registration have not prevented the emergence of politicians like Yudhoyono, Prabowo or Jokowi. Yet I would argue that Indonesia's electoral rules have, in fact, had important qualitative effects in terms of rendering presidencies effectively non-populist.

As we can see clearly in the case of Jokowi, the party-strengthening effects of the electoral system have disciplined this outsider populist president, such that any ambitions he may have had to assert his presidential prerogatives at the expense of parties faded away almost as soon as he became president. I argue that the at-best 'partial' populism (Kenny 2019b: 8) Jokowi exemplifies is a product of the electoral rules that force populists into alliances with parties, blunting their ability to campaign credibly on an anti-party, anti-establishment platform and raising the costs and risks of activating populist strategies once in office, given how enmeshed they are in quid pro quo relationships with parties. The populist movements rooted in civil society, notably the 212 movement, face precisely the same challenges in turning their sporadic acts of mobilisation into viable political vehicles: witness the strained relationship between the religious leaders spearheading the Jokowi-era Islamic populism and their allies-of-convenience in political parties. The politicians realise they have a privileged position in opening up opportunities to appear on a ballot; the religious leaders, meanwhile, resent being relegated to the position of intermediaries between those same politicians and the Islamic populist base.

Indeed, the very plurality of the Indonesian elite makes it inimically opposed to the personalisation of power that is so frequently a part of populist governing strategies. Jokowi and that elite are entrenching a collectively driven process of democratic regression whereby growing 'executive illiberalism' and weakening of liberal institutions coexist with the preservation of the autonomy and political prerogatives of key oligarchic actors: political parties, security agencies, religious and business interests, and subnational oligarchs. Indonesian politicians have proven themselves happy to approve of executive-led erosion of democratic norms and civil liberties *to the extent* that such erosion of democracy does not impinge upon their organisational autonomy and their access to patronage resources. Just as the 'anarchy of interests at the grassroots rebels against any attempt to re-establish authoritarian models of political centralisation' (Mietzner 2019), the sheer plurality of the distribution of power within Indonesia's national oligarchy—encompassing such players as parties, the military, the police force and the bureaucracy—rebels against a president's efforts to personalise power and the distribution of patronage at the apex of the political system, in the style of so many populist autocrats in other presidential systems. The consistent attempts by parties to write electoral laws so as to guarantee for themselves leverage over presidents through their control of presidential nominations should be seen in this light.[5]

Indeed, even an authoritarian ideologue like Prabowo would likely have found himself similarly constrained in office, given the strength of elite resistance to any possible erosion of party and institutional prerogatives in service to a president's personalising mission. While a hypothetical Prabowo presidency would, unlike Jokowi's, be rooted in a personal vehicle party with significant representation in the legislature, it is difficult to predict the outcome of a confrontation between the anti-personalising biases of the oligarchy and Prabowo's obvious drive for personalised power.

Be that as it may, it is precisely the non-populist nature of the state-directed elements of Indonesia's democratic regression under

---

5   A prominent Indonesian politician told an academic conference that parliament's move to increase the presidential threshold to its current high level in 2008 was prompted primarily by the parties' desire to ensure that the then very popular Yudhoyono would nevertheless be forced into coalition arrangements with them ahead of his 2009 re-election campaign (author's notes of a speech made under the Chatham House rule, Jakarta, June 2019).

Jokowi that makes it so worrying. Dan Slater (2013) has proposed that poorly consolidated democracies experience what he calls 'democratic careening', whereby countries oscillate between populist and liberal models of democracy, experiencing an autocratisation phase at the hands of a populist leader, followed by a democratising phase in which establishment elites seek to depersonalise the concentration of power, rehabilitating their own prerogatives and with it many of the rudiments of democracy. The implication of my argument, however, is that Indonesia is *not* experiencing the 'populist' phase of this 'democratic careening'; the collectively driven nature of the erosion of democracy suggests that something more enduring is under way than in the case of a temporary shift towards the personalisation of power under populist rule.

Further reinforcing this trend is the effect that populist mobilisation is having at the societal level. Many of the elite's collective efforts to crack down on Islamists in state institutions and limit freedom of expression and organisation pose potential and immediate risks for democracy, but the damage is being replicated at the grassroots as well. The sense of heightened stakes in political contestation, while clearly deleterious for Indonesia's democratic quality, has yet to carry Indonesia anywhere near the sort of sociopolitical polarisation that has infected civil society and grassroots communities in countries such as Thailand or Egypt, where the liberal backlash against a populist (Thaksin) or Islamists (in Egypt) has been a critical ingredient in the outright reversal of democracy at the hands of anti-populist elites. Nevertheless, the dynamic created by recurrent attempts at populist mobilisation on identity lines, and the incumbent elite's backlash to such mobilisation, appears to be posing a serious threat to the quality of Indonesian democracy over the medium term, one that may well outlive the Jokowi presidency if the current ideological divisions in Indonesian politics grow still more salient. Populism, once assumed to pose a threat to Indonesian democracy if and when propagated from the heights of the political system, may instead be weakening it from the grassroots upward.

REFERENCES

Aspinall, E. 2005. 'Elections and the normalization of politics in Indonesia'. *South East Asia Research* 13(2): 117–56.

Aspinall, E. 2013. 'Popular agency and interests in Indonesia's democratic transition and consolidation'. *Indonesia* 96: 101–21.

Aspinall, E. 2015. 'Oligarchic populism: Prabowo Subianto's challenge to Indonesian democracy'. *Indonesia* 99(April): 1–28.

Aspinall, E. and M. Mietzner. 2014. 'Indonesian politics in 2014: democracy's close call'. *Bulletin of Indonesian Economic Studies* 50(3): 347–69.

Aspinall, E. and M. Mietzner. 2019. 'Southeast Asia's troubling elections: non-democratic pluralism in Indonesia'. *Journal of Democracy* 30(4): 104–18.

Barr, R.R. 2009. 'Populists, outsiders and antiestablishment politics'. *Party Politics* 15(1): 29–48.

Boas, T.C. 2005. 'Television and neopopulism in Latin America: media effects in Brazil and Peru'. *Latin American Research Review* 40(2): 27–49.

Daud, A. and D.J. Bayu. 2017. 'Presidential threshold 20% sejak 2009, Jokowi: kenapa dulu tak ramai?'. *Katadata*, 28 July. https://katadata.co.id/berita/2017/07/28/presidential-treshold-20-sejak-2009-jokowi-kenapa-dulu-tak-ramai

Fachrudin, A.A. 2018. 'Notes on 212 in 2018: more politics, less unity'. *New Mandala*, 10 December. https://www.newmandala.org/notes-on-212-in-2018-more-politics-less-unity/

Fealy, G. 2016. 'Bigger than Ahok: explaining the 2 December mass rally'. *Indonesia at Melbourne*, 7 December. https://indonesiaatmelbourne.unimelb.edu.au/bigger-than-ahok-explaining-jakartas-2-december-mass-rally/

Gammon, L. 2014. 'Meet Joko Widodo'. *New Mandala*, 17 March. https://www.newmandala.org/the-enigmatic-mr-widodo/

Gidron, N. and B. Bonikowski. 2013. 'Varieties of populism: literature review and research agenda'. *Weatherhead Working Paper Series* No. 13-0004. Cambridge, MA: Weatherhead Center for International Affairs, Harvard University.

Hadiz, V.R. 2016. *Islamic Populism in Indonesia and the Middle East*. Cambridge: Cambridge University Press.

Houle, C. and P. Kenny. 2018. 'The political and economic consequences of populist rule in Latin America'. *Government and Opposition* 53(2): 256–87.

Huber, R.A. and C.H. Schimpf. 2016. 'Friend or foe? Testing the influence of populism on democratic quality in Latin America'. *Political Studies* 64(4): 872–89.

IPAC (Institute for Policy Analysis of Conflict). 2018. 'After Ahok: the Islamist agenda in Indonesia'. *IPAC Report* No. 44. Jakarta: IPAC. 6 April.

IPAC (Institute for Policy Analysis of Conflict). 2019a. 'Anti-Ahok to anti-Jokowi: Islamist influence on Indonesia's 2019 election campaign'. *IPAC Report* No. 55. Jakarta: IPAC. 15 March.

IPAC (Institute for Policy Analysis of Conflict). 2019b. 'Indonesian Islamists and post-election protests in Jakarta'. *IPAC Report* No. 58. Jakarta: IPAC. 23 July.

Kenny, P.D. 2017. *Populism and Patronage: Why Populists Win Elections in India, Asia and Beyond*. Oxford: Oxford University Press.

Kenny, P.D. 2019a. ' "The enemy of the people": populists and press freedom'. *Political Research Quarterly* 00(0): 1–15. https://doi.org/10.1177/1065912918824038

Kenny, P.D. 2019b. *Populism in Southeast Asia*. Cambridge: Cambridge University Press.

Kyle, J. and Y. Mounk. 2018. 'The populist harm to democracy: an empirical assessment'. London: Tony Blair Institute for Global Change. 26 December.

Levitsky, S. and M.A. Cameron. 2003. 'Democracy without parties? Political parties and regime change in Fujimori's Peru'. *Latin American Politics and Society* 45(3): 1–33.

Levitsky, S. and J. Loxton. 2013. 'Populism and competitive authoritarianism in the Andes'. *Democratization* 20(1): 107–36.

Mietzner, M. 2009. 'Indonesia's 2009 elections: populism, dynasties and the consolidation of the party system'. *Analysis*. Sydney: Lowy Institute for International Policy. May. https://www.files.ethz.ch/isn/100187/Mietzner_0509LowyAnalysis.pdf

Mietzner, M. 2014. 'Jokowi: rise of a polite populist'. *Inside Indonesia* 116(April–June). https://www.insideindonesia.org/jokowi-rise-of-a-polite-populist

Mietzner, M. 2016. 'Coercing loyalty: coalitional presidentialism and party politics in Jokowi's Indonesia'. *Contemporary Southeast Asia* 38(2): 209–32.

Mietzner, M. 2018. 'Fighting illiberalism with illiberalism: Islamist populism and democratic deconsolidation in Indonesia'. *Pacific Affairs* 91(2): 261–82.

Mietzner, M. 2019. 'Indonesia's elections in the periphery: a view from Maluku'. *New Mandala*, 2 April. https://www.newmandala.org/indonesias-elections-in-the-periphery-a-view-from-maluku/

Mietzner, M., B. Muhtadi and R. Halida. 2018. 'Entrepreneurs of grievance: drivers and effects of Indonesia's Islamist mobilization'. *Bijdragen tot de Taal-, Land- en Volkenkunde* 174(2–3): 159–87. https://doi.org/10.1163/22134379-17402026

Muhtadi, B. 2015. 'Jokowi's first year: a weak president caught between reform and oligarchic politics'. *Bulletin of Indonesian Economic Studies* 51(3): 349–68.

Muhtadi, B. 2019. *Vote Buying in Indonesia: The Mechanics of Electoral Bribery*. Singapore: Palgrave Macmillan. https://link.springer.com/book/10.1007/978-981-13-6779-3

Mujani, S. and R.W. Liddle. 2010. 'Indonesia: personalities, parties, and voters'. *Journal of Democracy* 21(2): 35–49.

O'Donnell, G. 1994. 'Delegative democracy'. *Journal of Democracy* 5(1): 55–69.

Power, T.P. 2018. 'Jokowi's authoritarian turn and Indonesia's democratic decline'. *Bulletin of Indonesian Economic Studies* 54(3): 307–38.

Raile, E.D., C. Pereira and T.J. Power. 2011. 'The executive toolbox: building legislative support in a multiparty presidential regime'. *Political Research Quarterly* 64(2): 323–34.

Ruth, S. 2018. 'Populism and the erosion of horizontal accountability in Latin America'. *Political Studies* 66(2): 356–75.

Self, D. and A. Hicken. 2018. 'Why populism? How parties shape the electoral fortune of populists'. V-Dem Working Paper 76. Gothenburg: Varieties of Democracy Institute. https://www.v-dem.net/media/filer_public/d8/eb/d8ebc26f-733e-4fa9-b48a-e50a4833c9a7/v-dem_working_paper_2018_76.pdf

Setijadi, C. 2017. 'Ahok's downfall and the rise of Islamist populism in Indonesia'. *Perspective* No. 38, 8 June. Singapore: ISEAS – Yusof Ishak Institute.

Slater, D. 2013. 'Democratic careening'. *World Politics* 65(4): 729–63.

Slater, D. 2014. 'Unbuilding blocs: Indonesia's accountability deficit in historical perspective'. *Critical Asian Studies* 46(2): 287–315.

Tapsell, R. 2015. 'Indonesia's media oligarchy and the "Jokowi phenomenon"'. *Indonesia* 99: 29–50.

Warburton, E. 2016. 'Jokowi and the new developmentalism'. *Bulletin of Indonesian Economic Studies* 52(3): 297–320.

Weyland, K. 1993. 'The rise and fall of President Collor and its impact on Brazilian democracy'. *Journal of Interamerican Studies and World Affairs* 35(1): 1–37.

Weyland, K. 2001. 'Clarifying a contested concept: populism in the study of Latin American politics'. *Comparative Politics* 34(1): 1–22.

7   Islamic populism and Indonesia's illiberal democracy

Abdil Mughis Mudhoffir

As a variant of populist politics, Islamic populism is a response to disillusionment and grievance with the ruling elites that is made distinctive by the use of Islamic rhetoric. Such rhetoric can unite different and contradictory interests within the Muslim community, and forge cross-class alliances—even if such alliances are tenuous in nature (Hadiz 2016; Hadiz and Chryssogelos 2017; Robison and Hadiz 2020). In Indonesia, the phenomenon of Islamic populism found its most dramatic expression during the 2017 Jakarta gubernatorial election when hundreds of thousands of Muslims staged a series of mass rallies known as the Defence of Islam movement (Aksi Bela Islam) against incumbent Basuki Tjahaja Purnama, popularly known as Ahok, who was accused of blaspheming Islam. This movement not only helped defeat Ahok electorally, but it was also instrumental in ensuring Ahok was charged with blasphemy and subsequently jailed, thereby paving the way for the use of Islamic populist narratives in a number of other political contests, including the 2019 presidential election.

Some studies on Indonesian Islamic populism employ actor-centred analysis focusing on the style of populist actors and their effect on democratic quality (Aspinall and Warburton 2018; Lindsey 2017; Mietzner 2018; Power 2018). Others utilise cultural-oriented analysis, explaining Islamic populist mobilisation as a result of increasing intolerance (Arifianto 2019; Assyaukanie 2017; Nuraniyah 2018). While both forms of analyses contribute to understanding facets of the Islamic populist phenomenon, they overlook the structural conditions linked to the broader prevalence of illiberal politics and to the kinds of social bases that make possible the rise of populist politics in the first place. According to Robison and Hadiz

(2020), varieties of populist politics, including Islamic populism, 'must be understood in the context of widespread failure of governments and elites to deal with larger structural crises that threaten their societies and with the disruption of old class or patronage-based politics by the rise of new cross class alliances'. Without attention to these sorts of structural forces, analyses tend to lead to over-anxiety about Islamist threats. Such analyses have also led to the view employed by the Indonesian government to justify its own form of reactionary populist politics. In this chapter I develop three main arguments on the basis of such observations.

First, I argue that contemporary Islamic populism in Indonesia is a symptom of the dysfunction of democratic institutions, which have been unable to respond to growing social–political discontent among many Indonesian Muslims. This discontent is due to the expansion of neoliberal policies and associated economic inequality in the absence of a viable leftist stream of politics. This means that the rise of various forms of populist politics in Indonesia is a symptom—and not the root cause—of Indonesia's illiberal politics, while it is also having the effect of deepening illiberalism by further constraining discourses on rights, including of various minorities (Hadiz 2017).

Second, although Islamic populism is on the rise, it is fragmented and incoherent, and therefore its representatives are in no position to challenge for control over the state. They also lack the ability to monopolise political discourses that refer to Islamic cultural references, since actors from a broad ideological spectrum have made claims to represent the interests of the Muslim community (*ummah*). As I will explain below, this is evident in the case of the largely secular nationalist politician Prabowo Subianto, the candidate of choice for many conservative Muslims in the 2019 presidential election. Consequently, Islamic populism remains on the political margins, subordinated by opportunistic but powerful politico-economic elites.

Third, undemocratic responses by the Indonesian government towards individuals and groups associated with Islamic populism have been justified by a narrative that exaggerates the rising threat of state Islamisation, despite the inability of Islamist organisations or movements to dominate the institutions of state power. This narrative conceals and distracts the public from the fact that Indonesian democracy itself is incapable of channelling a variety of grievances about systemic inequality, which in turn has facilitated the emergence of Islamic populism.

To substantiate these arguments, this chapter is presented in three parts. The first section outlines existing debates on Islamic populism in Indonesia and its link to the illiberalism of Indonesian democracy. It is followed by a discussion about the way that Islamic populist alliances are constituted and about the perceived threats of state Islamisation. The last section discusses the government's response to Islamic populism drawn from a view that validates the existence of a more-or-less imminent Islamist threat. It also elaborates on the argument that already entrenched illiberal politics has conditioned the way the government has sought to contain Islamic populism by further accentuating those same illiberal trends.

POPULISM IN INDONESIA

Concern about populist politics in Indonesia has come to the fore as anti-establishment narratives have increasingly been deployed by political leaders in many electoral contests. During the 2014 presidential election campaign, rivals Prabowo and Joko Widodo (Jokowi) both articulated the rhetoric of responding to popular demands and serving a (greatly homogenised) understanding of the nationalist interest in their respective campaigns. Aspinall (2015: 2), for example, categorises Prabowo as representing an 'oligarchic populism', as he is a member of the same oligarchic elite that he criticises. Aspinall (2015; see also Mietzner 2015) also identifies Prabowo as an authoritarian populist who portrayed himself as the sort of strong leader needed to address the socioeconomic problems that have created popular discontent. Jokowi, meanwhile, is characterised by some scholars as representing a soft technocratic populism due to his emphasis on 'inclusivism, technocratic competence and moderation' (Mietzner 2015: 4). For Mietzner, Jokowi's technocratic populism constitutes a new form of populism not only in Indonesia but also in the developing world. It is new, according to Mietzner (2015: 3), because Jokowi's technocratic populism 'was inclusive rather than focused on the exclusion of an identified enemy [and] it was nationalist, but used none of the anti-foreign rhetoric so many Asian and Latin American populists rely on'.

With their focus on the leadership style and rhetoric used by populist leaders, those studies have provided important insights into the way populists conduct politics. Using the same framework, Mietzner (2019: 371) distinguished between populists of different historical periods: 'anti-colonial populists of the 1950s, the developmental populists of the 1960s to 1990s and today's electoral populists'. Studying 'differences between the various forms of populism', according to Mietzner (2019: 370), is more important than identifying a common strand within these populisms. Yet, these works are more limited in providing an understanding of what makes possible the emergence of populist politics and the limits of specific populist projects. While Mietzner (2019: 375) has explored cases that illustrate the success and failure of populist projects, by emphasising the capacity of elites to mobilise poor voters he overlooks the sociological bases that help determine the different trajectories of populism.

As observed by Hadiz (2016) in his extensive study of Islamic populism in Indonesia and the Middle East, populist trajectories have much to do with the constitution of alliances that attempt to merge the often-contradictory interests of different social classes. The populist project is more likely to gain ascendency when cross-class alliances expressed as populist politics can 'suspend' such differences of interests, even if this is an inherently tenuous endeavour. A successful trajectory is identified by Hadiz (2016) in the case of the Islamic populist project led by Turkey's Justice and Development Party (AK Parti), which has dominated the state for nearly two decades, in contrast to the failure of its Indonesian counterparts. Hadiz emphasises the absence of a culturally Islamic bourgeoisie in Indonesia, which differs from the presence of a rising Anatolian bourgeoisie in Turkey that provided crucial material resources for the building of an effective cross-class Islamic populist alliance there. Rather than identifying the leadership style and personalities of populist leaders, Hadiz shows the importance of analysing the social bases of populist politics and the structural conditions that make possible the emergence and limitations of populist projects.

Such social bases need to be understood in relation to the way institutions associated with the workings of democracy have failed to address widespread social grievances associated with inequality. Such failure provides the opportunity to mobilise grievances by using a political lexicon that can unite different social classes. However, in Indonesia's oligarchic democracy (Robison and Hadiz 2004), it is the powerful politico-economic elites that can best exploit such grievances by employing cultural tropes associated with ethnic, religious or nationalist identity—but to serve their interests in concentrating, rather than redistributing, wealth and power. This is where populist politics becomes reactionary: being fuelled by culture wars that obscure problems of socioeconomic injustice. As such, the dysfunction of liberal democratic institutions in addressing problems of injustice not only aggravates sociopolitical disillusionment as one ingredient of populist politics but also delineates populism as a mere instrument of oligarchy.

In the case of Islamic populism in Indonesia, sociopolitical discontent is mobilised by using Islamic rhetoric and identity to serve oligarchic interests, rather than to further the project of state Islamisation. The nationalist populist reaction of the Jokowi government (Hadiz 2017) to contain Islamic populist politics must also be understood in the context of a social order in which liberal and social democratic discourses are bereft of effective vehicles, together with the absence of a viable leftist one. It must be understood in relation to a long historical legacy of elements of nationalist populisms being deployed by state officialdom to quell dissent, arising from anywhere, in the name of national integrity.

Populism as a symptom (not a cause) of illiberal democracy

Actor-centred approaches place great emphasis on the effect of populist politics upon the quality of democracy. Mietzner (2019: 381), for example, argues that 'most polities governed by populists have seen further democratic decline since they took office'. Aspinall and Warburton (2018) state that the illiberal drift of Indonesia's democracy has accelerated dramatically under Jokowi as seen from the rising political manipulation of laws to undermine government adversaries associated with sectarian populism (see also Setiawan, this volume). The implication is that Indonesian democracy has deteriorated in part due to the rise of populism since 2014.

Prior to the 2014 presidential election, Indonesia was widely praised as a stable democratic country. Diamond, for example, lauded Indonesia as a 'political success story' (2010: 23). Even though global trends showed that 'the number of democracies has been steadily ... in decline' since 2006, he claimed that Indonesian democracy had 'not only survived but also improved' (ibid.). Aspinall and Mietzner (2010) also assert that, in general, during Susilo Bambang Yudhoyono's first presidential term (2004–2009), Indonesian democracy was stable despite endemic corruption and anti-reformist elite domination. Aspinall and Warburton (2018: 1) also conclude that, until 2014, Indonesia's democracy was 'relatively liberal, and faced no serious existential threats'. They acknowledge problems especially associated with systemic corruption during that period, but as pointed out by Mietzner (2012), attempts to undermine Indonesian democracy by anti-reformist elites had been successfully challenged by 'strong civil society'. There was even an optimism among those scholars when Jokowi—often praised as a successful small-town leader who has no ties to the New Order elites—won the 2014 presidential election against the threat from authoritarian-populist leader, retired general and Suharto's former son-in-law, Prabowo. Prabowo's defeat was viewed by some as evidence that 'democratisation and improvements in public services' in Indonesia were advancing (Aspinall and Mietzner 2014; Mietzner 2015: 39).

However, such characterisations are problematic, because they underplay longstanding and endemic problems within Indonesian democracy, whereby consecutive governments have failed to address demands for wealth redistribution and socioeconomic justice in general.

These features have made possible the rise of a reactionary populist politics that brings Indonesia—even under a 'reformist' president (Aspinall and Mietzner 2014; Hamayotsu 2015; Mietzner 2015)—to a period of deepening illiberalism. From this point of view, populism is a symptom rather than a cause of Indonesia's illiberal democracy.

This chapter homes in on the structural pathologies of Indonesia's democracy that existed long before the so-called 'illiberal drift' that Aspinall and Warburton (2018) identify as beginning during Yudhoyono's second term. This characterisation is problematic because it tends to exaggerate the 'relatively liberal' (Aspinall and Warburton 2018: 1) nature of Indonesian democracy in the mid to late 2000s.

Most conceptions of liberal democracy would accord with Fukuyama's (2015) definition, which emphasises security, law and accountability. In line with Weberian tradition, the state must be able to monopolise the legitimate use of physical force. Meanwhile, the rule of law constitutes a set of rules that are binding not only on the common citizens, but also 'on the elites who wield power' (Fukuyama 2015: 13). Democratic accountability means that the government should be able to act 'in the interests of the whole communities, rather than simply in the self-interests of the rulers', and is 'usually achieved through procedures such as free and fair multiparty elections' (ibid.). In other words, equality before the law and checks on elite power are essential ingredients for a liberal democracy.

Except for the electoral aspect, those criteria have for the most part not been fulfilled by Indonesian democratic institutions since the beginning of *reformasi*. This can be seen from the fact that various non-state organisations coexist with formal coercive institutions and are able to exercise violence largely without state punishment. In the democratic era, vigilante groups as well as ethnic and religious militias have proliferated and, in some cases, have played significant roles in sociopolitical arenas (Wilson 2015; Jaffrey, this volume). Meanwhile, laws and other legal institutions continue to favour the dominant class instead of serving and protecting public interests.

As such, the rule of law and democratic accountability that 'constrain[s] [state] power and ensure[s] it is used in the public interests' (Fukuyama 2015: 13) has always been weak in Indonesia. Corruption and various forms of clientelism and predation are prevalent, creating disorder and legal uncertainty. Such disorder and legal ambiguity have enabled politico-business actors to continue to accumulate and concentrate power and wealth (Mudhoffir 2019; Robison and Hadiz 2017). In this way, Indonesia's democracy has also produced sociopolitical discontent that forms an important raw material for the emergence of populist politics.

Socioeconomic precarity and the rise of populism

The circumstances described above have meant that the government and formal representative institutions have failed to address increasing socioeconomic precarity in the face of expanding neoliberal markets. This provides perfect ingredients for rising populist politics that mobilises sectarian sentiments in electoral contests.

Studies on precarity have shown that neoliberal policies manifested especially through flexible labour regimes have led to a global increase in the number of people working in the informal labour sector who lack access to social security (Kalleberg and Hewison 2013; Standing 2011). In Indonesia in 2015, 51.9 per cent of the workforce was engaged in informal labour (ILO 2015). The informalisation of the formal labour sector also increased from 6.7 per cent in 2009 to 11 per cent in 2011 (Matsumoto and Veric 2011). This informalisation affects not only the 9.2 per cent of the population in 2018 that is under the absolute national poverty line (BPS 2018), but also some of those identified as middle class. Such people have suffered from 'the uncertainty, instability, and insecurity of work in which employees bear the risks of work ... and receive limited social benefits and statutory entitlements' (Kalleberg and Hewison 2013: 271; Vosko 2010). Although the middle class expanded 'from 25 percent of the population in 1999 to 45 percent in 2010' and is expected to reach 85 per cent by 2020 (Rakhmani 2017), the middle-class status of many Indonesians is uncertain amid enduring social inequalities that ensure that the fruits of economic growth are enjoyed mainly by a tiny elite.

The way in which such economic uncertainty feeds into Islamic populism in Indonesia is illustrated by examining the socioeconomic backgrounds of those who joined the Defence of Islam rallies. A survey of 600 Aksi Bela Islam participants showed that this was primarily a middle-class movement—but many of these middle-class actors did not have career or financial security. In other words, it was largely a movement of those who were precariously part of the middle class and whose life circumstances positioned them nearer to those placed lower in the social hierarchy. For example, although 97.5 per cent of participants were at least high school graduates, they did not necessarily hold a steady job (Hadiz and Rakhmani 2017).[1] Of those surveyed, 60 per cent were aged

---

1 Thanks to Vedi Hadiz and Inaya Rakhmani, the principle investigator and co-principle investigator, respectively, of a research project titled 'Islamic Morality and Challenges to Democracy: A Study of Urban Lower and Middle Class Responses', who allowed me to use primary data from their survey in developing the argument made in this chapter.

in their twenties and only 44 per cent could afford household expenses of Rp 4.5–7 million (A$450–700) per month, which falls within the middle-class category according to the World Bank (2019). Among those with only high school degrees, 27 per cent were university students, 14 per cent were skilled labourers and the rest were precariously employed, unemployed or housewives. Furthermore, among those with a tertiary education (just over 50 per cent), 23 per cent were employed by private companies, 10 per cent were civil servants and the rest were precariously employed.

These numbers show that educational attainment does not correspond to job security. This is reinforced by the fact that 46 per cent of the respondents lived with their parents or in-laws and 22 per cent lived in leased houses. In other words, their aspirations of 'social mobility and improved material circumstances' have often been blocked, despite improving educational credentials, constituting what Hadiz and Chryssogelos (2017) have termed 'the broken promises of modernity'.[2] The state's inability to provide social services and effective infrastructure contributes to their grievances. Mietzner et al. (2018: 161) suggest that those who were radicalised by these mobilisations were disadvantageously positioned in the social hierarchy, characterising them as 'Muslims from lower socio-economic strata'. Thus, many analysts appear to agree on the link between economic exclusion and disenchantment with social circumstances within sections of Indonesian society, and the dramatic political developments of 2016–17.

Facing such increasingly widespread precarity, in the absence of class-based politics, many Indonesian Muslims have looked to Islam for an answer, resulting in more conspicuous displays of piety. One indicator of this is the increasing cultural consumption of Islamic commodities since the late 1980s. As stated by Rakhmani (2017), 'Islamic fashions, Islamic housing compounds, and Islam-themed films and television programs have become common', demonstrating that Islamic consumerism is on the rise. Many middle-class Muslims prefer to send their children to Islamic schools and live in Islamic gated communities, for example, to secure and maintain their social status while at the same time expressing their piety. For lower-class Muslims, the consumption of Islamic commodities

---

2 Data on socioeconomic background are used to roughly ascribe an individual's class position. The data do not represent the whole picture of class status as they are not combined with data on perceptions of economic circumstances. However, it should be noted that the use of data on socioeconomic background (occupation, education, and household income and expenditure) to identify an individual's class position in relation to political behaviour has a long tradition in sociological research (McCall and Manza 2011; Saenger 1945).

reflects conditions of economic hardship. For example, the increasing consumption of Islamic medicines is in part a response to unaffordable public health services.

The flourishing of Islamic study groups (*majelis taklim*) and Islamic prayer recital groups (*majelis dzikir*) in both rural villages and urban neighbourhoods is also an indication that many Indonesian Muslims perceive these institutions as providing an 'Islamic narrative' that could address their anxieties and aspirations. Celebrity preachers such as Aa Gym, Yusuf Mansyur, Abdul Somad Batubara, Khalid Basalamah and Dedeh Rosidah (popularly known as Mamah Dedeh) have also become increasingly popular among Indonesian Muslims. However, their narratives mostly conceal socioeconomic insecurity by foregrounding cultural problems articulated through the rejection of ideas linked to liberalism, pluralism, secularism and communism, which are positioned as a threat to Islam.

From a sociological point of view, therefore, many Indonesian Muslims can be said to have become increasingly conservative. But that does not mean they can transform themselves into an independently coherent political force. In fact, their influence relies on the mobilisation of their aspirations and grievances by powerful politico-economic elites in contests over power and resources. Consequently, although the increasing piousness of Indonesian Muslims at the societal level is not reflected in greater power in the political realm, Islam has become a powerful resource for populist mobilisation. The driving forces of the resultant Islamic populism are an unorganised *ummah* and the powerful opportunistic politico-economic elites who are able to frame a diversity of aspirations and grievances within a narrative underpinned by Islamic cultural references.

FRAGMENTATION OF THE ISLAMIC POPULIST ALLIANCE

The Islamic populist alliance is fragmented and incoherent and therefore unable to constitute a direct threat to the current regime. This observation challenges culture-oriented analyses that point to the recent upsurge of Islamic mobilisations as a sign of the rising threat of Islamisation, a view that is also embraced by the government as a pretext for containing Islamic opposition figures. In fact, Islamic morality has been increasingly articulated by a variety of politicians in electoral contests, including by those from notionally 'secular nationalist' parties. But the prominence of Islamic morality in political discourse does not necessarily mean that Islamic politics will come to dominate powerful state institutions.

One example of such an opportunistic embrace of Islam comes from Jakarta. The success of Anies Baswedan in the 2017 Jakarta gubernatorial election was partly due to the support from conservative Muslims associated with the movement to defend Islam against the incumbent Ahok and his alleged blasphemy (*Tempo* 2017). Anies's victory does not represent a victory for an Islamic populist project aimed at Islamising the state, however. There have been no concrete policies directed at Islamising Jakarta since that victory, except for the largely symbolic closing down of some well-known brothels, which had been operating illegally anyway. Buehler (2016) has demonstrated that the proliferation of sharia by-laws across Indonesia is driven primarily by the pragmatic efforts of elites to mobilise political support, rather than the ideological goal of Islamising political institutions. However, the Islam-oriented regulations and policies produced by such processes are largely unenforceable, affirming the limited ability of Islamic groups to seize control of state institutions.

The fragmented and incoherent character of Islamic populism means that the agenda of state Islamisation remains marginal in Indonesia, even though it has become a prominent narrative in political mobilisations. In truth, such an agenda remains subordinated to the interests of opportunistic and powerful politico-economic elites, who are generally more pluralist and secular in orientation than their Islamist clients and supporters. While Islamist constituencies can be important during election season, when contending politico-economic elites will compete for their support, Islamist aspirations can be easily ignored post-election. This suggests that the Islamic narrative mobilised during electoral contests is merely rhetoric that serves to glue together alliances between the fragmented elements of Islamist voters and organisations and powerful, non-Islamist elites. Before the 2017 Jakarta gubernatorial election, for example, Anies was widely known as a pluralist scholar, but he turned to advocate a conservative Islamic narrative after recognising the impact of the 2016–17 sectarian mobilisations, and then made overtures to the Islamist movement in order to siphon support away from another rival, Agus Yudhoyono. Conservative Muslim supporters also largely ignored Anies's previously pluralist views by lauding him as the better Muslim leader and the figure most likely to bring victory for Islam.

In the 2019 presidential election, the Islamist alliance—which primarily comprised elements of the anti-Ahok movement assembled in the National Movement to Guard the Fatwa of Ulama (Gerakan Nasional Pengawal Fatwa Ulama, GNPFU)—backed Prabowo and his nationalist-oriented party, Gerindra. For the vice-presidential candidate in Prabowo's coalition, the Islamist alliance proposed two prominent Muslim figures: popular preacher Abdul Somad Batubara (known as UAS) and Salim

Segaf al-Jufri (advisory board chairman of the Prosperous Justice Party [Partai Keadilan Sejahtera, PKS]) through a meeting of *ulama* organised by GNPFU and called *ijtima ulama* I (Ramadhani 2018). After UAS refused to be nominated as the vice-presidential candidate, al-Jufri was the only name pushed by *ulama* for the position. As a coalition member, PKS had threatened to break ranks with Prabowo and to abstain from backing any ticket in the election if al-Jufri was not nominated as the vice-presidential candidate (Hakim 2018). Prabowo nevertheless ignored this ultimatum by unexpectedly appointing another secular figure—Sandiaga Uno, a wealthy businessman and the then deputy governor of Jakarta alongside Anies. Yet following this rebuke, GNPFU held another meeting (*ijtima ulama* II), which endorsed the appointment of Sandiaga as the vice-presidential candidate, confirming the weakness of Islamist political actors in formal political negotiations with powerful secular elites (*Jakarta Post* 2018b).

Meanwhile, the leaders of this Islamist alliance continued to fabricate unconvincing narratives to consolidate political support from their grassroots constituents. They emphasised the Islamic credentials of Prabowo and Sandiaga: PKS president, Sohibul Iman, for example, declared Sandiaga a post-Islamist scholar, a term used to describe a pious Muslim who also embraces pluralist values (*Jakarta Post* 2018a). PKS deputy chairman, Hidayat Nur Wahid, also gave Sandiaga the title of *ulama*, a term meaning an Islamic religious scholar (*Tempo* 2018). Enjoying the support of conservative Muslims, Prabowo and Sandiaga also frequently presented themselves as better Muslims than Jokowi during the campaign to reinforce their alliance with exponents of Islamic populism.

In an interview, one of the participants of the second reunion of the Defence of Islam movement, who is also a lecturer at a Jakarta university, explained that 'Prabowo might not be a true Muslim, but he could bring hope for the *ummah*' (interview with Lia [pseudonym], Defence of Islam movement participant, 4 December 2018). Another participant also justified the GNPFU's endorsement of the Prabowo–Sandiaga candidacy on the grounds that it was a valid assessment of costs and benefits (*mudharat dan manfaat*) for the *ummah*, although she expressed some doubts when admitting: 'I have no idea if *ulama* are also politicising us' (interview with Dali [pseudonym], Defence of Islam movement participant, 5 December 2018). This manipulation was further illustrated in the aftermath of the election, when Islamic leaders and politicians from this alliance constantly tried to shape the opinion of their grassroots supporters including by producing hoaxes about the election results. Prabowo also called for diehard supporters to protest the result, and these protests descended into riots that killed ten people and injured hundreds more (Halim 2019).

However, several days after the Constitutional Court rejected Prabowo's appeal against the election result, he abandoned the Islamist alliance and initiated rapprochement with the victorious coalition. Prabowo conducted several meetings with Jokowi and the leadership of the Indonesian Democratic Party of Struggle (Partai Demokrasi Indonesia-Perjuangan, PDI-P), which they framed as a post-election reconciliation (*Jakarta Post* 2019). Many Islamist leaders reacted negatively to these meetings. Another element of the anti-Ahok movement, the Brotherhood of 212 Alumni (Persaudaraan Alumni 212), planned to organise a fourth *ijtima ulama* to respond to Prabowo's manoeuvre (Nugroho 2019). On social media, Prabowo's supporters—many of them former participants in the anti-Ahok movement—similarly protested the reconciliation attempt. They also revoked their support for Prabowo and condemned him for betraying the *ummah*. Nonetheless, some leaders in this alliance continue to justify the reconciliation in the hope that it will lead to the cessation of criminal cases targeting prominent Islamist figures, including the leader of the Islamic Defenders Front (Front Pembela Islam, FPI), Habib Rizieq Shihab—although these hopes were dampened by government spokespeople (Ihsanuddin 2019).

As in the aftermath of the 2017 Jakarta election, the Islamic populist constituency had been manipulated during an election campaign and then cut loose by their main political patron. Another participant in the Defence of Islam movement expressed his anger and disappointment with all politicians and many religious leaders that he claimed had politicised Islam for self-serving purposes:

> I just realised that I was being fooled not only by the politicians like Prabowo, but also by *ulamas*, including Rizieq Shihab. I had admired FPI and Habib Rizieq for their *nahi munkar* ['anti-vice' vigilante activities] movement and how this organisation had successfully organised the *ummah* in defending Islam against Ahok. I thought the anti-Ahok movement could unite Muslims from many different regions and was promising for Islam. But it was just a tool used by opportunist politicians like Anies. His victory is only benefiting him, not the *ummah*. Now Prabowo has betrayed the *ummah*. We should never believe that Prabowo could bring hope for *ummah*, but we have been manipulated by the *ulamas*. I just realised that there is no organisation and figure that can represent the interests of the *ummah*. (Hamad [pseudonym], bank employee, Bekasi, personal communication, 14 August 2019)

This is not a new story. Elements of the Islamist constituency have been misled by powerful politicians since the early years of the New Order. Many of them were mobilised to suppress the left, while others were incorporated within the regime so that the secular state could also claim to represent the interests of the fragmented *ummah*. With this fragmented quality, Islamic populism has never been an important driver of policy change. Although expressions of Islamic conservatism in the public arena have been on the rise for the past three decades, there is no coherent political vehicle that represents Muslim hopes and grievances. However, rising conservatism at the societal level has made Islam a powerful source for political mobilisation. These conservative Muslims have also attracted opportunist politicians looking to gain electoral support.

As such, the rising trend of political articulation by using Islamic sentiments is indicative of how the alliance between the fragmented conservative Muslims and opportunist politicians is established in the democratic context; it is not a symptom of rising Islamism as is argued by those who take the 'cultural perspective', a view that is also embraced by the government. Anxiety about Islamic radicalism and religious intolerance emerges from a lack of attention to the origins and features of Islamic populism.

REINFORCING ILLIBERALISM

As a response to the perceived threat from Islamic populism, the Jokowi administration has, first, manipulated state institutions to silence political opponents associated with the Islamic groups and, second, promoted an alternative brand of reactionary populist politics that leverages a hypernationalist discourse about Pancasila and the undisputed conception of the unitary state of the Republic of Indonesia (NKRI [Negara Kesatuan Republik Indonesia] *harga mati*).

The government promotes the national ideology Pancasila—considered an authentically Indonesian way of regulating a tolerant and inclusive society—as a counter-narrative to Islamism (Nathalia 2019). The government and its supporters also advocate an alternative stream of Islam considered more genuinely Indonesian, and constructed as tolerant, moderate and civilised. Despite various and contradictory interests within the organisation, Nahdlatul Ulama (NU), the biggest Islamic group in Indonesia, is often described as a representation of the moderate Indonesian Islam, opening the way for its *ulamas* and activists to enjoy direct access to state institutions and resources. In 2017, for example, the Ministry of Finance signed a memorandum of understanding with the NU central board, delivering Rp 1.5 trillion (A\$159 million) in microcredit funds (Gumelar 2017). Meanwhile, the Ministry of Agriculture (2018) appointed the NU central board as a partner in a farming program in Java, Sumatra and Kalimantan. In November 2018, the government also launched a scholarship program targeting boarding school students (*santri*) associated with NU (Idhom 2018). Most recently, a bill was introduced that gives more opportunities to *pesantren*—educational institutions affiliated mostly to NU—to access state funding. The bill was passed by a legislature that is dominated by government-aligned parties (Permana 2019).

Unsurprisingly, NU has become the frontline agent that consistently supports any government attempts to address perceived Islamist threats, including in the enactment of the controversial Regulation in Lieu of Law (Peraturan Pemerintah Pengganti Undang Undang, Perppu) on Societal Organisations (Perppu Ormas) and the disbanding of non-violent organisation Hizbut Tahrir Indonesia (HTI) (Sapiie 2018). The Perppu Ormas was enacted soon after the 2017 Jakarta gubernatorial election as a reaction to the series of Islamic mobilisations against Ahok's alleged blasphemy (A'yun 2018). This law provides a legal framework to disband social organisations considered by the government to contradict the national ideology of Pancasila. It was meant to block the rise of Islamic populist mobilisation, as many HTI members had been foot soldiers of the Defence of Islam movement. Nevertheless, the FPI—a frequently violent Islamic vigilante group that initiated the Defence of Islam movement—has escaped proscription, perhaps because it advocates a more characteristically Indonesian form of Islamism seen as less hostile to Pancasila.

The manoeuvre targeting HTI resonates with the interests of NU, 'which had long been frustrated with the spreading influence of the organisation and its campaign for a caliphate' (Mudhoffir and A'yun 2017). Interestingly, those who defended this move strongly opposed the politicisation of the Blasphemy Law, which had led to the Defence of Islam rallies. The Perppu that they supported, however, replicates blasphemy provisions as it regulates defamation of religion conducted by mass organisations. The main problem with this regulation is that it removes 'almost all meaningful legal protections of freedom of association' (Hamid and Gammon 2017), leaving it open to manipulation by powerful state institutions. The enactment of the Perppu Ormas also reflects the cultural understanding of Islamic populism in that it responds to the perceived rise of Islamism and intolerance without considering 'the complex aspects that nurture and spread' religious radicalism (Mudhoffir and A'yun 2017). This law regulates conditions under which mass organisations can be disbanded, and thus provides the government with an instrument to target social organisations that challenge it ideologically or politically. Indeed, the government viewed the law as an effective way to curb intolerant groups that gained prominence after the Ahok case. Many liberal civil society activists support draconian measures, including the Perppu, for the sake of defending democracy from Islamist threats.

According to Mietzner (2018), this amounts to 'fighting illiberalism with illiberalism', and contributes to the deterioration of Indonesia's democracy.

Other government efforts also consistently reproduce such cultural antagonism. Any measures, including the manipulation of state institutions, are deemed acceptable for the sake of defending status quo politics from perceived Islamist threats. A state agency focused solely on the promotion of Pancasila, for example, has been created by the government, mirroring Suharto-era indoctrination policies (Halim 2017). The government has also proposed a regulation that gives the president the power to appoint university rectors based on their ability to control the spread of Islamic radicalism on campuses (Rahadian 2017). Many state universities have declared themselves 'Pancasila campuses' to take an active role in controlling the perceived spread of Islamic radicalism and religious intolerance among academics (Gadjah Mada University 2017). Most recently, the government has also mobilised a narrative of deradicalisation in undermining the Corruption Eradication Commission (Komisi Pemberantasan Korupsi, KPK), claiming that this agency has been infiltrated by Islamists. This narrative obscures fundamental issues regarding the appointment of the agency's new commissioners, individuals with poor track records, and the controversial revisions to the KPK law that have removed much of the agency's independence and authority (A'yun and Mudhoffir 2019).

Indonesian democracy already had strongly illiberal characteristics before Jokowi came to power, and so the responses adopted by the Jokowi administration are in many ways unsurprising. An established pattern of illiberal politics limits the options available to address the challenges faced by the ruling coalition in its efforts to consolidate power. Jokowi has chosen to constrain Islamist organisations rather than embrace them in the manner of his predecessor Yudhoyono. In doing so, Jokowi has deepened, rather than challenged, the illiberal nature of Indonesian politics. Efforts to further liberal democratic causes are not in the interests of the dominant politico-economic actors, who benefit from established illiberal structures. Instead, the government frames Islamist threats as a cultural and ideological problem—a result of growing religious intolerance—which in turn ignores the manifold shortcomings of Indonesian democracy that led to the emergence of Islamic populism.

CONCLUSION

Much of the work to date on Islamic populism in Indonesia has paid limited attention to how increasing socioeconomic insecurity underpins populist appeals (Hadiz is the most prominent exception to this rule). In this chapter, I have argued that a sense of injustice about the privileges enjoyed by elites and upper class citizens can be easily manipulated and mobilised as populist politics articulated through the language of religious and cultural difference, rather than class struggle. I maintain that this is a major shortcoming in the literature because the origins of Islamic populism in Indonesia must be firmly understood in relation to such a context.

Understanding the origins of Islamic populism is important in relation to how it expresses cross-class alliances, which are often forged in the heat of electoral contests. As discussed above, such alliances are fragile, as there is no single political vehicle in Indonesia that can claim to effectively channel the aspirations of an increasingly sociologically diverse *ummah*. Yet, for oligarchic interests, Islam still provides a powerful cultural resource for political mobilisation. As such, Islamic populism gains in importance only during electoral contests that pit different, and easily shifting, oligarchic factions against one another. The result is that Islamists remain excluded from dominant power structures despite their increasing visibility in electoral politics and the attention they have received from analysts.

Furthermore, the state's framing of Islamic populism as part of a broader threat posed by radicalism and intolerance is part of an effort to obscure fundamental structural problems in Indonesian society. The state foregrounds cultural threats that distract from the elite concentration of wealth.

These observations suggest that Islamic populism and the anti-democratic responses to it are not indicative of a tilt towards illiberal democracy in Indonesia, as some studies would have it. Instead, I have argued that Islamic populism is the product of an already illiberal regime. However, these illiberal features of Indonesian democracy are now being accentuated by the anti-democratic response of the Jokowi government, predictably made in the name of safeguarding national integrity.

REFERENCES

Arifianto, A.R. 2019. 'Rising Islamism and the struggle for Islamic authority in post-*reformasi* Indonesia'. *TRaNS: Trans-Regional and -National Studies of Southeast Asia*. https://doi.org/10.1017/trn.2019.10

Aspinall, E. 2015. 'Oligarchic populism: Prabowo Subianto's challenge to Indonesian democracy'. *Indonesia* 99(April): 1–28.

Aspinall, E. and M. Mietzner. 2010. *Problems of Democratisation in Indonesia: Elections, Institutions and Society*. Singapore: Institute of Southeast Asian Studies (ISEAS).

Aspinall, E. and M. Mietzner. 2014. 'Indonesian politics in 2014: democracy's close call'. *Bulletin of Indonesian Economic Studies* 50(3): 347–69.

Aspinall, E. and E. Warburton. 2018. 'Indonesia: the dangers of democratic regression'. *Proceedings of the Third International Conference on Social and Political Sciences*, Advances in Social Science, Education and Humanities Research 129. Atlantis Press.

Assyaukanie, L. 2017. 'Unholy alliance: ultra-conservatism and political pragmatism in Indonesia'. *Thinking ASEAN* 19(January).

A'yun, R.Q. 2018. 'Behind the rise of blasphemy cases in Indonesia'. *The Conversation*, 14 May. https://theconversation.com/behind-the-rise-of-blasphemy-cases-in-indonesia-95214

A'yun, R.Q. and A.M. Mudhoffir. 2019. 'The end of the KPK—at the hands of the "good" president'. *Indonesia at Melbourne*, 24 September. https://indonesiaatmelbourne.unimelb.edu.au/the-end-of-the-kpk-at-the-hands-of-the-good-president/

BPS (Badan Pusat Statistik). 2018. 'Profil kemiskinan di Indonesia Maret 2018'. *Berita Resmi Statistik* 57/07/Th.XXI: 1–8.

Buehler, M. 2016. *The Politics of Shari'a Law: Islamist Activists and the State in Democratizing Indonesia*. Cambridge: Cambridge University Press.

Diamond, L. 2010. 'Indonesia's place in global democracy'. In *Problems of Democratisation in Indonesia: Elections, Institutions and Society*, edited by E. Aspinall and M. Mietzner, 21–49. Singapore: Institute of Southeast Asian Studies (ISEAS).

Fukuyama, F. 2015. 'Why is democracy performing so poorly?'. In *Democracy in Decline?*, edited by L. Diamond and M.F. Platter, 11–24. Baltimore: Johns Hopkins University Press.

Gadjah Mada University. 2017. 'UGM Meneguhkan Kembali sebagai Universitas Pancasila', 22 May. https://ugm.ac.id/id/berita/13958-ugm-meneguhkan-kembali-sebagai-universitas-pancasila

Gumelar, G. 2017. 'Gandeng PBNU, pemerintah salurkan bantuan investasi Rp1,5 T'. CNN Indonesia, 23 February. https://www.cnnindonesia.com/ekonomi/20170223183635-78-195737/gandeng-pbnu-pemerintah-salurkan-bantuan-investasi-rp15-t

Hadiz, V.R. 2016. *Islamic Populism in Indonesia and the Middle East*. Cambridge: Cambridge University Press.

Hadiz, V.R. 2017. 'Indonesia's year of democratic setbacks: towards a new phase of deepening illiberalism?'. *Bulletin of Indonesian Economic Studies* 53(3): 261–78.

Hadiz, V.R. and A. Chryssogelos. 2017. 'Populism in world politics: a comparative cross-regional perspective'. *International Political Science Review* 38(4): 399–411.

Hadiz, V.R. and I. Rakhmani. 2017. *Islamic Morality and Challenges to Democracy: A Study of Urban Lower and Middle Class Responses*. Melbourne: Australia–Indonesia Centre.

Hakim, R.N. 2018. 'PKS ancam pecah kongsi dengan Gerindra jika tak dapat posisi cawapres'. *Kompas*, 11 July. https://nasional.kompas.com/read/2018/07/11/05150031/pks-ancam-pecah-kongsi-dengan-gerindra-jika-tak-dapat-posisi-cawapres

Halim, D. 2019. 'Polri: 9 korban meninggal dunia rusuh 21–22 Mei 2019 kami duga perusuh'. *Kompas*, 11 June. https://nasional.kompas.com/read/2019/06/11/20190081/polri-9-korban-meninggal-dunia-rusuh-21-22-mei-2019-kami-duga-perusuh

Halim, H. 2017. 'Jokowi inaugurates chief, advisors of Pancasila working unit'. *Jakarta Post*, 7 June. https://www.thejakartapost.com/news/2017/06/07/jokowi-inaugurates-chief-advisors-of-pancasila-working-unit.html

Hamayotsu, K. 2015. 'Indonesia in 2014: the year of electing the "people's president" '. *Asian Survey* 55(1): 174–83.

Hamid, U. and L. Gammon. 2017. 'Jokowi forges a tool of repression'. *New Mandala*, 13 July. https://www.newmandala.org/jokowi-forges-tool-repression/

Idhom, A.M. 2018. 'Beasiswa santri LPDP 2018: kuota, syarat dan jadwal pendaftaran'. *Tirto*, 13 November. https://tirto.id/beasiswa-santri-lpdp-2018-kuota-syarat-dan-jadwal-pendaftaran-c9TN

Ihsanuddin. 2019. 'Pemulangan Rizieq Shihab syarat rekonsiliasi Prabowo, ini kata istana'. *Kompas*, 9 July. https://nasional.kompas.com/read/2019/07/09/16070941/pemulangan-rizieq-shihab-syarat-rekonsiliasi-prabowo-ini-kata-istana?page=all

ILO (International Labour Organization). 2015. *Labour and Social Trends in Indonesia 2014–2015: Strengthening Competitiveness and Productivity through Decent Work*. Jakarta: ILO.

Jakarta Post. 2018a. 'Post-Islamism what? Sandiaga confused by PKS campaign slogan'. *Jakarta Post*, 30 August. https://www.thejakartapost.com/news/2018/08/30/post-islamism-what-sandiaga-confused-by-pks-campaign-slogan.html

Jakarta Post. 2018b. 'Prabowo–Sandiaga signs pact with GNPF, promises to uphold religious values'. *Jakarta Post*, 17 September. https://www.thejakartapost.com/news/2018/09/16/prabowo-sandiaga-signs-pact-with-gnpf-promises-to-uphold-religious-values.html

Jakarta Post. 2019. 'Political parties appreciate Jokowi–Prabowo meeting, hope for peace'. *Jakarta Post*, 14 July. https://www.thejakartapost.com/news/2019/07/14/political-parties-appreciate-jokowi-prabowo-meeting-hope-for-peace.html

Kalleberg, A.L. and K. Hewison. 2013. 'Precarious work and the challenge for Asia'. *American Behavioral Scientist* 57(3): 271–88.

Lindsey, T. 2017. 'Is Indonesia sliding towards a 'Neo-New Order'?' *Indonesia at Melbourne*, 4 October. https://indonesiaatmelbourne.unimelb.edu.au/is-indonesia-sliding-towards-a-neo-new-order/

Matsumoto, M. and S. Veric. 2011. 'Employment trends in Indonesia over 1996–2009: casualization of the labour market during an era of crises, reforms and recovery'. *Employment Working Paper* No. 99. Geneva: International Labour Organization.

McCall, L. and J. Manza. 2011. 'Class differences in social and political attitudes in the United States'. In *The Oxford Handbook of American Public Opinion and the Media*, edited by G.C. Edwards III, L.R. Jacobs and R.Y. Shapiro. Oxford University Press. https://doi.org/10.1093/oxfordhb/9780199545636.003.0034

Mietzner, M. 2012. 'Indonesia's democratic stagnation: anti-reformist elites and resilient civil society'. *Democratization* 19(2): 209–29.

Mietzner, M. 2015. 'Reinventing Asian populism: Jokowi's rise, democracy, and political contestation in Indonesia'. *Policy Studies* 72. Honolulu: East-West Center.

Mietzner, M. 2018. 'Fighting illiberalism with illiberalism: Islamist populism and democratic deconsolidation in Indonesia'. *Pacific Affairs* 91(2): 261–82.

Mietzner, M. 2019. 'Movement leaders, oligarchs, technocrats and autocratic mavericks: populists in contemporary Asia'. In *Routledge Handbook of Global Populism*, edited by C. de la Tore, 370–84. New York: Routledge.

Mietzner, M., B. Muhtadi and R. Halida. 2018. 'Entrepreneurs of grievance: drivers and effects of Indonesia's Islamist mobilization'. *Bijdragen tot de Taal-, Land- en Volkenkunde* 174(2–3). 159–87. https://doi.org/10.1163/22134379-17402026

Ministry of Agriculture. 2018. 'Kementan dan NU berdayakan 91 juta umat'. https://www.pertanian.go.id/home/?show=news&act=view&id=2589

Mudhoffir, A.M. 2019. 'The state of disorder: non-state violence in post-authoritarian Indonesia'. PhD thesis. Melbourne: University of Melbourne.

Mudhoffir, A.M. and R.Q. A'yun. 2017. 'Law on mass organizations is merely about power'. *Jakarta Post*, 30 August. https://www.thejakartapost.com/news/2017/08/30/law-mass-organizations-merely-about-power.html

Nathalia, T. 2019. 'Jokowi says growing radicalism threatens Pancasila'. *Jakarta Globe*, 16 August. https://jakartaglobe.id/context/jokowi-says-growing-radicalism-threatens-pancasila/

Nugroho, M.R.A. 2019. 'Jokowi bertemu Prabowo, PA 212 akan gelar Ijtima Ulama Ke-4'. *Tempo*, 14 July. https://nasional.tempo.co/read/1224344/jokowi-bertemu-prabowo-pa-212-akan-gelar-ijtima-ulama-ke-4

Nuraniyah, N. 2018. 'After Ahok: the Islamist agenda in Indonesia'. *IPAC Report* No. 44, 6 April.

Permana, R.H. 2019. 'Kontroversi UU pesantren: kitab kuning dan dana abadi'. *DetikNews*, 24 September. https://news.detik.com/berita/d-4719881/kontroversi-uu-pesantren-kitab-kuning-dan-dana-abadi

Power, T.P. 2018. 'Jokowi's authoritarian turn and Indonesia's democratic decline'. *Bulletin of Indonesian Economic Studies* 54(3): 307–38.

Rahadian, L. 2017. 'Mendagri jelaskan ide pelibatan presiden di pemilihan rektor'. CNN Indonesia, 5 June. https://www.cnnindonesia.com/nasional/20170605134327-32-219514/mendagri-jelaskan-ide-pelibatan-presiden-di-pemilihan-rektor

Rakhmani, I. 2017. 'Mainstream Islamic narratives and their divisive consequences'. *Indonesia at Melbourne*, 14 March. https://indonesiaatmelbourne.unimelb.edu. au/mainstream-islamic-narratives-and-their-divisive-consequences/

Ramadhani, N.F. 2018. 'Group of ulemas pushes for VP slot in Prabowo coalition'. *Jakarta Post*, 7 August. https://www.thejakartapost.com/news/2018/08/07/ group-of-ulemas-pushes-for-vp-slot-in-prabowo-coalition.html

Robison, R. and V.R. Hadiz. 2004. *Reorganising Power in Indonesia: The Politics of Oligarchy in an Age of Markets*. London and New York: RoutledgeCurzon.

Robison, R. and V.R. Hadiz. 2017. 'Indonesia: a tale of misplaced expectations'. *Pacific Review* 30(6): 895–909.

Robison, R. and V.R. Hadiz. 2020. 'Populism in Southeast Asia: a vehicle for reform or a tool for despots?'. In *The Political Economy of Southeast Asia: Politics and Uneven Development under Hyperglobalisation*, 4th edition, edited by T. Carroll, S. Hameiri and L. Jones, 155–75. Cham, Switzerland: Palgrave Macmillan.

Saenger, G.H. 1945. 'Social status and political behavior'. *American Journal of Sociology* 51(2): 103–13.

Sapiie, M.A. 2018. 'Hundreds rally decrying the burning of "HTI flag" by NU's youth wing'. *Jakarta Post*, 26 October. https://www.thejakartapost.com/ news/2018/10/26/hundreds-rally-decrying-the-burning-of-hti-flag-by-nus-youth-wing.html

Standing, G. 2011. *The Precariat: The New Dangerous Class*. London: Bloomsbury.

Tempo. 2017. 'Anies Baswedan denies plans to issue sharia bylaws'. *Tempo*, 21 April. https://en.tempo.co/read/868381/anies-baswedan-denies-plans-to-issue-sharia-bylaws

Tempo. 2018. '3 controversial nicknames of Sandiaga Uno'. *Tempo*, 27 October. https://en.tempo.co/read/922924/3-controversial-nicknames-of-sandiaga-uno

Vosko, L. 2010. *Managing the Margins: Gender, Citizenship, and the International Regulation of Precarious Employment*. Oxford: Oxford University Press.

Wilson, I.D. 2015. *The Politics of Protection Rackets in Post–New Order Indonesia: Coercive Capital, Authority and Street Politics*. Abingdon: Routledge.

World Bank. 2019. 'Global consumption database: table, charts and technical notes'. http://datatopics.worldbank.org/consumption/detail

PART 3

Popular Support
for Democracy

8 Electoral losers, democratic support and authoritarian nostalgia

Burhanuddin Muhtadi

The Joko Widodo (Jokowi) regime has conducted fraudulent elections, which damage the image of Indonesia in the eyes of the world. Democracy is already dead in Indonesia.

This is the caption that accompanies the video released by Prabowo Subianto's camp after all exit polls by reputable pollsters forecast Prabowo's defeat in the 2019 presidential election. The video went viral on social media platforms and WhatsApp group chats under the title 'Al Jazeera TV broadcast election fraud in Indonesia'. Al Jazeera immediately issued a letter of clarification regarding the viral video, arguing that it had been edited and assigned a caption that was taken out of context and given emphasis not in the original (Ishaq 2019). Although their allegations of electoral fraud were disputed, many of Prabowo's supporters firmly believed they had been cheated, triggering massive protests outside the headquarters of the Elections Supervisory Agency (Badan Pengawas Pemilu, Bawaslu) shortly after the General Elections Commission (Komisi Pemilihan Umum, KPU) announced the result of the presidential election. The demonstrations quickly turned violent, leading to the deaths of ten protestors, and hundreds more were injured in Jakarta's worst riots since the 1998 unrest that toppled long-time dictator Suharto (*Jakarta Post* 2019).

Democratic stability is determined not only by the conduct of electoral winners, but also by the responses of electoral losers. When election losers become disillusioned with democracy, and then fail to subscribe to democracy as the only game in town, this can ultimately lead to democratic deconsolidation (Rich and Treece 2018). The problem gets worse if they also incite 'violence, encourage a coup, or support the revival of the

141

former regime' (Grewal and Monroe 2019: 497). In this chapter, I bring the Indonesian case into conversation with a rich comparative literature on the relationship between electoral outcomes and democratic support. While Indonesia regularly holds multi-level elections, spanning local and national legislatures and direct presidential elections, surprisingly little work has been done to investigate how electoral losers react to defeat, and whether they remain committed to democracy after having cast a vote for the losing side. Studies of electoral losers typically measure support for the political system using surveys, in which respondents are asked whether they are satisfied with the way democracy works. This democratic satisfaction indicator, however, is problematic, because while citizens may be dissatisfied with how democracy is working in their country, they may nevertheless continue to support democracy as the preferred system of government (Grewal and Monroe 2019).

Beyond democratic satisfaction, this chapter uses two other measures of support for democracy: people's preferred system of government, and whether the current democratic situation is perceived as being better than the authoritarian New Order regime. I also explore less direct dimensions of democratic support, including support for principles and norms often considered to be foundational to a democratic political system, as well as perceptions of the authoritarian past. In doing so, this chapter distinguishes *democratic satisfaction*, understood as an indicator of democratic performance, from *democratic preference*, measured as the belief that democracy is the best form of government (Dalton 2004; Norris 1999). If there is a significant gap between the democratic satisfaction of election winners and losers, it is crucial to explore whether such a gap is antithetical to, or congruent with, the belief that democracy is the only game in town.

Using pre- and post-election survey data, I find that, for most presidential elections between 2004 and 2019, being a supporter of the losing presidential candidates significantly increased the likelihood of disillusionment with the way democracy works. However, in 2019 specifically, democratic satisfaction decreased dramatically for *all* voters. The results of post-election surveys in 2019 indicated a change from previous post-election surveys, which had typically found that the successful conduct of elections produced increased satisfaction with democratic performance. The conclusion of the 2019 election saw the opposite pattern, preceding an across-the-board drop in satisfaction with the functioning of democracy. Further, electoral losers in 2019 were also more likely to perceive the election as less free and fair. The losers were also convinced that their freedoms of speech and association had been undermined.

Nonetheless, if we include citizens' regime preferences as another measure of democratic support, the findings are far more nuanced than we might expect. While electoral losers perceive democratic deterioration across multiple indicators, their preference for democracy as the best regime type remained quite stable before and after the election. Despite their painful electoral defeat, they still think that democracy is the best form of government. My post-election data also found that levels of authoritarian nostalgia among Prabowo supporters did not increase significantly compared to pre-election surveys. In short, while their electoral loss affects how they evaluate the way democracy works, they are not losing faith in democracy as an ideal type of political system, and they appear unwilling to endorse authoritarian alternatives.[1]

This chapter is organised into four parts. The first section briefly presents previous work on the winner–loser gap with respect to attitudes towards the political system. In the second section, I briefly describe my method and its operationalisation. In the third section, I present the level of satisfaction over time, measured before and after presidential elections in 2004, 2009, 2014 and 2019. I then look at the effect of losing on perceptions about other aspects of democracy, and I explain the reasons why the gap between winners and losers was so big in 2019. I employ regression analyses to test whether supporting the losing candidates affects personal satisfaction with democracy. In the fourth section, I show consistent findings that despite their disillusionment with its functioning during the 2019 election, Prabowo supporters still hold that democracy is preferable to any other kind of government, and do not express higher levels of nostalgia for the authoritarian past. I conclude with a discussion about these findings and their implications for democratic (de)consolidation in Indonesia.

ELECTORAL LOSERS AND DEMOCRATIC DECONSOLIDATION

The issue of how democracy becomes consolidated has long been central to democratisation scholarship. Diamond (1996: 238) argues that democracy is consolidated when it 'becomes so broadly and profoundly legitimate among its citizens that it is very unlikely to break down'. We know a democracy is viewed as legitimate by its citizens when 'no one

---

1   This finding complements earlier works (Mujani et al. 2018; Norris 2011) that the public believes that democracy is the best system of government, but they are critical of the practice and implementation of democracy.

can imagine action outside the democratic institutions' (Przeworski 1991: 26). As a defining feature of democracy, elections produce losers. It is therefore crucial to investigate how voters react to electoral loss, because those reactions have implications for democratic stability. Winning an election oftentimes generates a range of positive emotions in individuals; conversely, losing can bring about anger, bitterness and disillusionment (Anderson et al. 2005: 23–6; Singh et al. 2012: 202). Dahlberg and Linde (2017: 626) argue that democracy is consolidated when electoral losers continue to support democracy and accept elections as 'the avenue to political power rather than consider approaches outside democratic rules … in the hope that today's losers can become tomorrow's winners'.

Much of the literature measures democratic support by examining levels of satisfaction with democracy among electoral winners and losers (e.g. Blais et al. 2017; Curini et al. 2011; Dahlberg and Linde 2017; Singh et al. 2012). However, democratic satisfaction is not the only measure of democratic support. Norris (1999), for example, argues that mass attachment to a political regime should be further divided into three dimensions of support: regime principles, which measures the extent to which citizens think democracy is a suitable form of government in all circumstances; regime performance, which tracks popular satisfaction with the way democracy works; and regime institutions, which measures people's level of trust in key political institutions. In this study, I employ Norris's categories and examine Indonesians' support for democratic regime principles and performance both before and after elections. Unfortunately, citizens' levels of trust in institutions are not available in the cross-sectional data used in this study, so this dimension is left out.

However, I add one more dimension to democratic support—the expression of nostalgic sentiments about authoritarian rule. Scholars have long stated that democracy in Asian countries is 'burdened with authoritarian nostalgia, generating unreasonably high expectations about the performance of a new democratic regime' (Chang et al. 2004: 3). When many citizens harbour reservations about democracy, and instead view an authoritarian past as appealing, democracy is in trouble (Chang et al. 2007). What remains unclear is whether those who lose elections demonstrate higher levels of nostalgia by looking back through rose tinted lenses at the authoritarian period—remembering fondly (or imagining, in the case of younger constituents born after the New Order era) a supposedly higher level of social stability and security, dynamic economic growth, admired international reputation and other positive attributes of Indonesia under non-democratic rule—and yearning to return to that system.

This is an important question for Indonesia. Since the fall of the authoritarian regime in 1998, Indonesian democracy has faced multiple challenges, including a weak party system, clientelism, corruption and uneven law enforcement. Indonesia nonetheless made important advances towards democratic consolidation by holding five consecutive national parliamentary elections since 1999, four direct presidential ballots since 2004, and thousands of local elections since 2005. But despite elections becoming a routine feature of Indonesian democracy, and producing a great many political losers since 1999, the issue of the losers' consent— whether political leaders and supporters remain committed to democracy after losing an election—has not received much systematic scholarly attention.

RESEARCH DESIGN AND OPERATIONALISATION

In this study, I draw upon original data derived from nationally representative surveys that took place before and after the 2019 presidential elections. The pre-election surveys were conducted twice in partnership with Indikator Politik Indonesia (Indikator), one of Indonesia's leading independent public opinion research institutes, from 12 to 30 September 2018 and from 8 to 21 February 2019. The first survey was conducted after two presidential candidate pairs, Joko Widodo–Ma'ruf Amin and Prabowo Subianto–Sandiaga Uno, had been registered. The second survey was conducted six weeks before the election. Using a questionnaire, the two surveys were conducted face to face using a randomly selected sample of 1200 individuals in each. Respondents were selected with multistage random sampling, proportionally distributed over the 34 provinces.[2] My post-election survey took place after the Constitutional Court (Mahkamah Konstitusi, MK) rejected Prabowo's legal challenge to the election result, and confirmed Jokowi's victory based on an earlier decision by the KPU. In the post-election survey, conducted in July 2019, the Indonesian Survey Institute (Lembaga Survei Indonesia, LSI) interviewed 1520 randomly selected respondents using the same questions and methodology. Given the sample underestimates support for the losing Prabowo–Sandiaga and abstention, a weighting scheme is applied to reflect the actual outcome of the election.

Direct presidential elections have been held regularly in Indonesia every five years since 2004. As a director of two prominent polling organisations, Indikator and LSI, I have been able to access multi-year datasets held by these institutes covering the period 2004 to 2019. In

---

2 Based on this sample size, the estimated margin of error is ±2.9 per cent at the 95 per cent confidence level, assuming a simple random sampling design.

election years, LSI and Indikator usually have an opportunity to organise two waves of surveys, with approximately 1200 to 2000 voting-age adults responding to the pre-election questionnaire and around 1200 to 1520 persons responding to the post-election questionnaire. For the purposes of this study, I used post-election data that were collected after the Constitutional Court had issued its decisions on election disputes, putting an end to any further legal challenge to that year's election results.[3] All the surveys were conducted through face-to-face interviews and covered the entire territory of Indonesia. All samples were taken proportionally based on population in each province, rural and urban areas, and gender. Given my involvement with LSI and Indikator began in 2003, I can be confident in the method, quality and consistency of the survey data I use in this chapter.

To examine how election outcomes shape people's satisfaction with and preference for democracy, I asked two questions that are commonly used in cross-national surveys like the Comparative Study of Electoral Systems, and that were asked in both pre- and post-election surveys in 2004, 2009, 2014 and 2019. I first asked whether people are 'very satisfied', 'fairly satisfied', 'unsatisfied' or 'very unsatisfied' with how democracy is working in their country. Second, I asked respondents about their preferred system of government: 'Of the following three opinions, which is closest to your own? (1) Under some circumstances, an authoritarian government can be preferable for our country to a democratic one; (2) Whatever system of government we adopt, a democratic or a non-democratic regime makes no difference; and (3) Although democracy is not perfect, it is still the best form of government.'[4]

To measure the extent of New Order nostalgia, respondents were given a series of statements and asked to agree or disagree. These statements were: 'During the New Order: (1) Indonesia was more respected by other countries than it is today; (2) Economic performance was better than it is today; (3) The government was more effective than it is today; (4) The economy was more just and equitable than it is today; (5) In general, people were more prosperous than they are today; (6) There was less corruption than there is today; (7) Ethnic and religious minorities were

---

3   LSI and Indikator have no post-election survey data after the Constitutional Court decision to reject Prabowo's lawsuit (late August 2014). Accordingly, I used Saiful Mujani Research & Consulting's post-election data collected in October 2014.

4   My thanks to LSI's senior colleague, Saiful Mujani, for introducing these democratic satisfaction and democratic preference measures and allowing me to use previous data on this for the purposes of this study.

better protected than they are today; and (8) People at that time were more free to voice their aspirations than they are now.' These questions about authoritarian nostalgia were asked only in 2019, before and after the elections.[5]

THE WINNER–LOSER GAP AND SATISFACTION WITH DEMOCRACY

As in many countries around the world, elections in Indonesia generally boost public satisfaction with democracy (Anderson et al. 2005; Singh et al. 2012). Figure 8.1 presents the aggregate levels of satisfaction with the way democracy works in Indonesia at thirteen points in time—from before the first presidential election in 2004 to after the most recent election in 2019—for a period of fifteen years. While the level of satisfaction fluctuates substantially over time, a pattern emerges: Indonesians generally tend to be more satisfied with democracy after an election. This is particularly evident in 2004 and 2009. In 2004, democratic satisfaction ratings rose significantly from 41.1 per cent pre-election to 65 per cent post-election. Similarly, in 2009 satisfaction increased from 61.7 per cent before to 72.7 per cent after the election. In 2014, satisfaction rose slightly from 58.2 per cent before to 60.8 per cent after the election.

This pattern holds for both winners and losers. As Figure 8.2 shows, even losers' levels of satisfaction increase after an election, especially in 2004 and 2009. Still, the data show that electoral winners overall express higher levels of satisfaction than the losers.

This is particularly the case in 2004 and 2014. Prior to the 2004 presidential election, those who supported incumbent Megawati Soekarnoputri's bid for re-election expressed higher levels of satisfaction than those who supported Susilo Bambang Yudhoyono. Even the survey from early September 2004—conducted after Megawati lost the first round of the election, but was yet to compete in a run-off with Yudhoyono— shows that Megawati's supporters still displayed more positive evaluations of the political system. The picture changed, however, when the run-off resulted in Yudhoyono's victory. Those who voted for Megawati suddenly became more disillusioned, while previously dissatisfied Yudhoyono voters expressed greater satisfaction with democracy after the election. This pattern was replicated in 2014. Before the 2014 election, there was little difference in levels of satisfaction with democracy among Jokowi or

---

5   These authoritarian nostalgia measures were based on input from Edward Aspinall.

Figure 8.1   Satisfaction with the way democracy works, 2004–2019 (%)

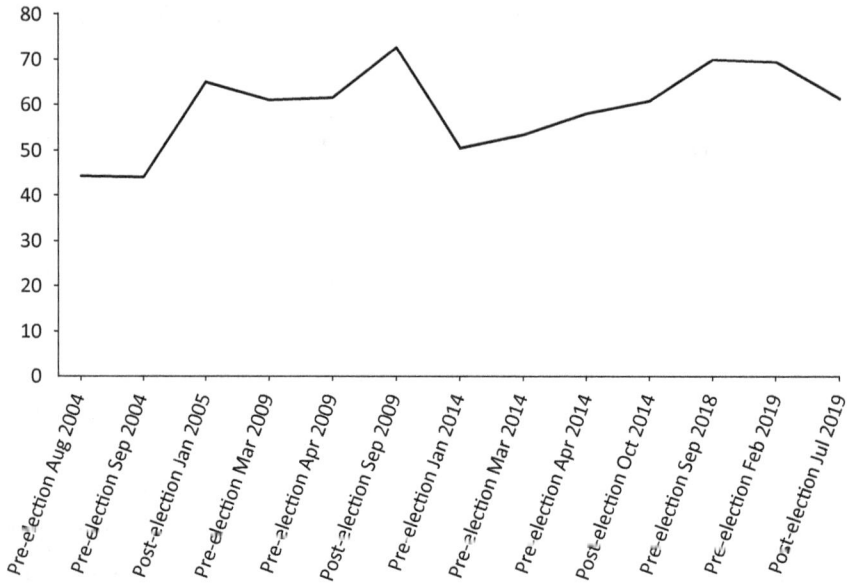

Prabowo supporters. After the Constitutional Court decision had been made and Prabowo had conceded, Jokowi voters tended to be happier with the functioning of democracy than Prabowo supporters.

The 2019 figures, however, represent a dramatic shift in patterns of satisfaction.[6] For the first time in one and a half decades, overall satisfaction dropped significantly after the election (Figure 8.1). When levels of satisfaction based on electoral results are disaggregated, Figure 8.2 clearly demonstrates that electoral losers are more likely than the winners to be dissatisfied with the functioning of the political system—and the gap is the largest it has ever been.

Studies on winner–loser gaps in democratic satisfaction can be divided into two camps: those that propose a 'stability' hypothesis, and those that advance a 'rational response' argument. The former holds that the effect of winning and losing on democratic satisfaction is not short-lived, but rather relatively permanent and long-lasting so that the gap in satisfaction between winners and losers will be stable over time (Dahlberg and Linde 2017). The rational response camp suggests the opposite. According to this school, the gap in satisfaction should level out over the course of the

---

6   In 2014, the level of satisfaction among losers is relatively flat before and after the election.

Figure 8.2   Satisfaction among electoral winners and losers, 2004–2019 (%)

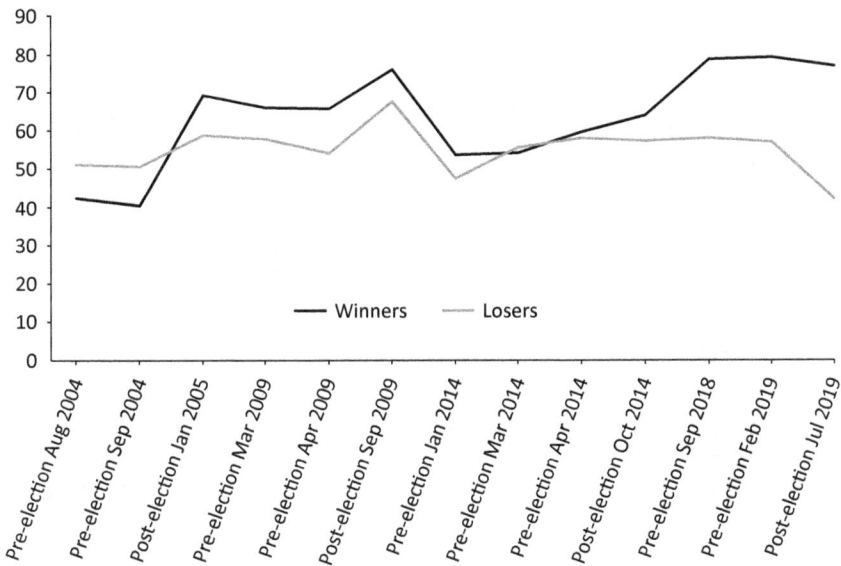

electoral cycle as the winners and losers will make rational judgements about the performance of new governments (Cutler et al. 2013).

The initial evidence, presented in Figure 8.2, paints a picture largely consistent with the stability hypothesis rather than the rational response perspective, as the gap in satisfaction is quite constant throughout the whole period.[7] Such a pattern may be harmful for democratic stability, as citizens' emotional responses to election results are the key determinants of democratic satisfaction. Democratic quality may be considered more robust when voters retain trust in the functioning of democratic institutions regardless of whether their favoured candidate wins or loses.

The multi-year datasets also allow us to measure attitudes among 'repeat losers'. Scholars have become increasingly interested in how different types of winners or losers might hold different attitudes to democracy (Anderson et al. 2005; Chang et al. 2014). Chang and his colleagues (2014) argue that, contrary to perceived general wisdom, there is no relationship between being satisfied with democracy and the number of electoral victories an individual experiences. Individuals who supported the winning side in just one election have the same level

---

7   For the Sweden case, see Dahlberg and Linde (2017).

Figure 8.3   Satisfaction among Yudhoyono, Megawati and Kalla voters in 2009 (%)

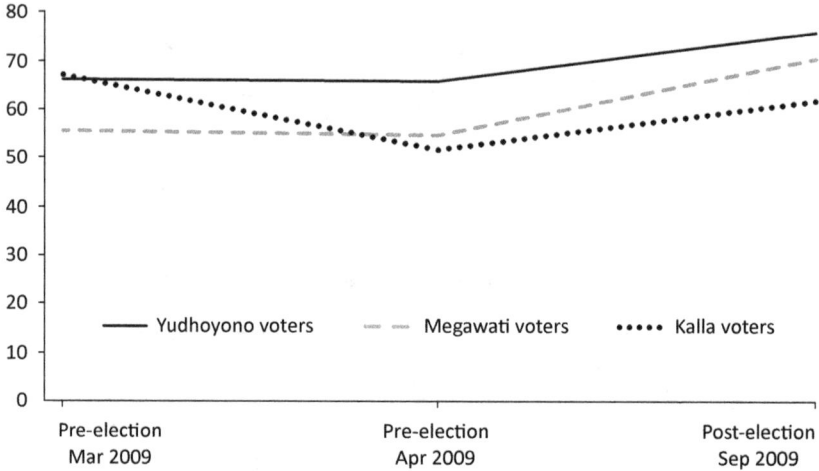

of satisfaction as repeat winners (i.e. those who supported the winning party several times). They admitted, however, that being a *repeat loser* can have a significant effect on political attitudes. Similarly, Anderson and his colleagues (2005) found that repeat losers become much more disillusioned with democracy after two consecutive electoral defeats.

Up until 2014, it was difficult to assess the impact of being a repeat loser in Indonesia. This is because multiple candidates lost in these elections. More specifically, those who lost in 2009 were not only Megawati supporters, who experienced their second straight electoral defeat, but also those who voted for Jusuf Kalla. Kalla in 2004 paired with Yudhoyono and won the election. In 2009, he ran against Yudhoyono with Wiranto, a former general and chair of the Hanura Party, and lost. However, by disaggregating the 2009 data into groups of voters who supported each of the three presidential candidates, we find that Megawati voters expressed lower levels of satisfaction than Yudhoyono voters throughout the election process. Meanwhile, those who voted for Kalla became more disillusioned with democracy as their candidate failed to gain traction with the wider electorate, and in the April pre-election and post-election surveys their satisfaction levels were even lower than those of 'repeat loser' Megawati voters (Figure 8.3). Hence, the 2009 results are inconsistent with the expectation that losing repeatedly engenders further disappointment; indeed, levels of dissatisfaction aligned more closely to the *scale* of a preferred candidate's defeat.

The 2014 and 2019 elections provide a more straightforward comparison, however, because the same two candidates ran against one another. Unlike 2009, the 2019 figures do support the notion that satisfaction among the supporters of a losing candidate is particularly eroded by repeated losses. Figure 8.2 clearly shows that Prabowo supporters expressed substantially lower levels of satisfaction following their 2019 defeat than they had following their first defeat in 2014. In the post-2014 election survey, 57.4 per cent of Prabowo supporters were still happy with the way democracy works, but the satisfaction level dropped dramatically after the 2019 election to only 42 per cent. Indeed, in 2019 satisfaction among losers was at the lowest point since 2004. Additionally, the gap in satisfaction between losers and winners was remarkably large in 2019, both before and after the election.

The winner–loser gap and perceptions of democratic quality

The effect of losing is not only apparent in terms of democratic satisfaction, but can also colour people's perceptions about other aspects of democracy. Table 8.1 compares electoral losers' and winners' perceptions about whether an election was free and fair based on exit polls conducted immediately after the respondents cast their votes, and on post-election surveys that were fielded after official results were released. Given that respondents of the exit polls were still optimistic that their preferred candidates would win the election, an overwhelming majority considered the election 'fair and free'. However, data collected after the announcement of results show that electoral losers from the past three elections were more likely to think that elections were unfair or fraudulent. In 2019, losers dramatically reassessed their views about the integrity of the election. The total effect of losing in 2019 amounted to a 53 per cent decline in confidence in elections, compared to a 22 per cent drop in 2014 and 10 per cent in 2009. Put simply, the proportion of Prabowo supporters who displayed negative evaluations of electoral processes in 2019 was more than double that found following their first electoral defeat in 2014.

A dramatic decline in public confidence on other indicators of the quality of democracy was noted in 2019. A post-election survey by Saiful Mujani Research & Consulting (SMRC) conducted in May–June 2019 found people were feeling much more cautious when discussing political issues, and more uneasy due to arbitrary or biased crackdowns by the law enforcement apparatus. At the same time, they also felt that freedom of assembly has come under pressure due to increasingly heavy-handed measures taken by the state apparatus. They also admit that freedom

Table 8.1   Elections were considered to be free and fair (%)

Status	Election year*	Base	Exit Poll	Post-election	Change
Loser†	2009	39.2	89.8	79.3	−10.5
Winner	2009	60.8	95.1	91.7	−3.4
Loser	2014	47.0	96.5	74.3	−22.2
Winner	2014	53.0	94.2	82.1	−12.1
Loser	2019	44.5	91.9	38.6	−53.3
Winner	2019	55.5	95.3	88.9	−6.4

* The three post-election surveys used here were conducted before the Constitutional Court made decisions, but after the Elections Commission announced the election results. The first and second surveys were conducted by LSI in July 2009 and July 2014, and the third was administered in May–June 2019 by SMRC. The question used in both exit polls and post-election surveys was the same: 'In general how fair, free, direct, and confidential is the General Election held today?'. In the 2009, 2014 and 2019 exit polls as well as the post-election surveys in 2014 and 2019, the choices were: 'very fair', 'quite fair', 'less fair' or 'not fair at all'. In the 2009 post-election survey, the choices were slightly different: 'very fair and honest', 'quite fair and honest with a few problems', 'somewhat fair and honest but a lot of problems', or 'not fair and honest at all'.

† For 2009, those who voted Megawati–Prabowo and Kalla–Wiranto are classified in one category as losers.

to practise religion is undermined by increasing intolerance within Indonesian society at large.

As shown in Table 8.2, the 2019 figures recorded a 26 per cent increase in being afraid to talk about politics, a 14 per cent increase in fear about arbitrary crackdowns by law enforcement agencies, an 11 per cent increase in perceptions of declining organisational freedom and an 18 per cent rise in perceptions of declining religious freedom compared with 2014. As expected, Prabowo supporters in 2019 are much more likely to express negative views about these indicators of democracy than Jokowi supporters (Table 8.3).

In theory, voters are more likely to assess democracy in a positive fashion when it produces the results they desire (Singh et al. 2011: 697). Yet in 2009 and 2014 there was almost no difference between winners' and losers' feelings about multiple indicators of democratic deterioration. In 2019, however, winners and losers began to think differently about their democratic system. Those who voted for the losing candidate were much more likely to believe there was a rise in arbitrary state crackdowns on freedom of speech and organisation and a deterioration in the protection of minority rights.

Table 8.2   Indicators of democratic deterioration (% of those who said always and often)

Indicators of democratic deterioration	2009	2014	2019
Feeling more cautious when discussing political issues	16	17	43
Feeling uneasy due to arbitrary crackdowns by law enforcement	24	24	38
Freedom of assembly is under pressure	10	10	21
Freedom to practise faith is undermined	3	7	25

Note: For each item surveyed, SMRC provided four choices: 'always', 'often', 'rarely' and 'never'.

Table 8.3   Democratic deterioration among electoral winners and losers (% of those who said always and often)

Indicators of democratic deterioration	2009		2014		2019	
	Win	Lose	Win	Lose	Win	Lose
Feeling more cautious when discussing political issues	16.5	15.9	17.6	15.2	36.4	57.0
Feeling uneasy due to arbitrary crackdowns by law enforcement	24.8	25.7	24.0	22.9	26.3	61.6
Freedom of assembly is under pressure	11.0	9.2	12.0	8.8	15.7	31.5
Freedom to practise faith is undermined	3.6	2.5	7.9	5.2	10.3	20.7

Note: For each item surveyed, SMRC provided four choices: 'always', 'often', 'rarely' and 'never'.

Explaining the 2019 results

Why was the gap between winners and losers so big in 2019? I argue that the contentious nature of the 2019 election produced dramatically different responses from voters than at previous points in Indonesian history. This election campaign was especially polarising. The Jokowi government's hardline approach to opposition figures in the lead-up to voting day, and Prabowo's rejection of the election result in the wake of his defeat, contributed to the widening gap between losers and winners.

Many scholars characterised 2019 as the most polarised election campaign in Indonesian history marked by the rise of populism, identity politics and hoaxes largely associated with Prabowo supporters.

Warburton and Aspinall (2019: 271) argue that the 2019 campaign reignited old divisions between Islamist and pluralist camps. Back in 2014 the race between Jokowi and Prabowo was divisive, close and bitterly fought; but in 2019 both sides relied more heavily on competing Islamic organisations and the mobilisation of identity politics. Specifically, Prabowo faced limited political support and financial issues in his second presidential bid, and so he relied more upon Islamist groups like the Islamic Defenders Front (Front Pembela Islam, FPI) in 2019 than in 2014. On the other side, Jokowi invested much more in the organisational support of Nahdlatul Ulama (NU), and NU's network of *pesantren* and mosques around East Java and Central Java were a critical resource during the campaign and helped bring Jokowi to victory. As Eve Warburton and Nava Nuraniyah explain in this volume, both sides used a narrative that painted the other as an 'existential threat'. In doing so they each raised the stakes of electoral competition. Such a campaign was unique in the context of Indonesia's democratic history. Against this backdrop, it is understandable that the losers would feel far more disillusioned and discontent with the democratic system in 2019.

Further, in response to the challenges from an Islamist-linked opposition, the Jokowi administration had taken several harsh measures, including the banning of Hizbut Tahrir Indonesia via the Regulation in Lieu of Law on Societal Organisations (Perppu Ormas) and the use of the Electronic Information and Transactions (ITE) Law to criminalise political opponents (Warburton and Aspinall 2019). Ironically, the heightened sense of polarisation caused many Jokowi supporters to accept such a heavy-handed approach. The administration's actions may, therefore, have eroded perceptions of democratic quality among Prabowo supporters.

At the same time, Prabowo continuously discredited the 2019 election, claiming that it was rigged and full of fraud and deceit. While there was little evidence to back up such claims, it is clear that Prabowo's rhetoric influenced how his constituents viewed the election—recall there was a 53 per cent drop in the number of Prabowo voters who felt the elections were fair between the exit poll and the survey conducted after the Constitutional Court decision. Once exposed to Prabowo's campaign to discredit the elections, his supporters lost faith in the electoral process.

All of these factors help to explain why the gap between losers and winners was so pronounced in 2019. Extreme polarisation during electoral competition can inadvertently lead voters to lose faith in the democratic status quo, especially when the situation ironically provokes an incumbent to employ all kinds of repressive measures to contain opposition forces (Somer and McCoy 2018: 6). The survey results presented here appear to show that such processes are under way in the wake of the 2019 elections.

Testing 'the loser effect'

Having painted the picture of how electoral losers feel about their democracy, we are now in a position to examine the strength of this relationship and to compare it with other sorts of factors that shape citizens' feelings about democracy. To do so, I use multiple regression analyses to reveal the determinants of democratic satisfaction based on four different points in time from post-election survey data.[8]

In all of these surveys a number of attitudinal variables were included that have been linked in the literature to democratic support, including a person's level of political interest, their trust towards political parties, and whether they feel close to a political party (Dahlberg and Linde 2017). I also account for whether political efficacy affects democratic perceptions, which is measured by three items: (1) People like me cannot influence decisions by government, (2) Political and government affairs are too complex, so people like me cannot understand what is going on, (3) I think I am able to participate in politics. The regressions also include demographic variables potentially linked to assessments of democratic performance and preference (Singh et al. 2012). Some research shows, for example, that having a higher level of education is linked to greater support for democracy (ibid.). I also include standard controls for gender, level of income, rural–urban domicile and religion.

The independent variable of primary interest is respondents' status as a winner or loser. The bivariate analyses, as shown in Model 1 in Table 8.4, suggest that being a loser does indeed lead to a decrease in democratic satisfaction in 2004, 2009, 2014 and 2019, and the effects are large and significant.

Model 2 shows that the relationships hold in 2004, 2009 and 2019 even when controlling for other variables that include political attitudes and socioeconomic factors. This was not the case for 2014, however, where the loser effect loses its significance when other variables are introduced.

Most of the other variables have either inconsistent effects, or their effects were not significant. An exception is trust in political parties which, as expected, significantly increases satisfaction with democracy. But given the variable is only available in 2004, 2014 and 2019, we cannot tell whether the effect of trust in parties on democratic satisfaction is stable over time. Among the sociodemographic variables included in the equation, there

---

8 The LSI post-2004 election survey was fielded in January 2005. The second round of the 2004 presidential election took place at the end of September 2004. LSI, in fact, had a nationwide survey in November 2004, but the democratic satisfaction question was not included.

Table 8.4   *The winner–loser gap and satisfaction with democracy,*
            2004–2019

	2004		2009	
Variable	Model 1	Model 2	Model 1	Model 2
Loser	−0.117*** (0.040)	−0.170*** (0.043)	−0.109*** (0.034)	−0.134*** (0.034)
Party identification		0.042** (0.018)		0.005 (0.025)
Political interest				0.002 (0.014)
Trust in political parties		0.099*** (0.019)		
Political efficacy				
Gender (male)		−0.003 (0.041)		0.015 (0.035)
Age		0.001 (0.002)		0.000 (0.001)
Education		0.014 (0.010)		−0.007 (0.009)
Income		−0.001 (0.008)		−0.001 (0.006)
Rural		0.023 (0.042)		0.091*** (0.036)
Muslim		−0.176*** (0.055)		−0.194*** (0.050)
Intercept	2.775*** (0.025)	2.409*** (0.129)	2.848*** (0.021)	2.969*** (0.100)
n	1,031	1,021	1,049	1,046
R^2	0.008	0.055	0.010	0.036

Note. The coding of the variables is done as follows: satisfaction with democracy is coded from very unsatisfied (1) to very satisfied (4); loser is coded as dichotomous variables with the values 1 (loser) and 0 (winner); party identification is coded as 1 = don't feel close at all to any party, 2 = feel somewhat close, 3 = feel quite close, 4 = feel very close; political interest is a four-point scale ranging from not interested at all (1) to very interested (4); trust in political parties in 2019 is a seven-point scale ranging from (1) = no trust at all to (7) = high trust, while the 2015 data is a five-point scale with (1) = no trust at all to (5) = high trust; political efficacy is an additive scale based on three items described above. Each of these items is a five-point scale, so by adding the score of all three items the efficacy runs from 5 to 15 so that the highest values correspond to a greater level of efficacy; gender is coded 1 if the respondent is a male and 0 if the respondent is a female; age is

Table 8.4   (continued)

Variable	2014		2019	
	Model 1	Model 2	Model 1	Model 2
Loser	−0.088*** (0.032)	−0.034 (0.033)	−0.475*** (0.031)	−0.385*** (0.034)
Party identification				0.033 (0.027)
Political interest				0.012 (0.013)
Trust in political parties		0.107*** (0.013)		0.062*** (0.011)
Political efficacy				0.022** (0.009)
Gender (male)		−0.029 (0.032)		0.064** (0.032)
Age		0.000 (0.001)		0.002* (0.001)
Education		−0.025*** (0.008)		−0.011 (0.008)
Income		−0.007 (0.005)		0.000 (0.006)
Rural		−0.081** (0.034)		0.056* (0.033)
Muslim		−0.074 (0.052)		−0.185*** (0.054)
Intercept	2.692*** (0.022)	2.641*** (0.103)	2.886*** (0.020)	2.396*** (0.150)
n	1,403	1,380	1,391	1,283
R^2	0.005	0.073	0.148	0.198

a continuous variable that reports the respondent's age in years, ranging from the youngest to the oldest; education is coded 1–10, where 1 indicates that the respondent never attended school and 10 indicates that the respondent had a bachelor's degree or higher; income is a continuous variable which reports the respondent's gross household income per month coded on a scale from 1 to 12, where 1 indicates that the respondent's income per month is less than Rp 200,000 and 12 indicates more than Rp 4,000,000; rural is a dummy variable where respondents who live in a rural area are coded 1 and 0 if they live in an urban area; Muslim is a dummy variable coded 1, and 0 otherwise.

Standard errors are in parentheses. *** $p < 0.01$; ** $p < 0.05$; * $p < 0.1$.

are no variables that have a consistent, significant relationship with satisfaction. Interestingly, non-Muslims were more likely to be satisfied with democracy in 2004, 2009 and 2019, but this effect was not significant in 2014. The generally lower levels of satisfaction among Muslim voters may reflect the discomfort of many Muslims with liberal democratic practices that are designed to constrain majoritarianism (Assyaukanie 2004: 37). Indonesian democracy has not facilitated the ascent to power of Islamic parties and leaders (with the short-lived exception of Abdurrahman Wahid), at once disappointing Muslims with majoritarian inclinations and reassuring non-Muslims about the continued protection of religious pluralism.

Overall, being an electoral loser has a substantial, significant and relatively consistent effect on democratic satisfaction. The opposite is also true: being part of the winning political majority leads to an increase in satisfaction. The effects that appear in 2004, 2009 and 2019 are very large ($p < 0.001$).

Despite the relatively consistent pattern of the winner–loser gap in satisfaction, the 2014 election was an exceptional case where despite the loser variable being statistically significant based on bivariate analysis, its significance disappears in the multivariate analysis. Why might this be the case? One reason may relate to the absence of an incumbent in the 2014 election. Jokowi, whose party Indonesian Democratic Party of Struggle (Partai Demokrasi Indonesia-Perjuangan, PDI-P) was in opposition during the Yudhoyono presidency (2004–2014), was supported by one of the governing parties, National Awakening Party (Partai Kebangkitan Bangsa, PKB). Similarly, Prabowo, who is the chairman of another opposition party, Gerindra, was also backed by some ruling parties, including Golkar, the Prosperous Justice Party (Partai Keadilan Sejahtera, PKS) and the National Mandate Party (Partai Amanat Nasional, PAN). This partly explains why the winner–loser gap in satisfaction was not especially strong in 2014.

An alternative, similarly plausible explanation is that despite having lost the 2014 presidential election, Prabowo's Red and White Coalition (Koalisi Merah Putih, KMP) managed to secure a 63 per cent majority of national parliamentary seats, enabling it to pass amendments to Law No. 27/2009 on Legislative Institutions (known as the MD3 law) that allowed the KMP to monopolise legislative leadership posts within the House of Representatives (Dewan Perwakilan Rakyat, DPR), People's Consultative Assembly (Majelis Permusyawaratan Rakyat, MPR) and in many regional parliaments (Muhtadi 2015). This differed from 2009 and 2019, when Yudhoyono's and Jokowi's presidential election victories were accompanied by their coalitions retaining control over the parliament.

Thus, the divergence of the presidential and legislative election results in 2014 may have initially ameliorated the winner–loser effect upon satisfaction with democracy.

DEMOCRACY YES, AUTHORITARIAN NOSTALGIA NO

I have shown that losing elections can induce strong feelings of dissatisfaction and higher levels of distrust in the integrity of elections, as well as a feeling that democratic liberties have been eroded. What remains unclear is whether such disillusionment leads to the rejection of democracy as a regime type. Previous studies have indicated that losers not only tend to be more disillusioned with democracy, but their commitment to democracy as an ideal type of political system erodes. My data, however, show no evidence for this. Instead, overall support for democracy as the best form of government was high and relatively stable both before and after the 2019 election (Figure 8.4).

When we break down the results by winners and losers, there is no big difference in the state of normative commitment to democracy over time (Figure 8.5). In 2019, losers' support for democracy remained high at 71.5 per cent, even after the election. Simply put, despite Prabowo's supporters' anger over their political defeat, and although they were more likely to view democratic performance in negative terms, they still saw democracy as the only game in town.

Figure 8.4   Democratic preferences before and after the 2019 election (%)

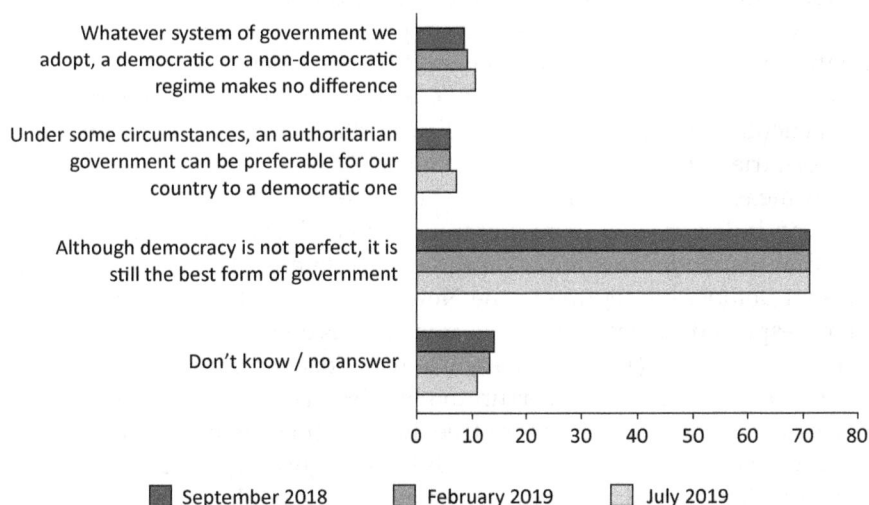

Figure 8.5   Democratic preferences among winners and losers, 2009–2019 (%)

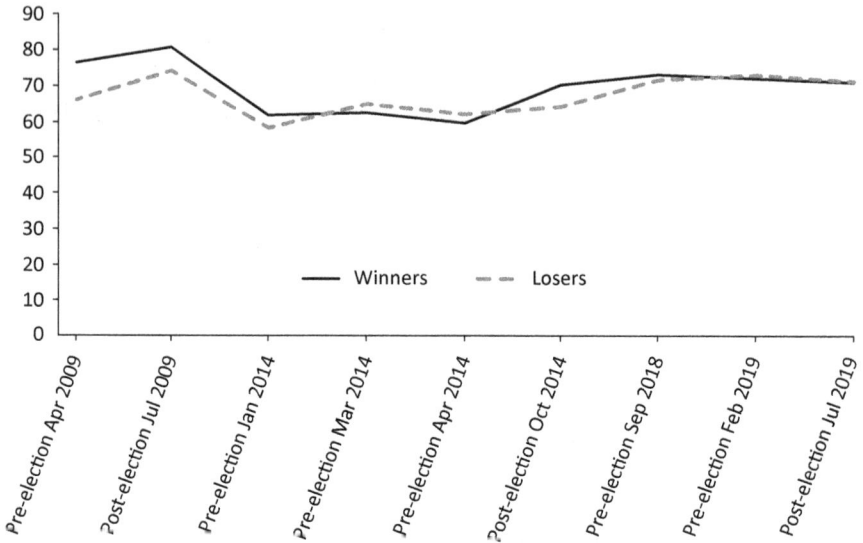

In order to become consolidated, democracy also requires the public to distance themselves from the authoritarian past (Chang et al. 2004). A final test, therefore, measures the prevalence of nostalgia for the New Order period. Given his status as a former general, Special Forces Commander and son-in-law of Suharto, it is reasonable to imagine that Prabowo's supporters would be more inclined towards authoritarian nostalgia. However, there are also reasons to hypothesise that Jokowi supporters might hold such views: first, they are the incumbents, and incumbents want to stay in power; and second, members of the Jokowi government in particular have openly expressed authoritarian ideas, and taken some authoritarian steps (Mietzner 2018; Power 2018).

To measure popular nostalgia about the past authoritarian regime I use an index created from eight questions. These questions inquired whether respondents agree or disagree with statements that compare the present democratic regime to the New Order period: (1) Indonesia was more respected; (2) economic performance was better; (3) the government was more effective; (4) the economy was more just and equitable; (5) people were more prosperous; (6) corruption was less; (7) minorities were better protected; (8) people were more free. Each of these items is a five-point scale, with responses ranging through 1 = strongly disagree, 2 = somewhat disagree, 3 = neutral, 4 = fairly agree and 5 = strongly agree. The 'don't

Figure 8.6   Authoritarian nostalgia index before and after the 2019 election (%)

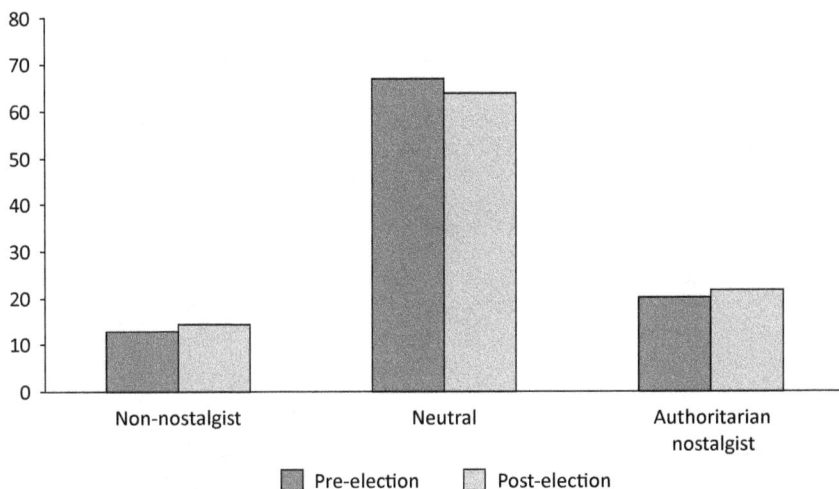

know' or 'no response' answers were coded 'neutral' (3). I then recoded the responses to be: 1 = 0, 2 = 25, 3 = 50, 4 = 75 and 5 = 100. An authoritarian nostalgia index is then developed based on answers to the eight questions. A score of between 66.67 and 100 (that is, if a respondent answered all or almost all questions in the affirmative) led to the classification as 'authoritarian nostalgist'; a score of between 33.33 and 66.67 led to a 'neutral' categorisation and a score of 0 to 33.33 placed respondents in the 'non-nostalgist' category.

Based on this classification scheme, 21.8 per cent of Indonesians in the post-election survey had strong feelings of authoritarian nostalgia and 14.4 per cent were non-nostalgist (Figure 8.6). Almost two-thirds of respondents had no strong feelings either way about the authoritarian period.[9] Overall, these numbers deviated only slightly from the pre-election surveys. Although the proportion of respondents who were inclined to authoritarian nostalgia showed a slight increase from 20.2 per cent in the September 2018 pre-election survey to 21.8 per cent after the election, the difference was not statistically significant (Table 8.5).

---

9   Given that a majority of respondents were not firmly committed either way, the challenge remains to prove that the performance of the current democratic regime is better than authoritarian rule. If not, such respondents may fall into the category of authoritarian nostalgist.

Indeed, a close analysis of the post-election cross-tabulations demonstrates that Prabowo supporters were more likely to express nostalgia for the authoritarian past: 33.7 per cent of Prabowo voters were categorised as authoritarian nostalgists, compared to just 12.3 per cent of those who voted for Jokowi (Table 8.6). The pre-election survey data showed a similar trend: 31.6 per cent of Prabowo supporters were nostalgists compared to only 14.1 per cent of Jokowi voters. But compared

Table 8.5   The mean difference between the pre- and post-election surveys

Category	Pre-election survey			Post-election survey		
	Mean	95% confidence interval for mean		Mean	95% confidence interval for mean	
		Lower bound	Upper bound		Lower bound	Upper bound
Non-nostalgist	12.9	12.2	13.7	14.4	12.6	16.2
Neutral	66.9	65.9	68.0	63.8	61.4	66.3
Authoritarian nostalgist	20.2	19.2	21.1	21.8	19.7	23.9

Table 8.6   Estimated numbers of authoritarian nostalgists by presidential choices (%)

Category		Presidential choice		
		Joko Widodo–Ma'ruf Amin	Prabowo Subianto–Sandiaga Uno	Will not vote/Abstain
Base	Sept 2018	55.2	34.4	10.4
	July 2019	55.5	44.5	0
Non-nostalgist	Sept 2018	18.8	6.1	4.4
	July 2019	21.2	5.9	0
	Change	2.4	−0.2	−4.4
Neutral	Sept 2018	67.1	62.3	81.3
	July 2019	66.6	60.4	0
	Change	−0.5	−1.9	−81.3
Authoritarian nostalgist	Sept 2018	14.1	31.6	14.3
	July 2019	12.3	33.7	0
	Change	−1.8	2.1	−14.3

to the pre-election data, the percentage of Prabowo supporters who were inclined to authoritarian rule increased only slightly after the election from 31.6 per cent to 33.7 per cent, which is not a statistically significant change. Therefore, the conclusion still holds that despite their electoral defeat, feelings of authoritarian nostalgia did not significantly increase among Prabowo supporters.

CONCLUSION

In this chapter I have presented the first attempt at a detailed examination of the relationship between electoral outcomes and democratic support in Indonesia. It is especially striking that despite elections being held regularly since 1999, little scholarly attention has been paid to the question of how electoral winners and losers respond to the election results. Previous comparative studies suggest that losing an election has negative effects on how voters regard the functioning of the democratic system and undermines their commitment to democracy. Taking these findings as my point of departure, this chapter used multi-year opinion poll data to investigate Indonesians' attitudes towards democracy when their preferred presidential candidate loses or wins. Overall, my study found that while being a winner increases satisfaction with democracy, being part of a political minority undermines satisfaction. Electoral losers are also more likely to believe that the political process is unfair and democracy is deteriorating.

However, levels of commitment to democracy as the best available regime type—and nostalgia for the authoritarian past—were not significantly affected by election outcomes, despite electoral losers' grievances about the *conduct* of those elections. All of this suggests that Indonesians' attitudes towards democracy as a system are cognitively distinct from their assessments of democratic performance.

However, their willingness to support democracy should not be taken for granted. If democracy continues to deteriorate, and citizens continue to experience growing limitations on free speech and freedom of association as described above, they might feel increased disillusionment and anger about the status quo. In other words, the perceptible decline in Indonesia's democratic performance over a variety of indicators must be reversed to ensure that electoral losers continue to have faith in democracy and do not become more sympathetic to nondemocratic systems of government.

When the winning party or candidate emerges after an intense and heated electoral competition, it is imperative to strike what Anderson and colleagues (2005) call a 'democratic bargain' between the opposing parties or candidates, so that the winners don't harass the losers in the name of political payback. Likewise, the losing parties or candidates and their supporters need to concede power and allow the legitimate winners to rule. This democratic culture is important in order to ensure the survival and legitimacy of the democratic political system. When the reciprocal gestures above do not occur after an electoral competition concludes, an acute sense of disillusionment towards the democratic system may arise, especially among the losing party or candidate's supporters, which could potentially lead to civil disobedience, violence and a crisis of democratic legitimacy. In this regard, it is important to distinguish between the post-election, patronage-based bargains brokered among political elites, on one hand, and the treatment of opposition groups and supporters at the grassroots level on the other. Additional research will be required in order to properly evaluate the effects of elite-level grand coalitions upon patterns of popular democratic support beyond election cycles.

REFERENCES

Anderson, C.J., A. Blais, S. Bowler, T. Donovan and O. Listhaug. 2005. *Losers' Consent: Elections and Democratic Legitimacy*. New York: Oxford University Press.

Assyaukanie, L. 2004. 'Democracy and the Islamic state: Muslim arguments for political change in Indonesia'. *Copenhagen Journal of Asian Studies* 20: 32–46.

Blais, A., A. Morin-Chassé and S.P. Singh. 2017. 'Election outcomes, legislative representation, and satisfaction with democracy'. *Party Politics* 23(2): 85–95.

Chang, E., Y.-H. Chu and W.-C. Wu. 2014. 'Consenting to lose or expecting to win? Inter-temporal changes in voters' winner-loser status and satisfaction with democracy'. In *Elections and Representative Democracy: Representation and Accountability*, edited by J. Thomassen, 232–53. Oxford: Oxford University Press.

Chang, Y.-T., Y. Chu, F. Hu and H. Shyu. 2004. 'How citizens evaluate Taiwan's new democracy'. *Asian Barometer Working Paper Series* 18. Taipei: National Taiwan University.

Chang, Y.-T., Y. Chu and C.-M. Park. 2007. 'The democracy barometers (part 1): authoritarian nostalgia in Asia'. *Journal of Democracy* 18(3): 66–80.

Curini, L., W. Jou and V. Memoli. 2011. 'Satisfaction with democracy and the winner/loser debate: the role of policy preferences and past experience'. *British Journal of Political Science* 42(2): 241–61.

Cutler, F., A. Nuesser and B. Nyblade. 2013. 'Evaluating the quality of democracy with individual level models of satisfaction: or, a complete model of satisfaction with democracy'. Paper presented to the ECPR General Conference, 4–7 September. Bordeaux.

Dahlberg, S. and J. Linde. 2017. 'The dynamics of the winner–loser gap in satisfaction with democracy: evidence from a Swedish citizen panel'. *International Political Science Review* 38(5): 625–41.

Dalton, R.J. 2004. *Democratic Challenges, Democratic Choices: The Erosion of Political Support in Advanced Industrial Democracies*. Oxford: Oxford University Press.

Diamond, L. 1996. 'Toward democratic consolidation'. In *The Global Resurgence of Democracy*, 2nd edition, edited by L. Diamond and M.F. Plattner, 227–40. Baltimore: Johns Hopkins University Press.

Grewal, S. and S.L. Monroe. 2019. 'Down and out: founding elections and disillusionment with democracy in Egypt and Tunisia'. *Comparative Politics* 51(4): 497–539.

Ishaq, Z. 2019. 'Benarkah TV Al-Jazeera telah menyiarkan kecurangan pemilu di Indonesia?'. *Tempo*, 15 May. https://cekfakta.tempo.co/fakta/282/fakta-atau-hoaks-benarkah-tv-al-jazeera-telah-menyiarkan-kecurangan-pemilu-di-indonesia

Jakarta Post. 2019. 'Post-election unrest grips Jakarta'. *Jakarta Post*, 22 May. https://www.thejakartapost.com/news/2019/05/22/post-election-unrest-grips-jakarta.html

Mietzner, M. 2018. 'Fighting illiberalism with illiberalism: Islamist populism and democratic deconsolidation in Indonesia'. *Pacific Affairs* 91(2): 261–82.

Muhtadi, B. 2015. 'Jokowi's first year: a weak president caught between reform and oligarchic politics'. *Bulletin of Indonesian Economic Studies* 51(3): 349–68.

Mujani, S., R.W. Liddle and K. Ambardi. 2018. *Voting Behavior in Indonesia since Democratization: Critical Democrats*. Cambridge: Cambridge University Press.

Norris, P. 1999. *Critical Citizens: Global Support for Democratic Governance*. Oxford: Oxford University Press.

Norris, P. 2011. *Democratic Deficit: Critical Citizens Revisited*. New York: Cambridge University Press.

Power, T.P. 2018. 'Jokowi's authoritarian turn and Indonesia's democratic decline'. *Bulletin of Indonesian Economic Studies* 54(3): 307–38.

Przeworski, A. 1991. *Democracy and the Market: Political and Economic Reforms in Eastern Europe and Latin America*. Cambridge: Cambridge University Press.

Rich, T. and M. Treece. 2018. 'Losers' and non-voters' consent: democratic satisfaction in the 2009 and 2013 elections in Germany'. *Government and Opposition* 53(3): 416–36.

Singh, S., I. Lago and A. Blais. 2011. 'Winning and competitiveness as determinants of political support'. *Social Science Quarterly* 92(September): 695–709.

Singh, S.P., E. Karakoc and A. Blais. 2012. 'Differentiating winners: how elections affect satisfaction with democracy'. *Electoral Studies* 31(March): 201–11.

Somer, M. and J. McCoy. 2018. 'Déjà vu? Polarization and endangered democracies in the 21st century'. *American Behavioral Scientist* 62(1): 3–15.

Warburton, E. and E. Aspinall. 2019. 'Explaining Indonesia's democratic regression: structure, agency and popular opinion'. *Contemporary Southeast Asia: A Journal of International and Strategic Affairs* 41(2): 255–85. https://www.muse.jhu.edu/article/732138

9 How popular conceptions of democracy shape democratic support in Indonesia

Diego Fossati and Ferran Martinez i Coma

The path to democracy is rarely steady or linear. Countries can perform well on some indicators of democratic consolidation, while improvements in other areas remain elusive. Indonesia, for example, holds regular and competitive elections, but still confronts real challenges when it comes to protecting the rights of minorities. In other words, democracy is multidimensional. Democratic quality can be evaluated from different perspectives, and the conclusions analysts reach are often contingent on exactly what aspect of democratic consolidation they are analysing.

In this chapter, we focus on the multidimensionality of democracy. Specifically, we study how different dimensions of democracy are *understood* by Indonesian citizens. Public opinion research has painted a mixed picture of public support for democracy in Indonesia. On one hand, it shows that Indonesians are highly supportive of democracy. Although the results vary depending on how specific survey questions are formulated, scholars have shown that support for and satisfaction with democracy in Indonesia are generally high (Mietzner 2013; Mujani and Liddle 2015). On the other hand, some studies show that Indonesians do not understand democracy in *liberal* terms, as they equate democracy with good governance and policy outcomes rather than with a system of checks, balances and limited government (Aspinall et al. 2020; Warburton and Aspinall 2019). This is consistent with other cases in East and Southeast Asia (Chu and Huang 2010).

These findings point to the importance of investigating democracy as a concept, in a context where support for democracy is widespread but the meaning of 'democracy' is contested. Existing research, however, does not account for some of the important dimensions of democracy, such as deliberation and informal participation. Given Indonesia's long tradition of progressive politics (Dibley and Ford 2019) and relatively high levels of civic participation (Lussier and Fish 2012), this is a potentially important omission.

In this chapter, we draw on the comparative literature to describe and delimit five different dimensions for assessing democratic quality: electoral, liberal, deliberative, participatory and egalitarian. We then develop a new measure of how ordinary Indonesians conceive of democracy, which we use to address a series of research questions. First, we ask to what extent these five dimensions resonate in the minds of ordinary Indonesians as coherent and distinct ideological constructs. We identify two distinct conceptions of democracy among the Indonesian public. The first is a blend of liberal and egalitarian elements. While the liberal dimension complicates some of the existing research on public opinion in Indonesia, the widespread emphasis on egalitarianism is consistent with studies suggesting that economic performance and substantive outcomes are central to how Indonesians conceive of democracy. The second conception, which we describe as participatory, suggests that some Indonesians associate democracy with informal practices of political participation.

Second, we ask to what extent the different conceptions of democracy have implications for how Indonesians assess, evaluate and support democratic institutions. The answers shed light on whether variation in conceptions of democracy shapes how Indonesians evaluate their political system, and help us to identify deficiencies in democratic practice that may undermine the legitimacy of democratic institutions in the eyes of the public. We find that the two conceptions of democracy outlined above are indeed closely related to satisfaction with democracy—but not with whether people support democracy as a political regime. Most importantly, we find that the two conceptions are related to satisfaction with democracy in different ways: while egalitarian–liberal democrats are more likely to be dissatisfied with democracy in Indonesia, participatory democrats are significantly more likely to be satisfied with democracy.

The remainder of this chapter is structured as follows. We start by discussing the conceptual framework that will guide the analysis. In the first part of the empirical section, we demonstrate the utility of a multidimensional conception of democracy. We do so by analysing country-level data that show how the trajectory of Indonesian democratic development has varied along different dimensions, both over time and relative to other young democracies. Based on an original public opinion survey using those dimensions, we then transition to an analysis of our data. We conclude by commenting on the relevance of our findings for research on democratic consolidation in Indonesia.

A MULTIDIMENSIONAL CONCEPTION OF DEMOCRACY

Following the framework adopted by the Varieties of Democracy (V-Dem) Project (Coppedge and Gerring 2011), we distinguish between electoral, liberal, participatory, deliberative and egalitarian conceptions of democracy. A necessary condition for a political regime to be called a democracy is that different parties or candidates compete for the votes of the citizenry in free and fair elections. Schumpeter (1942), Przeworski et al. (2000) and others have proposed a 'minimalist' idea of democracy in which elections are the essential element. This electoral conception of democracy entails multiparty competition in an even field in which electoral institutions are transparent and the media provides reliable information to citizens.

There is more to democracy than elections, however. The second conception of democracy is the liberal—also sometimes known as the pluralist—variant, which emphasises limits on elected governments, and the principles of individual rights (Fawcett 2018). Protection against the 'tyranny of the majority' is important in this dimension of democracy. Thus, the protection of civil liberties, the establishment of legal constraints on power—that is, rule of law—and limitations on the exercise of power by the government through additional institutional checks and balances are essential to the liberal view of democracy.

Although voting is important in the participatory conception of democracy, this dimension places greater primacy on direct rule by the citizens and their involvement in determining public policies (Barber 2003; Huber et al. 1997). As participatory democracy rests on the principle that democracy is government *by* the people, scholars working from this perspective have been critical of the fact that contemporary democracies rely heavily on representation of the people through intermediary institutions and formal electoral channels. This dimension emphasises the importance of direct avenues of political participation, such as town hall meetings, public hearings, citizen assemblies and other mechanisms such as referendums and plebiscites, as well as engagement through civil society organisations.

The deliberative dimension of democracy focuses on whether political decisions are the product of public deliberation (Cohen 1997; Fishkin 1991). In this conception, government decisions should be reached through a process of dialogue with citizens. Such dialogue should be informed and respectful, not guided by emotions and social identities as in politics. In an ideal deliberative democracy, competing views are placed alongside each other and accompanied by reliable information, participants are open to persuasion through compelling argument, and political decisions are the product of deliberation. This dimension is typically measured by experts' assessments of whether decision-making in a given country conforms to this ideal type, focusing especially on interactions among political elites and the quality of public discourse.

Finally, the egalitarian dimension asks whether all citizens are equally empowered. In this perspective, inequalities—economic or otherwise— are an impediment to the full development and exercise of rights and liberties (Huber et al. 1997; Young 2002). While citizens may enjoy equal political rights on paper, inequalities based on economic disparities, or on social identities such as religion, ethnicity or gender, may exclude substantial sectors of the population from political participation. An egalitarian perspective on democracy thus probes the fairness of the distribution of material and non-material resources in a society. It asks, for example, if citizens are protected from poverty, if access to basic rights such as education and healthcare is guaranteed for all, and if people have the same opportunities in life regardless of their social background.

While some of these dimensions of democracy are closely related and may evolve simultaneously (Coppedge and Gerring 2011), this is not always the case. For example, political equality may or may not be closely associated with the development of the checks and balances emphasised in the liberal dimension, as the relationship between the two may be contingent on a country's specific historical trajectory. In short, the dimensions are conceptually distinct and empirically independent from one another. Assessing them both individually and in contrast to each other can provide new insights into the performance of democracy.

A MULTIDIMENSIONAL APPROACH TO INDONESIA'S DEMOCRATIC TRAJECTORY

How has Indonesia fared on V-Dem's various dimensions of democratic quality? In this section, we look at Indonesia's V-Dem scores over time, and compare them with the more conventional aggregate scores estimated by Freedom House and Polity.[1] The main strength of Freedom House and Polity is that they aggregate different dimensions of democracy into a single value, which helps analysts make parsimonious comparisons of democratic quality in countries around the world. But this is also their main limitation, because a single value does not allow us to disentangle and analyse different democratic arenas. For example, if two countries were to obtain the same score—say, a score of 1 on the Freedom House scale, as South Africa and Sweden did in 2018—we might conclude that there are no significant differences between the forms of democracy that exist in these two countries, but this would be problematic.

V-Dem, on the other hand, offers hundreds of indicators that researchers can use to 'build' the indexes that are most relevant for their purposes. To illustrate the utility of such multidimensional data, Figure 9.1 shows changes in Indonesia's democracy scores over time as measured by Freedom House, Polity and V-Dem's Electoral Democracy Index.[2] The correlation of the V-Dem indicator with Freedom House and Polity is above 0.9 in both cases, suggesting that Polity and Freedom House primarily rely on an electoral conception of democracy.

According to Freedom House, Indonesia's democracy performed best between 2005 and 2012, with a slight decline in the subsequent period (Figure 9.1). V-Dem also records a rise in democratic quality until 2005, followed by a gradual decline. The Polity data, however, indicate that Indonesia's democracy strengthened between 2014 and 2017. These indexes, therefore, do not paint a uniform picture: Indonesian democracy strengthened according to the Polity data, declined according to the V-Dem figures and stagnated according to Freedom House. Such divergent conclusions justify a closer look at each of the dimensions outlined above.

In Figure 9.2, we display Indonesia's scores on the five dimensions of democracy measured by V-Dem. Since its democratic transition in 1998–99, Indonesia has performed best on the electoral dimension and worst on the participatory and egalitarian dimensions. The trends for the various dimensions have been quite uniform over time. From 2000 until approximately 2006, the estimates of democratic quality increase for

---

1   Freedom House and Polity are two of the most widely used indexes of democratic quality. Freedom House has been grading countries' democratic quality since the early 1970s. It gives a score of 1–2.5 for free countries, 3–5 for partially free countries and 5.5–7 for non-free countries. Polity scores countries on a range from full autocracies (–10) to full democracies (10), beginning in 1800. V-Dem's dataset covers 202 countries, starting in 1789.

2   All indexes are rescaled to the 0–1 interval. The scores for the two subcategories in the Freedom House index (political rights and civil liberties) are averaged and reversed.

Figure 9.1   Evolution of electoral democracy in Indonesia, 1990–2018

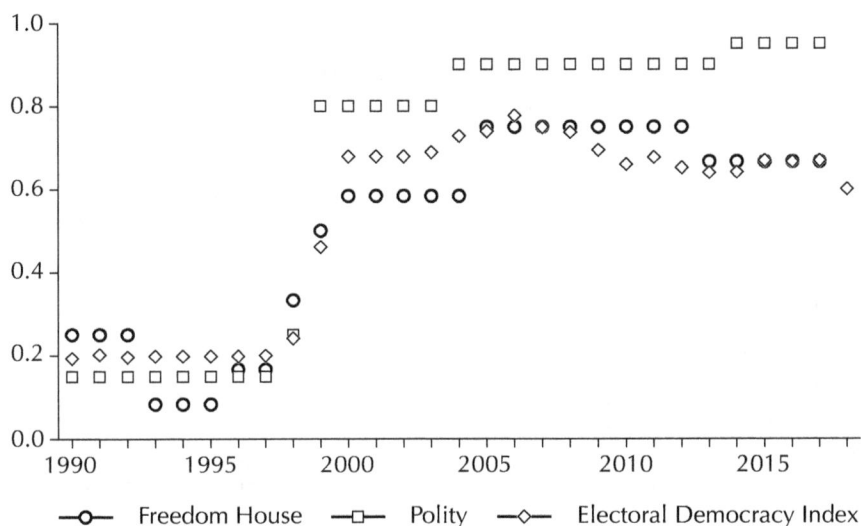

Source: Coppedge et al. (2019).

all dimensions. They then decline from 2006 until about 2014, increase slightly until 2017 and again decrease in 2018. So, despite some fluctuations, Indonesia's democracy has been remarkably stable over the past 20 years. After reaching a peak in 2005–08, the quality of democracy in Indonesia has declined in small increments, and today looks as imperfect (and with as much room for improvement) as it did in the wake of the first democratic elections in 1999.

To better appreciate the achievements and shortcomings of Indonesia's post-1998 reforms, it is valuable to place the Indonesian case in a comparative context. How has Indonesia performed compared with other countries that democratised in the same period? To address this question, we gathered information on all countries that underwent a democratic transition in 1994–2004, that is, during a window of five years before and after Indonesia's foundational democratic elections in 1999.[3]

---

3 These countries are Macedonia, Mozambique, Panama, Ukraine, Moldova and Malawi in 1994; Ghana in 1996; Indonesia, Nigeria and Armenia in 1999; Croatia in 2000; Peru and East Timor in 2001; and Sierra Leone and Lesotho in 2002.

*Figure 9.2   Evolution of electoral, liberal, participatory, deliberative and
              egalitarian democracy in Indonesia, 1990–2018*

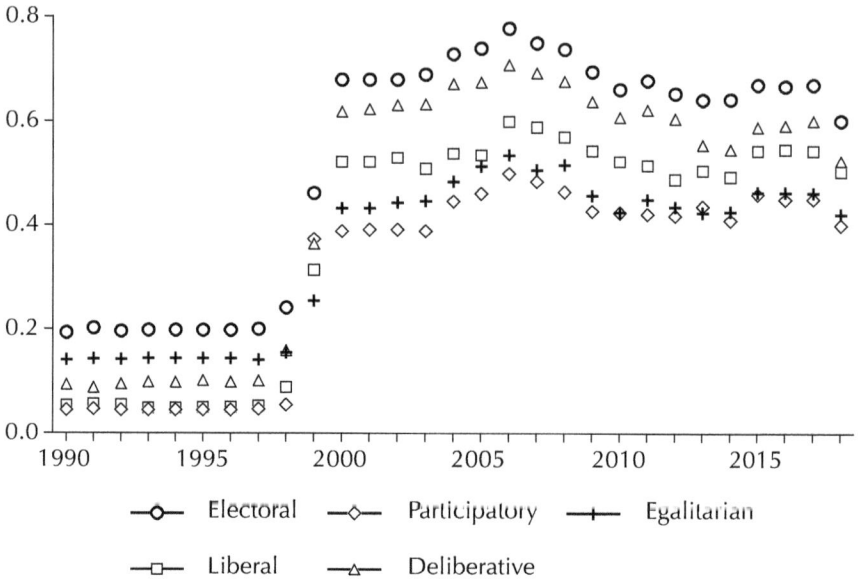

Source: Coppedge et al. (2019).

Figure 9.3 shows how Indonesia's scores on the Electoral Democracy Index compare with those of this diverse set of young democracies.[4] Since its transition to democracy ended in 1999, Indonesia has been one of the top performers on this dimension (with an average score of 0.69 since 2000), alongside Croatia (0.78), Peru (0.77) and Ghana (0.69), and has avoided the fluctuations seen in countries such as Ukraine (0.48), Sierra Leone (0.44) or Mozambique (0.47).[5]

Indonesia performs less well on the Liberal Democracy Index (with an average score of 0.53) (Figure 9.4). However, this is also the case for every other country included in the comparison. For example, Peru and Croatia perform around the 0.6 mark, and several other countries have substantially lower scores, including Ukraine (0.30), Sierra Leone (0.33)

---

4 To facilitate visual inspection of cross-country and chronological variation, Figure 9.3 shows a more limited set of six countries (including Indonesia), which we selected to ensure that various world regions are represented.

5 These values are calculated as averages from the end of the democratic transition to the last available data point.

Figure 9.3   Indonesia in comparative perspective: Electoral Democracy Index

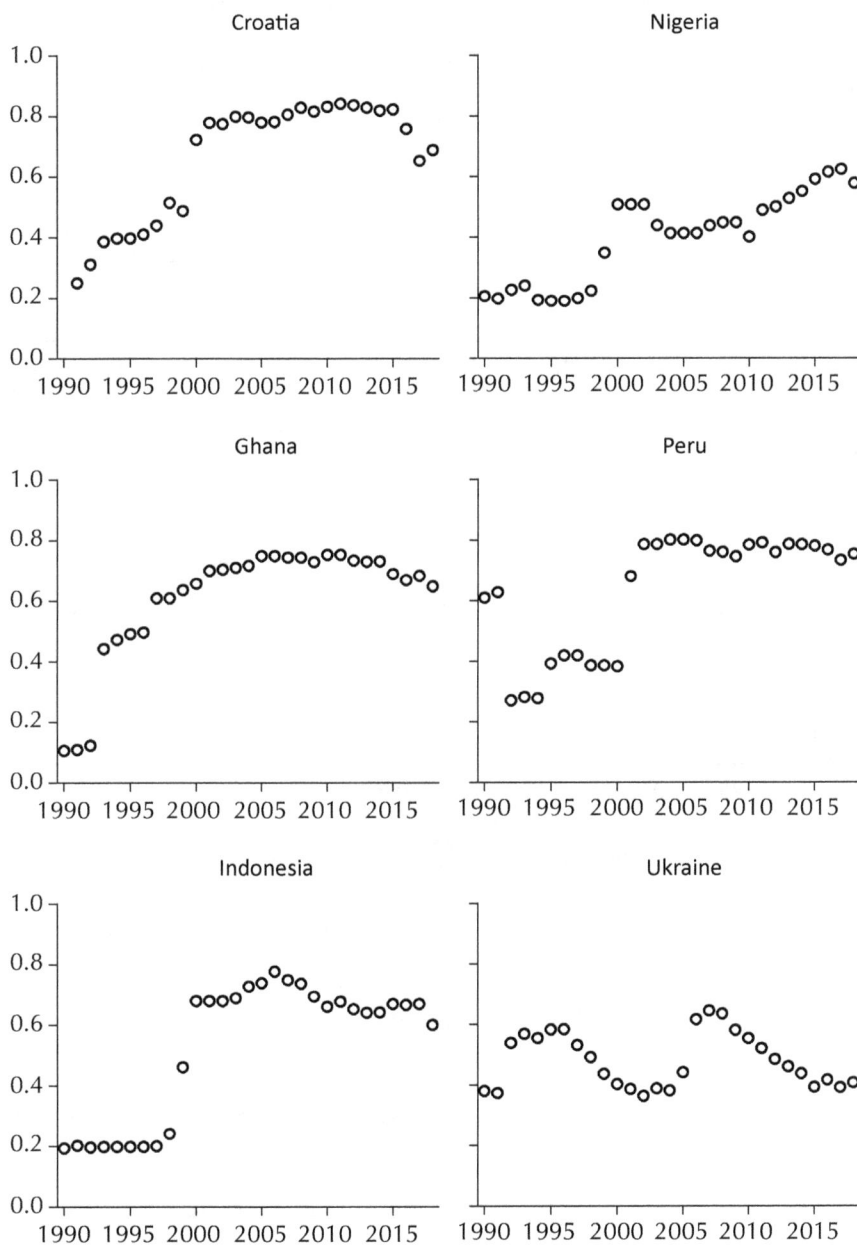

Source: Coppedge et al. (2019).

Figure 9.4   Indonesia in comparative perspective: Liberal Democracy Index

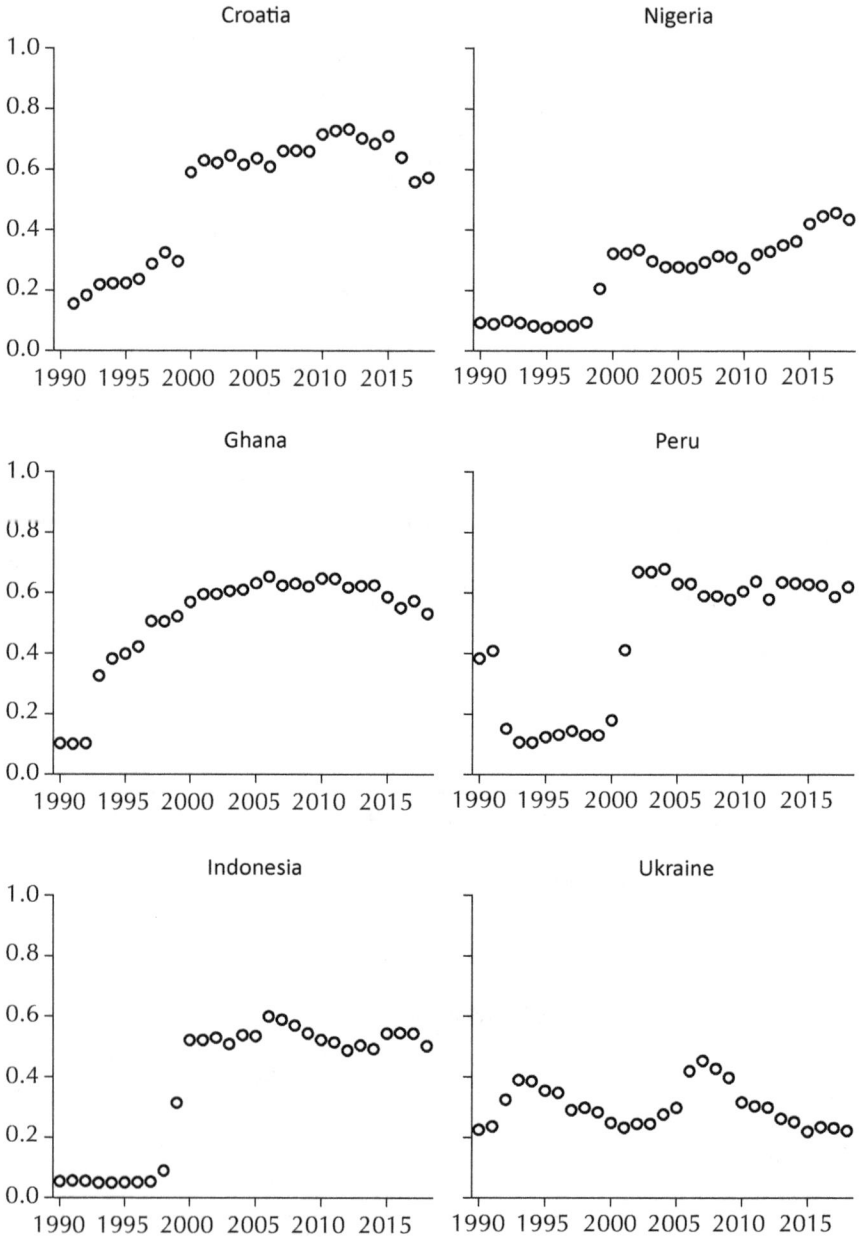

Source: Coppedge et al. (2019).

and Mozambique (0.32). Moreover, top-performing countries such as Croatia and Ghana seem to have experienced declining performance in this area over the past few years, as is the case for Indonesia.

To summarise the trends for the remaining three dimensions, Croatia and Peru (both 0.53) perform better than Indonesia (0.42) on the participatory dimension of democracy; Ghana (0.61) and Indonesia (0.6) outrank most other countries on the deliberative dimension of democracy; and Indonesia (0.44) ranks in the middle of the selected group of countries on the egalitarian dimension of democracy, where it is preceded by Croatia (0.62), Ghana (0.5) and Peru (0.47).

Overall, our analysis of aggregate-level data on the dimensions of democracy is revealing in three important ways. First, the data tell a relatively positive story about Indonesia's democratic trajectory. Indonesia has been performing well on all dimensions relative to other young democracies, and the evolution of its scores over time seems more stable than in most other countries. Second, the conclusion as to whether Indonesia is following a global trend of democratic regression (Lührmann and Lindberg 2019) is contingent on the time frame adopted as a reference. While V-Dem picks up a noticeable decline in index values from the peaks of 2005–08, the prevailing pattern is one of stability. Finally, the country-level data suggest that it is important to distinguish between the various dimensions of democracy because, at least to a certain extent, they are empirically distinct. Although many studies rely on indexes that use single scores to assess and compare countries' democratic quality, we believe that disaggregating democracy into its different dimensions provides a more fine-grained, more sensitive and, we argue, more accurate picture of both quality and change over time.

A LOOK AT THE MASS PUBLIC: CONCEPTIONS OF DEMOCRACY IN INDONESIA

In this section, we ask whether ordinary citizens perceive the multidimensional nature of democracy outlined above. Analysing the mass public's conceptions of democracy is an important endeavour for academic research, because ideas about what a democracy should be and expectations of what it should deliver are plausibly associated with levels of satisfaction with democracy. When a democratic political regime fails to ensure the delivery of basic outcomes such as civic freedoms, rule of law and economic prosperity to most of the population, citizens' dissatisfaction with democratic institutions may grow. If people attribute such failures, not to incumbent politicians, but to democracy itself, support for authoritarianism may rise and pose a threat to democratic consolidation (Huang et al. 2008; Magalhães 2014). This idea is highly relevant in the context of Indonesia, where satisfaction with democracy appears to be closely related to evaluations of government performance (Mujani and Liddle 2015; Mujani et al. 2018).

With this in mind, we designed a survey to investigate public conceptions of democracy in Indonesia, and the extent to which they are related to satisfaction with and support for democracy. While some international survey research programs, such as Afrobarometer and Asian Barometer, do ask questions about conceptions of democracy, they typically suffer from two shortcomings. First, they do not account for the whole range of conceptions of democracy. Each of the five dimensions discussed above entails several components that cannot be thoroughly investigated by distilling them into just the handful of questions typically included in such large-scale survey programs. Second, survey questions on conceptions of democracy usually ask respondents to make a choice between different alternatives. In doing so, they may be forcing an artificial choice on respondents that could produce unreliable data, because the various dimensions of democracy, while distinct in theory, might overlap in the minds of ordinary citizens.

We therefore developed a novel instrument to measure conceptions of democracy in mass publics, based on two premises: first, that democracy can usefully be conceptualised as incorporating the five dimensions discussed above; and second, that these dimensions are not mutually exclusive. Drawing on the indicators used in the V-Dem project to measure the various dimensions of democracy, we designed a total of 36 survey items, each of which could be ascribed to a specific conception of democracy (five to the deliberative conception, eight to the egalitarian conception, ten to the electoral conception, eight to the liberal conception and five to the participatory conception).

We recruited a sample of 2,027 Indonesians of diverse demographic backgrounds as survey respondents and administered the survey through a web-based platform between July and August 2019. Respondents were prompted that people usually think about a number of different things as being important for a democracy. They were then asked their views on the importance of each of the 36 items (presented in randomised order) for a political regime to be considered a democracy. This approach permitted a fuller range of possibilities in terms of what conceptions of democracy might resonate with the Indonesian public, while at the same time allowing for the possibility that the various dimensions might be closely intertwined in public understandings of what democracies are and should do.

Table 9.1 reports the average scores for the 36 items on a scale ranging from 1 (not important at all for being a democracy) to 10 (very important). It shows that there is substantial variation across both items and dimensions. Most respondents agree that certain aspects are crucial for democracy (for instance, 'All adult citizens have the right to vote in elections'), while others are less essential (for example, 'People participate in politics and civic life beyond elections'). Overall, respondents are most likely to identify the egalitarian and liberal statements with democracy (with average scores of 8.01 and 7.98, respectively) and least likely to identify the participatory items with democracy (7.29), while the deliberative (7.86) and electoral (7.68) items fall in between. As the figures in the table indicate, however, there is also some variation across items within each dimension, indicating that respondents differentiate between aspects that are commonly identified as belonging to the same conception of democracy.[6]

These average scores alone, however, do not tell us if ordinary Indonesians think of democracy as incorporating our five distinct dimensions. To gain a better understanding of this, we perform factor analysis. Factor analysis is a data reduction technique for analysing patterns of variation among a series of variables, in this case our 36 items. In a nutshell, this technique examines correlations among the various items in order to identify categories of 'similar' statements, meaning that they may be attributable to a common underlying factor. This technique allows us to test whether survey responses can be reduced into groups that reflect our five dimensions of democracy.[7]

Results from factor analysis suggest that two distinct conceptions of democracy can be identified among the Indonesian public: egalitarian–liberal and participatory. To identify the meanings of democracy associated with these two dimensions, we turn again to Table 9.1 and examine the reported factor loadings for the 36 items, where higher values indicate a closer correlation between item and factor.

The first factor is closely associated with several egalitarian items (five of the ten items with loadings above 0.75 are found in this category), but also with some liberal ones (the statement 'Citizens have the same rights regardless of their race and ethnicity' has the highest loading of any of

---

6   For example, looking at the electoral dimension, respondents appear to consider the role of the media or the role of opposition parties to be less important to democracy than universal suffrage or the absence of intimidation during elections.

7   Factors are extracted using principal components.

Table 9.1   Conceptions of democracy in Indonesia: results from factor analysis

Dimension & item	Average score	Factor 1	Factor 2
Deliberative			
1 Decisions are taken on the basis of rational discussion	7.34	0.0869	0.2014
2 Decisions are taken to advance the common good, not to protect special interests		**0.5358**	−0.0064
3 Political adversaries respect each other even when they disagree	8.04	**0.6922**	−0.0116
4 When taking an important decision, all points of view are considered	8.12	**0.7375**	0.0488
5 The government explains its decisions to voters	7.80	**0.6992**	0.2572
Egalitarian			
6 Citizens have the same rights and opportunities in life, regardless of the social group they are from	8.01	0.3097	−0.0070
7 Government policies help to reduce the difference between the rich and the poor	7.72	0.4269	0.0060
8 Access to education is guaranteed for all	8.24	**0.7567**	−0.0439
9 Access to healthcare is guaranteed for all	8.27	**0.8238**	−0.0667
10 The government protects all citizens against poverty	8.12	**0.8340**	0.0432
11 The government ensures law and order for all	8.22	**0.8401**	−0.0064
12 An employment subsidy is given to those who do not have a job	7.45	**0.5880**	0.3331
13 Public goods such as roads and other infrastructure are provided	8.19	**0.8440**	0.0257
Electoral			
14 The media provides citizens with reliable information to judge the government	7.49	0.0996	0.1999
15 All adult citizens have the right to vote in elections	8.39	**0.7892**	0.0282
16 Opposition parties are free to operate, to criticise the government and to run for elections	7.16	−0.1798	**0.6456**
17 Elections are free from fraud	7.95	**0.5998**	−0.1162

Table 9.1   (continued)

Dimension & item	Average score	Factor 1	Factor 2
18 People are free to discuss politics in public	7.20	−0.0496	**0.6744**
19 Elections are free from intimidation	8.10	**0.7334**	−0.0026
20 People are free to demonstrate and protest	7.15	0.1347	**0.7120**
21 Elections are free from vote buying	7.97	**0.7716**	−0.0168
22 Political parties offer clear policy alternatives	7.63	**0.6402**	0.2931
23 Governments are punished in elections when they have done a bad job	7.91	**0.8156**	0.1319
Liberal			
24 Laws are applied in the same way for all citizens	7.85	0.2803	−0.0346
25 Citizens have the right to own property	7.84	0.3773	0.1780
26 Citizens have the same rights regardless of their sexual orientation	7.54	0.4205	0.2318
27 The courts can stop the government if it acts against the constitution	7.86	**0.6065**	0.2560
28 Men and women have equal rights	8.23	**0.6351**	0.1119
29 Citizens have the right to choose and profess any religion	8.38	**0.7779**	−0.0014
30 Citizens have the same rights regardless of their race and ethnicity	8.31	**0.8569**	−0.0296
31 The parliament keeps the government accountable for what it does	7.94	**0.7262**	0.1883
Participatory			
32 People participate in politics and civic life beyond elections	7.00	−0.1315	**0.5419**
33 Voters discuss politics with people they know before deciding how to vote	7.02	−0.0187	**0.6437**
34 Women participate in politics as much as men do	7.81	0.3973	0.3186
35 Citizens are interested in political issues	7.07	0.1803	**0.7351**
36 Citizens have the final say on the most important political issues by voting on them directly in referendums	7.61	**0.5550**	0.4471

Note: Factor analysis with N = 1,939. Principal-component factors are obtained with oblique rotation (promax).

the items associated with this factor). Factor 1 can thus be described as representing a multilayered, egalitarian–liberal conception of democracy.[8]

These findings resonate with previous research on Indonesian public opinion showing that egalitarian conceptions of democracy are widespread (Aspinall et al. 2020). In contrast to past research, however, our analysis suggests that the liberal and egalitarian views of democracy are intimately related. While these dimensions are distinct in the minds of political theorists and in the analysis of empirically oriented political scientists, they are not so clearly distinguished in the minds of Indonesian people, who think of them as being inextricably linked. Furthermore, scholars of voting behaviour have argued that support for democracy in Indonesia is contingent on government performance, or on the democratic regime's ability to deliver desirable socioeconomic outcomes (Mujani et al. 2018). We find that the relationship between performance and democracy is even closer. When it comes to expressing a view of what democracy means, Indonesians see egalitarian elements related to socioeconomic development as being constitutive of the concept of democracy itself.

The second factor reflects the participatory dimension, with three of the five participatory items having high loadings. This factor is also closely associated with two items from the electoral dimension measuring informal aspects of participation: 'People are free to demonstrate and protest' and 'People are free to discuss politics in public'. The prominence of this dimension in public opinion points to the importance of political participation in the minds of many Indonesians. While some scholars of Indonesia portray the country's politics as being dominated by oligarchs (Hadiz and Robison 2013; Winters 2013)—and indeed the V-Dem scores for participatory democracy are the lowest among all five dimensions of democracy—many people continue to see political participation and civic engagement as central to democratic life. These findings resonate with analyses highlighting the importance of civic engagement for the resilience of Indonesian democracy (Lussier and Fish 2012), and indicate the continuing relevance of the legacy of informal, progressive politics in Indonesia (Dibley and Ford 2019).

---

8   Some items representing the deliberative conception of democracy, however, also load strongly on this first factor.

WHAT EXPLAINS DIFFERENT CONCEPTIONS OF DEMOCRACY?

Having established that two dominant conceptions of democracy exist among the Indonesian public, one egalitarian–liberal and the other participatory, we now turn to the question of variation. Do these two conceptions of democracy vary significantly across social groups, or according to political preferences and ideology? To answer this question, we estimate simple multiple regression models that test the sociodemographic, attitudinal and political factors that may explain variation in conceptions of democracy.[9] The results of this exercise are reported in Table 9.2.

First, we find that education and age are positively associated with both conceptions of democracy. Respondents who are better educated and older are more likely to have a clearly defined conception of democracy, be it egalitarian–liberal or participatory. The association with education suggests that conceptions of democracy may be related to political sophistication or knowledge about politics, as highly educated individuals may be better able to appreciate the meanings of the 36 indicators and evaluate them. The association with age may indicate that conceptions of democracy develop and consolidate over time as part of a person's political socialisation process, although there may also be historical factors that drive differences across cohorts, such as differences in the political, socioeconomic and technological conditions in which voters first develop their conceptions of democracy. Sociodemographic factors therefore have an important effect on conceptions of democracy, in that they determine whether a person has a coherent idea of what democracy is about. However, they alone do not tell us *which* conception of democracy a person might have.

Second, two ideological orientations that loom large in Indonesian politics, namely political Islam and populism, are associated with noteworthy variation in conceptions of democracy. Respondents who

---

9 Respondents are grouped into four age groups, five educational levels and five income brackets, as reported in Table 9.2. Gender and region are measured with a binary variable (0 = male, 1 = female; 0 = urban, 1 = rural). Support for the incumbent president, Joko Widodo (Jokowi), is measured by asking respondents if they are satisfied with how the president is handling his job, and life satisfaction (or happiness) by asking respondents to rate their level of life satisfaction on a scale ranging from 1 to 10, where higher values denote higher levels of satisfaction. In the case of political Islam and populism, we follow existing work that has measured these two constructs in the Indonesian context (Fossati 2019; Fossati and Mietzner 2019).

Table 9.2   Determinants of conceptions of democracy

Variable	Egalitarian–liberal conception (1)	Participatory conception (2)
Age group = 2, 25–34	0.0220 (0.0501)	0.0495 (0.0515)
Age group = 3, 35–44	0.155*** (0.0573)	0.115* (0.0589)
Age group = 4, 45 or older	0.281*** (0.0715)	0.214*** (0.0735)
Gender	0.0779* (0.0420)	−0.0470 (0.0431)
Muslim	0.0969* (0.0585)	0.105* (0.0602)
Rural area	−0.115** (0.0460)	−0.0817* (0.0472)
Education = 2, junior secondary school	0.226** (0.0990)	−0.0559 (0.102)
Education = 3, senior secondary school	0.345*** (0.0891)	0.158* (0.0916)
Education = 4, diploma	0.398*** (0.102)	0.224** (0.105)
Education = 5, college/postgraduate	0.403*** (0.106)	0.291*** (0.109)
Income = 2, Rp 2,000,000–3,999,000	0.0452 (0.0617)	−0.0867 (0.0634)
Income = 3, Rp 4,000,000–5,999,000	−0.0507 (0.0605)	−0.165*** (0.0622)
Income = 4, Rp 6,000,000–7,999,000	−0.0611 (0.0780)	−0.0446 (0.0802)
Income = 5, Rp 8,000,000 or more	0.0498 (0.0712)	−0.0391 (0.0732)
Jokowi	0.00581 (0.0248)	0.0317 (0.0255)
Political Islam	−0.0970*** (0.0190)	0.0102 (0.0195)
Populism	0.0340 (0.0213)	0.0885*** (0.0219)
Happiness	0.173*** (0.00943)	0.158*** (0.00969)
Constant	−1.623*** (0.170)	−1.776*** (0.175)
Observations	2,027	2,027
R^2	0.209	0.164
Log-likelihood	−2593	−2649

Note: Models include fixed effects for islands (not reported). Standard errors are in parentheses.
*** = $p < 0.01$; ** = $p < 0.05$; * = $p < 0.10$.

could be characterised as Islamist (that is, they believe strongly that the Indonesian government should prioritise Islam over other religions) are much less likely than pluralist individuals to subscribe to the conception of democracy captured by the egalitarian–liberal factor. This reassures us that this dimension can indeed be labelled liberal as well as egalitarian, since previous research has highlighted a connection between Islamism and illiberalism in both political discourse (Hadiz 2018) and mass attitudes (Fossati 2019).

Populism, meanwhile, is positively associated with the participatory conception of democracy. Populists tend to perceive the social–political world as being divided into two homogeneous camps of elites and masses, and they generally hold a negative view of elites (Fossati and Mietzner 2019). According to our results, such people are more likely to have a strong participatory conception of democracy. One interpretation of this result is that populist Indonesians are more critical of prevailing, established views of democracy, especially the notion of consensus building and compromise making extolled by deliberative democrats. Instead, populists value direct participation in political life beyond elections, through civic organisations and community meetings.

SATISFACTION WITH AND SUPPORT FOR DEMOCRACY

Finally, we explore the implications of conceptions of democracy for how Indonesians evaluate their political regime. To do so, we rely on the responses to three questions from our survey.

The first question asks whether respondents believe Indonesia to be a democracy. Specifically, respondents are asked whether Indonesia is best described as: (1) not a democracy; (2) a democracy with major problems; (3) a democracy with minor problems; or (4) a full democracy. Most respondents in our sample are quite critical of the state of democracy in contemporary Indonesia, with more than half describing their country either as not a democracy (5.3 per cent) or as a democracy with serious flaws (45 per cent). A minority of respondents consider Indonesia to be a full democracy (15 per cent), and the remainder (34.7 per cent) believe Indonesia to be a democracy with minor problems.

The second question asks whether respondents are satisfied with how democracy is working in Indonesia. Again, four choices are provided, ranging from 'very dissatisfied' to 'very satisfied'. The answers to this question overlap only partially with the responses to the previous one:

a clear majority of 61 per cent of the sample is satisfied or very satisfied with how democracy is working in their country, while a smaller share is either somewhat dissatisfied (30 per cent) or very dissatisfied (9 per cent).

Finally, we ask about support for democracy as a political regime with the following question: 'Do you agree or disagree with the following statement: "Democracy may have its problems, but it is still the best form of government for Indonesia" '. Support for democracy is very high in Indonesia, as several studies have shown (Fossati et al. 2017). Our sample aligns with this consensus: 24.7 per cent of the respondents strongly agree with this statement, 61.0 per cent agree and only 14.3 per cent disagree or strongly disagree.

Table 9.3 estimates the effect of conceptions of democracy on evaluations of Indonesia's political regime. The first two columns (assessments of whether Indonesia is a democracy, and satisfaction with how democracy is working in Indonesia) show that both the egalitarian–liberal and participatory conceptions of democracy are significantly associated with evaluations of Indonesia's political system—but in different directions. Thus, respondents with a stronger egalitarian–liberal conception of democracy are less likely to believe that Indonesia is a democracy or to be satisfied with how democracy is working, whereas respondents with a participatory conception of democracy are more likely to describe the current political system in Indonesia as a democracy, and to be satisfied with it.

These strong empirical associations suggest that conceptions of democracy are crucial in shaping public satisfaction with democracy. Indonesians who are dissatisfied with their country's democracy are more likely to have a strong egalitarian–liberal conception of democracy than to view democracy as a matter of informal participation. Yet, the third model shows us that this bifurcation in the relationship between conception of and satisfaction with democracy does not extend to *support* for democracy. Both conceptions of democracy are positively associated with the belief that democracy, while imperfect, is the best form of government for Indonesia. Having strong, clearly defined ideas about what it means to be a democracy is therefore conducive to higher levels of public support for democracy as a suitable political regime for Indonesia, regardless of what the specific conception of democracy may be.

Table 9.3   *Effect of conceptions of democracy on evaluations of Indonesia's political system*

Variable	Believe Indonesia is a democracy (1)	Satisfied with how democracy is working (2)	Support Indonesia's democracy (3)
Egalitarian–liberal	−0.244***	−0.280***	0.150**
	(0.0600)	(0.0609)	(0.0635)
Participatory	0.262***	0.371***	0.265***
	(0.0584)	(0.0598)	(0.0622)
Age group = 2, 25–34	0.0505	0.0984	−0.0794
	(0.111)	(0.113)	(0.119)
Age group = 3, 35–44	−0.00229	0.0727	0.0508
	(0.127)	(0.129)	(0.136)
Age group = 4, 45 or older	0.159	0.309*	0.0220
	(0.158)	(0.160)	(0.170)
Gender	−0.348***	−0.211**	0.0443
	(0.0934)	(0.0945)	(0.0992)
Muslim	0.418***	−0.0261	−0.390***
	(0.129)	(0.134)	(0.139)
Rural area	0.0924	−0.0704	−0.0970
	(0.101)	(0.103)	(0.109)
Education = 2, junior secondary school	−0.00972	−0.0251	0.253
	(0.226)	(0.231)	(0.237)
Education = 3, senior secondary school	0.0204	−0.246	0.230
	(0.205)	(0.209)	(0.214)
Education = 4, diploma	0.0521	−0.244	−0.0473
	(0.233)	(0.237)	(0.245)
Education = 5, college/postgraduate	−0.259	−0.0656	0.435*
	(0.242)	(0.247)	(0.255)
Income = 2, Rp 2,000,000–3,999,000	−0.208	−0.0427	0.161
	(0.136)	(0.138)	(0.145)
Income = 3, Rp 4,000,000–5,999,000	−0.522***	−0.126	0.104
	(0.135)	(0.136)	(0.143)
Income = 4, Rp 6,000,000–7,999,000	−0.304*	−0.227	0.323*
	(0.172)	(0.174)	(0.185)
Income = 5, Rp 8,000,000 or more	−0.372**	−0.319**	0.458***
	(0.157)	(0.161)	(0.170)
Jokowi	0.831***	1.290***	0.619***
	(0.0606)	(0.0642)	(0.0620)
Political Islam	−0.0221	0.128***	−0.00573
	(0.0430)	(0.0439)	(0.0462)
Populism	0.0799*	0.142***	0.197***
	(0.0476)	(0.0491)	(0.0526)
Happiness	0.102***	0.124***	0.0647***
	(0.0238)	(0.0239)	(0.0250)
Observations	2,027	2,027	2,027
Log-likelihood	−2147	−2025	−1811

Note: Models include fixed effects for islands (not reported). Standard errors are in parentheses.
*** = $p < 0.01$; ** = $p < 0.05$; * $p < 0.10$.

CONCLUSIONS

This chapter adopted a conceptual framework that treats democracy as a multidimensional construct and applied it to the Indonesian case, studying both the trajectory of Indonesia's democratic development over the past 20 years and conceptions of democracy among the mass public. Distinguishing between the various dimensions of democracy should sharpen our ability to identify areas of weakness in the practice of Indonesian democracy that risk fuelling public grievances and undermining democratic governance. Our analysis of public opinion suggests that this is a fruitful avenue for further research, as conceptions of democracy have important implications for democratic consolidation from a public opinion perspective.

It is often argued that Indonesians view democracy primarily in terms of policy outcomes—that their support for democracy is contingent on democracy's ability to deliver economic development (Mujani et al. 2018). Our first contribution to the debate is to suggest that this view should be reconsidered. If we allow that various conceptions of democracy are not alternatives to one another, and that ordinary citizens can simultaneously hold different views about what a democracy is and should do, then a different picture of popular democratic preferences emerges. Policy outcomes are important, but ordinary Indonesians do not distinguish between the egalitarian and liberal conceptions of democracy: rather, they see them as being inseparable. There is also, however, a segment of the public that acknowledges a different conception of democracy, which we have defined as participatory. This indicates that there is indeed some diversity in how Indonesians conceive of democracy.

Our second contribution is to show that there is an association between conceptions of democracy and different ideological persuasions: Islamists are less likely to embrace liberal egalitarianism, and populists are more likely to conceive of democracy in participatory terms.

Finally, we demonstrate that different conceptions of democracy have implications for how Indonesians make judgements about the quality and performance of democratic government. While a strong majority of Indonesians remain committed to democracy as a political regime, many are dissatisfied with how democracy is being practised. Indonesians who hold a strong participatory view of democracy are more likely to be satisfied with how democracy works, while those who see democracy in egalitarian–liberal terms are less likely to be satisfied. This is surprising, as the V-Dem data indicate that the participatory dimension is the most poorly consolidated one—instead, prominent analyses of Indonesia's democracy cast it as a regime dominated by predatory elites (Hadiz and

Robison 2013). Yet, we find that those who see democracy primarily as a matter of public participation are more, rather than less, satisfied with Indonesia's democracy. This finding calls for further research on the practice of public participation in Indonesian democracy, especially its informal dimensions. Overall, however, when asked whether other types of regime would be preferable to a democratic one, Indonesians reaffirm their commitment to the status quo. For most Indonesians, appreciation for the democratic progress made so far seems to trump frustration about the work that still needs to be done.

REFERENCES

Aspinall, E., D. Fossati, B. Muhtadi and E. Warburton. 2020. 'Elites, masses, and democratic decline in Indonesia'. *Democratization* 27(4): 505–26.

Barber, B. 2003. *Strong Democracy: Participatory Politics for a New Age.* Berkeley, CA: University of California Press.

Chu, Y. and M. Huang. 2010. 'The meanings of democracy: solving an Asian puzzle'. *Journal of Democracy* 21(4): 114–22.

Cohen, J. 1997. 'Procedure and substance in deliberative democracy'. In *Deliberative Democracy: Essays on Reason and Politics*, edited by J. Bohman and W. Rehg, 407–38. Cambridge: MIT Press.

Coppedge, M. and J. Gerring. 2011. 'Conceptualizing and measuring democracy: a new approach'. *Perspectives on Politics* 9(2): 247–67.

Coppedge, M., J. Gerring, C.H. Knutsen, S.I. Lindberg, J. Teorell, D. Altman, M. Bernhard, et al. 2019. 'V-Dem dataset—version 9'. Gothenburg: Varieties of Democracy Institute. https://doi.org/10.23696/vdemcy19

Dibley, T. and M. Ford 2019. *Activists in Transition: Progressive Politics in Democratic Indonesia.* Ithaca, NY: Cornell University Press.

Fawcett, E. 2018. *Liberalism: The Life of an Idea.* Princeton, NJ: Princeton University Press.

Fishkin, J.S. 1991. *Democracy and Deliberation: New Directions for Democratic Reform.* New Haven, CT: Yale University Press.

Fossati, D. 2019. 'The resurgence of ideology in Indonesia: political Islam, *aliran* and political behavior'. *Journal of Current Southeast Asian Affairs* 38(2): 119–48.

Fossati, D. and M. Mietzner. 2019. 'Analyzing Indonesia's populist electorate: demographic, ideological and attitudinal trends'. *Asian Survey* 59(5): 769–94.

Fossati, D., Y.-F. Hui and S.D. Negara. 2017. 'The Indonesia National Survey Project: economy, society and politics'. *Trends in Southeast Asia* No. 10. Singapore: ISEAS – Yusof Ishak Institute.

Hadiz, V.R. 2018. 'Imagine all the people? Mobilising Islamic populism for right-wing politics in Indonesia'. *Journal of Contemporary Asia* 48(4): 566–83.

Hadiz, V.R. and R. Robison. 2013. 'The political economy of oligarchy and the reorganization of power in Indonesia'. *Indonesia* 96(1): 35–57.

Huang, M., Y. Chang and Y. Chu. 2008. 'Identifying sources of democratic legitimacy: a multilevel analysis'. *Electoral Studies* 27(1): 45–62.

Huber, E., D. Rueschemeyer and J.D. Stephens. 1997. 'The paradoxes of contemporary democracy: formal, participatory, and social dimensions'. *Comparative Politics* 29(3): 323–42.

Lührmann, A. and S.I. Lindberg. 2019. 'A third wave of autocratization is here: what is new about it?' *Democratization* 26(7): 1,095–113.

Lussier, D.N. and M.S. Fish. 2012. 'Indonesia: the benefits of civic engagement'. *Journal of Democracy* 23(1): 70–84.

Magalhães, P.C. 2014. 'Government effectiveness and support for democracy'. *European Journal of Political Research* 53(1): 77–97.

Mietzner, M. 2013. 'Fighting the hellhounds: pro-democracy activists and party politics in post-Suharto Indonesia'. *Journal of Contemporary Asia* 43(1): 28–50.

Mujani, S. and R.W. Liddle. 2015. 'Indonesia's democratic performance: a popular assessment'. *Japanese Journal of Political Science* 16(2): 210–26.

Mujani, S., R.W. Liddle and K. Ambardi. 2018. *Voting Behavior in Indonesia since Democratization: Critical Democrats*. Cambridge: Cambridge University Press.

Przeworski, A., M.E. Alvarez, J.A. Cheibub and F. Limongi. 2000. *Democracy and Development: Political Institutions and Well-being in the World, 1950–1990*. Cambridge: Cambridge University Press.

Schumpeter, J.A. 1942. *Capitalism, Socialism and Democracy*. London: Routledge.

Warburton, E. and E. Aspinall. 2019. 'Explaining Indonesia's democratic regression: structure, agency and popular opinion'. *Contemporary Southeast Asia: A Journal of International and Strategic Affairs* 41(2): 255–85. https://www.muse.jhu.edu/article/732138

Winters, J.A. 2013. 'Oligarchy and democracy in Indonesia'. *Indonesia* 96(1): 11–33.

Young, I.M. 2002. *Inclusion and Democracy*. Oxford: Oxford University Press.

PART 4

Democratic Institutions

10 Indonesian parties revisited: systemic exclusivism, electoral personalisation and declining intraparty democracy

Marcus Mietzner

As key actors in democratic states, political parties are necessarily part of the crisis that is affecting democracy (Cyr 2017; Lisi 2018). Even in the established democracies of the West, the increasing inability of parties to represent the aspirations of a broad spectrum of voters has given rise to anti-party, anti-establishment populism (Lochocki 2017). In newer democracies, this trend has been even more pronounced, with the weakness of institutional checks and balances making it hard for such polities to constrain authoritarian populists in the way that most established democracies still manage to do (Lupu 2016). Rodrigo Duterte in the Philippines, whose drug war has killed thousands of people, and Narendra Modi in India, who initiated citizenship policies that discriminated against Muslims, have used widespread anti-system sentiments to pursue illiberal agendas that might have been softened or prevented by a stronger tradition of party-based deliberative democracy. In the Philippines and India, but elsewhere too, the crisis of democracy is thus primarily a crisis of conventional party politics (Invernizzi-Accetti and Wolkenstein 2017).

Indonesia is no exception in this regard. In both the 2014 and 2019 elections, a moderate populist (Joko Widodo) faced off against a radical one (Prabowo Subianto), and while the moderate prevailed (Aspinall and Mietzner 2014, 2019), the absence of established party actors in both presidential races highlighted the parties' increasing marginalisation and deterioration. Under President Widodo (Jokowi), the trend of party and party system weakening continued, and expressed itself in three major ways. First, it became apparent that the post-Suharto party system was excluding significant segments of the electorate by erecting ever-increasing hurdles to the formation of new parties. Second, the entrenchment of the proportional, open party-list electoral system led to an escalation in the personalisation of elections, with parties forced to pick non-party figures to represent them in both executive and legislative elections. And third, the already weak procedures governing intraparty democracy were hollowed out further, with even formerly contested party leaderships now often in the hands of incumbents who could easily engineer reappointment to their posts. Overall, then, Indonesia's party system has become less representative, while the parties have been institutionally weakened.

To be sure, some of these trends were already in place before the 2014 elections, but they have accelerated significantly since then. In a 2013 book, I analysed the state of the party system and its parties at the time (Mietzner 2013). I concluded that while Indonesian parties were not substantially weaker than many of their new-democracy counterparts in Latin America and Eastern Europe, they faced two major threats that could undermine them—and democracy—in the future. The first was the absence of a functioning party financing system, which made parties dependent on oligarchs and corrupt fundraising methods. This dysfunction in the party financing regime was both deliberate and debilitating, with many elites preferring informal patronage channels to institutionalised and transparent fundraising mechanisms. This defect also aggravated the impact of the second threat: the repercussions of the open party-list electoral system introduced in 2009. Under this system, legislative candidates had to use personalised rather than party-based campaign styles, driving up costs and distancing parties from the electoral process. In combination, I asserted back then, these two trends could seriously harm what was otherwise a relatively stable party system with a number of core parties that were better institutionalised than many others in East and Southeast Asia (Mietzner 2013: 43, 239–40).

This chapter reviews post-2014 developments in Indonesia's political parties against some of the analyses offered in my 2013 book. It emphasises that the decline of parties as leading actors of political representation has been faster, and more comprehensive, than I anticipated at the time. Based on an analysis of the three issues pinpointed above—exclusivism in the party system, personalisation even of legislative campaigns, and erosion of already feeble procedures governing intraparty democracy—the chapter concludes that the defects of party system and party organisation are no longer just potential threats to democracy. Rather, they are already seriously damaging it, and thus speeding up the process of democratic regression in Indonesia. At the same time, the chapter highlights that many of these deficiencies were caused by institutional decisions made in the 2000s and 2010s—and thus could be addressed by corrective regulatory reforms focused on restrengthening the role of parties in democratic life.

THE PARTY SYSTEM: REDUCED REPRESENTATIVENESS

A main point of my 2013 book was that, measured by a wide range of quantitative indicators of party system institutionalisation, Indonesia's party system did not exhibit signs of an imminent crisis. Indeed, Indonesia compared moderately well to other young democracies, including in Latin America and Eastern Europe. For instance, electoral volatility (the net electoral change in the party vote between two consecutive elections) was lower in Indonesia than in the latter two regions; turnout in elections was high and stable; support for both the principle and practice of democracy remained solid; and the number of effective political parties was comparatively high but did not fluctuate wildly. The only two indicators that hinted at an increasing alienation between the electorate and parties were the low number of citizens who identified closely with a party (which dropped from 86 per cent in 1999 to 14 per cent in 2012), and the low trust voters generally placed in political parties (Mietzner 2013: 44). But both indicators had fallen not just in Indonesia. They had collapsed around the world, pointing to a structural shift in global voter–party relations rather than a specific problem in Indonesia.

Not much has changed in Indonesia's quantitative indicators of party system institutionalisation since 2013. Electoral volatility remained virtually unchanged in 2014, at 26.3 (Higashikata and Kawamura 2015: 36), and even improved in 2019, to 12.7 (Kawamura and Higashikata, forthcoming); turnout is slightly up, reaching a record for presidential elections in 2019 (at 79 per cent); support for democracy is high— 76 per cent of Indonesians backed it as a principle in 2017, and 70 per cent were satisfied with the way it was being practised (LSI 2017: 19, 105); and while the number of effective political parties increased in 2014 (from 6.2 to 8.2), it decreased again in 2019 (to 7.5) (Gallagher 2019). Levels of party identification and citizen distrust of parties were also almost unchanged (LSI 2017: 33). In one sense, this continued stability of key positive indicators (and the stagnation of the negative ones) is important: it helps to explain why Indonesia, despite its democratic *regression*, has not experienced a democratic *reversal*.

Yet, in another, more nuanced sense, the stability of the indicators has masked distortive trends in the party system that are difficult to quantify. Most crucially, behind the façade of stable institutionalisation, large segments of the electorate were gradually being excluded from the party system. This affected not just the political left and liberal voters, who have had no natural home in the party system since the destruction of the Communist Party in 1965–66. In a more recent sign of the growing alienation of a key electorate from the party system, conservative Muslims began to mobilise outside it. This trend became visible in the Islamist mobilisation against the Christian Chinese governor of Jakarta, Basuki Tjahaja Purnama (known as Ahok), in late 2016. In what came as a surprise to many observers (and certainly to the government), about a million people filled the streets of Jakarta to express support for Islamist ideas. For instance, the protesters insisted that non-Muslims should not occupy political leadership posts, and that the Qur'an should take precedence over the constitution. Such demands had previously all but disappeared from the political discourse of mainstream parties—including the Islamic parties. Foreign journalists, too, seemed astonished to gain a glimpse of a puritan Muslim electorate they thought had become more moderate through its inclusion in the post-Suharto party system (Cochrane 2016).

Polling research carried out during and after the anti-Ahok demonstrations showed that many of the conservative Muslims who had mobilised during the protests would vote for a more Islamist party if such a choice were available. In an August 2017 poll, 13.3 per cent of Muslim respondents (or 11.7 per cent of the whole sample) stated that they would cast a ballot for the ultraconservative Islamic Defenders Front (Front Pembela Islam, FPI) if it were allowed to stand as a party in elections (LSI 2017: 121). FPI was one of the initiators of the anti-Ahok demonstrations, and its leader, Habib Rizieq Shihab, was the public face of the movement. If this polling result had carried over into the 2019 elections, a hypothetical FPI party would have become the fourth-largest party, with about 70 seats in parliament. Further polling results showed that many FPI supporters had chosen not to vote in previous elections (Mietzner and Muhtadi 2018: 488), underlining the alienation of this right-wing, Islamist constituency from the existing party system.

The Indonesian party system, then, has become increasingly unrepresentative, excluding both the left and right ends of the political spectrum. The reason for this trend lies in an initially well-meaning decision by the designers of the post-Suharto party system. In order to promote inclusiveness and moderation, they required all electoral parties to have branches across the archipelago (in 1999, in half of all provinces, and in half of the districts in those provinces). This was done to prevent the rise of ethnic parties, which had helped to splinter the party system in the 1950s (Reilly 2007). Moreover, lawmakers obligated parties to have ideological foundations that were in line with the state ideology, Pancasila. Intended to make parties ideologically pluralist in outlook, this regulation echoed a deep-seated anxiety that democracy could be brought down by ideological divisions, as it had in the 1950s.

For about a decade and a half, it *appeared* as if this approach was serving Indonesia well. It delivered the stability expressed in many indicators of party system institutionalisation, and it helped the country to portray itself to the outside world as a moderate Muslim democracy. But by 2014, the long-term unviability of the forced-moderation paradigm had become palpable. There were two main triggers for this. First, the decision-makers of the mid-2010s escalated the initial 1999 model of party regulation to a new level. For the 2014 elections, parties were required to have regional branches in 100 per cent of provinces, and in 75 per cent of the districts in those provinces—a unique regime in the democratic world. Given the stability of the overall system at the time, it is implausible that increased concern over ethnic or ideological fragmentation was the primary motivation for this increase in the hurdle to new party formation. Rather, it was the self-interest of incumbent party elites to exclude new competitors that led to the increased barriers. In the same vein, party and state elites increased the threshold for a party to enter parliament from 2.5 per cent in 2009 to 3.5 per cent in 2014 and 4.0 per cent in 2019. Thus, what had initially been an attempt at positive electoral engineering was now a transparent and self-preserving manoeuvre by party leaders that distorted the representativeness of the party and electoral systems.

The second trend that increasingly isolated Indonesia's middle-of-the-road party system from the electorate was the movement of many Muslim parties into the ideological centre. Motivated by President Susilo Bambang Yudhoyono's success as a centrist political figure who appealed to both pluralist and Islamist voters, and guided by the existing regulations on party ideologies, Muslim-based parties such as the Prosperous Justice Party (Partai Keadilan Sejahtera, PKS) shifted in the early 2010s from their original Islamist position to a more pragmatic, moderate posture. While praised by many as a further step towards stabilising the party system—including by this author (Mietzner 2008)—the end effect of this moderation was that principled Islamist voters were no longer accommodated by the party system and drifted off to non-party actors. Prabowo's strong showing in the 2014 presidential election was a first sign of the increasing support for politicians who promoted Islamist interests not through a party platform, but through a populist campaign. Rizieq's leadership of the anti-Ahok movement then made it perfectly clear that the epicentre of political Islamism was no longer located in Indonesia's Islamic parties. PKS, together with the United Development Party (Partai Persatuan Pembangunan, PPP) and the Crescent Moon and Star Party (Partai Bulan Bintang, PBB), had become part of the mainstream (Tomsa 2012)—or, as their former supporters saw it, had been domesticated by the establishment.

While the limits imposed on new party entries and the ideological shift of many parties to the centre were in themselves undermining the representativeness of the party system, the impact of these trends was worsened by the dysfunction of the political financing regime. Given that this regime was essentially based on the necessity of self-funding, only oligarchs could clear the institutional hurdles set for new party registrations—and they viewed political centrism as the most attractive option available to them. The Islamist, leftist and liberal-progressive constituencies, which generally lacked oligarchic backing, thus found it almost impossible to create new parties. Consequently, the new parties that *did* get approved in 2014 and 2019 were those founded or backed by tycoons with a moderate political orientation—the very parties that Indonesia already had in excess. Surya Paloh, a media tycoon, saw his NasDem party enter parliament in 2014, and fellow media mogul Hary Tanoesoedibjo tried the same with his Perindo party in 2019—but failed. In a telling sign of the increasingly closed nature of Indonesia's contemporary party system, none of the four new, tycoon-funded parties that made it past the high entry requirements cleared the raised parliamentary threshold in 2019. Significantly, this included the Indonesian Solidarity Party (Partai Solidaritas Indonesia, PSI), the only quasi-liberal party in the 2019 elections. It had the backing of a wealthy (and unusually progressive) financier, but it too was too weak to overcome the obstacles erected to keep new parties out (Abdulsalam 2018).

These developments left the Indonesian party system of the late 2010s in an ambiguous state. Viewed from the outside, the system continues to show signs of stability—especially when compared with many of its Southeast Asian neighbours. But its foundations are in the process of crumbling, as the system is failing to capture a wide variety of electoral constituencies. Currently, Indonesia has a party system that many of its centrist elites *wish* were representative of Indonesia's political reality— but it isn't. Especially since the mid-2010s, groups have come to the fore that rebel against the party system's prescribed centrism and its built-in privileging of oligarchs who alone have the necessary cash to found new parties. Having been excluded from the party system, these groups instead mobilise on the streets (as in the case of the 2016–17 Islamist rallies) or withdraw into absenteeism (such as the human rights activists calling for a boycott of the 2019 elections). These forms of extra-institutional mobilisation and activist disengagement have both contributed, in different but meaningful ways, to the visible decline of democratic culture in the late Yudhoyono and early Jokowi periods.

THE PARTIES: ELECTORAL PERSONALISATION

We have seen above how ever-increasing (and ever more costly) party registration regulations, coinciding with a trend towards electoral centrism under Yudhoyono, limited the entry of new political parties to a certain party type. This type comprises parties that are founded by tycoons to serve their own political interests, and that are equipped with catch-all policy platforms designed to maximise the vote base. To call these parties 'presidentialist', as has often been done in the past (Mietzner 2013: 54), is now somewhat misleading, as only a few of them have any realistic prospect of delivering the presidency to their founders. In most cases, they have opened the door to cabinet representation or involvement in government distribution of patronage. Thus, they are personalist parties with a limited life expectancy (the only incumbent party to fall short of the 2019 parliamentary threshold was Hanura, founded by former armed forces commander Wiranto). Whereas the party market has been flooded with such personalist–centrist parties, the electorate itself has moved in different directions—some voters have shifted to the liberal fringe, but even more have moved to the conservative Islamic end of the politico-ideological spectrum.

This personalisation at the party system level—initiated by the 2004 change in the electoral system to direct presidential elections, and deepened by the tightening of party entry rules—has found its equivalent in internal party organisation. In my 2013 book, I had already noted an increasing personalisation of electoral campaigns that was weakening parties organisationally (Mietzner 2013: 43). Driven by changes in the electoral system, an increase in campaign costs and the absence of a functioning political financing regime, parties were forced to turn more and more to party outsiders to run for them in elections. While this trend began during the 2004 presidential elections, it consolidated in 2005 with the switch to direct elections of local government heads. This new local elections arrangement replaced the previous system of election by party-controlled legislatures. In post-2005 local elections, parties retained the authority to nominate candidates, but often lacked cadres with sufficient funds, networks and popularity to run for them. Consequently, party leaders handed nominations to bureaucrats, businesspeople and retired military and police officers who had the resources and name recognition to be successful in elections (Buehler 2010). In order to conceal their non-party status, candidates who succeeded in becoming local government heads were often asked to chair local party boards, giving the impression that the parties were in charge.

This shift away from parties towards personalities as the key actors in elections accelerated further in 2009, when the system of legislative elections changed to a proportional, open party-list regime. In 1999 and 2004, closed and semi-open party-list systems had been in place, leading to party-based legislative campaigns. In the 2009 elections, the open party-list system was practised for the first time; in this system, voters are able not only to vote for parties, but also to express their preference for a candidate from the party they support. If parties win seats, these are given to the candidates with the highest numbers of individual votes. This change, which was introduced abruptly by a Constitutional Court decision several months before the 2009 elections, moved the focus of campaigns from interparty competition to intraparty contestation between individual candidates. In terms of campaign organisation, this meant that candidates had to highlight their personal characteristics rather than party platforms; that nominees had to entirely self-fund their campaigns; and that vote buying became rampant, as it was one of the most effective ways to beat candidates from the same party who were indistinguishable in policy and ideological terms.

While the 2009 elections (the last national polls covered in my 2013 book) had already altered the way legislative elections were fought, the abrupt manner in which the open party-list system was introduced had mitigated its impact somewhat. Its full repercussions would only be felt in the 2014 and 2019 elections. The 2014 elections were the first in which the open party-list system was used from the very beginning of the electoral process (that is, from the nomination of candidates). As a consequence, the legislative campaign was almost entirely decentralised, with self-funded candidates concentrating on winning their own seats rather than connecting with the broader goals of their parties (Aspinall and Sukmajati 2016). Campaign posters, which in 1999 and 2004 had prominently featured party symbols as well as national party leaders and slogans, now highlighted the candidate's personal background and individual promises—party symbols were far less conspicuous. One of the most important results of this shift towards personalised campaigns was a significant increase in vote buying from 2009. Indeed, the 2014 elections made Indonesia the country with the third-highest level of vote buying in the world (Muhtadi 2018).

The 2019 elections saw a further loosening of the ties between parties and their legislative candidates. Discouraged by the high costs of campaigning and the big personal risk associated with losing, many local party leaders refrained from seeking candidacies for themselves and instead invited applications from outside their parties. Interviewed during the campaign in March 2019, the chair of the Golkar branch in the subdistrict of Banda Islands (Maluku) explained that he had cast a wide net when trying to recruit candidates for the Central Maluku district parliament. 'I can't afford to run', he said, 'and not many high-quality Golkar members here want to run either. At the same time, those cadres who do want to run don't have good prospects of winning because they are not wealthy enough or are unpopular.'[1] The local branch ended up picking those non-party candidates who had the best chance of winning— which in most cases meant having sufficient financial resources and/or established personal networks within the local constituency. The problem for parties, therefore, was not the inability to find candidates in general— parties filed approximately 245,000 nominations at all levels in the 2019 elections. Rather, many parties struggled to find willing (and capable) candidates from within their own ranks, thus pushing them to opt for non-party nominees.

Not surprisingly, then, many of these external recruits refused to campaign for the presidential candidate supported by the national chapters of their nominating parties. This was despite the fact that the 2019 elections were the first in Indonesia's history in which legislative and presidential elections were held on the same day. (Previously, legislative elections were held before the presidential ballot.) Most party leaderships had hoped for a presidential coattail effect, whereby presidential candidates lift the vote shares of their nominating parties. Hence, most parties ordered their legislative candidates to adorn their campaign posters with a picture of the party's presidential nominee. But in the eyes of the majority of parliamentary nominees, for whom victory or defeat could rest on a handful of votes, tying themselves to a particular presidential candidate in a deeply polarised electoral landscape was disadvantageous; most saw such an approach as more likely to alienate potential voters than to attract them. Therefore, few campaign posters featured presidential candidates, and the coattail effect was minimal.

Naturally, there were exceptions to this pattern. The better-institutionalised parties, such as PKS and the Indonesian Democratic Party of Struggle (Partai Demokrasi Indonesia-Perjuangan, PDI-P), were

---

1   Interview, Banda Neira, 15 March 2019.

more successful in nominating their own cadres and forcing them to comply with strategic orders from party headquarters. But even in the case of these parties, the number of party outsiders among legislative nominees increased over the years, and many decided not to include a picture of the party's presidential candidate in their campaign material.

The increasing dealignment between parties and candidates was also reflected in voter attitudes and behaviour. When asked during the 2019 campaign who they would support in the upcoming legislative elections, many voters responded by mentioning the names of people rather than parties. In remote and rural areas, these were often the names of a relative, boss at work, local religious authority, tribal leader or community activist. This pattern was particularly strong at the district level, where many voters had a personal relationship with the candidate they intended to support. One voter in Maluku remarked that 'the legislative elections are now exactly like the local executive elections—we vote for people rather than parties'.[2] This attitude led to an increase in split-ticket voting: whereas in 1999 voters tended to vote for the same party in the district, provincial and national-level legislative elections, in 2019 it was not uncommon for them to vote for a different party at each level. In the city of South Tangerang in Banten, for instance, PDI-P received 14.3 per cent of the vote at the district level; 16.4 per cent at the provincial level; and 21.7 per cent at the national level.[3] This trend was also evident in the fact that the share of voters casting a vote for an individual candidate rather than the party symbol consistently increased over time. In the case of the national parliament, this percentage increased from 69 per cent in 2009 to 70 per cent in 2014, and to 75 per cent in 2019.[4]

The shift from party-based to candidate-centred elections—which accelerated in 2014 and intensified further in 2019—has seen levels of political party institutionalisation decline considerably since the publication of my book in 2013. At the party system level, regulatory change and the continued dysfunction of political financing mechanisms favoured the consolidation of personalised, tycoon-led and centrist parties, while similar pressures at the party organisation level dissociated electoral candidates from their parties and thus institutionally disempowered the latter. When parties are forced to recruit a significant proportion of their electoral candidates from outside their organisational structures, and struggle to maintain even a basic working relationship with their

---

2 Interview, Namlea, 20 March 2019.
3 Data provided by Titi Anggraini Masudi; percentages calculated by the author.
4 Data provided by Titi Anggraini Masudi.

nominees once elected, a key element of the representative function of political parties is damaged.

In short, while the contemporary party system fails to accommodate important electoral constituencies by constantly raising the existing entry barriers for participation, the dynamics of party organisation increasingly marginalise the parties themselves from electoral contestation. The beneficiaries of these concurrent processes are national-level, cashed-up actors who can build or buy themselves parties in the centre, or local strongmen who can use the weakness of parties to gain parliamentary seats for the pursuit of their personal interests—rather than those of the party they ran for.

INTRAPARTY DEMOCRACY: FROM WEAK TO PARALYSED

The third area in which parties became weaker in the second half of the 2010s is that of intraparty democracy. To be sure, the relative weakness of internal party democracy is a longstanding feature of Indonesian parties. But as I explained in my 2013 book, in the first decade after Indonesia's democratic transition, local party branches had a variety of mechanisms they could use to pressure central party boards (Mietzner 2013: 124–32). In many parties, grassroots cadres elected local party branch heads who subsequently expressed their self-confidence at national party congresses by threatening to withhold support for national leaders if certain demands (often related to the rights of branches) were not fulfilled. Specifically, branch heads asked for a significant say in local candidate selection, the formulation of party policies and matters related to branch autonomy. This often led to tensions between the national party boards and their branches, and it was not uncommon for local chapters to prevail. Thus, while it was true back then that Indonesian parties had for a long time been highly personalised and their internal decision-making processes distorted by clientelism and patronage (Hellmann 2011), national party leaders had to accommodate demands from their branches in order to secure their rule.

At the same time, there was often fierce competition for the position of party chair. Even in PDI-P, which has been under the control of the Sukarno family since the early 1990s, chairperson Megawati Sukarnoputri faced tough challenges to her leadership in 2005. In other, non-personalist parties such as Golkar, PPP, PKB, PKS and the National Mandate Party (Partai Amanat Nasional, PAN), party congresses often saw tight races for the leadership. In some cases, such close contests also occurred in personalist parties: in 2010, then president Yudhoyono experimented with a competitive election to choose his successor at the helm of the Democratic Party (Partai Demokrat, PD). At the time, this was widely seen as a laudable effort by a leader of a personalist party to institutionalise the organisation beyond his presidency and political life (Honna 2012).

But in many ways, Yudhoyono's experiment—or, more precisely, its failure—marked the end of this phase of competitive intraparty leadership contests. Yudhoyono's decision to open up the contest for his succession sparked a bribery-soaked election at the 2010 Democratic Party congress in Bandung. The person who succeeded in being elected chair, Anas Urbaningrum, was arrested for corruption in 2013, as was Andi Mallarangeng, one of his 2010 competitors (and the one Yudhoyono had favoured). Both were accused of illicitly raising funds for (among other things) the contest at the 2010 congress, and both were sentenced to prison terms. After Anas's resignation, Yudhoyono took the position of party chair for himself, and put the party onto a dynastic path. His youngest son, Edhie Baskoro, had already been the party's secretary-general since 2010, but in 2016 Yudhoyono persuaded his older and politically more talented son Agus to give up his military career and run for the governorship of Jakarta. After this attempt proved unsuccessful, Agus was given day-to-day management roles in the party, and he became its chairman in March 2020. If Yudhoyono had ever intended a non-dynastic future for the Democratic Party, that endeavour ended soon after Anas Urbaningrum's election—and definitively with his arrest.

In PDI-P, too, the grip of Megawati Sukarnoputri over her party continued to strengthen during this period. At the 2010 congress, her brother Guruh Sukarnoputra had still been able to launch a campaign to replace her, creating a semblance of intraparty (and intradynastic) competition for the leadership. But by 2019, even that shadow of competitiveness had vanished. The congress in that year did not even schedule an election for the leadership, only a 'confirmation' (*penetapan*). Indeed, delegates were told prior to the congress that Megawati's position was not up for election, as no other candidates had emerged. At the congress, Megawati confirmed her daughter, Puan Maharani, and her son, Prananda Prabowo, as deputy chairs. This was widely understood— both within and outside the party—as a signal that she was planning a dynastic succession scenario for PDI-P (Ucu 2019).

This consolidation of dynastic patterns in parties with high levels of personalisation was accompanied by a notable decline in leadership contestation within other, non-personalist parties. Two manifestations of this decline in the competitiveness of party leadership races were particularly prominent. First, there was increasing intervention by President Widodo in internal party affairs, aiming to place pro-government loyalists in the top leadership of key parties. In the cases of Golkar and PPP, Jokowi's government drove initiatives between 2015 and 2019 to remove party heads who had sided with the opposition and replace them with politicians who promised to support the incumbent (Mietzner 2016). In April 2016, pro-Jokowi PPP politician Muhammad Romahurmuziy replaced former party leader Suryadharma Ali, who had supported Jokowi's adversary, Prabowo. Almost at the same time, pro-Jokowi Golkar functionary Setya Novanto replaced Aburizal Bakrie, who had also supported Prabowo in the 2014 elections. When Novanto had to step down two years later because of a corruption case, a Jokowi cabinet minister replaced him. Romahurmuziy also had to resign after being arrested for corruption in 2019, and he too was replaced with a Jokowi-friendly politician who had been endorsed by the president.

The PPP and Golkar cases pointed to presidential patronage as the most important political asset for candidates running for the leadership of non-personalist and non-dynastic parties. Of course, support by the president had long been an important factor in post-Suharto party leadership races. But the aggressiveness with which the Jokowi government used legal instruments to intervene in party affairs and engineer the election of its preferred candidates marked a new phase in this process. In both the PPP and Golkar cases, the government exploited its authority to recognise or disavow party leaderships as legal representatives of their organisations. In Indonesia, the government—through the minister of justice—holds the authority to register the version of a party's central board it views as legitimate. If the legality of a party's leadership is questioned, therefore, the government has considerable power in deciding the outcome of such disputes. Through this technique, the government was able to force the pro-Prabowo leadership boards of both parties to resign, opening the door to the election of pro-Jokowi boards. These manoeuvres constituted the first major signs of Jokowi's executive illiberalism (which intensified substantially after the anti-Ahok mobilisation), and they further reduced intraparty democracy.

The second manifestation of diminishing party leadership contestation is related less to government intervention than to the increasing concentration of power in the hands of an individual at the top of previously competitive parties. The most significant case in this regard is PKB. While Abdurrahman Wahid, Indonesia's president between 1999 and 2001, was the party's dominant figure until about 2007, under him there had been much competition for the leadership. When Muhaimin Iskandar, his nephew, was running to become chair of PKB in 2005, he had faced three other candidates. Wahid tried to remove Muhaimin in 2007, but the latter resisted this move successfully in the courts. After Wahid's death in 2009, Muhaimin systematically consolidated his grip over the party, using his access to government resources under Yudhoyono and Jokowi as well as his family relationship with Wahid as crucial political assets. By 2019, he had such a stranglehold over the party—and had removed anyone who opposed him with such precision—that he faced no internal dissent. Consequently, the PKB congress of 2019 resembled that of PDI-P's in the speed with which the 'confirmation' of the chair was administered (Sabrini 2019).

In Golkar, similar patterns took hold. After his installation as chair in 2017 (with Jokowi's support), Airlangga Hartarto resorted to increasingly illiberal measures to stay in power: he refused to hold party plenary meetings for much of 2019 to fend off potential challenges to his rule, and his campaign team asked branches to swear on the Qur'an that they would re-elect him (Prihatin 2019). He was re-elected by acclamation, without facing a competitor, at the Golkar congress in December 2019.

Importantly, the increasing power of national-level party elites was institutionalised through gradual changes to internal party regulations that weakened local party branches PDI-P, for instance, introduced provisions in 2019 that gave its central board full authority for the appointment of the chairs, secretaries and treasurers of local party branches. This meant that the branches could no longer elect their own leaders, but only had the right to submit the names of candidates to the centre for consideration (Septianto 2019).[5] Moreover, for 2019, most branch 'elections' were clustered in regional hubs, so that central board representatives could 'handle' a number of elections at the same time. Occasionally, there was protest over this centralisation of power—especially in Surabaya, where PDI-P's national leadership picked a candidate who had not even been nominated by the lower levels of the branch. But most PDI-P branches grudgingly accepted their institutional emasculation, which removed powers they had held for the first two decades of the post-Suharto era.

Other central party boards have not taken such drastic steps, instead using their already existing authority to temporarily suspend local party leaders seen in violation of national-level instructions. In 2019, associates of Golkar chair Airlangga Hartarto suspended leaders of the Maluku branch after they declared their support for the latter's opponent in the upcoming leadership contest (Putra 2019). A similar pattern was visible before the 2015 congress of the Democratic Party, when several

---

5   While the provisions gave stronger rights to branches that had achieved above-average results in the 2019 elections, in practice those rights were often ignored.

branch chairs believed to be loyal to former chair Anas Urbaningrum were dismissed in order to clear the way for Yudhoyono's re-election by acclamation. While such dismissals also occurred in previous periods, they have now become part of a larger process of recentralising party authority in the hands of central leaderships.

The ability of local branches to select electoral candidates has also been reduced, particularly as far as local executive and national legislative candidates are concerned. In his thesis on this subject, Arya Budi (2016) investigated the changing dynamics of nominations for local executive elections in PDI-P and Golkar between 2005 and 2015. He found a trend of gradual recentralisation of nomination processes in both parties. Thus, not only have local party branches been confronted by the personalisation of elections and the corresponding erosion of their influence over legislative polls, but they have also been forced to surrender much of their authority over candidate selection to the central party board. The only exception is legislative elections at the district level, where the sheer number of candidates makes it impossible for the central leadership to screen them all.

Two longer-term factors have contributed to the decline of intraparty democracy in the second half of the 2010s. First, the type of party produced by rising costs and increased registration barriers is one in which oligarchs cover most expenses, but demand full control in return. Even if—like Muhaimin, Megawati or Airlangga—party chairs are not leading business tycoons, they secure the financing of the party through their elite connections and expect recognition of their superiority in return. Intraparty democracy, in other words, is incompatible with a party type in which the leader pays most of the bills (with the exception of the bills for elections, which are 'subcontracted' to self-funded candidates). Second, there is also an increased tolerance among party cadres for autocratic party leadership. Opposition to dynastic and otherwise exclusivist party leadership has declined since the time when even figures such as Wahid, Yudhoyono and Megawati faced internal dissent. Arguably, this has to do with the general erosion of democracy in Indonesia, which has been accompanied by the re-emergence of ideas of 'strong' leadership in some elite circles. Thus, whereas many parties in the West have responded to the crisis of public trust by democratising their internal decision-making through member plebiscites (Detterbeck 2013), Indonesian parties have moved in the opposite direction.

CONCLUSION: WEAKENED PARTY SYSTEM, WEAKENED PARTIES

How, then, have Indonesia's party system and parties changed since the early 2010s? As we have seen, the party system has become less representative, with many voters shifting to the margins but the existing party system allowing the entry only of new parties that are ideologically centrist and controlled by wealthy financiers. In the same vein, the parties have been weakened by the accelerating personalisation of elections, which has loosened the ties between parties and elected representatives. Finally, parties have become less democratic in their internal organisation, with party leaders tightening their grip over the branches and presidential interventions reducing the pool of politicians who have a realistic chance of becoming leader.

At the same time, it is important to emphasise the continuities. Indonesian parties remain in a constitutionally strong position: they nominate presidential candidates; they are the only vehicle for participation in legislative elections; they can recall their parliamentarians at any time; they have significant bargaining powers vis-à-vis the president; and they remain important recruitment avenues for people seeking political careers. Similarly, Indonesia's party system continues to run on a two-track system: one track that comprises ideologically and culturally rooted parties such as PDI-P, PKS and PKB, which are stronger than most of their Asian counterparts; and a personalist track that is increasingly crowded with catch-all, tycoon-led parties.

These constitutional strengths, and the social rootedness of some parties, have somewhat mitigated the factors that are driving the weakening of Indonesian parties: the ever-increasing costs of political operations amid a dysfunctional party financing system; the continuing shift from party-based to personality-centred elections; and the increasing alienation of voters from the party system charged with representing them. Indeed, the fact that Indonesia has not gone down the path of full populist rule, as in the Philippines, or military-backed semi-authoritarianism, as in Thailand, is to no small extent the result of the controls parties have put on populists and the military. In Indonesia, democratic quality is declining, but not as strongly as in the Philippines and Thailand—and this is true for party strength as well.

Nevertheless, it is clear that Indonesian parties are now experiencing a process of deinstitutionalisation. Page Johnson Tan (2006) made this claim as early as 2006, pointing to the direct presidential and local executive elections of the previous year. At that time, this assessment was overdrawn: Yudhoyono (in contrast to Jokowi) built his own party organisation, recognising the continued importance of parties. Equally, the pre-2005 mechanism for electing local government heads (through parliaments) had not benefited the parties either, as independent candidates often bribed legislators to elect them—this was the reason parties agreed to the switch to direct elections in the first place. The crucial development that put Indonesia's parties on a trajectory of deinstitutionalisation came later, with the introduction of the open party-list system in 2009. Even then, the impact of this system was reduced by its sudden implementation in that year. It was only in 2014 and 2019 that the system developed its full potential, distancing parties from their legislative nominees. Johnson Tan was right, of course, that the direct presidential and local executive polls were the first step in the personalisation of Indonesian politics; but had Indonesia retained a closed or semi-open party-list system for legislative elections, and worked to develop a better party financing system, the deinstitutionalisation of parties could arguably have been prevented or at least moderated.

The hopeful aspect of this connection between changes to the electoral regime and party deinstitutionalisation is that the latter process is not irreversible. Past electoral system reform caused some of the phenomena related to party decline, and thus future electoral reform could help to restrengthen the parties. At the moment, the *structural* causes of party weaknesses (that is, a society prone to patronage and clientelism) combine in a toxic manner with *institutional* decisions (that is, a personalised electoral system and a political financing system that encourages self-funding). While the structural deficiencies of Indonesian politics are difficult to overcome quickly, institutional change could be agreed upon in a relatively short period of time. Electoral reforms that put parties, not individuals, at the centre of political contestation, and the creation of a functional party financing system, would go a long way towards reversing the current trend of party decline and, by implication, the erosion of democratic quality accompanying it.

REFERENCES

Abdulsalam, H. 2018. 'Klise parpol baru: status quo PSI, oligarki Perindo dan Berkarya'. *Tirto*, 8 August.
Aspinall, E. and M. Mietzner. 2014. 'Indonesian politics in 2014: democracy's close call'. *Bulletin of Indonesian Economic Studies* 50(3): 347–69.
Aspinall, E. and M. Mietzner. 2019. 'Indonesia's democratic paradox: competitive elections amidst rising illiberalism'. *Bulletin of Indonesian Economic Studies* 55(3): 295–317.

Aspinall, E. and M. Sukmajati, eds. 2016. *Electoral Dynamics in Indonesia: Money Politics, Patronage and Clientelism at the Grassroots*. Singapore: NUS Press.

Budi, A. 2016. 'Less democracy, more centralism: changing patterns in the nomination of Golkar and PDIP candidates for local executive elections, 2005–2015'. Master's thesis. Canberra: Australian National University.

Buehler, M. 2010. 'Decentralisation and local democracy in Indonesia: the marginalisation of the public sphere'. In *Problems of Democratisation in Indonesia: Elections, Institutions and Society*, edited by E. Aspinall and M. Mietzner, 267–85. Singapore: Institute of Southeast Asian Studies (ISEAS).

Cochrane, J. 2016. 'Islamists march in Jakarta, demanding Christian governor be jailed'. *New York Times*, 4 November.

Cyr, J. 2017. *The Fates of Political Parties: Institutional Crisis, Continuity, and Change in Latin America*. Cambridge: Cambridge University Press.

Detterbeck, K. 2013. 'The rare event of choice: party primaries in German land parties'. *German Politics* 22(3): 270–87.

Gallagher, M. 2019. 'Election indices dataset'. https://www.tcd.ie/Political_Science/people/michael_gallagher/ElSystems/Docts/ElectionIndices.pdf, accessed 20 September 2019.

Hellmann, O. 2011. *Political Parties and Electoral Strategy: The Development of Party Organization in East Asia*. London: Palgrave Macmillan.

Higashikata, T. and K. Kawamura. 2015. 'Voting behavior in Indonesia from 1999 to 2014: religious cleavage or economic performance?'. *IDE Discussion Paper* No. 512. Chiba: Institute of Developing Economies.

Honna, J. 2012. 'Inside the Democrat Party: power, politics and conflict in Indonesia's presidential party'. *South East Asia Research* 20(4): 473–89.

Invernizzi-Accetti, C. and F. Wolkenstein. 2017. 'The crisis of party democracy, cognitive mobilization, and the case for making parties more deliberative'. *American Political Science Review* 111(1): 97–109.

Johnson Tan, P. 2006. 'Indonesia seven years after Soeharto: party system institutionalization in a new democracy'. *Contemporary Southeast Asia* 28(1): 88–114.

Kawamura, K. and T. Higashikata. Forthcoming. 'Voting behavior in the 2019 elections'. In *The 2019 Elections in Indonesia*, edited by K. Kawamura. Chiba: Institute of Developing Economies (in Japanese).

Lisi, M., ed. 2018. *Party System Change, the European Crisis and the State of Democracy*. London: Routledge.

Lochocki, T. 2017. *The Rise of Populism in Western Europe: A Media Analysis on Failed Political Messaging*. Heidelberg: Springer.

LSI (Lembaga Survei Indonesia). 2017. 'National survey on radicalism, corruption, and presidential election'. Jakarta: LSI.

Lupu, N. 2016. *Party Brands in Crisis: Partisanship, Brand Dilution, and the Breakdown of Political Parties in Latin America*. Cambridge: Cambridge University Press.

Mietzner, M. 2008. 'Comparing Indonesia's party systems of the 1950s and the post-Suharto era: from centrifugal to centripetal inter-party competition'. *Journal of Southeast Asian Studies* 39(3): 431–54.

Mietzner, M. 2013. *Money, Power, and Ideology: Political Parties in Post-authoritarian Indonesia*. Singapore: NUS Press.

Mietzner, M. 2016. 'Coercing loyalty: coalitional presidentialism and party politics in Jokowi's Indonesia'. *Contemporary Southeast Asia* 38(2): 209–32.

Mietzner, M. and B. Muhtadi. 2018. 'Explaining the 2016 Islamist mobilisation in Indonesia: religious intolerance, militant groups and the politics of accommodation'. *Asian Studies Review* 42(3): 479–97.

Muhtadi, B. 2018. 'A third of Indonesian voters bribed during election—how and why'. *The Conversation,* 20 July.

Prihatin, I.U. 2019. 'Airlangga sebut sumpah dukungan pakai Alquran kebijakan DPD Golkar Jabar'. *Merdeka,* 3 September.

Putra, P.M.S. 2019. 'Pendukung Bamsoet dipecat, Airlangga sebut itu tanggung jawab DPD I Golkar'. *Merdeka,* 13 July.

Reilly, B. 2007. *Democracy and Diversity: Political Engineering in the Asia-Pacific.* Oxford: Oxford University Press.

Sabrini, I.D. 2019. 'PKB bakal aklamasi tunjuk Cak Imin jadi ketua umum di muktamar'. *iNews,* 20 July.

Septianto, B. 2019. 'Jelang kongres, PDIP bentuk kepengurusan baru di semua DPC dan DPD'. *Tirto,* 1 August.

Tomsa, D. 2012. 'Moderating Islamism in Indonesia: tracing patterns of party change in the Prosperous Justice Party'. *Political Research Quarterly* 65(3): 486–98.

Ucu, K.R. 2019. 'Puan & Prananda dinilai sulit samai karisma Megawati'. *Republika,* 12 August.

11   The media and democratic decline

Ross Tapsell

A free and robust media is central to any democracy. Traditionally, the media's role is as a 'fourth estate': an institution that can comment on and objectively criticise other 'estates' such as the government, judiciary and religious organisations (Bulla 2008). There are, of course, problems with this definition and much to debate about the precise power journalists and editors should be given, but as a general rule in any functioning democracy the media plays a vital role in enhancing the transparency and accountability of powerful actors and institutions (ibid.).

Indonesia's transition from authoritarian rule to democracy in 1998 saw its media landscape become significantly more free than it had been under Suharto's authoritarian rule. Janet Steele (2012: 2) described this immediate post-*reformasi* period as one in which the media moved 'from darkness into light'. Among the political and economic chaos that accompanied the collapse of the New Order, media owners, press freedom activists and ordinary Indonesians began to produce and enjoy a wider diversity of news and views. The lasting exceptions in this story of transformation are the provinces of Papua and West Papua, where, due to a simmering separatist movement, the local media operates under a subnational authoritarian regime and international journalists face stringent regulatory restrictions (Tapsell 2015).

The Papua exception aside, many scholars and observers frame Indonesia's current media landscape by comparing it to the previous New Order period (Kitley 2008; Steele 2010). If seen through this prism, the Indonesian media operates in a largely free environment. News outlets publish stories of government corruption, and journalists comment on and criticise government policies. The media can now report on certain topics that were 'taboo' under Suharto, including race and religion. The emergence of social media as a prominent form of communication in Indonesia has undoubtedly played a significant role in allowing greater freedom of expression for individuals to air their grievances; in some cases, social media activism has helped bring about important changes to laws and issues that affect civil society (Fortuna Anwar 2015: 28). Thus, when compared with the New Order, Indonesia's contemporary media landscape looks vibrant and free.

Yet this chapter will show how the declining quality of Indonesia's media has contributed to a broader decline in the quality of democracy in the country. In many ways the media is a prism for understanding the broader changes in Indonesia's sociopolitical life: it tells us about the power of elites, increasing limits to individual freedoms, and the shaping (and manipulating) of political discourse.

This chapter reviews recent developments in Indonesia's media industry against some of the analyses offered in my book *Media Power in Indonesia* (Tapsell 2017). In that volume, I argued that while violence against journalists and the application of draconian laws play a role in shaping journalists' professional practice, the biggest influence on the media industry in the past ten years has been the digital revolution— which has simultaneously enabled media companies to combine, merge, consolidate and centralise media content and businesses, as well as allowing citizens to create and share their own content on social media and internet platforms. The effects of the digital revolution, I suggested, have been complex: on one hand, the expansion of established media corporations into the digital sphere has further consolidated the influence of a small coterie of owners within the media industry; on the other, the emergence of social media and new avenues of online discourse challenge the power of media oligarchs (Tapsell 2017). Since that book was published, however, both traditional and online forms of media have become more politicised, and subject to increasing state intervention and regulation.

I begin this chapter by briefly reviewing this previous research, and discussing the ways in which media oligarchs contributed to the decline of the Indonesian media from a high point in the mid-2000s. I then put forward two further arguments emerging from the first term of president Joko Widodo (Jokowi): first, the coercion of media owners by the Jokowi government has led to the reduction of fair and balanced coverage of political campaigns and government policy, and to less contestation and competition; as such, the media is declining as a key space for diverse political conversations. Second, the failure of media oligarchs to provide independent, critical coverage of Indonesia's political elite has meant discourse has rapidly moved online to social media and messenger platforms. As in many contemporary democracies, the shortcomings of corporate media and the sweeping changes brought about by the digital revolution have contributed to the online intermingling of legitimate critical discourse with fake news and disinformation. The Jokowi government's response has been to try to control this space through its own social media campaigners, known locally as 'buzzers', and to crack down on dissent and opposition forces online through implementation of existing laws and by overly corrective regulatory reforms that undermine important democratic norms. Thus, this chapter argues that Indonesia's media landscape is becoming increasingly concentrated, more beholden to the influence of oligarchic owners, and more constrained by the state's illiberal regulatory interventions.

MEDIA CONCENTRATION, POWER AND PARTISANSHIP

To understand how Indonesia's media environment has undermined democratic quality over the past ten years, we must first understand the impact of the digital revolution on the media industry itself. Contrary to some more positive expectations, digitalisation has not enabled a diverse professional media realm to flourish in Indonesia. Rather, it has enabled big media to become bigger. Across the television, print and online media sectors, power has become increasingly concentrated in the hands of a few extremely wealthy and politically active tycoons; far from enhancing democratic transparency and accountability, the new media oligopolies generally serve the narrow political agendas of their owners.

In the early 2000s, it seemed that the growth of the internet as a major avenue for mass communication would threaten the power of wealthy, politically connected media moguls (Couldry and Curran 2003). In many ways it did, as those moguls who relied on printed newspapers as their flagship news platforms saw profits and circulation decline rapidly. Detik.com and other pioneer online news sites challenged the market dominance and power of print newspapers like *Kompas* and *Jawa Pos*, for example. The corporate media sector needed to drastically change its business models in order to keep up with the evolution of audiences and advertising revenues, or risk becoming redundant.

Indonesian media owners successfully adapted to this challenge. A select group of businessmen quickly managed to consolidate much of the industry into a small number of multi-platform companies. Indonesia's major media corporations became 'digital conglomerates': leaders in 'convergent' news production, a process that encourages the purchasing of smaller competitors. The effective mobilisation of existing capital reserves was crucial to this process of consolidation. Much of the communications infrastructure in the digital era is expensive, and smaller companies found they did not have the capital to keep up with the far better-funded media behemoths. Even very successful new companies succumbed to this process of conglomerate expansion and consolidation: Detik.com, for example, was sold in 2011 to a larger conglomerate owned by one of Indonesia's richest tycoons, Chairul Tanjung. The result through the 2010s was an increasingly oligopolistic media market.

A major corollary of this process is the centralisation of media power. Media conglomeration is occurring predominantly by larger Jakarta companies swallowing up smaller, regional companies through centralised national newsrooms based in the capital. While it is true that similar media conglomeration occurs in other countries with a large capital city that is the nation's hub of business and government (e.g. Vartanova and Smirnov 2010), in Indonesia this process has been exacerbated by a regulatory environment favourable to Jakarta elites. One pertinent example of this is the delivery of Indonesia's 'multiplexing' digital television licences. As a result of this process, approximately two-thirds of regional television stations are now owned by large Jakarta-based digital conglomerates (SPS Media Directory 2014). These digital conglomerates maintain offices in Jakarta and increasingly expand their coverage to broadcast nationwide. Although they generate only around 5–8 per cent of television audience share, 24-hour television news stations TVOne (owned by Aburizal Bakrie) and MetroTV (owned by Surya Paloh) have significant influence on shaping coverage of political events, election campaigns and presidential candidates because they are influential among educated and elite audiences. Entertainment-oriented broadcasters like TransCorp (owned by Chairul Tanjung) and MNC Group (owned by Hary Tanoesoedibjo) are also very influential in framing popular opinion towards political narratives, debates and contests.

The process of media conglomeration has occurred concurrently with the growing political clout of Indonesia's media owners. The mainstream media landscape has become far more partisan in its coverage of politics, reflecting the political interests of the owners and their factional allies. By the end of Susilo Bambang Yudhoyono's presidency, the penetration of media moguls into the formal political arena was a well-established phenomenon. Aburizal Bakrie began his reign as Golkar party chairman in 2009. Dahlan Iskan, of the Jawa Pos Group; and Chairul Tanjung, owner of two popular free-to-air television stations, the most popular online news portal in Detik.com and the CNN Indonesia franchise; were both ministers in the Yudhoyono government. Dahlan also won the

Democratic Party (Partai Demokrat, PD) presidential convention ahead of the 2014 election (though the party did not proceed with his nomination). Moreover, two media owners established personal party vehicles in the first half of the 2010s: Surya Paloh founded the National Democratic Party (Partai Nasional Demokrat, NasDem) in 2012, and Hary Tanoesoedibjo established Perindo (Partai Persatuan Indonesia, Indonesian Unity Party) in 2015 (having previously been active in two other parties). Owning a media company was important for these individuals' political careers, and as their media companies grew so too did their involvement in formal politics. Political power and media influence were mutually reinforcing.

The 2014 election reflected this state of affairs, with Indonesian audiences witnessing the most partisan coverage of candidates that the post-*reformasi* period had yet seen. Prabowo Subianto's coalition had the support of moguls Aburizal Bakrie (Visi News) and Hary Tanoesoedibjo (MNC Group), who dominated the television ratings with five stations between them. Jokowi had the support of coalition partner Surya Paloh (and thus his news station MetroTV), while Dahlan Iskan and Sofyan Wanandi (*The Jakarta Post*) were both on Jokowi's campaign team. The extreme partisanship of television coverage reached its height on the night of the presidential election, as TV stations that favoured Prabowo only broadcast 'quick count' results that showed a Prabowo victory. Aburizal Bakrie's TVOne election night coverage stood out for its particularly overt rejection of the notion of fair and balanced journalism. Live in the TVOne studio, Prabowo claimed victory on the basis of dubious quick counts provided by several little-known polling organisations hired to deliberately misinform the public about the election outcome. The station's coverage seemed to have been planned long before election night, with guests supporting Prabowo's claim of victory already in the studio and primed for comment. One far more reputable polling firm, Poltracking Institute, cancelled its agreement with TVOne in the aftermath of the election in order to 'maintain its professionalism' (Mietzner 2015). Jokowi's declaration of victory was broadcast live on Surya Paloh's MetroTV, but given MetroTV had aggressively campaigned for Jokowi throughout, many Indonesians treated its published quick counts with similar scepticism.

Even the respected magazine *Tempo*, whose reporting is usually exemplary, struggled to convince many Indonesians that it was indeed fair and balanced in its coverage. After the election, its journalists placed Jokowi on their shoulders as he crowd-surfed throughout the newsroom (*Tempo* 2014a). *Tempo* journalists likely believed that Jokowi was the better candidate for democracy, clean government and human rights, which are longstanding concerns of *Tempo's* reportage, but the perception of bias during the 2014 contest threatened to tarnish even *Tempo's* reputation for independence and journalistic rigour. So even if some of these media outlets ostensibly endorsed the candidate they saw as better for Indonesian democracy, they nonetheless risked their reputation for political impartiality. The English-language *Jakarta Post* explicitly supported Jokowi, the first time it had supported a candidate in its thirty-year history, with one editorial stating:

> There is no such thing as being neutral when the stakes are so high ... One [candidate—Jokowi] is determined to reject the collusion of power and business, while the other [Prabowo] is embedded in a New Order-style of transactional politics that betrays the spirit of reformasi. (*Jakarta Post* 2014)

Thus, we can conclude a number of key points relating to mainstream media and politics in the 2014 election. First, some of the print media justified the support of Jokowi on ideological grounds relating to concerns about protecting democratic institutions. Second, and more importantly for our analysis of the media, in 2014 almost all major media owners overtly supported one of the two presidential candidates, with the contestation between pro-Prabowo and pro-Jokowi tycoons leading to a highly partisan and polarised media landscape.

An oligarchic media is of course not unique to Indonesia, and the nature and influence of media ownership is discussed and debated around the world. However, the implications of oligarchic media control can vary substantially, depending on the degree of divergence—or convergence—between the interests and agendas of media owners. In 2017, I described Indonesia's media landscape as a 'multi-oligarchic or competitive oligarchic system, where individual owners predominantly push their own interests rather than the interests of a broader "cartel" ' (Tapsell 2017: 75). If Indonesians wanted to switch between television channels, or read a wide variety of newspapers or online news outlets, they would have obtained a reasonably broad view of events and perspectives in 2014. That is, where a multi-oligarchic media landscape exists, there is reasonable diversity of political information in the public sphere for the concerned media consumer with access to a range of news outlets. Unlike other countries in Southeast Asia where there is strong control over media by the government, most political topics in Indonesia were covered somewhere at some point by some mainstream media organisation in 2014. To know why this changed in 2019, we need to understand how Jokowi coerced various media owners into his coalition during his first presidential term.

JOKOWI'S FIRST TERM: CO-OPTING MOGULS

One of Jokowi's first challenges as president was dealing with the media oligarchs who had supported his campaign, who looked to reap significant rewards for themselves. Surya Paloh's NasDem had won 6.7 per cent of votes in its first legislative election, and Paloh was reportedly visiting the palace numerous times a day (*Tempo* 2014b). A week after his inauguration, Jokowi appointed HM Prasetyo from Paloh's NasDem party to the position of attorney general, an office with the prosecutorial power to function as a 'political weapon' (Power 2018: 330). In turn, MetroTV continued its often laudatory reportage of Jokowi's presidency. Journalists and editors who had hoped that MetroTV would 'resume normal programming' after the election were left disappointed. At its worst, MetroTV resembled the programming of state television broadcaster TVRI under the New Order—opening news broadcasts with triumphant declarations of the president's achievements, and broadcasting his speeches at regular intervals throughout the day's programming. The disquiet this provoked inside newsrooms became public in 2017 when MetroTV's star newscaster and an important critical voice, Najwa Shihab, left the station and moved her popular political talk show, *Mata Najwa*, first to YouTube and later to a rival broadcaster (Khoiri 2018).

While Surya Paloh's political fortunes seemed to benefit greatly from a Jokowi victory, Dahlan Iskan's political fortunes fell drastically. Once regarded as the 'king-maker' of East Javanese politics (Ida 2011) and a rising star under Yudhoyono's administration, Dahlan's influence in politics declined more than any other media mogul in the country, a sign of the cut-throat nature of politics and media in Indonesia, and served as a warning to others (such as Hary Tanoesoedibjo) of the way in which legal instruments can be employed, even against powerful media owners. Concurrently, Dahlan's media businesses underwent difficulties from 2014, even if his overall wealth reportedly did not drastically change.[1] Debts mounted in the electricity companies he owned, while some regional Jawa Pos Group newspapers were in debt. Although he had maintained no official role in Jawa Pos Group for some time, he was still considered a key voice in its direction and his son continued to maintain the position of managing director. Presumably distracted by corruption cases and financial stresses, in 2017 Dahlan faced a disgruntled board of

---

1   In June 2016 Dahlan's wealth was reported as US$445 million, Indonesia's 90th richest person (https://www.globeasia.com/cover-story/150-richest-indonesians/). In 2018 he had dropped to 95th place with a wealth of US$481 million (https://www.globeasia.com/cover-story/150-richest-indonesians-3/).

directors and discussion over whether he should sell his shares (*Jakarta Globe* 2017).

Dahlan had been appointed CEO of Indonesia's state-owned electricity company, Perusahaan Listrik Negara (PLN), in 2009 by then-president Yudhoyono, and he went on to be minister of state owned enterprises in Yudhoyono's government in 2011. He was widely seen as a possible successor to Yudhoyono in his Democratic Party in 2014. In May 2014, Dahlan emerged as the leading candidate in the Democratic Party's inaugural presidential convention. However, with his party winning only 10.9 per cent of the vote in the legislative elections, Yudhoyono was unable to secure a presidential nomination from within his party in the 2014 elections, and instead preferred to remain notionally 'neutral' (while tacitly channelling support to Prabowo). He later appointed his son Agus as 'heir' to his party leadership. Dahlan then chose to give support to the Jokowi–Kalla 2014 campaign, including producing print materials in East Java to counter smear campaigns being run against Jokowi. Following Jokowi's victory, Dahlan's career looked set for further success. He controlled a large media empire; styled himself as a clean reformer, capable manager and popular political figure; and seemed an important ally for the new president.

But Dahlan was not offered a position in Jokowi's cabinet, nor did he win access to the various other forms of presidential patronage regularly distributed to allied media tycoons. Indeed, far from enjoying increased access to state largesse, from mid-2015 to 2019 Dahlan found himself embroiled in numerous corruption cases. Notably, these cases did not involve the Corruption Eradication Commission (Komisi Pemberantasan Korupsi, KPK), which had become popular during the Yudhoyono era for its independent prosecution of well-connected and high-profile graft suspects. Rather, the cases against Dahlan were overseen by the police and the Attorney General's Office—institutions that lacked the KPK's reputation for political independence. Throughout these cases, Paloh's MetroTV produced numerous reports of Dahlan's corruption trial (e.g. MetroTV News.com 2017), while his own *Jawa Pos* newspaper generally portrayed him as innocent (Setiawan 2017). Dahlan was acquitted in both corruption cases in 2019, but he had suffered severe reputational and financial damage, which ruined his political career. This all suggests that, despite his previous efforts for both Yudhoyono and Jokowi, Dahlan was not able to rely on the protection of his presidential patrons—particularly given the presence of rival media tycoons within the governing coalition. In an interview with *Tirto* in 2016, Dahlan said he wanted to 'forget' his time in politics and understood that Jokowi was 'busy' with other matters and would not help him recover from his various setbacks (Nugroho 2016).

Having been deprived of the privileges extended to other pro-Jokowi tycoons, Dahlan publicly changed sides and backed the Prabowo–Sandiaga Uno ticket in the 2019 election (Erdianto 2019).

Despite Dahlan's apparent failure to benefit from his endorsement of Jokowi, the co-option of media tycoons behind the incumbent presidential coalition was nevertheless a notable feature of Jokowi's first term. Having won the 2014 election in the context of a highly partisan but competitive media landscape, Jokowi set about bringing previously pro-Prabowo media owners into his fold or engineering their political marginalisation. One early target of these tactics was Aburizal Bakrie. Starting in 2015, the Jokowi government used its authority over party registrations to exacerbate a factional split within Golkar and undermine Bakrie's chairmanship of the party. By mid-2016, government powerbrokers were able to engineer the election of a new pro-Jokowi chairman, Setya Novanto (who was replaced in late 2017 by Airlangga Hartarto, following Setya's arrest on corruption charges). This meant that Bakrie's influence over the party dwindled (though he remained head of the Advisory Board). With Golkar having switched its allegiance to Jokowi, Bakrie's alliance with Prabowo was also at an end, and his media companies TVOne and ANTV softened in their coverage of Jokowi.

The Jokowi government deployed still more overtly coercive tactics in securing the support of the ethnic Chinese tycoon Hary Tanoesoedibjo. His MNC media conglomerate hosts 3 free-to-air television stations, 46 local television stations, 19 pay TV channels and the cable television provider companies IndoVision, TopTV and OKVision (Tapsell 2017: 31–2). In addition, Tanoesoedibjo founded Perindo in early 2015, following dalliances with Paloh's NasDem in 2011–13 and the People's Conscience Party (Partai Hati Nurani Rakyat, Hanura) during the 2014 legislative election. After backing Prabowo in 2014, Tanoesoedibjo remained antagonistic towards Jokowi's administration through the first half of his first presidential term. This peaked when Tanoesoedibjo's media companies provided extensive and positive coverage of the Islamist opponents of Basuki Tjahaja Purnama ('Ahok')—Jokowi's ally and former deputy governor—during the 2016–17 Jakarta campaign. In early 2017, police investigators opened a case against Tanoesoedibjo for threatening a prosecutor in an earlier legal matter. Shortly afterwards, Tanoesoedibjo announced he would abandon Prabowo and support Jokowi's re-election, and MNC channels switched to positive coverage of the president (Aspinall and Mietzner 2019). While there may have been other factors in Tanoesoedibjo's realignment, its timing in the midst of a criminal investigation—and the subsequent stalling of the case—suggest that fear of repercussions from the state was an important factor in his decision.

The Jokowi government efforts to forge alliances with media moguls was not a new phenomenon. During Yudhoyono's presidency, both Bakrie and Chairul Tanjung held ministerial portfolios, and other moguls like Tanoesoedibjo were offered similar positions (Tapsell 2017: 68). But whereas Yudhoyono's alliance-building rested on the distribution of cabinet posts and government largesse, Jokowi showed with Bakrie and Tanoesoedibjo that he was willing to adopt a more coercive strategy when dealing with media oligarchs, an approach that seems to have strengthened these media owners' fealty to the president.

This is not to say, however, that Jokowi eschewed the distributive coalition-building strategies of his predecessor in his efforts to co-opt Indonesia's media tycoons. Ahead of his 2019 re-election bid, Jokowi appointed Erick Thohir, Bakrie's business partner in his VisiNews Asia media group, as his campaign chairman. Thohir also owns several television and radio channels as well as *Republika*, the leading Islamic daily newspaper. In addition, Chairul Tanjung was sounded out as a potential vice-presidential candidate (Aspinall and Mietzner 2019).

Skewed coverage has led to more robust discussion among Indonesians around the partisan nature of mainstream media, and in turn eroded public trust in this important democratic institution. For example, a 2006 survey showed 86 per cent of Indonesians trusted mainstream media (GlobeScan 2006). In a 2017 survey on trust in major institutions in Indonesia, the lowest ranked were political parties (45 per cent), the parliament (55 per cent) and the courts (65 per cent), followed closely by the mass media (67 per cent). Even the notoriously corrupt Indonesian police (70 per cent) ranked higher than the media (Fossati et al. 2017). A 2018 survey found trust in media was as low as 62 per cent (LSI 2018: 46) (Table 11.1).

A number of incidents also point to a rising trend of dissatisfaction and distrust in mainstream media. In 2015, for example, TransTV journalists were not allowed to enter a media briefing resulting from a factional meeting within the Democratic Party that was critical of Yudhoyono, because Chairul Tanjung was believed to be too close to Yudhoyono (*Kompas* 2015). Mainstream television's decision not to live broadcast the Islamist '212 protests' in late 2016, which were at the time the largest protest movements in Indonesia since *reformasi*, saw television companies heavily criticised by Islamist groups. A number of print newspapers, including *Kompas*, relegated the story to back pages of the newspaper, which led Prabowo to allege that they were manipulating the news (*Kompas* 2018). At a number of 212 'reunion' rallies, journalists from MetroTV were attacked by protestors, as they were seen as partisan operators for the Jokowi government.

Table 11.1   Indonesians' trust in media (%)

	Trust	Do not trust	No answer/don't know
January 2005*	70	15	15
May 2007*	62	30	8
September 2009*	55	25	20
January 2014**	69	26	5
April 2014**	72	23	5
October 2018*	62	19	19
May 2019*	62	33	5

Sources: *Lembaga Survei Indonesia, **Indikator Politik Indonesia.

Thus, Jokowi's first term saw the continued entrenchment of the media partisanship that arose during the 2014 election; however, it also saw a shift from the polarised media landscape of 2014 towards a consolidation of support for the incumbent government among mainstream media companies. This broad amalgamation of support had two consequences for the democratic contests of 2019. First, the incumbent president secured a major advantage over his opponent in terms of the amount and tone of media coverage and support from owners. Whereas Jokowi's campaign events were covered by all the major television stations, members of Prabowo's campaign team complained there was little purpose in conducting regular campaign events because the mainstream media would not cover them (Gerindra official, personal communication, Jakarta, 2019). Second, and more importantly, because one side (Jokowi) had come to dominate the mainstream media, there was little critical and informed discussion about the candidates' strengths and weaknesses, or about differences in their respective policy platforms. In addition, five publicly televised debates were broadcast, but they were formatted in a highly contrived, stilted fashion that seemed remote from the general mood among grassroots supporters and averted issues of sensitivity (such as the role of Islam within the state, a topic regarded as being crucial to such a polarised election campaign) (Aspinall 2019; Warburton 2019). With traditional media organisations offering little opportunity for meaningful debate and critical discourse, these elements of the 2019 election were increasingly confined to digital media platforms.

Will support from media moguls help Jokowi run a more stable, productive government? Jokowi seems to think so. In his second cabinet of 2019–24, two media owners were appointed as ministers—Erick Thohir (VisiNews and Mahaka Group) and Wishnutama Kusubandio (NETTV)—while Surya Paloh's NasDem party secured control over the Ministry of Communications and Information with the appointment of senior NasDem politician Johnny Plate. The daughters of Hary Tanoesoedibjo and Chairul Tanjung were also assigned positions in government. Yudhoyono similarly tried to manage media tycoons and massage coverage by rewarding cooperative owners with prestigious and influential appointments (Aspinall et al. 2015). However, critical coverage of Yudhoyono grew as media moguls, their political allies and their parties began to make plays for the 2014 presidential election, and as new faces—such as Jokowi circa 2012—became ratings winners. To the extent that we should expect similar tendencies during Jokowi's second term, it may seem unlikely that the major media companies will collectively trumpet Jokowi's achievements through to the final days of his presidency, or that they will continue to lavish attention on a president in the final months in office as a new generation of politicians comes to the fore. However, during his first term Jokowi showed far less patience in handling media and online criticism than Yudhoyono, and proved far more ready to respond with the adoption of authoritarian strategies. Should Jokowi and his allies maintain these coercive strategies, independent and critical media may continue to be stifled, with much political coverage in mainstream media increasingly resembling pro-government propaganda.

DIGITAL MEDIA: FROM INNOVATION TO POLARISATION

As trust in mainstream media declines, many citizens turn to online media content for alternative sources of information, news and views. This turn is also shaped by the way in which increasingly ubiquitous social media usage encourages citizen participation in debates and discussions. Urban areas of Indonesia are a place for burgeoning social media use among youth. DataReportal estimates that by 2019 Indonesia had 150 million social media users. For Indonesians who have access to the internet, a vast majority watch YouTube (88 per cent) and use social media platforms like WhatsApp (83 per cent), Facebook (81 per cent), Instagram (80 per cent) and Twitter (52 per cent) (Kemp 2019). Sensing the decline of mainstream media and the concurrent rise of social media platforms, Indonesian politicians have increasingly turned their attention to adopting various new forms of online political campaigning in order to reach voters. Digital volunteer groups were important campaigners for Jokowi and Ahok in the 2012 Jakarta election (such as the group Jasmev: Jokowi–Ahok social media volunteers) and in the 2014 presidential election for Jokowi.

The change in this space occurred in the highly polarised Jakarta gubernatorial election of 2017. As Lim (2017) showed, throughout this campaign social media discourse produced 'algorithmic enclaves' of supporters and partisan commentary. Online campaigners produced material that they encouraged citizens to share through their own networks on Facebook and WhatsApp, rather than solely relying on official campaign networks and mainstream media to spread campaign messages. Anti-Ahok groups used social media to send racially and religiously charged material. One such group, which called itself the 'Muslim 212 cyber army', aggressively campaigned against Ahok (and Jokowi) (Juniarto 2018; Lamb 2018). A large amount of material it produced during 2017 was anti-Chinese and anti-communist in character. On the other side, Ahok's digital-savvy group Teman Ahok (Friends of Ahok) used online platforms to try to neutralise the campaign against him and depict Ahok as a martyr. All of this led to a highly febrile, sectarian campaign where voters were encouraged to ally themselves to candidates who shared their religious affiliation. Another important trend that began in the Jakarta election was the greater adoption of digital media campaigners within formal political party campaign structures. For example, after Ahok's nomination by the Indonesian Democratic Party of Struggle (Partai Demokrasi Indonesia-Perjuangan, PDI-P), the party moved to acquire much of the digital campaign infrastructure developed by Teman Ahok. Hasan Hasbi, who had been a chief creator (and funder) of Teman Ahok, concluded that he and others 'were moved to the side' in the 2017 election, where the party 'took control of everything' (Hasan Hasbi, personal communication, October 2017).

In the 2019 presidential election, Warburton (2019) noted there was a 'heightened sense of polarisation' due to the way in which Islamic groups associated with either side of the pluralist–Islamist cleavage in Indonesia had 'crystallised into more cohesive blocs behind their chosen candidate'. Islamist groups got behind Prabowo and campaigned on his behalf, while Nahdlatul Ulama (NU) played a major role in Jokowi's campaign in the Javanese heartland. Each side 'raised the stakes and framed their political enemy as a threat. The result [was] a much more divisive election, both online and in the communities where people live and work' (Warburton 2019). The algorithmic enclaves described by Lim in 2017 continued through to the 2019 presidential elections, and the result was a highly polarised and tense campaign. Disinformation via social media drove much of this campaign, where explicit and often crude messages of race and religion were distributed on social media platforms. Such material did not come from official political party pages and candidate profiles on social media, but rather from third parties presumably enlisted by campaign teams. The mechanics of this type of campaign, and the influence it had on voters, is still being debated and discussed by scholars and policy analysts. Certainly, the rise of 'buzzer teams' consisting of a larger network of underground 'black campaign' teams set up by presidential advisers is a large factor in this trend. As one pro-Jokowi social media campaigner told me: 'Michele Obama said "when they go low, we go high". But it didn't work. Trump won. So here, when they go low, we go lower' (anonymous, personal communication, March 2019). After the announcement of the presidential election result in May 2019, thousands of Prabowo supporters protested (and rioted) in front of the election commission in Jakarta, claiming the election had been rigged by the incumbent president. In response, the Indonesian government chose to reduce WhatsApp, Facebook and Instagram content, essentially 'slowing down' the use of the platforms by limiting functions such as video and photo uploading and downloading.

The Jokowi government has increasingly used Law No. 11/2008 on Electronic Information and Transactions (ITE Law) to crack down on those who produce and share what the government sees as 'fake news'. Indonesia has not introduced a controversial 'anti–fake news law' as has occurred in Malaysia and Singapore, and instead has politicised the ITE Law with arrests and prosecutions of opposition activists and supporters (Tapsell 2019). For example, singer-turned-activist Titi Widoretno was investigated by police on the suspicion she had created a WhatsApp group using the '2019 Change the President' (2019GantiPresiden) tag, which was adopted by many opposition activists in the months leading up to the formal nomination of presidential candidates (Power 2018: 331). Opposition politician Ahmad Dhani was sentenced to eighteen months jail for a series of tweets in which he criticised Ahok supporters, while other cases include Ratna Sarumpaet, a member of the Prabowo–Sandiaga campaign team who falsely claimed to have been assaulted by a group of men because of her political affiliation; Lieus Sungkharisma, Prabowo–Sandiaga campaign spokesperson, arrested 'on suspicion of subversion and spreading hoaxes' (*Jakarta Post* 2019); and National Mandate Party (Partai Amanat Nasional, PAN) politician Eggi Sudjana. At the same time that these sorts of cases were being launched against opposition figures, online attacks against the Prabowo side went largely unprosecuted (Potkin and Da Costa 2019).

The concern here is that institutions such as the Ministry of Communications and Police are so integrated in their information-sharing procedures that their professional practice becomes largely to crack down on dissent against the sitting government. In January 2018 Indonesia launched the National Cyber and Encryption Agency, tasked to help stop the spread of hoax news. It reports directly to the president. Thus, while social media disinformation and fake news circulation remains a difficult problem to be addressed in Indonesia and elsewhere, the Jokowi government is increasingly encroaching on online media freedom by arresting social media critics, restricting internet connectivity (as occurred during the post-election riots in Jakarta in 2019) or even shutting down internet access altogether on security grounds (as occurred in the Papua region in 2019), and is thus a further worrying sign for the health of democracy in the country.

CONCLUSION: THE STATE OF MEDIA INDEPENDENCE IN INDONESIA

This chapter has argued that the long-term trend of Indonesia's media freedom is one of decline, caused by both the way in which oligarchs have capitalised on the digital revolution, and a government that has hardened its stance on restricting critical expression and political opposition—both in traditional and online media—while at the same time employing state-sponsored 'buzzers' to manipulate the social media realm.

These trends are now being reflected in international indexes. Indonesia is ranked 124 in Reporters Without Borders 2019 World Press Freedom Index (https://rsf.org/en/ranking), a downgrade from its score of 100 in 2009. The latest Freedom House Freedom of the Press report was in 2017, which rated Indonesia's media as 'partly free' (https://freedomhouse. org/report-types/freedom-press); the 2019 Freedom on the Net report had the same status, citing declines in internet freedom (https://www. freedomonthenet.org/explore-the-map). This is not to say that Indonesia's media does not produce high-quality, critical journalism. Once the 2019 elections were over, outlets like *Tempo* magazine, *Tirto* and *Kumparan*, founded by the previous owners of Detik.com, returned to publishing sharp critiques of the incumbent administration.

However, the purpose of this chapter has been to assess the media landscape two decades on from *reformasi* against the media landscape of the mid-2000s, as the digital revolution was just getting under way and as Yudhoyono—Indonesia's first directly elected president—began his first term. Seen through this comparative lens, the trends outlined in this chapter suggest that the media today is less diverse and increasingly beholden to oligarchs, and subject to growing government influence. The implications of these trends for Indonesia's democratic quality have been serious: the independence and reliability of media is reduced, which in turn undermines an important check on executive government and abuse of power; the norm of free and critical expression is eroded; and the quality of democratic debate is diminished. Whether Indonesia's media landscape can recover from the damage wrought by powerful media oligarchs, an increasingly coercive and illiberal government, and the spread of hoaxes and buzzer campaigns remains to be seen. Now that these forces have been unleashed on Indonesian democracy, however, they will not easily be reined in.

REFERENCES

Aspinall, E. 2019. 'Indonesia's election and the return of ideological competition'. *New Mandala*, 22 April. https://www.newmandala.org/indonesias-election-and-the-return-of-ideological-competition/

Aspinall, E. and M. Mietzner. 2019. 'Indonesia's democratic paradox: competitive elections amidst rising illiberalism'. *Bulletin of Indonesian Economic Studies* 55(3): 295–317.

Aspinall, E., M. Mietzner and D. Tomsa. 2015. 'The moderating president: Yudhoyono's decade in power'. In *The Yudhoyono Presidency: Indonesia's Decade of Stability and Stagnation*, edited by E. Aspinall, M. Mietzner and D. Tomsa, 1–22. Singapore: Institute of Southeast Asian Studies (ISEAS).

Bulla, D.W. 2008. 'Fourth estate, media as'. In *Encyclopedia of Political Communication*, edited by L.L. Kaid and C. Holtz-Bacha. SAGE Publications. http://dx.doi.org/10.4135/9781412953993.n217

Couldry, N. and J. Curran. 2003. *Contesting Media Power: Alternative Media in a Networked World*. Lanham: Rowman and Littlefield.

Erdianto, K. 2019. 'Pilpres 2014 dukung Jokowi, ini alasan Dahlan Iskan kini Prabowo'. *Kompas*, 12 April. https://nasional.kompas.com/read/2019/04/12/15434361/pilpres-2014-dukung-jokowi-ini-alasan-dahlan-iskan-kini-pilih-prabowo?page=all

Fortuna Anwar, D. 2015. 'Yudhoyono's legacy: an insider's view'. In *The Yudhoyono Presidency: Indonesia's Decade of Stability and Stagnation*, edited by E. Aspinall, M. Mietzner and D. Tomsa, 23–31. Singapore: Institute of Southeast Asian Studies (ISEAS).

Fossati, D., Y.-F. Hui and S.D. Negara. 2017. 'The Indonesia National Survey Project: economy, society and politics'. *Trends in Southeast Asia* No. 10. Singapore: ISEAS – Yusof Ishak Institute.

GlobeScan. 2006. 'BBC/Reuters/Media Center Poll: trust in the media'. GlobeScan. http://news.bbc.co.uk/2/shared/bsp/hi/pdfs/02_05_06mediatrust.pdf

Ida, R. 2011. 'Reorganisation of media power in post-authoritarian Indonesia: ownership, power and influence of local media entrepreneurs'. In *Politics and the Media in Twenty-First Century Indonesia: Decade of Democracy*, edited by K. Sen and D.T. Hill, 13–26. London: Routledge.

Jakarta Globe. 2017. 'Media mogul Dahlan Iskan gives up entire stake in Jawa Pos: report'. *Jakarta Globe,* 15 November. https://jakartaglobe.id/business/media-mogul-dahlan-iskan-has-sold-entire-stake-at-jawa-pos-group-report/?fbclid=IwAR2XQVEirOSNNDGhSkIfV2IK5V4fNBDqUG7J Kwm-BcewtGjYBMj4zTuAtmc

Jakarta Post. 2014. 'Editorial: endorsing Jokowi'. *Jakarta Post,* 4 July. http://www.thejakartapost.com/news/2014/07/04/editorial-endorsing-jokowi.html

Jakarta Post. 2019. 'Prabowo campaign spokesman arrested on subversion charges'. *Jakarta Post,* 21 May. https://www.thejakartapost.com/news/2019/05/21/prabowo-campaign-spokesman-arrested-on-subversioncharges.html

Juniarto, D. 2018. 'The Muslim cyber army: what is it and what does it want?'. *Indonesia at Melbourne,* 20 March. https://indonesiaatmelbourne.unimelb.edu.au/the-muslim-cyber-army-what-is-it-and-what-does-it-want/

Kemp, S. 2019. 'Digital 2019: Indonesia'. DataReportal, 31 January. https://datareportal.com/reports/digital-2019-indonesia

Khoiri, A. 2018. 'Cerita Najwa Shihab soal "Mata Najwa" kembali tayang di TV'. CNN Indonesia, 5 January. https://www.cnnindonesia.com/hiburan/20180105 182432-220-267048/cerita-najwa-shihab-soal-mata-najwa-kembali-tayang-di-tv

Kitley, P. 2008. 'Civil society and the media in Indonesia'. In *Islam beyond Conflict: Indonesian Islam and Western Political Theory,* edited by A. Azra and W. Hudson, 211–22. Aldershot: Ashgate Publishing.

Kompas. 2015. 'Wartawan "Trans Corp" dilarang masuk acara kader demokrat penentang SBY'. *Kompas,* 30 April. https://nasional.kompas.com/read/2015/04/30/14133161/Wartawan.Trans.Corp.Dilarang.Masuk.Acara.Kader.Demokrat.Penentang.SBY

Kompas. 2018. 'Menurut Prabowo, saat ini banyak media massa beritakan kebohongan'. *Kompas,* 5 December. https://nasional.kompas.com/read/2018/12/05/15193531/menurut-prabowo-saat-ini-banyak-media-massa-beritakan-kebohongan?page=all

Lamb, K. 2018. 'Muslim cyber army: a "fake news" operation designed to derail Indonesia's leader'. *The Guardian,* 13 March. https://www.theguardian.com/world/2018/mar/13/muslim-cyber-army-a-fake-news-operation-designed-to-bring-down-indonesias-leader

Lim, M. 2017. 'Freedom to hate: social media, algorithmic enclaves, and the rise of tribal nationalism in Indonesia'. *Critical Asian Studies* 49(3): 411–27.

LSI (Lembaga Survei Indonesia). 2018. 'National survey result: trends in public perception of corruption in Indonesia'. Jakarta: LSI. 8–24 October. http://www.lsi.or.id/riset/442/rilis-survei-nasional-lsi-101218

MetroTV News.com. 2017. 'Dahlan Iskan menangis saat bacakan Pledoi'. MetroTV News.com, 14 April. https://www.metrotvnews.com/play/NL0U938d-dahlan-iskan-menangis-saat-bacakan-pledoi

Mietzner, M. 2015. 'Reinventing Asian populism: Jokowi's rise, democracy, and political contestation in Indonesia'. *Policy Studies* 72. Honolulu: East-West Center.

Nugroho, K.B. 2016. 'Jabatan lama yang memangsa Dahlan Iskan'. *Tirto,* 21 December. https://tirto.id/jabatan-lama-yang-memangsa-dahlan-iskan-camo

Potkin, F. and A.B. Da Costa. 2019. 'Fact-checkers vs. hoax peddlers: a fake news battle ahead of Indonesia's election'. Reuters, 11 April. https://www.reuters.com/article/us-indonesia-election-fakenews-insight/fact-checkers-vs-hoax-peddlers-a-fake-news-battle-ahead-of-indonesias-election-idUSKCN1RM2ZE

Power, T.P. 2018. 'Jokowi's authoritarian turn and Indonesia's democratic decline'. *Bulletin of Indonesian Economic Studies* 54(3): 307–38.

Setiawan, V.A. 2017. 'Analisis framing pemberitaan Dahlan Iskan dalam kasus dugaan korupsi gardu induk listrik di koran Jawa Pos edisi bulan Juni–Agustus 2015'. Program Studi Ilmu Komunikasi, Universitas Muhammadiyah Surakarta. http://eprints.ums.ac.id/56282/3/Naskah per cent20Publikasi per cent202.pdf

SPS Media Directory. 2014. '2013–2014: Integrasi multiplatform and monetisasi digital'. Serikat Perusahaan Pers, 22.

Steele, J. 2010. 'Indonesian journalism post-Suharto: changing ideals and professional practices'. In *Politics and the Media in Twenty-First Century Indonesia: Decade of Democracy*, edited by K. Sen and D.T. Hill, 85–103. London: Routledge.

Steele, J. 2012. 'The making of the 1999 Indonesian press law'. *Indonesia* 94 (October): 1–22.

Tapsell, R. 2015. 'The media and subnational authoritarianism in Papua'. *Southeast Asia Research* 23(3): 319–34.

Tapsell, R. 2017. *Media Power in Indonesia: Oligarchs, Citizens and the Digital Revolution*. London: Rowman and Littlefield.

Tapsell, R. 2019. 'Indonesia's policing of hoax news increasingly politicised'. *Perspective* 75, 20 September. Singapore: ISEAS – Yusof Ishak Institute. https://www.iseas.edu.sg/images/pdf/ISEAS_Perspective_2019_75.pdf

Tempo. 2014a. 'Winning signs'. *Tempo*, 14–20 July.

Tempo. 2014b. 'Dalam bayang-bayang Paloh'. *Tempo*, 24–30 November.

Vartanova, E. and S. Smirnov. 2010. 'Contemporary structure of the Russian media industry'. In *Russian Mass Media and Changing Values*, edited by A. Rosenholm, K. Nordenstreng and E. Trubina, 21–40. Oxon: Routledge.

Warburton, E. 2019. 'Polarisation in Indonesia: what if perception is reality?'. *New Mandala*, 16 April. https://www.newmandala.org/how-polarised-is-indonesia/

12 The economic dimensions of Indonesia's democratic quality: a subnational approach[1]

Puspa Delima Amri and Mochamad Pasha

Prior to the third wave of democratisation, regimes considered to be democratic were a minority in the world stage; fast-forward five decades, and more than 50 per cent of today's states are considered democratic (Coppedge et al. 2019). Experience with democratic transition has not been smooth, however. During periods of democratic transition and consolidation, political and economic reforms often stagnate, breeding widespread disappointment. Even where democratic transitions appear relatively successful, the threat of backsliding often remains: the past decade has seen a global decline in the health of democracy (Bermeo 2016; Mounk 2019). Increasingly, democratic regimes have deteriorated under the stewardship of democratically elected leaders—in Hungary, Turkey and the Philippines, to name a few—rather than falling to the types of authoritarian takeover so readily conjured in the popular imagination (Aspinall and Berenschot 2019; Bermeo 2016). As this book demonstrates, Indonesia is quickly catching up to this global trend as it backslides into an increasingly illiberal form of democracy.

Among the many theories that explain why some democracies consolidate while others regress, economic arguments—and especially variants of modernisation theory—have been especially influential. Przeworski et al. (2000), for example, contend that income per capita is the strongest predictor of whether democracy or dictatorship prevails. Indeed, a cursory glance around the world suggests that many authoritarian countries are poorer than the wealthy democracies of Europe and North

1 For help on various aspects of this chapter we thank Mulya Amri, Arya Fernandes, Indira Hapsari, Melissa Rogers, Nathanael Sumaktoyo, M. Zulfan Tadjoeddin and the editors of this volume. The views expressed here are those of the authors and do not necessarily reflect those of the authors' affiliations, including Sonoma State University, the World Bank, its executive directors or the countries they represent.

America. Within democracies, a lack of economic progress can also reduce public satisfaction with the political and institutional status quo. For example, a 2018 poll by Pew Research Center conducted in 24 countries, including Indonesia, revealed that respondents with negative views of the economy are on average 36 per cent points more likely to be dissatisfied with democracy, compared to those with favourable views of the economy (Wike et al. 2019). A large body of research also suggests that a high level of inequality has negative implications for democratic participation and support (e.g. Solt 2008).

This chapter explores the economic dimensions of Indonesia's democratic quality. Our main goal is to analyse how economic conditions—specifically, income per capita, income inequality and unemployment—correlate to variations in democratic quality in Indonesia over the past decade. We do so by focusing on subnational variation among Indonesia's 34 provinces. We look at the provincial rather than the national level for several reasons. First, province-level observations provide a much larger number of cases and more reliable conclusions. Second, comparative research shows that subnational variation in democratic quality exists in many countries—for example, Russia (Lankina 2010), Argentina (Gervasoni 2010) and Mexico (Benton 2012)—and such variation can offer important insights into the conditions that determine domestic democratic health. We can certainly expect such variation in Indonesia; one likely point of subnational difference arises from the tendency of local governments to pass religious regional regulations, which are often seen as threatening minority rights (Künkler and Stepan 2013). By taking a subnational approach, we aim to account for important variations in the protection of civil liberties and political rights, the quality of electoral processes, and other factors that make democracy meaningful (Lankina 2010).

To do so, we use the Indonesia Democracy Index (IDI), which to our knowledge is the only subnational time-series dataset measuring democratic quality in Indonesia. A secondary goal of this chapter, however, is to comment on the validity of the IDI as a measure of provincial democratic quality, and to highlight the strengths and weaknesses of a dataset that is used regularly by the Indonesian government and by civil society as a basis for policy recommendations.

We find that several development indicators do have a positive and significant effect on democratic quality at the provincial level—particularly urbanisation and literacy rates—but that those effects are not always consistent. We also draw only tentative conclusions about the economic foundations of subnational democracy, given our concerns about the quality and reliability of the IDI dataset. Prompted by these concerns, we put forward a set of recommendations to improve the IDI. If acted upon, these could ensure policymakers, analysts and activists are equipped with a quality tool for developing pro-democracy policy recommendations and interventions into the future.

The rest of this chapter proceeds as follows: we first review the literature that connects economic development and democracy, and make the case for testing this connection at the local level. The next section explains the data and methods used to implement our research questions. Next, we report the results of our statistical analysis. Finally, we comment on the reliability of the IDI for research purposes, before offering our concluding remarks. Pointing out caveats related to coding, weighting and operationalisation of the concepts of democracy in the IDI dataset, we call on Indonesian researchers and public policy analysts to further develop and improve this dataset.

DEMOCRACY AND DEVELOPMENT: A LITERATURE REVIEW

The relationship between economic development and political regimes is one of the most debated topics in the democratisation literature.[2] Notably, across multiple countries and time periods, scholars have found a positive link between income per capita and democratic outcomes. As societies become more affluent they undergo social transformations that reduce the structural viability of autocracy (Lerner 1958; Lipset 1959; Przeworski et al. 2000). Modernisation theory argues, for example, that industrialisation changes modes of production in ways that require the active cooperation of employees in production. These processes additionally empower the middle class to rise as champions of democracy. Further, in a capitalist setting, so the argument goes, democracies are valued for providing features supportive of the market economy such as accountability, third-party arbitration and the enforcement of contracts and law (Heller 2000). Proponents of modernisation theory even suggest that economic progress can encourage cultural shifts, promoting values that are more receptive towards democracy (Almond and Verba 1963; Diamond 1992). These include the values of secularism and self-expression associated with egalitarian social structures (Inglehart and Welzel 2005). Given that these cultural shifts are found more often in urban than rural

---

2   For a summary of these studies and other factors that determine democracy see, for example, Teorell (2010), Waldner and Lust (2018), and Wucherpfennig and Deutsch (2009).

areas (Lipset 1994), it is unsurprising that multiple studies have found a positive correlation between levels of education and urbanisation, and the likelihood of democratic transition (Barro 1999; Lupu and Murali 2009).

Although the dominant stream of research diagnoses a positive relationship between development and democracy (Wucherpfennig and Deutsch 2009), a number of prominent studies have found the opposite.[3] There is also much debate over questions of causality: that is, whether economic development helps overturn dictatorship (i.e. endogenous modernisation, a hypothesis supported by Boix and Stokes 2003), or whether it functions only to sustain already existing democracy (i.e. exogenous modernisation, a theory championed by Przeworski et al. 2000). Both theories have received statistical support (Inglehart and Welzel 2005; Przeworski et al. 2000), and it is now common to test both the endogenous and exogenous versions of the modernisation theory (Waldner and Lust 2018).[4] Finally, according to some studies, both endogenous and exogenous modernisation suffer from reverse causality: it is democratic regimes that produce greater economic development, not the other way around (Acemoglu et al. 2008). The latter argument holds that democracy promotes development by encouraging a more open society with more robust policy commitments to education and health.[5]

Income inequality is also touted as a factor that affects democratisation although, once again, existing theories offer contending views. Using a game-theory model, Boix (2003) shows that low levels of income inequality enhance the prospects for democratisation. Boix argues that elites are more willing to 'allow' democratisation when income inequality is low, as this is correlated with a low demand for fiscal redistribution. Ansell and Samuels (2010) disagree. In their view, demands for democratisation are more likely to arise and succeed when income inequality is high—a common by-product of economic growth—as more unequal societies

---

3   Among those who found a negative or no relationship are Sirowy and Inkeles (1990) and Hadenius (1992). One reason for the contradictory results are different countries and time period samples as well as different measures of democracy (Przeworski and Limongi 1997).

4   Take the case of Indonesia, for example. As argued by Tadjoeddin (2012), democratisation in 1998 was the result of factors other than economics (exogenous modernisation) but, ever since, Indonesia's democratic development seems to be a case of endogenous democratisation.

5   Another channel raised by Acemoglu and co-authors (2008) is that democracies provide a formal avenue for people to express political dissatisfaction and demand accountability of their leaders, which then helps business communities to retain (and even grow) their investment in the country.

often contain pockets of industrialisation and urban middle classes that are ripe for mobilisation against autocratic rule.

Aspects of modernisation theory and its variants have, of course, been criticised over the years, with analysts pointing to cases such as Singapore or China, where rising wealth has not led to democratic openings. Many emphasise that income inequality and redistributive urges are *insufficient* to explain democratic breakdowns and transitions; Slater et al. (2014) make this case in specific reference to Southeast Asia. Others have questioned the notion that urban educated citizens are especially likely to embrace democratic values, as studies of rural societies in developing countries show that such communities are often just as active and engaged in democratic processes (Krishna 2008; Lankina 2010). One should note that critics of the modernisation hypothesis often overlook that Lipset's (1959) seminal work on this subject is one of correlation, not of causation (Wucherpfennig and Deutsch 2009). Lipset identified possible correlates of economic development, such as industrialisation, urbanisation and education, as factors *supportive* of democracy. Modernisation theory continues to occupy a central role in the study of political regimes, and its application has been extended to cross-country, time-series studies as well as with reference to particular countries.

Our present interest is in the intersection between economic and democratic outcomes in Indonesia. As noted earlier, we do so by looking at province-level data. We take our lead from other studies of subnational democratisation—a growing subfield within comparative politics. There is increasing recognition that democratic islands can exist within undemocratic regimes (Lankina 2010); and, at the same time, subnational authoritarian enclaves can survive well beyond national-level democratic transitions. Indeed, work on India (Beer and Mitchell 2006; Harbers et al. 2019; Heller 2000), Mexico (Benton 2012), Argentina (Gervasoni 2010, 2018) and Russia (McMann and Petrov 2000) has demonstrated the possibility of subnational political units with a level of democracy that is quite different from the centre.

Some of this work on subnational regime variation tests aspects of the modernisation thesis.[6] Here, the results have also been mixed. While Linz (1994) and O'Donnell (1993) associate low quality subnational democracy with factors such as poverty and low levels of urbanisation, Gervasoni (2010) found no consistent association with development-related variables

---

6   Other studies could be classified as rentier theories of democracy (see Waldner and Lust 2018 for a review), where it is not income per capita that matters for democracy, but rather the source of regional income, such as natural resources and fiscal transfers.

(e.g. literacy rates and infant mortality rates). Using expert surveys in Russia, both Lankina (2010) and McMann and Petrov (2000) found urbanisation to positively affect democratic quality, but income-related variables were not significant (although this was possibly due to weak measures of income; regional gross domestic product (GDP) was not used). Tadjoeddin's (2012) study of 282 local elections in Indonesia found a correlation between economic indicators—including income and poverty indices—and 'electoral hostility' (i.e. electoral conflict).

We also argue that a subnational study is valuable because Indonesia is highly decentralised. While provinces, districts and municipalities do not have their own constitutions, local leaders have the resources and authority to create regional laws. In practice this has led to a proliferation of by-laws, some of which narrow personal freedoms and threaten the rights of religious minorities (Salim 2007). These are not easy to repeal, even though many of them contradict national-level laws (Lindsey and Butt 2013). There is little doubt that these local regulations can meaningfully impact democratic quality. In fact, local political outcomes may have greater consequences for citizens' daily lives compared to political changes at the more distant national level (Tadjoeddin 2012). Most citizens' first point of political contact is with their local government (Benton 2012). Finally, the sheer size and diversity of Indonesia's political, social and economic landscape render the study of subnational variation in democratic quality an important endeavour (Rauf et al. 2013).

THE DATA AND METHOD

The Indonesia Democracy Index (IDI) is the only comprehensive dataset that measures the quality of democratic institutions and practices at the subnational level. The project began around 2007 through cooperation between the Indonesian government and the United Nations Development Programme.[7] The main agencies involved are the Ministry of National Development Planning (Badan Perencanaan Pembangunan Nasional, Bappenas), the Coordinating Ministry of Politics, Law and Security (which oversees the Ministry of Home Affairs) and Statistics Indonesia (Badan Pusat Statistik, BPS). A team of experts (academics, non-government organisation activists, politicians and journalists) contributed to the design of the framework and to the weighting of the index, leaving BPS primarily in charge of data collection and processing. The initial goal

---

7 https://www.undp.org/content/dam/indonesia/Project%20Docs/IDI/Fast_ Facts_Indonesia.pdf

of the IDI project was to equip the national government with the data necessary to monitor democracy in the regions, and enable it to pressure provincial governments into maintaining and improving democratic quality. Results from the IDI project were also designed to be used for planning purposes by Bappenas (Rauf et al. 2013). Provinces are ranked according to their level of democratic attainment in each year's official data release, much as countries are ranked in international democracy indices.

IDI indicators are inspired by the conception and operationalisation of democratic indicators used by Freedom House. Specifically, the IDI uses a weighted average of indicators that fall under 'civil liberties' ('the freedom of citizens and groups of individuals to come together and to associate or organize, to voice their opinions or speak up and to have a belief or faith in something', Rauf et al. 2011: 16), 'political rights' ('the right to vote and the right to get elected in a general election … [and] political participation in decision making', Rauf et al. 2011: 18) and 'institutions of democracy' ('state institutions formed with the intention of supporting a democratic political system', Rauf et al. 2013: 18). Figure 12.1 displays the average combined IDI scores for each province from 2009 to 2018 and Table 12.1 lists the variables and indicators (28 in total) that make up the IDI.

To test whether changes in economic factors influence the quality of democracy across Indonesia's provinces, we employ a panel-data regression analysis with robust standard errors clustered at the province level, using data from 2009 to 2018. Much like correlations, panel-data regression is a statistical tool for the investigation of relationships between variables, observed across different entities (in our case, the Indonesian provinces) and over multiple time periods (in our case, 2009–2018). We do not include North Kalimantan, which only became a separate province in 2012. Papua, West Papua and Aceh are mostly excluded,[8] mainly because these are provinces with special autonomy status, which likely have different political dynamics compared to the other provinces.

Our statistical analyses are represented by the equation:

$$Democracy_{i,t} = \alpha + \beta_1 GDP/capita_{i,t-1} + \beta_2 Inequality_{i,t-1} + \beta_3 Unemployment_{i,t-1} + \beta_4 X_{i,t-1} + \varepsilon_{i,t}$$

where *Democracy*$_{i,t}$ refers to the democracy score for province *i* in year *t*. We use four different forms of *democracy*: the overall/combined IDI and

---

8 As a comparison, we include one specification which includes these provinces (column 5, Table 12.3). We have concerns about the reliability of the IDI scores for these three provinces as they suggest an extremely positive assessment of civil liberties in Papua and West Papua in particular, which is hardly consistent with independent reports.

Figure 12.1   Regional variations in the Indonesian Democracy Index (average combined scores for civil liberties, political rights and institutions of democracy), 2009–2018

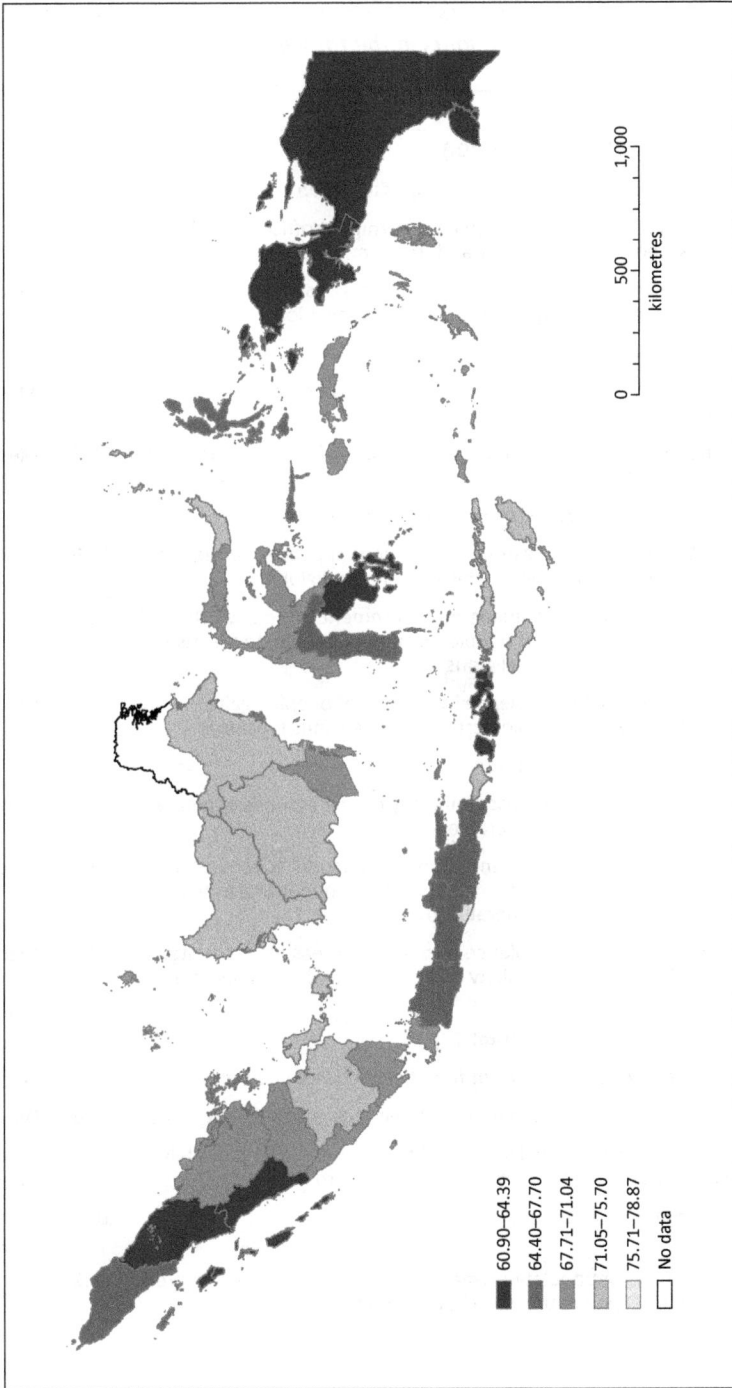

60.90–64.39
64.40–67.70
67.71–71.04
71.05–75.70
75.71–78.87
No data

0   500   1,000
kilometres

Source: Authors' calculations based on BPS data.

Table 12.1   The 28 indicators of the Indonesia Democracy Index and their respective weights in the total index

Indicator	Weight	Source
A. Civil liberties (32.7% of total IDI)		
I. Freedom of assembly and freedom of association		
1 Threats of or use of violence by government officers which curbs freedom of assembly and freedom of association	2.4	Media
2 Threats of or use of violence by members of society which curbs freedom of assembly and freedom of association	0.3	Media
II. Freedom of expression		
3 Threats of or use of violence by government officers which curbs freedom of expression	2.5	Media
4 Threats of or use of violence by members of society which curbs freedom of expression	0.5	Media
III. Freedom of belief/faith (freedom of religion)		
5 Written rules which restrict the freedom of people, or require people, to practise the teachings of their religions	13.6	Document
6 Actions or statements made by government officers which restrict the freedom of people, or require people, to practise the teachings of their religions	2.2	Media
7 Threats of or use of violence by a group of people against another group of people pertaining to religious teachings	3.4	Media
IV. Freedom from discrimination		
8 Written rules that are discriminatory on the grounds of gender, ethnicity or against vulnerable groups	3.1	Document
9 Actions taken, or statements made, by regional government officers which are discriminatory on the grounds of gender, ethnicity or against vulnerable groups	2.2	Media
10 Threats of or use of violence by people for reasons associated with the gender or ethnicity of the victim and/or vulnerable groups	2.6	Media
B. Political rights (41.3% of total IDI)		
V. The right to vote and the right to get elected in a general election		
11 Incidents in which people's right to vote or get elected is curbed	3.6	Document
12 Incidents which show lack of facilities for people with disabilities such that they cannot exercise their rights to vote	1.6	Expert Judgement
13 The quality of the permanent voter list	10.2	Expert Judgement
14 Percentage of population who use their right to vote compared to the total population who have the right to vote (voter turnout)	3.2	Document

Table 12.1   (continued)

Indicator	Weight	Source
15 Percentage of women elected as members of provincial parliament compared to the total members of provincial parliament	2.0	Document
VI. Political participation in decision making and watchdog		
16 Percentage of demonstrations/strikes that turn violent compared to the total number of demonstrations/strikes	10.3	Media & Document
17 Complaints on the running of government	10.3	Media & Document
C. Institutions of democracy (26% of total IDI)		
VII. Free and fair general elections		
18 Incidents that indicate the partiality of regional general elections commissions in organising and administering elections	2.0	Media & Document
19 Incidents or reporting of the fraudulent counting of votes	2.0	Media & Documents
VIII. The role of regional parliament (Dewan Perwakilan Rakyat Daerah, DPRD)		
20 The amount of budget allocated for education and health per capita	3.4	Documents
21 Share of regional regulations originating from the right to initiate a regulation exercised by DPRD	0.8	Documents
22 Recommendations put forward by DPRD to the executive	0.9	Document
IX. The role of political parties		
23 Cadre formation activities carried out by political parties which participate in general elections	4.6	Media & Documents
24 Percentage of women in the stewardship of political parties at provincial level	0.5	Documents
*X. The role of regional government bureaucracy**		
25 Reports and news concerning the use of government facilities for the interests of certain nominees/candidates/political parties in legislative general elections	2.9	Media & Documents
26 Reports and news concerning the involvement of civil servants in political activities of political parties in legislative general elections	2.9	Media & Documents
XI. The role of an independent judiciary		
27 Controversial rulings handed down by judges	2.9	Media
28 Terminations of controversial investigations by prosecutors or police	2.9	Media

* Indicators 25 and 26 in this table were used from 2009 to 2014.

Source: Rauf et al. (2013).

its three components. The respective betas (β) in the equation refer to the estimated coefficients for each independent variable. For example, β1 captures the average estimated effect of gross domestic product (GDP) per capita on the quality of democracy. As is common practice (e.g. Lupu and Murali 2009), all the independent variables are lagged by one year, as marked by the subscript t–1. Regional GDP per capita is measured in constant 2010 prices (in natural log form, to account for nonlinearity effects), inequality is a measure of income dispersion as captured by the Gini index,[9] and the unemployment rate is the percentage of the labour force that is unemployed.

As the level of democracy is affected by other factors, we included several control variables ($X_{i,t-1}$) previously found to be important determinants of democratisation (see earlier literature review). These are the urbanisation rate, literacy rates for people aged 15 and above, and the share of the manufacturing sector in the local GDP. We use fixed effects estimators to control for unobserved province-specific and year-specific characteristics that may affect the relationship between economic factors and democracy. While this, together with lagged independent variables, helps lower possible reverse causal directions (i.e. higher democratic quality leads to better economic progress), we cannot fully eliminate endogeneity and thus are careful in making causality claims. It should be noted that the control variables included here are not necessarily complete. For example, when Indonesian leaders resorted to policies that contributed to democratic stagnation, those policies could be responses to the changing nature of electoral competition in the very fierce marketplace for votes (Davidson 2018; Power 2018). Therefore, future work should consider the degree of electoral competition as a control variable.

All independent variables were extracted from the Indonesia Database for Policy and Economic Research (INDO-DAPOER), the National Socio-economic Survey (Survei Sosio-Ekonomi Nasional, Susenas) and CEIC Data (https://www.ceicdata.com/en).

We introduce two simple robustness checks. First, given the changes in coding rules from 2015 for indicators 25 and 26 (which will be further explained after a discussion of our findings), we conduct additional ordinary least squares regressions with two separate time periods. We averaged the overall/combined IDI from 2009 to 2014 and regressed it on the average of the independent variables from 2008 to 2013 (column 7,

---

9   An index between 0 and 100 that measures the extent to which the distribution of income (or, in some cases, consumption expenditure) among individuals or households within an economy deviates from a perfectly equal distribution (a score of 0 is a perfectly equal distribution).

Table 12.2); the dependent variable is averaged from 2015 to 2018, while the independent variables are averaged from 2014 to 2017 (column 8, Table 12.2) (accordingly, these columns have lower numbers of observations). The second test is reported in Table 12.3, where we replace real income per capita with average growth of real GDP since 2000, to capture economic progress since the beginning of the democratic transition, following Mainwaring and Bizzarro (2019).

FINDINGS

Overall, the results show a fairly inconsistent relationship between economic development and subnational democracy. As Table 12.2 shows, while we found that provinces with stronger economic indicators are indeed more likely to receive higher IDI scores, results are highly sensitive to the type of democracy index used. For example, income per capita has positive effects on democracy outcomes, but is statistically significant only for institutions of democracy (column 4).[10] On the other hand, unemployment is negatively related to democratic quality, but the effect is only significant when political rights is the dependent variable. Meanwhile, income inequality is not significant in any of the regression models we tested.[11]

The income variable's significance does not appear to be very robust to alternative specifications. In Table 12.3, instead of GDP per capita, we tested for the effects of real GDP growth rate since 2000, which do not appear to have significant effects. Using our second robustness measure (we divided the analysis into two periods: 2009–2014 and 2015–2018, columns 7 and 8 of Table 12.2), real GDP per capita was insignificant in both periods. However, the unemployment rate continues to register significantly negative effects on political rights (column 3, Table 12.3) and also to the overall/combined IDI for 2015–2018 (column 8, Table 12.2).

Surprisingly, the variables most commonly shown to be significant across the different models are not conventional economic variables, but literacy and urbanisation rates. That more urbanisation is associated

---

10 Notably, many of the components of institutions of democracy under the IDI are variables commonly considered governance variables (see Table 12.1).

11 Models using political rights as dependent variables (column 3, Table 12.2 and column 3, Table 12.3) have the highest R-squared among the similar family of regressions, suggesting it is a better fit compared to the rest. An R-squared of 0.75 means that 75 per cent of the variations in the political rights index can be explained by the independent variables in that model.

Table 12.2   Determinants of provincial democracy and its various components

Variable	Civil liberties	Political rights	Institutions of democracy	IDI combined	IDI (with Aceh and Papua)	IDI 2009–2014	IDI 2015–2018
Income per capita	4.329 (7.809)	-6.846 (5.421)	22.003** (8.354)	4.260 (4.618)	7.161** (3.049)	1.750 (1.646)	-0.920 (1.746)
Unemployment rate	0.374 (0.434)	-1.301** (0.517)	1.283 (0.834)	-0.098 (0.258)	0.188 (0.264)	-0.671 (0.416)	-1.279** (0.475)
Inequality	6.351 (19.439)	-4.468 (25.579)	-31.557 (26.405)	-8.672 (15.252)	-7.565 (14.282)	25.22 (30.42)	-0.373 (23.83)
Literacy rate	0.913 (0.582)	1.779** (0.766)	1.398 (0.829)	1.381*** (0.375)	0.378 (0.496)	0.445** (0.162)	0.542*** (0.178)
Urbanisation	8.643* (4.910)	10.875** (4.452)	3.039 (5.736)	8.562*** (2.801)	3.529 (3.797)	4.720 (2.916)	9.540*** (2.820)
Manufacturing	-9.542 (5.892)	-2.665 (4.216)	0.255 (4.831)	-4.415* (2.483)	-7.466*** (2.611)	-1.534 (1.274)	-2.983** (1.214)
Fixed effects	Yes	Yes	Yes	Yes	Yes	No	No
Observations	290	290	290	290	320	32	32
R^2	0.28	0.75	0.31	0.54	0.48	0.35	0.51

Note: Robust and clustered standard errors in parentheses. *** = $p < 0.01$; ** = $p < 0.05$; * $p < 0.10$; each regression has a constant term.

Table 12.3   *Determinants of provincial democracy and its various components using income growth*

Variable	Civil liberties	Political rights	Institutions of democracy	IDI combined
Income growth since 2000	2.992 (1.795)	0.335 (2.098)	−1.903 (2.698)	0.560 (1.092)
Unemployment rate	0.366 (0.422)	−1.241** (0.523)	1.091 (0.820)	−0.126 (0.260)
Inequality	−0.048 (0.066)	−0.046 (0.062)	−0.047 (0.070)	−0.049 (0.044)
Literacy rate	0.884 (0.609)	1.669** (0.730)	1.822** (0.843)	1.438*** (0.372)
Urbanisation	8.758 (5.566)	9.909** (4.681)	4.625 (6.883)	8.591*** (3.083)
Manufacturing	−9.230* (4.590)	−4.049 (4.631)	5.136 (5.342)	−3.608 (2.234)
Fixed effects	Yes	Yes	Yes	Yes
Observations	290	290	290	290
R^2	0.28	0.76	0.29	0.54

Note: Robust and clustered standard errors in parentheses. *** = $p < 0.01$; ** = $p < 0.05$; * $p < 0.10$; each regression has a constant term.

with higher democracy scores in Indonesia's provinces is consistent with findings in regional democracy studies in Russia (Lankina 2010; McMann and Petrov 2000), as well as multicountry studies (Barro 1999). The reasons for the causal direction from urbanisation to democracy are well documented; among others, urban density allows for easier communication and mobilising collective action (McMann and Petrov 2000). However, we should also take into account that income per capita is highly correlated with urbanisation and literacy rates, which may dampen the effect of income per capita on democracy scores. In some specifications, the size of the manufacturing sector appears weakly significant in the negative direction, contrary to expectations under the modernisation thesis.

The results lead us to draw the tentative conclusion that democracy in Indonesia is likely working better in regions with greater levels of urbanisation and higher literacy rates, particularly when it comes to ensuring the protection of citizens' political rights, including equality of access to political and electoral institutions. Given the way that political rights are measured in the IDI (non-electoral participation is included as an important aspect here), the findings also imply that in more urbanised provinces, democratic engagement may be more widely accessible, with citizens more able to voice complaints about local government performance. It follows that Indonesia's more isolated and rural areas require more investment into, and better monitoring of, electoral and non-electoral forms of political participation to ensure the nationwide protection of democratic rights. This serves to remind us that equality of economic opportunity must go hand-in-glove with equality of political rights; the pursuit of the former is intertwined with the development of the latter. Finally, in finding that urbanisation and literacy appear as more robust factors in determining democracy scores compared to income per capita, our result underscores the notion that democracy may be more sustainable when there is a well-informed and open society. However, these correlations do not imply—as some government policymakers have recently argued (*Jakarta Post* 2019)—that democracy can function only in more developed regions. Indeed, we firmly believe the government's proposal to 'solve' lower-quality democratic outcomes in less-developed regions by winding back direct elections would serve to exacerbate, rather than ameliorate, these democratic discrepancies.

IDI: AN IMPORTANT BUT IMPERFECT DATASET

While our conclusions are consistent with several key themes in the comparative literature, they must remain tentative due to our reservations about the quality of the IDI data. Given the importance of developing a credible subnational democratic dataset, and the role that the IDI plays in government policy planning, we believe it is necessary to delve into the IDI's weaknesses and the ways in which this resource can be improved.

First, some of the provincial scores raise red flags. As Table 12.4 suggests, provincial IDI scores are on average substantially higher for the civil liberties component than they are for political rights and institutions of democracy.[12] This is at odds with the overwhelming majority of qualitative national-level observations (e.g. Aspinall and Mietzner 2019; Warburton and Aspinall 2019) and data from global indices such as V-Dem (Coppedge et al. 2019). IDI scores also have substantial temporal fluctuations, while having low correlations across components of democracy. For example,

---

12   The civil liberties average score for all provinces from 2009 to 2018 is 80.38, while political rights scored 57.95 and institutions of democracy 70.75.

Jakarta went from the highest IDI score in 2015 to 24th place in 2016 due to the infamous 212 (2 December 2016) rally to 'defend Islam'.[13] In 2016 we also saw West Papua receive the sixth-highest score on civil liberties, while placing bottom of the chart in terms of political rights. These variations are even more extreme between different aspects used to score particular components. For instance, Jambi's 2015 scores for 'freedom of religion' and 'freedom of association', both of which are elements of the civil liberties component, were 86.61 and 7.81 respectively.

Some of this volatility must be attributed to the IDI's coding method. Unlike many other democracy indexes, the IDI does not rely on expert opinion surveys. Instead, BPS uses secondary sources, such as one major provincial newspaper and official government documents, to assign scores of 0–100 to each indicator.[14] For the most part, scores are based on the absence of incidents and regulations that are deemed harmful for democracy (Rauf et al. 2013).[15] The coding is done by the Jakarta-based, national BPS staff (using information collected by local enumerators), and is verified by a team of independent experts alluded to earlier (Mellisa et al. 2016). After this initial coding process, BPS organises focus group discussions to verify (or reject) the tabulated scores assembled by its analysts. At this stage, a province's score can be raised or lowered by up to 10 points, should the focus group discussions uncover incidents of democratic violations not previously recorded (Rauf et al. 2013). The focus group discussions are complemented with in-depth interviews of experts, focusing on cases which have not been resolved in the focus group discussions.

However, these processes often fall short in their implementation. Focus group discussions are not always well attended by stakeholders (Mellisa et al. 2016), and even when they are well attended, focus group discussions involve provincial government officials with a strong interest in ensuring their provinces rate highly. It is unclear how disagreements

---

13 Still, even with the 212 incident, where Muslim groups took to the streets to demand the arrest of then Jakarta governor Basuki Tjahaja Purnama ('Ahok') on grounds of blasphemy, the fluctuation appears excessive.

14 Scoring for each indicator varies, but a common method compares the number of incidents to the best and worst possible score (Rauf et al. 2011). For example, indicator 5 (written rules which restrict the freedom to practise religion) has 0 rules as the best possible score, while the worst possible score would be the average number of such rules across all provinces plus 5 standard deviations, which amounts to 23 regulations in 2009. Aceh reportedly had 5 such regulations in 2009, which leads to a score of $(5–23)/(0–23) \times 100 = 78.26$.

15 Except when it comes to numerical targets, like the quota for the proportion of women in regional parliament and in leadership positions of political parties.

Table 12.4   The Indonesia Democracy Index and its components: summary statistics by province, 2009–2018

Province	IDI		Civil liberties	
	Mean	SD	Mean	SD
Papua	60.90	1.73	88.66	3.43
West Sumatera	62.57	5.24	56.21	4.97
West Papua	62.60	2.99	93.18	4.64
West Nusa Tenggara	62.87	7.24	64.18	9.28
Southeast Sulawesi	64.00	7.79	86.74	5.47
North Sumatera	64.39	4.01	78.34	3.81
East Java	65.12	8.41	78.25	4.80
North Maluku	66.27	5.00	85.99	7.25
West Java	66.47	5.12	76.99	5.78
Aceh	66.82	7.87	74.65	13.37
South Sulawesi	67.06	5.24	79.16	5.71
Central Java	67.70	4.91	78.82	7.33
Lampung	68.40	4.22	79.89	12.14
West Sulawesi	68.74	3.94	87.62	6.66
Bengkulu	69.07	5.26	84.25	8.22
Banten	69.39	4.48	81.74	6.08
Jambi	69.41	2.77	84.20	6.96
Central Sulawesi	69.44	4.85	90.99	4.87
Gorontalo	70.24	6.22	82.35	5.76
Maluku	70.27	5.78	85.45	7.08
South Kalimantan	70.41	5.91	60.29	6.48
Riau Islands	70.64	5.02	86.31	5.25
Riau	71.04	3.80	80.67	8.43
Bangka Belitung Islands	72.24	5.79	86.17	4.69
Central Kalimantan	72.96	4.93	88.45	8.78
East Kalimantan	73.05	4.26	91.61	6.37
West Kalimantan	73.70	4.97	95.41	4.75
South Sumatera	74.11	4.47	91.15	5.43
East Nusa Tenggara	74.96	4.66	92.36	5.50
North Sulawesi	75.09	5.03	92.81	3.48
Bali	75.70	4.10	94.40	1.40
Yogyakarta	77.48	6.35	89.93	2.27
Jakarta	78.87	5.78	89.62	3.74

Table 12.4   *(continued)*

Province	Political rights		Institutions of democracy	
	Mean	SD	Mean	SD
Papua	38.49	6.44	61.58	7.08
West Sumatera	57.63	8.61	78.40	10.83
West Papua	40.30	3.27	59.57	6.09
West Nusa Tenggara	55.22	7.10	73.38	11.72
Southeast Sulawesi	45.58	15.01	64.68	8.83
North Sumatera	56.88	7.46	58.78	5.33
East Java	53.36	14.60	67.28	13.24
North Maluku	52.04	12.56	64.07	8.52
West Java	61.02	13.25	61.84	10.26
Aceh	60.06	8.72	67.71	10.00
South Sulawesi	53.68	13.77	73.09	8.04
Central Java	57.28	10.54	70.27	7.63
Lampung	57.59	6.86	71.12	9.20
West Sulawesi	53.26	10.61	69.07	7.04
Bengkulu	59.39	6.63	65.36	11.35
Banten	55.45	9.82	74.37	9.90
Jambi	53.99	8.51	75.29	9.34
Central Sulawesi	51.57	12.05	70.74	9.66
Gorontalo	60.38	9.77	70.67	7.83
Maluku	58.90	12.27	69.21	5.81
South Kalimantan	71.84	12.10	80.86	7.07
Riau Islands	59.85	11.67	68.06	4.54
Riau	59.85	9.93	76.72	9.21
Bangka Belitung Islands	60.60	14.09	73.21	8.32
Central Kalimantan	58.56	7.57	76.34	9.45
East Kalimantan	62.09	12.24	67.11	4.79
West Kalimantan	57.93	13.07	71.44	9.59
South Sumatera	62.75	11.67	70.75	6.09
East Nusa Tenggara	62.47	11.24	72.91	9.69
North Sulawesi	64.83	11.35	69.08	7.02
Bali	59.25	10.82	78.33	7.39
Yogyakarta	66.00	13.54	80.05	8.06
Jakarta	66.74	11.48	84.98	9.44

Note: Author calculations based on IDI data from BPS. SD is standard deviation. Provinces are ranked in ascending order based on average IDI (2009–2018).

concerning the interpretation of the coding are resolved. Furthermore, local newspapers do not always report on the issues relevant to the IDI indicators and BPS researchers frequently encounter bureaucratic hurdles in obtaining official documents to review (Mellisa et al. 2016; Rauf et al. 2011).

Another problem concerns weighting. While the weight received by each indicator is public information, which we summarise in Table 12.1, it is unclear why certain indicators such as 'threats of or use of violence by members of society which curbs freedom of expression' carry as little as 0.5 per cent weight, while others, like 'written rules which restrict the freedom of people, or require people, to practise the teachings of their religions', carry as much as 13.6 per cent (the largest of any single indicator) in the overall index. A panel of experts (whose names are published in the IDI codebook published by Bappenas) determine this aspect of the IDI methodology, but there is no publicly available information on the theoretical or conceptual justification for this weighting. One can only infer that the panel views religious pluralism, as it is enshrined in written rules and also in reports of threats of or use of violence related to religious freedom, to be the single most important element of democracy.[16] Yet even here, there is ample evidence that informal social sanctions on citizens' behaviour, including religious expression, are often more consequential than formal laws in Indonesia (see Jaffrey, this volume).

There are other conceptual problems with how the IDI measures democratic quality. For example, the IDI counts the share of public protests that turned violent as an indicator of poor political participation, and allocates a weight of 10.3 per cent. While we agree that participatory democracy is important, we think it is misleading to interpret demonstrations that turned violent as a poor reflection of political participation per se; indeed, the absence or curtailment of popular protest may be an equally (if not more) alarming indicator of shortcomings in this area. Another example is the dimension of free and fair elections, which is judged using only local newspaper reports of ballot box fraud or bias on the part of Regional Elections Commission officials. Aside from the fact that the absence of *reports* of fraud does not necessarily mean no fraud occurred, the IDI overlooks multiple other forms of electoral manipulation, such as voter intimidation, vote buying and the suppression of opposition parties and candidates. As such, it is difficult to trust the accuracy of the score of 94.94 received by West Papua for free and fair elections in 2009,

---

16 Some possible explanations for this heavy emphasis on pluralism are raised by Nuraniyah in this volume.

or Jakarta's score of 100 in 2011, especially considering there were no province-wide elections in Jakarta in 2011.

One of the problems we diagnose with the IDI is the fact that it is compiled by government officials instead of independent researchers. We are sceptical that bureaucrats can be expected to make objective and unbiased judgements that reflect on the quality of the institutions that employ them, even though it has been acknowledged that BPS has a reputation as an independent agency with strong analytical capacity for socioeconomic data (Hill and Vidyattama 2014). To be sure, BPS reports often appear candid and critical in addressing various incidents that are deemed harmful for democracy at the regional level. For example, the 2016 IDI report stated that, across the board, 'threats to freedom of association' was mainly attributed to 'the terrible behaviour of local government officials in threatening and using force' (Rauf et al. 2017: 29). The 2015 report stated that one of the reasons for Aceh's very low score of 18.76 out of 100 for the variable 'freedom of expression' is because of a common coercive tactic used by regional administrations:

> IDI found many instances of Aceh civil servants who were relocated to remote offices with high living costs, not for a valid reorganisational purpose, but simply due to expressing differences of opinion with their superiors. (Rauf et al. 2016: 69)[17]

Meanwhile, the 2018 report commented thus on the 2016 collapse of Jakarta's political rights score:

> Jakarta's gubernatorial election was marked by intense competition, characterised by massive and emotional identity politics, which resulted in many violations of *pilkada* rules and democratic principles in general. (Rauf et al. 2018: 8).

However, the inclusion of these criticisms does not necessarily indicate independence and objectivity in IDI reporting. IDI's codebook does not provide a listing of all the events that may have contributed to very low or very high scores in a particular indicator; the above are only a few examples. Indeed, the IDI may also be subject to direct political influence from local government officials, who have the opportunity to revise BPS's assessment of the indicators during the focus group discussions. With no information on how often BPS assessments are revised following the focus group discussion stage, it is difficult to gauge the extent of influence potentially exerted by these local administrators. On occasion, local BPS

---

17 While the Islamist mobilisations of 2016 no doubt damaged political rights in Jakarta, it is at least worth noting that the IDI's criticism of 'identity politics' was wholly consistent with the national government's position.

officials have hinted that downstream interference is taking place, stating they are simply following guidelines passed down by the national agency and its independent expert team, and suggesting that disagreements about methodologies should be discussed between local government officials and those experts.[18] Indeed, the independent expert team also verified the initial scoring/coding done by the central BPS analysts (Mellisa et al. 2016).

One final note we raise is the lack of consistency in the indicators and coding rules. First, while the weights have not changed over time, two of the 28 indicators were replaced in 2015, both of which pertain to the effectiveness of local government bureaucracy. Specifically, indicator 25 'reports and news concerning the use of government facilities for the interests of certain nominees/candidates/political parties in legislative general elections' was replaced by 'local government policies deemed to have breached regulations by the State Administration Court', while indicator 26 'reports and news concerning the involvement of civil servants in political activities of political parties in legislative general elections' was replaced by 'local government provision of information regarding the local budget'. Not only did the new indicators refer to very different problems from those they replaced, the removed indicators had been important in reflecting local incumbents' attempts to tilt the electoral scales in their favour.[19]

Second, the scoring system for Aceh changed substantially in ways that overestimate the province's civil liberty scores. Starting in 2015, local regulations (and government actions to enforce these regulations) that infringe on freedom of religion no longer resulted in changes to Aceh's civil liberty score, as such provisions were deemed an essential part of Aceh's special autonomy status. In addition, Aceh's scores were not retroactively revised. For this reason alone, we recommend excluding Aceh from any time-series analysis of the IDI.

In our view, these concerns underscore the importance of having a more reliable measure of subnational democracy in Indonesia. An improved IDI would be based on more theoretically informed measures of democracy, be collected using sources that are more comprehensive in coverage (reliance on a single local media outlet is hardly appropriate for many of

---

18 See statement by the head of West Sumatera BPS, Sukardi, which deflected criticism regarding IDI methodology from West Sumatera officials (Candra 2018).

19 As a comparison, incumbents in less democratic provinces of Argentina often misuse their office to gain a competitive edge in elections, such as massively outspending challengers and excluding opponents from desirable public jobs (Gervasoni 2010).

the indicators) and adopt more clear and consistent coding rules. We also believe that awareness of the above concerns should guide researchers in exercising caution (and making necessary modifications) when using these data, rather than dismissing the data altogether. After all, some of the values do appear compatible with more widely accepted measures of democratic quality. Notably, aggregate scores from the provincial IDI—which, in effect, should provide a national-level overview of democratic quality—document a pattern consistent with the findings of international indices such as V-Dem: that is, a reduction of features associated with liberal democracy starting around 2010 (Coppedge et al. 2019).

CONCLUSION

This chapter looked at Indonesia's varied democratic conditions at the provincial level, and explored the economic foundations of that variation. This line of enquiry is important in the Indonesian context, given ongoing debates among state officials about whether Indonesia's poorer, less-developed regions are 'ready' or suited for electoral democracy. We find some evidence that democratic performance is associated with the variables of urbanisation, literacy rates and—to a more limited extent—per capita income and unemployment rates. However, we should emphasise that despite these associations, we do not find any *definitive* relationship between macroeconomic variables and regional scores on the IDI. Nor are our results uniform across components of democratic quality. For example, higher GDP per capita corresponds to stronger institutions of democracy, but no commensurate improvements to civil liberties or political rights. Finally, we found no significant correlation between democracy scores and income inequality.

An improved tool for the measurement of local democracy might be founded upon a relatively narrow conception of democracy—potentially one that focuses on the quality of electoral democracy—before incorporating a more extensive layer of liberal and participatory indicators. This would allow researchers to concentrate on finding theoretically relevant index attributes. While there are templates from other countries such as Argentina (Gervasoni 2010) and India (Harbers et al. 2019), it is important to design a framework that is locally sensitive to conditions in Indonesia, and that draws on qualitative insight into the characteristic features of local democracy, such as vote buying, patron–client relationships and political dynasties.

While it is true that Indonesia's subnational political regimes are extremely complex and multidimensional, and they are not easily understood, we also believe the IDI's coding relies on imperfect proxies for democratic quality. The limitations of the IDI—its variable coding rules, incomplete sources of secondary data and potential political interference, to name but the most obvious—necessarily temper any grand claims about the relationship between economic outcomes and democracy in Indonesia's provinces. Yet developing a valid and reliable regional democracy indicator—ideally, one that extends to the district level—will be extremely important if we are to better understand the origins, effects and shortcomings of democratic development in Indonesia, and the ways in which these relate to economic development.

REFERENCES

Acemoglu, D., S. Johnson, J.A. Robinson and P. Yared. 2008. 'Income and democracy'. *American Economic Review* 98(3): 808–42.

Almond, G.A. and S. Verba. 1963. *The Civic Culture: Political Attitudes and Democracy in Five Nations*. Princeton, NJ: Princeton University Press.

Ansell, B. and D. Samuels. 2010. 'Inequality and democratization: a contractarian approach'. *Comparative Political Studies* 43(12): 1543–74.

Aspinall, E. and W. Berenschot. 2019. *Democracy for Sale: Elections, Clientelism, and the State in Indonesia*. Ithaca, NY: Cornell University Press.

Aspinall, E. and M. Mietzner. 2019. 'Southeast Asia's troubling elections: nondemocratic pluralism in Indonesia'. *Journal of Democracy* 30(4): 104–18.

Barro, R.J. 1999. 'Determinants of democracy'. *Journal of Political Economy* 107(S6): S158–83.

Beer, C. and N.J. Mitchell. 2006. 'Comparing nations and states: human rights and democracy in India'. *Comparative Political Studies* 39(8): 996–1,018.

Benton, A.L. 2012. 'Bottom-up challenges to national democracy: Mexico's (legal) subnational authoritarian enclaves'. *Comparative Politics* 44(3): 253–71.

Bermeo, N. 2016. 'On democratic backsliding'. *Journal of Democracy* 27(1): 5–19.

Boix, C. 2003. *Democracy and Redistribution*. Cambridge: Cambridge University Press.

Boix, C. and S.C. Stokes. 2003. 'Endogenous democratization'. *World Politics* 55(4): 517–49.

Candra, S.A. 2018. 'Lonjakan indeks demokrasi Sumbar tertinggi di Indonesia'. *Republika*, 15 August. https://www.republika.co.id/berita/nasional/daerah/18/08/15/pdierk349-lonjakan-indeks-demokrasi-sumbar-tertinggi-di-indonesia

Coppedge, M., J. Gerring, C.H. Knutsen, S.I. Lindberg, J. Teorell, D. Altman, M. Bernhard, et al. 2019. 'V-Dem dataset—version 9'. Gothenburg: Varieties of Democracy Institute. https://doi.org/10.23696/vdemcy19

Davidson, J.S. 2018. *Indonesia: Twenty Years of Democracy*, Elements in Politics and Society in Southeast Asia. Cambridge: Cambridge University Press.

Diamond, L. 1992. 'Economic development and democracy reconsidered'. *American Behavioral Scientist* 35(4–5): 450–99.

Gervasoni, C. 2010. 'A rentier theory of subnational regimes: fiscal federalism, democracy, and authoritarianism in the Argentine provinces'. *World Politics* 62(2): 302–40.

Gervasoni, C. 2018. *Hybrid Regimes within Democracies: Fiscal Federalism and Subnational Rentier States.* Cambridge: Cambridge University Press.

Hadenius, A. 1992. *Democracy and Development.* Cambridge: Cambridge University Press.

Harbers, I., J. Bartman and E. van Wingerden. 2019. 'Conceptualizing and measuring subnational democracy across Indian states'. *Democratization* 26(7): 1,154–75.

Heller, P. 2000. 'Degrees of democracy: some comparative lessons from India'. *World Politics* 52(4): 484–519.

Hill, H. and Y. Vidyattama. 2014. 'Hares and tortoises: regional development dynamics in Indonesia'. In *Regional Dynamics in a Decentralized Indonesia,* edited by H. Hill, 68–97. Singapore: Institute of Southeast Asian Studies (ISEAS).

Inglehart, R. and C. Welzel. 2005. *Modernization, Cultural Change, and Democracy: The Human Development Sequence.* Cambridge: Cambridge University Press.

Jakarta Post. 2019. ' "Dilemma of democracy": Tito says nondemocratic countries have better economic growth'. *Jakarta Post,* 27 November. https://www.thejakartapost.com/news/2019/11/27/dilemma-of-democracy-tito-says-nondemocratic-countries-have-better-economic-growth.html

Krishna, A. 2008. 'Introduction: poor people and democracy'. In *Poverty, Participation, and Democracy,* edited by A. Krishna, 1–27. New York: Cambridge University Press.

Künkler, M. and A. Stepan, eds. 2013. *Democracy and Islam in Indonesia.* New York: Columbia University Press.

Lankina, T. 2010. 'Regional democracy variations and the forgotten legacies of western engagement'. In *The Politics of Sub-national Authoritarianism in Russia,* edited by V. Gel'man and C. Ross, 39–65. Farnham: Ashgate Publishing.

Lerner, D. 1958. *The Passing of Traditional Society: Modernizing the Middle East.* Free Press of Glencoe.

Lindsey, T. and S. Butt. 2013. 'Unfinished business: law reform, governance, and the courts in post-Suharto Indonesia'. In *Democracy and Islam in Indonesia,* edited by M. Künkler and A. Stepan, 168–86. New York: Columbia University Press.

Linz, J.J. 1994. 'Democracy, presidential or parliamentary: does it make a difference?'. In *The Failure of Presidential Democracy: The Case of Latin America,* edited by J.J. Linz and A. Valenzuela, 3–87. Baltimore: Johns Hopkins University Press.

Lipset, S.M. 1959. 'Some social requisites of democracy: economic development and political legitimacy'. *American Political Science Review* 53(1): 69–105.

Lipset, S.M. 1994. 'The social requisites of democracy revisited: 1993 Presidential Address'. *American Sociological Review* 59(1):1–22.

Lupu, N. and K. Murali. 2009. 'Development, democratization, and democratic deepening'. Paper presented to the annual meeting of the Midwest Political Science Association, 16 September. http://www.noamlupu.com/democratic_deepening.pdf

Mainwaring, S. and F. Bizzarro. 2019. 'The fates of third-wave democracies'. *Journal of Democracy* 30(1): 99–113.

McMann, K.M. and N.V. Petrov. 2000. 'A survey of democracy in Russia's regions'. *Post-Soviet Geography and Economics* 41(3): 155–82.

Mellisa, A., H. Mubarok, S. Mulyartono, A. Nursahid, I. Rafsadi and P.T. Chatami. 2016. 'Mengukur kebebasan beragama di Jawa Barat 2014: catatan dari Indeks Demokrasi Indonesia'. Washington, DC: Center for the Study of Islam and Democracy.

Mounk, Y. 2019. 'The dictators' last stand: why the new autocrats are weaker than they look'. *Foreign Affairs*, September/October. https://www.foreignaffairs.com/articles/world/2019-08-12/dictators-last-stand

O'Donnell, G. 1993. 'On the state, democratization and some conceptual problems: a Latin American view with glances at some postcommunist countries'. *World Development* 21(8): 1,355–69.

Power, T.P. 2018. 'Jokowi's authoritarian turn and Indonesia's democratic decline'. *Bulletin of Indonesian Economic Studies* 54(3): 307–38.

Przeworski, A. and F. Limongi. 1997. 'Modernization: theories and facts'. *World Politics* 49(2): 155–83.

Przeworski, A., M.E. Alvarez, J.A. Cheibub and F. Limongi. 2000. *Democracy and Development: Political Institutions and Well-being in the World, 1950–1990.* Cambridge: Cambridge University Press.

Rauf, M., S. Hidayat, A.M. Gismar, S.M. Mulia and A. Parengkuan. 2011. *Measuring Democracy in Indonesia: 2009 Indonesia Democracy Index.* Jakarta: United Nations Development Programme.

Rauf, M., S. Hidayat, A.M. Gismar and S.M. Mulia. 2013. *Indeks Demokrasi Indonesia (IDI) 2011: Demokrasi Indonesia: Ledakan Tuntutan Publik vs. Inersia Politik.* Jakarta: Bappenas.

Rauf, M., S. Hidayat, A.M. Gismar and S.M. Mulia. 2016. *Indeks Demokrasi Indonesia 2015: Urgensi Penguatan Kultur Demokrasi.* Jakarta: Bappenas.

Rauf, M., S.M. Mulia, S. Hidayat and A.M. Gismar. 2017. *Indeks Demokrasi Indonesia 2016: Tantangan Peningkatan Kualitas Partisipasi dan Representasi.* Jakarta: Bappenas.

Rauf, M., S.M. Mulia, A.M. Gismar and S. Hidayat. 2018. *Indeks Demokrasi Indonesia 2017: Citra Demokrasi, Minim Kapasitas.* Jakarta: Bappenas.

Salim, A. 2007. 'Muslim politics in Indonesia's democratisation'. In *Democracy and the Promise of Good Governance,* edited by R.H. McLeod and A. MacIntyre, 115–37. Singapore: Institute of Southeast Asian Studies (ISEAS).

Sirowy, L. and A. Inkeles. 1990. 'The effects of democracy on economic growth and inequality: a review'. *Studies in Comparative International Development* 25(1): 126–57.

Slater, D., B. Smith and G. Nair. 2014. 'Economic origins of democratic breakdown? The redistributive model and the postcolonial state'. *Perspectives on Politics* 12(2): 353–74.

Solt, F. 2008. 'Economic inequality and democratic political engagement'. *American Journal of Political Science* 52(1): 48–60.

Tadjoeddin, M.Z. 2012. 'Electoral conflict and the maturity of local democracy in Indonesia: testing the modernisation hypothesis'. *Journal of the Asia Pacific Economy* 17(3): 476–97.

Teorell, J. 2010. *Determinants of Democratization: Explaining Regime Change in the World, 1972–2006.* Cambridge: Cambridge University Press.

Waldner, D. and E. Lust. 2018. 'Unwelcome change: coming to terms with democratic backsliding'. *Annual Review of Political Science* 21: 93–113.

Warburton, E. and E. Aspinall. 2019. 'Explaining Indonesia's democratic regression: structure, agency and popular opinion'. *Contemporary Southeast Asia: A Journal of International and Strategic Affairs* 41(2): 255–85. https://www.muse.jhu.edu/article/732138

Wike, R., L. Silver and A. Castillo. 2019. 'Many across the globe are dissatisfied with how democracy is working'. Pew Research Center, 29 April. https://www.pewresearch.org/global/2019/04/29/many-across-the-globe-are-dissatisfied-with-how-democracy-is-working/

Wucherpfennig, J. and F. Deutsch. 2009. 'Modernization and democracy: theories and evidence revisited'. *Living Reviews in Democracy* 1:1–9.

13   A state of surveillance? Freedom of expression under the Jokowi presidency

Ken M.P. Setiawan

In May 2019, following the official announcement that Joko Widodo ('Jokowi') had been re-elected for a second term, supporters of his rival, former general Prabowo Subianto, took to the streets. While these protests were unlikely to alter broad public acceptance of the election results, they prompted a strong response from the Jokowi government. This included the large-scale mobilisation of security forces, mass arrests of demonstrators, and the blocking of video and image sharing on social media and messaging platforms such as WhatsApp.

Government representatives justified the actions by referring to national 'interests' and 'security'. Communications and Information Technology Minister Rudiantara stated that the restrictions on social media were imposed to contain the spread of fake news, hoaxes and provocative content that could prompt clashes between Prabowo supporters and security personnel. Other cabinet members, including Wiranto, the coordinating minister for politics, law and security, similarly argued the restrictions were born of necessity: '[for] three days, we won't be able to look at pictures. I think we'll be fine. This is for the national interests' (Kure 2019). After the protests had ended, Rudiantara suggested the police should be given the power to monitor WhatsApp. He dismissed concerns of civil society groups who argued that such monitoring would violate privacy rights. Rudiantara received support from presidential chief of staff Moeldoko, who said that national security should be prioritised over individuals' privacy (Lee 2019).

This case reflects a broader trend towards increasing limitations on the freedom of expression under the first term of Jokowi's presidency (2014–2019). The Jokowi administration's limited interest in civil and political rights has been well noted (McGregor and Setiawan 2019). In the early years of Jokowi's presidency, analysts attributed this apathy to Jokowi's prioritisation of economic programs and the need to consolidate his initially weak political position by accommodating conservative political forces (Muhtadi 2015; Warburton 2016). But these trends only intensified as Jokowi secured his hold on power: by late 2016 he had consolidated his political position, yet the government's protection of civil and political rights continued to deteriorate.

These developments are further evidence of what Diprose et al. (2019) describe as an 'illiberal turn' in Indonesian politics. As the introduction to this volume makes clear, Indonesia is not alone in sliding towards illiberalism; instead, the Indonesian case is consistent with a global pattern that has seen a gradual decline of freedom across the world for more than a decade, leading to the sombre conclusion that 'democracy is in retreat' (Shenkkan and Repucci 2019).

This chapter examines freedom of expression, one of the core democratic norms that has come under attack in much of the democratic world. It is legally defined as the freedom to hold opinions without government interference or censorship and to seek, receive and impart information and ideas through any media. The principle of freedom of expression, as enshrined in Article 19(2) of the International Covenant on Civil and Political Rights, has been ratified by Indonesia under Law No. 12/2005. Yet the erosion of freedom of expression is among the most prominent indicators of Indonesia's present democratic deterioration.

This chapter begins by looking back on key developments related to the freedom of expression from the end of authoritarianism in 1998 until the conclusion of Susilo Bambang Yudhoyono's presidency in 2014. It then moves to the Jokowi presidency, with a particular emphasis on developments in four key areas of freedom of expression: media freedom, religious freedom, academic freedom and the right to express personal political opinion. Through an examination of several important case studies, a range of factors are identified at institutional, societal and personal levels that have collectively contributed to regression in the protection of freedom of expression.

I argue that the Indonesian government has increased the use of surveillance—that is, the systematic monitoring of people to regulate and govern their behaviour—to facilitate the more draconian policing of citizens' behaviour and expression. As noted by Monahan (2011), while surveillance is commonly conducted by state institutions, societal actors are also involved. The surveillance of individuals—whether by state bodies or society at large—can have significant implications for the protection of human rights, freedom of expression and, as this chapter will argue, for the quality of democracy in contemporary Indonesia.

FREEDOM OF EXPRESSION AFTER REFORMASI: PROGRESS AND REGRESSION

The democratic transition that began at the end of the twentieth century gave Indonesian citizens, civil society organisations and the media new freedoms and liberties. However, the country's second democratic decade has seen those new freedoms slowly and steadily eroded, and new restrictions have been imposed. The use of both legal and non-legal instruments to limit freedom of expression have slowed—and even reversed—the important achievements of the *reformasi* period.

Under the authoritarian New Order regime (1966–1998), freedom of expression in the political arena was heavily constrained. Political activists and opposition leaders were arrested and disappeared. The state placed tight controls on the media, and legal restrictions on oppositional or ideologically non-conformist sentiment were strictly enforced. After the fall of President Suharto in May 1998, there was a strong public push for liberalisation and for reforms influencing all aspects of social and political life. This led to the creation of many new laws, including a number specifically focused on human rights and modelled on international human rights norms and standards.

Demands for greater freedom of expression, and particularly for press freedom, led successive post-Suharto administrations to review a number of old laws and regulations. Under President Habibie, the government passed Law No. 9/1998 on Freedom of Expression. Article 1 of this law defines freedom of expression as the 'right of citizens to express their thoughts orally, in writing, or by other means, freely and responsibly in accordance with existing legislation'. In 1999, parliament passed two national laws that included legal guarantees for freedom of expression: Law No. 39/1999 on Human Rights and Law No. 40/1999 on the Press. That same year, President Abdurrahman Wahid abolished the Ministry of Information, the New Order's main weapon for controlling the media. Amid a series of constitutional amendments carried out between 1999 and 2002, a specific chapter (Chapter XA) on human rights was incorporated into the Indonesian Constitution in 2000. Constitutional provisions on the freedom of expression include Articles 28E(2) and (3) as well as Article 28F. Together, these legal reforms dismantled many authoritarian-era restrictions and aided the development of a more substantive human rights framework.

However, from the outset, these new freedoms were also contested. The 1998 Law on Freedom of Expression, for instance, stipulated that in exercising the freedom of expression other considerations should be taken into account, with Article 3 referring to the balancing between rights and duties, as well as principles of deliberation and consensus. The conceptualisation of freedom of expression was thus never wholly 'liberal': from its initial formulation, this right was limited, open for potential abuse, and continued to reflect elements of New Order ideology. Additionally, the constitutional amendments allowed for the state to limit rights based on political, moral, religious and security considerations. While international human rights standards also allow for the limitation of rights in some circumstances, these limitations must be clearly prescribed by law and be reasonable, necessary and proportionate (UNHRC 2011). But Indonesia's constitutional provisions are broadly and vaguely formulated, meaning there has always been a risk that any limitations may not conform to the international provisions to which Indonesia is a signatory.

Under both the Habibie and Wahid presidencies, progress was made in the areas of freedom of expression, association and assembly. By the end of Wahid's tenure as president most political prisoners convicted during the New Order had been released. Most importantly, the 'era of politically motivated trials in Indonesia appeared to be over' (Human Rights Watch 2003: 3). However, under the presidency of Megawati Sukarnoputri (2001–2004), the first signs of regression became apparent, with a number of media editors brought to court for defaming politicians and business tycoons. The presidency of Susilo Bambang Yudhoyono (2004–2014) saw an increase in the number of violent attacks on journalists by vigilante groups, sometimes orchestrated by state officials (Wiratraman 2014).

But these shortcomings were offset by continued progress in the protection of freedom of expression, preventing any diagnosis of full-blown regression. For example, in 2007 the Constitutional Court declared unconstitutional the so-called *haatzaai artikelen* ('sowing of hatred articles'), which were a colonial-era relic in the Penal Code, on the grounds that they violated the right to free speech.[1] Under the New Order, the *haatzaai artikelen* were used to criminalise public expression considered offensive towards or critical of the government. These provisions were regularly used against political opponents and human rights defenders. The ruling

---

1 Constitutional Court Decision No. 6/PUU-V/2007.

of the court was highly significant and was welcomed by human rights organisations as a sign of Indonesia's continued democratic progress.

But then only a year later, a law was passed with far-reaching implications for the freedom of expression. Law No. 11/2008 on Electronic Information and Transactions (ITE Law)[2] was designed to provide both online businesses and individuals with protection in electronic transactions. However, it contains provisions that severely restrict and punish certain types of content and specific 'misuses' of electronic devices. Articles 27 and 28 are particularly problematic, because they outline criminal penalties for a broadly defined range of acts and activities that may be classified as 'defamation'. Article 45(1) of the ITE Law determines that anyone deemed guilty of defamation may be sentenced to up to six years' imprisonment and/or a fine of up to one billion rupiah. This combination of broad applicability and heavy punishment means that the ITE Law can be easily and effectively manipulated by politically or economically powerful actors as a tool for intimidation and coercion.

An alliance of non-government organisations responded to the defamation clauses by requesting a judicial review by the Constitutional Court, arguing that these provisions violate the constitutional right to free expression. However, the court rejected the challenge and determined that freedom of expression was trumped by the need to protect citizens from online defamation.[3] Defamation prosecutions under the ITE Law became increasingly frequent in the following decade, particularly during the Jokowi presidency. As pointed out by Hamid (2017), those targeted are often activists, lawyers, researchers, journalists and 'ordinary' social media users. The ITE Law has been used to punish citizens who make critical comments online about public figures, government institutions or companies, which in turn encourages self-censorship. This ultimately has a detrimental impact on the openness of Indonesia's democracy.

In sum, during the first decade of *reformasi*, Indonesia recorded many positive developments in the area of political rights in general and the freedom of expression in particular. However, the late 2000s saw the slowing of this reformist zeal, as well as setbacks such as the introduction of the ITE Law. While President Yudhoyono painted himself as an advocate for democratic norms and institutions, both he and forces within his governing coalition sought restrictions on particular types of expression, including expression deemed too critical of those in

---

2   In addition to the ITE Law, Law No. 44/2008 on Pornography may also pose a threat to artistic and cultural expression.

3   Constitutional Court Decision No. 2/PUU-VII/2009.

positions of power. This was indicative of the democratic 'stagnation' under Yudhoyono, which analysts have often attributed to the president's moderating approach, because he placed emphasis on avoiding conflict and accommodating all segments of the political elite, including those with regressive, illiberal agendas (Aspinall et al. 2015). This meant that opportunities to further consolidate and deepen democracy, protect hard-won freedoms, and ensure a more resilient set of democratic institutions were missed during Yudhoyono's tenure.

JOKOWI, HUMAN RIGHTS AND CIVIL LIBERTIES

Under the Jokowi government, protection of citizens' rights to freedom of expression has regressed far more dramatically than analysts anticipated. Regulatory reforms and trends in law enforcement policy have translated to increased criminalisation of speech and association, surveillance, and an extension of the powers of the executive to the detriment of human rights protections.

The 2014 presidential elections brought renewed attention to human rights issues, largely prompted by the obvious contrasts between Jokowi—a civilian and successful mayor—and the retired general Prabowo Subianto, who was complicit in human rights crimes in East Timor and in violence perpetrated against activists towards the end of the New Order regime. Unsurprisingly, many human rights activists endorsed Jokowi; not only were they alarmed by the spectre of a Prabowo presidency, but they were buoyed by Jokowi's promises to address ongoing human rights challenges and investigate unresolved past abuses. Nawa Cita, a nine-point agenda put forward by Jokowi and his running mate Jusuf Kalla during the 2014 campaign, included a commitment to freedom of information and public communication.

The early months of Jokowi's first term offered democracy activists some further cause for optimism. In 2015, the government announced it was lifting restrictions preventing foreign journalists from entering and writing about Papua (*Jakarta Post* 2015). The government also announced that sentences for criminal defamation, particularly in online cases, would be reduced (Hamid 2017). At the 2015 State of the Nation address, Jokowi reiterated his commitment to resolve human rights issues, with specific reference to past human rights crimes and Papua.

However, in reality the Jokowi administration did not fulfil this more progressive human rights agenda. For example, while foreign journalists were formally permitted to report from Papua, in practice access was still tightly regulated. The government sought to cultivate a more progressive image without carrying out substantive policy reform: in the words of Tedjo Edhy Purdijatno, then coordinating minister for political, legal and security affairs, '[foreign journalists] can change the idea the international community has of Papua. The message that violence and violations of human rights do not happen in Papua can be disseminated' (*Antara* 2015). In addition, while penalties for online defamation were reduced—with prison sentences under the ITE Law lowered from six to four years— prosecutions have become more frequent. Sentences for online defamation also remain harsher than those for offline defamation. Moreover, the definition of defamation has been expanded to include content published unintentionally or by third parties—for instance, through the tagging of Facebook posts. Private chat messages can also be considered a violation of the law.

The ITE Law has also been invoked to block websites that are deemed to spread radical ideas or other content the state considers offensive. In some instances, blocking has occurred in response to legitimate security concerns; for instance, in 2017 the government blocked eleven Telegram domain name systems due to terrorism-related content. However, in other instances the link to security is obscure or extremely tenuous. For example, online content relevant to the LGBT (lesbian, gay, bisexual and transgender) community is regularly blocked. In 2016, the Ministry of Communication and Information ordered internet service providers to block social networking apps used by the LGBT community, stating that these contained 'sexual deviance' (Bastian 2016). In 2018, Google responded to the government's request and removed more than seventy applications from the Google Play store that had LGBT-related content. The Ministry of Communication and Information's capacity to filter and block online content was increased in 2018 as a result of the introduction of Cyber Drone 9, a system that detects potential content violations. A specialised task force now monitors and identifies sites for blocking.

The increased restrictions on and surveillance of digital spaces is consistent with a global trend in the rise of 'digital authoritarianism' (Shenkkan and Repucci 2019). This has made life difficult for government critics, who often heavily rely on online mobilisation. They are now subject to increased monitoring and intimidation by the security forces. Scrutiny is particularly intense in Papua, where online surveillance of activists has led to arrests and political killings (Hamid 2017). As a result, while digital media offer many opportunities for people to publicise their opinions, the use of these tools also carries increasing risk.

Under the Jokowi government there has also been a renewed push to revise Indonesia's outdated Criminal Code. Following Jokowi's 2019 re-election, his coalition attempted to push a number of highly controversial revisions through parliament. Several of these proposed revisions, if passed, would have dire implications for freedom of expression. These include a clause criminalising defamation of the president and vice president, with penalties of up to five years' imprisonment. Another proposed article criminalises the broadcasting of fake news or hoaxes that 'result in a riot or disturbance', attracting a punishment of six years in prison. As with many of the provisions discussed above, a major concern is that the definitions of this clause have been poorly specified, meaning they are highly malleable and open to broad interpretation; in Indonesian parlance, these are known as 'rubber clauses' (*pasal karet*). While the spreading of fake news can have serious social consequences, criminalisation—especially where definitions are vague—restricts the freedom of the press and journalists (see Tapsell, this volume).

A further aspect of the assault on freedom of expression has been new restrictions on freedom of association. In 2017, the Jokowi government passed the Regulation in Lieu of Law (Peraturan Pemerintah Pengganti Undang Undang, Perppu) on Societal Organisations. This regulation amends Law No. 17/2013, and was designed to ban the transnational Islamist organisation Hizbut Tahrir Indonesia (HTI). HTI was a highly visible participant in the 2016 Islamist protests against Jakarta governor Basuki Tjahaja Purnama ('Ahok'), but its relatively small size and clandestine nature made it a prime target for repression as the Jokowi government moved to dismantle the oppositional Islamist coalition. However, rather than moving to disband the organisation through existing judicial channels, the government introduced a far-reaching and flexible decree that allows the executive to unilaterally ban any organisation considered to contravene the state ideology of Pancasila. The right of organisations to contest such bans in court was removed via this Perppu, taking away an essential avenue to check executive power. This general slide during the Jokowi era towards a more illiberal order, in which Indonesians' freedom of expression is increasingly restricted, has had particularly serious consequences for four groups of citizens: journalists, scholars, members of minority communities, and those considered part of a critical or threatening political opposition.

Table 13.1   Comparison of individuals charged by President Yudhoyono and President Widodo under the ITE Law

	President Yudhoyono (2008–2014)	President Widodo (2015–2019)
Private citizens	54	152
Journalists	3	22
Government officials	4	19
Politicians	2	3
Activists	9	12
Total	72	208

Source: SAFEnet (2019a).

CASE STUDY 1: THE MEDIA

Freedom of expression for Indonesia's journalists came under increasing threat through the 2010s. In large part, this was due to the ITE Law. As discussed above, of particular concern are the law's provisions on defamation in online media, which are exacerbated by the loose way in which 'defamation' is defined. Data collected by the Southeast Asia Freedom of Expression Network (SAFEnet) show that the number of people charged under the ITE Law has increased dramatically in comparison to the Yudhoyono years (Table 13.1).

SAFEnet data also show that the ITE Law is used particularly against private citizens, with most reports being lodged by state agencies. However, corporations have also increasingly resorted to the law to suppress criticism. According to these data, the number of journalists charged under the ITE Law remains limited—but the proportion doubled from 5 per cent of all cases during the Yudhoyono years to 11 per cent during Jokowi's first term. It is also notable that between 2015 and 2016 the Alliance of Independent Journalists (Aliansi Jurnalis Independen, AJI) recorded a sharp rise in cases of assault, threat and intimidation towards reporters (Figure 13.1). AJI end-of-year reports for 2015 and 2016 highlight acts of violence against journalists being committed by the police, members of the armed forces, and participants in the 2016 'Defence of Islam' rallies (AJI 2015, 2016). Representatives of AJI also claim there has been a steady rise in mob violence against journalists (Tuasikal 2019).

These trends suggest that the state has remained absent from protecting individuals (whether journalists or private citizens) from such threats, and

Figure 13.1   Number of acts of violence against journalists, 2009–2019

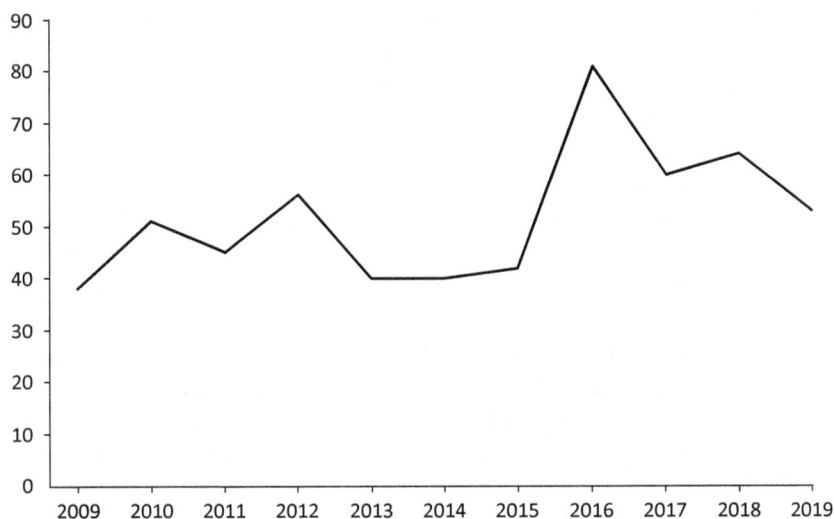

Source: AJI (2019).

is even complicit in the increased harassment of individuals who express their beliefs or thoughts publicly. This interpretation further underlines the Jokowi administration's lack of concern for civil and political rights (McGregor and Setiawan 2019).

CASE STUDY 2: ACADEMICS

Freedom to conduct, publish and discuss critical research is increasingly under threat as well. During the first term of the Jokowi presidency, academics experienced intense state scrutiny relating to their political affiliations, ideological inclinations and research outputs. In 2015 and 2016, SAFEnet recorded 22 and 36 incidents respectively in which freedoms of association and expression were violated (SAFEnet 2019b). A majority of these incidents related to academic events addressing the 1965–1966 mass violence. Many academic events (including seminars, book launches and film screenings) were organised related to the 50th anniversary of the mass violence, which also saw increased activism for and engagement with this issue. In many cases, this was met by hostile responses from state bodies and social groups. In addition, despite the important work being done by many Indonesian academics in opening dialogue on this particular topic, academic institutions in general—whether state, private or denominational—remain at best ambivalent and at worst directly opposed to publicly discussing this dark chapter of Indonesian history.

Examples include the October 2015 decision by Satya Wacana Christian University (Universitas Kristen Satya Wacana, UKSW) management to withdraw its student magazine *Lentera*, after the magazine published stories of the mass killings in Salatiga, where UKSW is located. The decision of the university was a response to police pressure, after the police accused the student journalists of inciting social unrest. The same month, there was international outcry when the Ubud Writers and Readers Festival was forced to cancel a series of 1965-related events following pressure from the local police (Setiawan 2015). In 2016, Gadjah Mada University (Universitas Gadjah Mada, UGM) banned a discussion on the International People's Tribunal 1965 at its campus. UGM resorted to this self-censorship following advice from state intelligence services, which in turn had been approached by Islamist groups. Similarly, the cultural festival Belok Kiri (Turn Left) was cancelled after strong opposition from mass organisations, such as the Indonesia Islamic Youth Movement, who claimed the festival would promote 'left wing ideology' (Setiawan 2016). The police granted a permit to the groups opposing the event to hold a demonstration against festival organisers. Then, in 2017, police broke up an academic discussion on the events of 1965 at the Indonesian Legal Aid Foundation (Lembaga Bantuan Hukum, LBH), one of the country's oldest and most influential civil society organisations. On this occasion police again sided with Islamic groups, who had also consulted with retired general Kivlan Zen, former chief of the Army Strategic Reserve Command (Komando Strategi Angkatan Darat, Kostrad) and close confidant of Prabowo Subianto.

These cases illustrate how state institutions have consistently endorsed the repressive and illiberal agendas of conservative groups rather than upholding the right to academic freedom. Indeed, they reveal how both state and non-state actors play a role in the erosion of freedom of expression. In the cases described above, police and academic institutions caved under the pressure of religious groups and community organisations, some of which had direct links to the security forces themselves. Close ties between institutions for law enforcement and hardline community actors and organisations allows for the unlawful harassment of academics and activists, and impunity for transgressors (Jaffrey 2017). So, rather than protecting victims, police often stand aside and enable such groups to decide the parameters of individual freedom at the local level.

CASE STUDY 3: MINORITIES

Indonesia's minorities have disproportionally felt the effects of Indonesia's illiberal drift. For example, the Blasphemy Law[4] constitutes a serious challenge to freedom of expression, and it gets weaponised against minorities in particular. Passed in 1965, the Blasphemy Law was intended to allow religious leaders to protect the privileged status and conventional interpretation of Indonesia's recognised religions. It also allowed for religious practice to be monitored and controlled by the state. The law identifies 'deviant' beliefs or teachings as a potential threat to social order.

Under the New Order, less than a dozen cases were brought before the courts under the Blasphemy Law. However, since 1998 prosecutions under the Blasphemy Law have rapidly increased (Crouch 2012), and it has often been used to intimidate and silence citizens—usually those from a minority religion. In 2016, for example, a joint decree of the ministers of religious affairs and home affairs banned activities of the heterodox Gafatar (Gerakan Fajar Nusantara) community and propagation of the group's beliefs. Punishment for violations include up to five years imprisonment based on the 1965 Blasphemy Law.

Under the Jokowi presidency, blasphemy attracted much attention when it was used to prosecute Basuki Tjahaja Purnama ('Ahok'), former governor of Jakarta, who possessed 'double-minority' status as an ethnic Chinese Christian. Ahok was investigated and prosecuted after the Indonesian Council of Islamic Scholars (Majelis Ulama Indonesia, MUI) declared that he had blasphemed against Islam during a speech uploaded to his YouTube channel. In May 2017, Ahok was found guilty and sentenced to two years imprisonment. While the Ahok case was unique in that the Blasphemy Law was used against a high-profile figure for political purposes, the guilty verdict was not: in cases where MUI deems an individual to have committed blasphemy, a conviction nearly always follows even if evidence is weak (Butt 2018).

The law is also used much more frequently against ordinary citizens involved in personal or community-level disputes. In 2018 Meliana, a Chinese Buddhist woman in North Sumatra, was sentenced to eighteen months imprisonment. Two years earlier she had complained about the volume of the call to prayer from the local mosque. Islamic vigilantes retaliated by attacking her house and vandalising Buddhist temples. Muslim groups requested a fatwa from the MUI in North Sumatra, which

---

4   Passed in 1965 as Presidential Decree No. 1/PNPS/1965 on the Prevention of the Misuse/Insulting of a Religion, in 1969 the decree was strengthened and upgraded to the status of law.

eventuated in January 2017. It was only then that the police continued their investigation of Meliana, leading to her trial and conviction (A'yun 2019).

The number of blasphemy trials increased during the Yudhoyono years. However, the Ahok crisis and emergence of the religiously charged demonstrations against him (also known as the 212 movement) brought the effects of the Blasphemy Law into sharp relief. These events revealed the ways in which such cases contribute to religio-political polarisation at local and national levels (see also Nuraniyah; Warburton, this volume), and how these laws are manipulated for the purpose of criminalising criticism of religious institutions and figures.

Indonesia's LGBT community has also felt their space for public expression severely restricted in recent years. Between 2016 and 2018 there was a sharp rise in anti-LGBT attacks and rhetoric, to a large extent fed by public figures—including senior government officials—who construed the LGBT community as a threat to the nation. Many called for criminalisation and 'cures' for homosexuality as well as censorship of information related to LGBT individuals (Human Rights Watch 2018). This has effectively granted social sanction and political cover to violence and discrimination. Social spaces for members of Indonesia's LGBT community, and publications with material considered supportive of LGBT rights, have been attacked or shut down. In one case, the rector of a university fired the student newspaper's entire executive for publishing a short story deemed to 'promote LGBT' (Widhana 2019). While Jokowi has called upon the police to protect the LGBT community (Parmar 2016), the lack of implementation underlines that aside from rhetoric the president has done little to ensure the protection of this group.

CASE STUDY 4: POLITICAL OPPOSITION

The Jokowi government is increasingly intolerant of opposition, and has used a range of legal weapons to contain critical expression and political challenges. The Jokowi government had used regulatory powers to curtail party-based opposition in 2015–16 (see also Mietzner; Power, this volume), but these tactics became more systematic following the anti-Ahok protests in late 2016. Ahok was a personal ally of Jokowi and their party coalitions were very similar, leading the Jokowi government to perceive the demonstrations as a serious political threat. The government responded to this threat by introducing a number of legal measures—including the aforementioned Perppu that disbanded HTI—and by arresting a number of figures associated with the protests. These figures were charged with various offences, including treason and breaches of the ITE Law. These arrests of government critics were clearly politically motivated, but the use of flexible legal provisions lent them a veneer of legitimacy.

A more high-profile case arose in 2017, when Habib Rizieq Shihab, head of the Islamic Defenders Front (Front Pembela Islam, FPI) and leader of the mass mobilisations against Ahok, was charged with a number of criminal offences including the dissemination of pornographic content (resulting in charges under the ITE Law and the 2008 Pornography Law). The latter case was lodged after screen captures emerged of explicit text messages between him and a woman to whom he was not married, though Rizieq denied the authenticity of the messages and claimed he had been framed by the government. Whether or not the texts were authentic, he was targeted for his role in mobilising public opposition to Jokowi's ally, and the case was obviously designed to stifle Rizieq's political influence in the lead-up to the 2019 presidential elections.

There are numerous other cases where the government targeted critics of Jokowi or opposition figures (see Power, this volume). Rocky Gerung, an academic and critic of Jokowi, was investigated under the Criminal Code in relation to comments made on national television that holy books were 'fiction'. Musician and Prabowo supporter Ahmad Dhani was charged after insulting NU-affiliated militia Banser. Dhani was also charged and given a prison sentence under the ITE Law, after tweeting that Ahok supporters were 'idiots' who deserved to be spat on.

Repression of grassroots opposition was evident in government responses against activists of the 2019 Change the President (2019 Ganti Presiden) movement. This movement, which drew largely from groups of the 212 movement but lacked its Islamist overtones, had its origins in the Twitter hashtag #2019GantiPresiden. Gradually, as Power (2018: 323) observes, this developed into 'a political vehicle with a strong social media presence ... and formal organisational structure'. The state apparatus, supported by government politicians and Jokowi, responded through investigations based on the ITE Law, the confiscation of merchandise and the prohibition of scheduled meetings, often with assistance from pro-government counter-protesters (Power 2018; also this volume).

In addition to oppression of political opponents in the context of elections, activists have also come under increasing pressure. Under the Jokowi presidency there has been a dramatic increase in prosecutions of anti-corruption and land-reform activists. Many activists have reported physical and social media surveillance as well as wire tapping by the security forces. Papuan pro-independence activists in particular remain at high risk of arbitrary detention, torture and extrajudicial killing (Hidayat et al. 2019). To a degree unprecedented during the *reformasi* era, the Jokowi government has sought to silence oppositional expression by using the state's coercive apparatus.

EXPLAINING THE NEW STATE OF SURVEILLANCE

The case studies discussed above reveal the variety of ways in which freedom of expression has been curtailed under the Jokowi presidency. However, this forces us to return to the question of why these developments have emerged—particularly under a president who was expected to provide new impetus for democratisation (Tomsa 2017).

Three factors can be distinguished that are at the root of recent setbacks. These are structural factors at levels of both state and society, as well as personal factors that relate to the agency of individual political leaders. While I discuss these factors separately, they interact with one another and I argue that ultimately it is the combination of these factors—rather than one in particular—that explains the ongoing erosion of freedom of expression.

In referring to structural factors at the level of the state or political institutions, I argue that lessons should be drawn from a critical reflection on the nature of Indonesia's democratic transition. As emphasised in this chapter, many liberal reforms were introduced after 1998, but these were often immediately contested or rolled back—both in law and in practice. These early pitfalls arose largely because democratic stabilisation after 1998 was secured by accommodating actors from the old authoritarian regime into new power structures. While these processes occurred well before Jokowi came to power, the maintenance of New Order figures in the contemporary system means there remains much resistance within the state to liberal ideals, including citizens' right to critique government and express a range of political and social ideas freely and openly. Over time, this has provided fertile ground for democratic regression (Warburton and Aspinall 2019).

Beyond the state, developments at the societal level have also undermined freedom of expression. Analysts have long noted a creeping religious and political conservatism among citizens themselves (e.g. van Bruinessen 2013), which has enabled certain aspects of the illiberal turn in Indonesia's legal and state institutions described in this paper and elsewhere (Hamid 2018; Warburton and Aspinall 2019). Survey data from Asian Barometer, for example, show that while Indonesians are committed to free and fair elections, they are more ambivalent when it comes to individual rights such as expression of political opinion and the right to protest (Warburton and Aspinall 2019). Indonesians have been broadly accepting of the ways in which blasphemy laws get deployed by politicians and citizens, and the Jokowi government's crackdowns on critics and opposition figures has made little dent in his popularity.

This is not to argue that societal groups have been bystanders to limitations of the freedom of expression. Civil society groups have used various strategies to counter the increasing limitations on freedom of expression, including appeals to the legal system. For instance, in 2017 HTI filed a petition with the Supreme Court for judicial review of the Regulation in Lieu of Law on Societal Organisations. In 2019, a coalition of human rights organisations lodged a complaint with the Administrative Courts regarding the blocking of internet services in Papua. Non-government organisations have made reports to the police of violence and threats against them, while some have also improved the physical protection of their premises after attacks by vigilante groups. Another strategy used by civil society groups is to make changes to terminologies they use in their work in order to avoid resistance and possible banning of their activities. LGBT activists, for example, have found that using the term 'gender diversity' is less likely to attract opposition. In a similar vein, human rights activists working on the 1965 massacres have found that avoiding key terms such as '1965' and 'communism' contributes to the peaceful organisation of events. It is troubling, however, that activists increasingly resort to self-censorship in an attempt to escape reprisals from state agencies or vigilante groups.

The revival of a robust democracy movement may provide the best prospects for resistance to the present attacks on freedom of expression. Hopes for such a revival were raised in September 2019, when a wave of student protests erupted across major cities in Indonesia and attracted global attention. These protests, which were the largest student mobilisations since those that brought down Suharto in 1998, were an extraordinary expression of political discontent among young Indonesians. The students protested a wide range of issues, but were most focused on newly passed legislation that substantially weakened the Corruption Eradication Commission (Komisi Pemberantasan Korupsi, KPK), as well as a number of highly illiberal articles that had been proposed for the revised Criminal Code. The protesters also demanded government action on environmental degradation, the end of military aggression in Papua, decriminalisation of activists, and resolution of cases of human rights violations by bringing those responsible to justice.

The protests enjoyed some success: the government postponed the revisions to the Criminal Code, citing popular opposition. This was an important achievement and the student protests have been lauded for their ability to generate social mobilisation over a wide range of everyday issues, thereby underlining that anyone can become a victim of these developments (Savirani 2019). At the same time, those protests did not achieve their key goal of annulling the amendments to the KPK law. Indeed, the government turned to force to break up the protests, with police deploying water cannons and tear gas against the students and injuring hundreds. Many demonstrators were arrested, including two leading organisers and, following ministerial instructions, universities threatened students with expulsion should they continue to mobilise against the administration.

It is thus important not to overstate the broader societal and political influence of this protest and of liberal civil society as advocates of democratic agendas and a defence against the current democratic regression. This is because this pro-democracy movement is not homogenous. As several other contributions to this volume point out, segments of the 'liberal' constituency tend to treat Islamist groups as their most dangerous enemies and have even endorsed illiberal government policies as long as these are primarily directed against the forces of Islamic fundamentalism. This tendency is illustrated, for instance, by the support of many human rights activists for the 2017 Regulation in Lieu of Law on Societal Organisations. Much as the shortcomings of Indonesia's democratic institutions were not merely a product of Jokowi-era policies, so the weakness of liberal civil society and in particular human rights groups is not something that emerged under the Jokowi presidency. Rather, Indonesia's 'human rights movement' has historically lacked cohesiveness (McGregor and Setiawan 2019), and this in turn limits civil society's ability to be a catalyst for progressive change.

Finally, regression can be explained by the role played by political leaders in democratic processes. Throughout his presidency, Jokowi has shown very little interest in the protection of civil and political rights. Why has Jokowi not lived up to the (misplaced) hope that his administration would bring positive changes to the protection of civil and political rights—or at least prevent regression? Early on, analyses of Jokowi's presidency have pointed to his primary interest in an economic agenda that favours infrastructure, deregulation and de-bureaucratisation (Warburton 2016). As a consequence, non-economic sectors have received far less attention. Meanwhile, the accommodation of conservative political forces, needed to secure his position, has led to 'silence on human rights issues' (McGregor and Setiawan 2019: 849).

However, it is not only a general disinterest in civil and political rights, a preference for economic programs, or Jokowi's alignment with powerful conservative forces that underlie the backsliding of human rights during the Jokowi government. Jokowi himself appears to have an ambivalent view of liberal democratic values. This ambivalence was best illustrated in 2017 when he commented at the inauguration of the leadership of the Hanura party that 'our democracy has gone too far' (*demokrasi kita sudah kebablasan*). He continued that this has meant 'there are opportunities for the articulation of extreme politics such as liberalism, radicalism, fundamentalism, sectarianism, terrorism, and other doctrines that are in contradiction with Pancasila' (Ihsanuddin 2017). The solution to overcome these excesses of Indonesian democracy, Jokowi argued, was law enforcement. This emphasis on law enforcement reflects Jokowi's fear of instability, and his belief that political disputes in turn inhibit his economic programs. Jokowi's approach recalls that of Suharto during the New Order and reflects a long history of Indonesian governments establishing legal instruments to limit personal freedoms and create a facade of legality (McGregor and Setiawan 2019).

Jokowi's anxieties about an Islamist-linked opposition have also motivated him to move closer to conservative Islamic organisations such as MUI, which has denounced pluralism and minority rights (Warburton and Aspinall 2019). This means that he is surrounded by illiberal actors to whom he has made political concessions. The result of this is that while Jokowi continues to profile himself as a pluralist (particularly compared to his 2014 and 2019 electoral rival Prabowo Subianto), he has largely refrained from condemning rising intolerance against certain minority groups. This is further supported by Jokowi's lack of personal commitment to civil and political rights and his consistent use of highly nationalist discourses that emphasise the importance of Pancasila and the unitary state of Indonesia. He has consistently presented these as overriding objectives that both further his economic and development agenda and justify the limitation of civil and political rights.

CONCLUDING REMARKS

This chapter has scrutinised developments in the area of freedom of expression under the Jokowi presidency. The four areas of regression discussed in this chapter reveal the heightened surveillance of individuals and increased limitations on free expression. Surveillance is conducted not only by state bodies, but also by other powerful forces including hardline or conservative social organisations. In many cases, it is the increasing entanglement of these state and non-state actors that underpins continued encroachment on individual liberties. As argued above, the increased pervasiveness of these trends under the Jokowi presidency can be attributed to an interplay between structural factors at the levels of political institutions and society, including the limitations of liberal civil society groups, as well as personal factors related to Jokowi himself.

More generally, this chapter has illustrated a key aspect of the growing illiberalism of Indonesian democracy. A liberal democracy is one in which free and fair elections take place alongside the protection of civil liberties, including the right to express one's opinions without fear of intervention or censorship. Even if Indonesian elections remain relatively free from direct fraud and manipulation, the protection of citizens' freedom of expression leaves much to be desired. Indonesia increasingly conforms to the model of illiberal democracy: one in which citizens choose their own leaders and representatives, but where there are serious limitations on civil liberties and the rule of law (Warburton and Aspinall 2019). Looking ahead into Jokowi's second term, this means that while there is no direct threat to the sustainability of electoral democracy, what is at stake is democratic quality and the place that individual rights hold within Indonesian democracy.

REFERENCES

AJI (Aliansi Jurnalis Independen). 2015. 'Catatan akhir tahun AJI: 2015 musim gugur pers Indonesia'. AJI, 20 December. https://www.kabarnusa.com/2015/12/catatan-akhir-tahun-aji-2015-musim.html

AJI (Aliansi Jurnalis Independen). 2016. 'Catatan akhir tahun AJI: jurnalis dalam tekanan rezim, kekerasan naik tajam'. AJI, 23 December. https://aji.or.id/read/press-release/592/catatan-akhir-tahun-aji-jurnalis-dalam-tekanan-rezim-kekerasan-naik-tajam.html

AJI (Aliansi Jurnalis Independen). 2019. 'Catatan akhir tahun AJI 2019'. AJI, 23 December. https://aji.or.id/read/press-release/1007/catatan-akhir-tahun-aliansi-jurnalis-independen-aji-2019

Antara. 2015. 'Foreign journalists in Papua must abide by Indonesian laws: minister'. *Antara*, 7 August.

Aspinall, E., M. Mietzner and D. Tomsa. 2015. 'The moderating president: Yudhoyono's decade in power'. In *The Yudhoyono Presidency: Indonesia's Decade of Stability and Stagnation*, edited by E. Aspinall, M. Mietzner and D. Tomsa, 1–22. Singapore: Institute of Southeast Asian Studies (ISEAS).

A'yun, R.Q. 2019. 'Blasphemy on the rise'. *Inside Indonesia*, 20 January. https://www.insideindonesia.org/blasphemy-on-the-rise

Bastian, A.Q. 2016. 'Kominfo blokir aplikasi Grindr, Blued, dan BoyAhoy'. *Rappler*, 16 September. https://www.rappler.com/indonesia/146413-kominfo-blokir-aplikasi-grindr-lgbt

Butt, S. 2018. 'Religious conservatism, Islamic criminal law and the judiciary in Indonesia: a tale of three courts'. *Journal of Legal Pluralism and Unofficial Law* 50(3): 402–34.

Crouch, M.A. 2012. 'Law and religion in Indonesia: the Constitutional Court and the Blasphemy Law'. *Asian Journal of Comparative Law* 7(1): 1–46. https://doi.org/10.1515/1932-0205.1391

Diprose, R., D. McRae and V.R. Hadiz. 2019. 'Two decades of *reformasi* in Indonesia: its illiberal turn'. *Journal of Contemporary Asia* 49(5): 691–712.

Hamid, S. 2018. 'Normalising intolerance: elections, religion and everyday life in Indonesia'. CILIS Policy Paper. Melbourne: Centre for Indonesian Law, Islam and Society. https://law.unimelb.edu.au/centres/cilis/research/publications/cilis-policy-papers/normalising-intolerance-elections,-religion-and-everyday-life-in-indonesia

Hamid, U. 2017. 'Laws, crackdowns and control mechanisms: digital platforms and the state'. In *Digital Indonesia: Connectivity and Divergence*, edited by E. Jurriëns and R. Tapsell, 93–109. Singapore: ISEAS – Yusof Ishak Institute.

Hidayat, N., M. Makarim and E. Nugroho. 2019. *Shrinking Civic Space in ASEAN Countries: Indonesia and Thailand*. Jakarta: Lokataru.

Human Rights Watch. 2003. *A Return to the New Order? Political Prisoners in Megawati's Indonesia*. New York: Human Rights Watch.

Human Rights Watch. 2018. *'Scared in Public and Now No Privacy': Human Rights and Public Health Impacts of Indonesia's Anti-LGBT Moral Panic*. New York: Human Rights Watch.

Ihsanuddin. 2017. 'Jokowi: demokrasi kita sudah kebablasan'. *Kompas*, 22 February. https://nasional.kompas.com/read/2017/02/22/12031291/jokowi.demokrasi.kita.sudah.kebablasan

Jaffrey, S. 2017. 'Justice by numbers'. *New Mandala*, 12 January. https://www.newmandala.org/justice-by-numbers/

Jakarta Post. 2015. 'Foreign journalists now "free" to report on Papua, says Jokowi'. *Jakarta Post*, 10 May. https://www.thejakartapost.com/news/2015/05/10/foreign-journalists-now-free-report-papua-says-jokowi.html

Kure, E. 2019. 'Gov't slows down WhatsApp to stop hoaxes'. *Jakarta Globe*, 22 May. https://jakartaglobe.id/context/govt-slows-down-whatsapp-to-stop-hoaxes/

Lee, C. 2019. 'Gov't supports plan to patrol WhatsApp group chats'. *Jakarta Globe*, 19 June. https://jakartaglobe.id/context/govt-supports-plan-to-patrol-whatsapp-group-chats

McGregor, K. and K. Setiawan. 2019. 'Shifting from international to "Indonesian" justice measures: two decades of addressing past human rights violations'. *Journal of Contemporary Asia* 49(5): 837–61.

Monahan, T. 2011. 'Surveillance as cultural practice'. *Sociological Quarterly* 52(4): 495–508.

Muhtadi, B. 2015. 'Jokowi's first year: a weak president caught between reform and oligarchic politics'. *Bulletin of Indonesian Economic Studies* 51(3): 349–68.

Parmar, T. 2016. 'Indonesia's president finally speaks out against worsening anti-LGBT discrimination'. *Time*, 20 October. https://time.com/4537925/indonesias-president-finally-speaks-out-against-worsening-anti-lgbt-discrimination/

Power, T.P. 2018. 'Jokowi's authoritarian turn and Indonesia's democratic decline'. *Bulletin of Indonesian Economic Studies* 54(3): 307–38.

SAFEnet (Southeast Asia Freedom of Expression Network). 2019a. 'Daftar kasus netizen yang terjerat UU ITE'. SAFEnet, 1 December. https://id.safenet.or.id/daftarkasus/

SAFEnet (Southeast Asia Freedom of Expression Network). 2019b. 'Daftar pelanggaran hak berkumpul dan berekspresi di Indonesia'. SAFEnet, 1 December. https://id.safenet.or.id/pelanggaranekspresi/

Savirani, A. 2019. ' "Continue the fight!": a '98 activist reflects on the 2019 student movement in Indonesia'. *The Conversation*, 26 September. https://theconversation.com/continue-the-fight-a-98-activist-reflects-on-the-2019-student-movement-in-indonesia-124184

Setiawan, K. 2015. 'Spectre of censorship casts a shadow over Ubud festival'. *Indonesia at Melbourne*, 27 October. https://indonesiaatmelbourne.unimelb.edu.au/spectre-of-censorship-casts-a-shadow-over-ubud-festival/

Setiawan, K. 2016. 'The fear of communism still haunts Indonesia'. *Indonesia at Melbourne*, 3 March. https://indonesiaatmelbourne.unimelb.edu.au/belok-kiri-fest-fear-of-communism-still-haunts-indonesia/

Shenkkan, N. and S. Repucci. 2019. 'The Freedom House survey for 2018: democracy in retreat'. *Journal of Democracy* 30(2): 110–14.

Tomsa, D. 2017. 'Regime resilience and presidential politics in Indonesia'. *Contemporary Politics* 24(3): 266–85.

Tuasikal, R. 2019. 'Press groups: regulations, violence constrain Indonesia's journalists'. VOA News, 10 August. https://www.voanews.com/press-freedom/press-groups-regulations-violence-constrain-indonesias-journalists

UNHRC (United Nations Human Rights Committee). 2011. 'General comment no. 34. Article 19: Freedoms of opinion and expression'. UNHRC, 12 September. https://www2.ohchr.org/english/bodies/hrc/docs/gc34.pdf

van Bruinessen, M., ed. 2013. *Contemporary Developments in Indonesian Islam: Explaining the 'Conservative Turn'*. Singapore: Institute of Southeast Asian Studies (ISEAS).

Warburton, E. 2016. 'Jokowi and the new developmentalism'. *Bulletin of Indonesian Economic Studies* 52(3): 297–320.

Warburton, E. and E. Aspinall. 2019. 'Explaining Indonesia's democratic regression: structure, agency and popular opinion'. *Contemporary Southeast Asia: A Journal of International and Strategic Affairs* 41(2): 255–85. https://www.muse.jhu.edu/article/732138

Widhana, D.H. 2019. 'Kasus "cerpen LGBT" suara USU: diberedel rector, didukung alumni'. *Tirto*, 4 April. https://tirto.id/kasus-cerpen-lgbt-suara-usu-diberedel-rektor-didukung-alumni-dkZQ

Wiratraman, H.P. 2014. *Press Freedom, Law and Politics in Indonesia: A Socio-legal Study*. Leiden: Leiden University Press.

PART 5

Law, Security and Disorder

14 Assailing accountability: law enforcement politicisation, partisan coercion and executive aggrandisement under the Jokowi administration

Thomas P. Power

Executive aggrandisement is among the most common modes of democratic backsliding in the post–Cold War era. The term refers to processes whereby elected governments weaken democracy from within by eroding institutional checks on the exercise of executive power (Bermeo 2016; Khaitan 2019). It entails the winding back of institutional accountability mechanisms, whether by hamstringing or dismantling independent state agencies, restricting criticism of the government, curtailing opposition activity within formal representative institutions, or otherwise undermining existing constraints on executive behaviour. Studies of executive aggrandisement tend to emphasise the horizontal expansion of executive authority, but the process is commonly accompanied by efforts to curb vertical accountability mechanisms, for instance by manipulating electoral processes or restricting popular protest (e.g. Sözen 2019).

Similarly, while formal institutional changes—particularly legal revisions introduced by elected officials—often provide the most visible evidence of executive aggrandisement (see Bermeo 2016: 10–11), incumbent executives may also concentrate political power by less overt means. In particular, the maintenance of democratic norms is especially important where laws are pliant or inconsistently enforced, or where the state's coercive apparatus is especially amenable to the direction of executive officeholders. In this vein, Levitsky and Ziblatt (2018) identify the principles of forbearance (that is, that governments should refrain from the punitive deployment of the law) and toleration (of political opposition and popular criticism) as essential to the maintenance of functioning democratic government. Thus, while legislative and constitutional revisions may often be the most visible embodiments of executive aggrandisement, the exploitation of longstanding democratic shortcomings—particularly those relating to the rule of law—is often essential in laying the groundwork for these more explicit changes.

In this chapter, I argue that at the heart of Indonesia's contemporary democratic decline is an assertive effort by the incumbent national executive to accrue and wield power in fundamentally anti-democratic ways. The presidency of Joko Widodo (Jokowi) has seen the increasingly coercive and punitive deployment of law enforcement agencies to silence government critics and restrict opposition activity, while also assailing reserves of independent legal and political authority that may otherwise serve to check the administration's powermongering. This process is evident in the strong-arming of subnational administrations, the defanging of the national anti-corruption agency, and the heavy-handed curtailment of opposition mobilisation and popular protest. Previous analyses of these trends have treated them as expressions of 'executive illiberalism' (Aspinall and Mietzner 2019) or as evidence of an 'authoritarian turn' (Power 2018); however, it is important to recognise that the ostensible goal of these tactics—and their apparent effect—has been to consolidate power within central government while reducing democratic restraints on executive behaviour. In this way, executive manipulation of the levers of law enforcement is both an expression of the increasingly unchecked exercise of government power, as well as a means by which to strip away the democratic checks and balances that yet remain.

The chapter proceeds as follows. Before examining particular manifestations of executive aggrandisement under the Jokowi administration, I outline specific shortcomings of Indonesia's democratic transition that have left the political system vulnerable to the deployment of authoritarian tactics. I then detail four key processes by which the national executive has used its regulatory authority and control of law enforcement agencies to strip away a variety of important checks and limitations on its power. First, I discuss the government's legal coercion of party-based opposition at the national level. Second, I explore the deployment of politicised law enforcement agencies as a means of pressuring notionally independent subnational executives into compliance with the government's partisan demands. Third, I turn to the executive-led decimation of the Corruption Eradication Commission (Komisi Pemberantasan Korupsi, KPK), Indonesia's only credibly impartial law enforcement agency. Finally, I consider the government's curtailment of popular protest and public criticism, ranging from the targeted prosecution of Islamist leaders following the Defence of Islam (Aksi Bela Islam) demonstrations in 2016–17, to the crackdown on opposition activists ahead of the 2019 election, to the late-2019 suppression of Indonesia's largest pro-democracy protests since the post-Suharto transition. Taken in sum, these measures have revealed the fragility of Indonesia's democratic institutions, consolidated power within executive government, and laid the foundations for a continued slide into deepening illiberalism.

PERVASIVE ILLEGALITY AND PARTISAN LAW ENFORCEMENT

Politically impartial law enforcement is a core tenet of democratic government. Some basic adherence to the rule of law—in particular, the principles that governments and their partisans should be subject to independent legal oversight, and that democratic opposition should not face prejudicial or coercive treatment—is essential to most modern conceptions of democracy (Dahl 1982; Diamond 2008; Habermas 1995; Schmitter and Karl 1991). Indonesia's shortcomings in this regard are of long standing. Executive intrusions into law enforcement and judicial institutions were apparent in its polarised post-independence democracy (Aidit 1964; Feith 1962), and became ubiquitous with its descent into authoritarianism in the late 1950s. During the New Order, interpenetration between the state's administrative and security apparatus and the regime vehicle, Golkar, underpinned a highly effective form of electoral authoritarianism. The state's regulatory powers and coercive apparatus functioned as weapons of the regime and were routinely wielded to suppress opposition activity. This underpinned a steep pyramidal political power structure with a dominant presidency at its apex (Liddle 1985).

Winding back the political roles of security and law enforcement agencies was essential to Indonesia's transition to democracy at the turn of the century: the military was stripped of its 'dual-function' sociopolitical role; the police force was extricated from the New Order umbrella organisation ABRI (Angkatan Bersenjata Republik Indonesia; the Armed Forces of the Republic of Indonesia); an independent judiciary was established; and new autonomous institutions such as the KPK and the Constitutional Court (Mahkamah Konstitusi, MK) were founded. These wide-ranging reforms were essential to Indonesia's democratic success. They reduced overt partisanship within law enforcement, promoted peaceful alternation in government and curbed the legal impunity of top political elites. This, in turn, produced a more competitive democratic playing field and established horizontal checks on executive power. The massive decentralisation program of the early 2000s further buttressed this diffusion of political authority: investing a new class of relatively autonomous regional elites with a strong stake in the maintenance of the democratic system seemed an effective means by which to insulate Indonesia's democratic gains against future authoritarian reversal (Aspinall 2010; Ziegenhain 2017; cf. Nordholt 2005).

Despite these achievements, students of Indonesian politics should be under no illusions about the limits of rule-of-law reform in the post-authoritarian period. Two features are particularly relevant to the present discussion: pervasive illegality and executive-controlled law enforcement. As other chapters in this volume point out, Indonesia's legal framework is awash with illiberal and malleable provisions open to anti-democratic abuse. The state security apparatus retains a raft of draconian powers enabling the arbitrary restriction of democratic activities, including basic forms of critical political expression, and the right to peaceful assembly and protest. Meanwhile, illegality—particularly corruption and administrative malfeasance—remains endemic at all levels of society and is especially rife among political and bureaucratic elites. Indeed, given the expense associated with party candidacies, election campaigns and bureaucratic promotion, political success is all but contingent on participation in various forms of illicit activity (see Mietzner 2007, 2015; McLeod 2008).

The upshot of this pervasive illegality is that every member of the political and bureaucratic elite is—almost inevitably—legally compromised. While hundreds of high-ranking officials have faced criminal prosecution over the past two decades—including many pursued by the independent KPK—institutionalised corruption continues unabated, with most elites able to escape sanction by levering extreme wealth and power imbalances. Writing early in Indonesia's second democratic decade, Robert Cribb (2011: 33) described the country's legal institutions as a 'system of exemptions' in which 'law matters, but only to some people and only in some circumstances'. Through much of the post–New Order era, unequal treatment by law enforcement has been understood most fundamentally as a function of economic and social disparities, rather than political partisanship. While the protection of well-connected patrons has contributed to the unevenness of law enforcement throughout the reformasi period (Tomsa 2015), the administrations that preceded Jokowi's did not take systematic advantage of endemic illegality to reward partisans and coerce or punish opponents. Under Jokowi, the legal implications of partisan affiliation have been magnified: presidential allies have enjoyed greater legal impunity even as the law has been deployed in a heavy-handed manner against opponents.

Equally relevant to the trends discussed in this chapter is the executive's top-down control over law enforcement agencies. Unlike civil administration, which underwent large-scale decentralisation at the turn of the century, the state's coercive apparatus has retained a vertical, centralised structure under executive control throughout the democratic era. The ubiquity of elite corruption and collusion ensure a lack of effective checks on presidential appointments to key offices within law enforcement agencies, the state security apparatus, or legally powerful ministries. As a result, law enforcement and regulatory bodies—including the Indonesian National Police (Polisi Republik Indonesia, Polri), the Attorney General's Office (Kejaksaan Agung, AGO), the Ministry of Home Affairs (Kementerian Dalam Negeri, Kemdagri) and the Ministry of Justice and Human Rights (Kementerian Hukum dan Hak Asasi Manusia, Kemkumham)—have remained institutionally vulnerable to partisan manipulation by incumbent executives.

The degree to which this vulnerability is leveraged for executive advantage has varied between administrations. Yudhoyono's desire to project an image of due process and professionalism saw him favour formally non-partisan appointees to these powerful offices. Under Jokowi, any real semblance of non-partisan oversight in law enforcement was discarded, with many key posts assigned to party hacks. The Indonesian Democratic Party of Struggle (Partai Demokrasi Indonesia-Perjuangan, PDI-P) and the National Democratic Party (Partai Nasional Demokrat, NasDem) benefited particularly, as their leaders deliberately sought to capture 'strategic' offices rather than focusing on more traditionally lucrative rent-seeking opportunities.[1] When Jokowi took office, he unveiled NasDem cadres Muhammad Prasetyo and Tedjo Edhy Purdijatno as attorney general and coordinating minister for politics, law and security, respectively. Meanwhile, the home affairs and justice and human rights ministries were handed to PDI-P politicians Tjahjo Kumolo and Yasonna Laoly. As Jokowi consolidated power these partisan appointments only accelerated. Presidential favourite Tito Karnavian received a series of rapid promotions in the first half of 2016 which culminated in his installation as national police chief. Hadi Tjahjanto—the commander of Solo airbase during Jokowi's mayoral tenure—enjoyed an even swifter ascent, rising from a one-star marshal heading the Airforce Information Department

---

1 Interviews with PDI-P politicians, 17 December 2015, 10 January 2016, 26 February 2016.

to newly minted commander of the Indonesian National Army (Tentara Nasional Indonesia, TNI) in just two years. Budi Gunawan, a close confidante of PDI-P chairperson Megawati Sukarnoputri, was appointed to head the formidable State Intelligence Agency (Badan Intelijen Negara, BIN) in late 2016, a year and a half after his abortive nomination as national police chief early in Jokowi's first term.

In short, Indonesia's post-authoritarian institutional landscape has preserved avenues for a renewed executive power grab. In particular, the combination of endemic illegality, an array of malleable laws and the retention of patrimonial structures within an executive-controlled law enforcement apparatus provide ready ingredients for anti-democratic encroachment. The non-partisanship of law enforcement agencies has often depended on the incumbent government's adherence to the norms of forbearance and toleration identified by Levitsky and Ziblatt (2018). As the result of tendencies outlined in other contributions to this volume (see also Warburton and Aspinall 2019), these principles have come under sustained attack since 2014. As Jokowi's first term progressed, the president and his senior coalition partners repurposed the state's coercive apparatus for narrowly partisan agendas, assailing both horizontal and vertical checks on executive power.

THE SUPPRESSION OF FORMAL OPPOSITION

The liberalisation of Indonesia's party system and the strengthening of its electoral institutions were among the most conspicuous democratic reforms to take place following Suharto's 1998 resignation. Competitive multiparty elections, pluralistic parliamentary representation and the introduction of direct presidential ballots in 2004 underpinned Indonesia's emergence as the healthiest electoral democracy in Southeast Asia. While the fragmented nature of post-1999 parliaments, the opaque and transactional character of legislative decision-making, and the tendency for oversized, cartelised governing coalitions have long plagued representative accountability mechanisms (Fionna and Tomsa 2017; Mietzner 2013; Slater 2004, 2018), executives had eschewed overtly coercive interventions in the party system and electoral institutions prior to 2014.

Jokowi's election that year saw a significant shift in the dynamics of presidential coalition-building, ostensibly prompted by the unusually unstable and hostile environment which greeted his new administration (Mietzner 2016). Though Jokowi's rival Prabowo Subianto had been defeated at the ballot box, the latter led a majority parliamentary coalition (the Red and White Coalition; Koalisi Merah Putih, KMP) that divvied up legislative leadership positions and briefly abolished direct executive elections at the subnational level in an attempt to capture regional administrations through its local parliamentary majorities (Aspinall and Mietzner 2014). Even before Jokowi's inauguration, then, Prabowo's opposition coalition had set out to hamstring his presidency through the anti-democratic manipulation of whichever institutional levers it could control.

Unlike his predecessors, Jokowi did not turn to patronage to buy off the opposition coalition. Before his election, Jokowi had repeatedly rejected the inclusive patronage distribution that underpinned previous presidential coalitions, suggesting that his popular support would be sufficient to cow recalcitrant political elites (Mietzner 2016: 215). Moreover, in the early months of his presidency, Jokowi was beset by growing discontent from within his own coalition, as party elites greedily squabbled over the spoils of government. Given the immediate need to appease his notional coalition allies, Jokowi had little scope to distribute patronage incentives to a wider array of parties. Thus, rather than relying on the disbursement of state largesse, the Jokowi administration sought to stabilise its political position through the coercive deployment of the legal instruments at its command. Early indications of this tactic emanated from the NasDem-controlled AGO. In early 2015, public prosecutors laid corruption charges against regional powerbrokers from several opposition parties in a deliberate warning to KMP elites (Muhtadi 2015: 365), foreshadowing an increasingly systematic pattern of political manipulation that would come to characterise the department's activities during Jokowi's first term.

A more profound illustration of this shift was provided by the government's manipulation of its longstanding (but previously perfunctory) power to determine the legal status of party leadership boards (Mietzner 2016). In the early months of Jokowi's presidency, the minister for justice and human rights—PDI-P's Yasonna Laoly—revived this dormant power to interfere in intraparty disputes by issuing legal endorsements of marginal pro-government factions in two opposition parties, Golkar and the United Development Party (Partai Persatuan Pembangunan, PPP) (Mietzner 2016: 211). This deprived the incumbent pro-opposition leaders of facilities, resources and legal standing, and severely undermined the cohesiveness of the KMP. Golkar and PPP were ultimately dragged into Jokowi's coalition, while other opposition parties were tamed: the National Mandate Party (Partai Amanat Nasional, PAN) declared its unconditional support for the government, and the Democratic Party (Partai Demokrat, PD) and the Prosperous Justice Party (Partai Keadilan Sejahtera, PKS) similarly moved to appease the new administration. As Mietzner (2016: 217) observes, this sort of government intervention in intraparty democracy—whereby state authority is deployed to engineer the replacement of incumbent party leaders by a marginal pro-government faction—had not occurred since the New Order's removal of Megawati as the Indonesian Democratic Party (Partai Demokrasi Indonesia, PDI) leader in 1996.

Thus, Jokowi was able to dismantle parliamentary opposition through the anti-democratic manipulation of legal powers. Mitigating this, however, were the opposition coalition's own efforts to disassemble even more fundamental elements of Indonesian democracy (Mietzner 2016; Muhtadi 2015). There was inescapable irony when KMP leaders labelled Laoly a 'hijacker of democracy' for his endorsement of Golkar's insurgent faction, only months after their own efforts to abolish direct executive elections (Ihsanuddin 2015). But the government's assault on the KMP established anti-democratic innovation as a core element of the Jokowi administration's strategic toolkit.

In the months and years that followed, similar coercion was deployed to weaken formal accountability mechanisms and narrow avenues for opposition activity. In 2017, the ruling coalition pushed through electoral rules requiring that all 2019 presidential nominees be nominated by a party or coalition that secured at least 20 per cent of national parliamentary (i.e. Dewan Perwakilan Rakyat, DPR) seats at the previous election in 2014. This closed off participation by new parties and, with the government controlling more than two-thirds of a fragmented parliament, effectively prevented any more than one challenger standing against Jokowi. The months that followed even saw negotiations between the president and his strongest potential rival, Prabowo, about the possibility of a joint ticket (Aspinall and Mietzner 2019: 297; Power 2018: 323). This briefly raised the spectre of an uncontested presidential election, which would have mirrored a phenomenon that has grown at the local level since 2015 (Lay et al. 2017; Power 2018: 320). When these negotiations fell through, executive powerholders turned to other measures to improve Jokowi's re-election prospects.

TAMING THE REGIONS: SUBNATIONAL CO-OPTION, GRASSROOTS COERCION AND PARTISAN PROTECTION

In the months before the 2019 elections, executive-controlled law enforcement agencies were deployed in an effort to 'recruit' subnational executives in support of the incumbent president and—in the case of the AGO—for the NasDem party. The details of police and AGO cases are not routinely publicised, and investigations are readily opened and closed at the direction of top officials. As the incumbent coalition sought to secure widespread political support from the regions, the absence of independence, transparency and accountability within the major law enforcement agencies rendered them viable instruments for the co-option of regional executives.

This pattern revealed the inherent tension between Indonesia's administrative and fiscal decentralisation, on one hand, and central control over law enforcement, on the other. The centralised structure of law enforcement agencies, combined with institutionalised illegality and a compromised rule of law, has ensured that national-level executive powerbrokers retain the means to exercise substantial leverage over subnational officeholders. This coercive capacity may be deployed alongside or in place of the more widely recognised incentives of material patronage. During the Yudhoyono era, national elites would occasionally deploy these tactics against opposition-aligned regional officeholders, but it is under Jokowi that we have seen a far more systematic effort by the central government to co-opt subnational executives through law enforcement operations.

The lead-up to the 2019 elections saw dozens of incumbent governors, regents and mayors announce their support for Jokowi's re-election bid, often departing from the political positions of their nominating parties. Ahead of the campaign period, Jokowi's team claimed that an unprecedented 31 of 34 governors and 359 of 508 elected district heads were actively endorsing the president's re-election bid (Dongoran 2018). Many regional officials who had previously been aligned to opposition parties suddenly announced their support for Jokowi's re-election bid amid swirling corruption scandals. These included the PD-aligned governors of West Nusa Tenggara and Papua provinces, who escaped ongoing criminal investigations after publicly endorsing Jokowi (Power 2018: 330).

In a telling indication of the role played by the AGO, many of these officials accompanied their declarations for Jokowi with a realignment to NasDem. By November 2018, as many as 195 regents and mayors had aligned to the party (Partai NasDem 2018), even though it held the second-smallest parliamentary caucus with just 6.5 per cent of DPR seats. It was widely understood—both in elite circles and in media reporting—that NasDem's recruitment drive relied heavily on clandestine pressure from prosecutors. An informant familiar with one such case reported that prosecutors presented a mayor with a charge sheet and told him to choose between aligning to NasDem or facing corruption charges.[2] In several areas, prosecutors allegedly carried out waves of coercive recruitment ahead of visits by NasDem chairman Surya Paloh, and en masse party switching by local executives to NasDem occurred in multiple regions. In North Sulawesi, for example, four incumbent executives left opposition parties to join NasDem in 2018 (Gatra 2018).

This pattern of partisan realignment to the governing coalition rests on a simple bargain: in return for their endorsement of the incumbent government, subnational executives are protected from prosecution by the police and AGO. The implications of this sort of protection racket are threefold. First—and most obviously—it further undermines an already flawed rule of law by enhancing the effect of partisanship on law enforcement. Second, it sets out to strengthen national executive influence over regional leaders, revealing the limitations of subnational administrations as bulwarks against central government–led democratic regression. Third, it threatens the quality of regional democracy by heightening incentives for regional executives to acquiesce to central government directives, even where these are inconsistent with the preferences of local constituents. Although the government's so called 'hostage politics' (*politik sandera*) did not produce consistent electoral swings to Jokowi in 2019, the longer-term ramifications of these tactics for regional autonomy remain to be seen.

In order to investigate the evolving relationship between partisanship and law enforcement at the subnational level, I assembled a dataset of 327 cases in which incumbent and former subnational executives have been named criminal suspects, either by police or public prosecutors, over a 15-year period from Yudhoyono's inauguration in October 2004 to Jokowi's second-term inauguration in October 2019. This is the most comprehensive analysis of criminal cases involving subnational executives yet published, but two caveats nevertheless apply. First, I rely on available government and media reports, which may not be exhaustive given the opacity of much police and AGO activity. Second, by including all cases where suspects have been named—rather than focusing only on indictments or prosecutions—I have sought to generate the largest possible sample size; this allows us to observe instances where cases have been initiated, only to stall or be withdrawn. However, there is no way to capture instances where legal pressure has been applied to subnational executives prior to their public identification as a suspect. Perhaps the only plausible proxy for the latter category is the overall number of cases: we

---

2 Interview, 5 August 2018.

can hypothesise that a reduction in the number of suspects being named may indicate the increased frequency of partisan protection-seeking.

Figure 14.1 illustrates total numbers of cases involving subnational executives while distinguishing cases involving members of the two presidential parties: PD in 2004–14 and PDI-P in 2014–19. First and foremost, it is noteworthy that the number of regional executives to be publicly identified as suspects in police or AGO investigations during Jokowi's first term dropped more than 40 per cent from the preceding five-year period. Moreover, alignment to the presidential party seems to have yielded substantially greater protection under Jokowi than under his predecessor. Whereas PD remained a small party during Yudhoyono's first term—which is likely reflected in the low number of cases in 2004–09 involving its members—PDI-P has been the largest party during Jokowi's tenure. The regional political map reflected its dominance: while the number of PDI-P members in subnational offices fluctuated according to election results, the party's own data recorded 207 cadres being elected (both in senior and deputy executive positions) during Jokowi's first term.[3] Thus, the dramatic post-2014 reduction in legal cases involving its members offers compelling prima facie evidence of the more acutely partisan character of law enforcement. In addition, two of the four PDI-P-aligned executives to be identified as police or AGO suspects during Jokowi's first term had already left office, while a third—Tasiya Soemadi—was only a deputy district head in Cirebon. Indeed, Rudy Erawan of East Halmahera was the sole incumbent PDI-P-aligned district head or mayor named a suspect by these agencies during this five-year period, and his 2016 case vanished shortly after it was initiated.[4]

Through Jokowi's first term, no governor, district head or mayor was successfully prosecuted by the police or AGO while holding PDI-P or NasDem membership.[5] In short, the two parties with greatest influence over law enforcement were not only able to co-opt subnational executives through clandestine legal coercion; they also rewarded their regional partisans with de facto impunity against investigation and prosecution by the largest and best-resourced agencies.

---

3   Totals of 86 in 2015, 50 in 2017 and 71 in 2018. These numbers were buttressed by PDI-P's expanded recruitment of incumbent officeholders.

4   Rudy was arrested by the KPK on separate charges in 2018.

5   Kotabaru district head Irhami Ridjani was a near exception: he was a NasDem member when charged by police in 2015, but had joined the Indonesian Justice and Unity Party (Partai Keadilan dan Persatuan Indonesia, PKPI) by the time of his 2017 conviction.

Figure 14.1   Alignment of current and former subnational executives named police/AGO suspects by presidential term, 2004–19

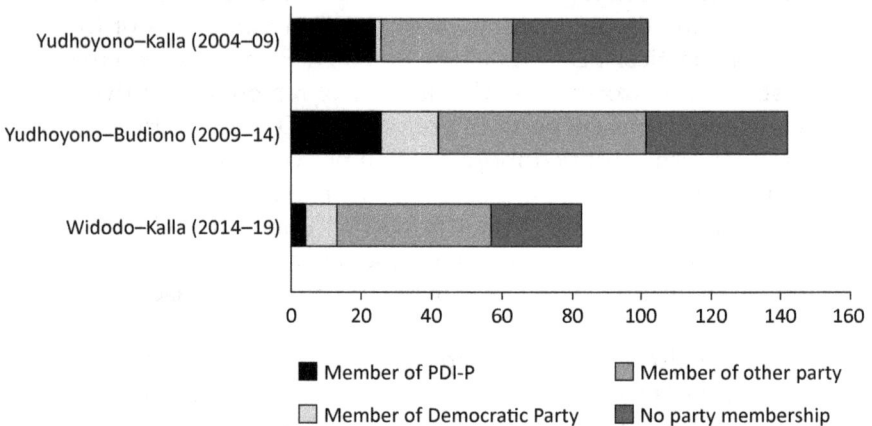

This government co-option of regional executives aimed to deliver electoral advantages to the incumbent coalition: Jokowi sought a landslide victory to match Yudhoyono's successes of 2004 and 2009 (Aspinall and Mietzner 2019). As the election approached, government representatives encouraged subnational administrations to mobilise local networks and resources in support of Jokowi. In March 2019, for instance, the PDI-P home affairs minister, Tjahjo Kumolo, publicly rejected the established principle of bureaucratic neutrality and demanded that civil servants show 'unswerving loyalty to their local executives [and] to the president', including by promoting government programs at the grassroots (Farisa 2019). On the other hand, even low-level officials seen to endorse Prabowo were vulnerable to sanction: in one notable case, a village head in Mojokerto who welcomed a campaign stop by Prabowo's running mate, Sandiaga Uno, was arrested and sentenced to two months' imprisonment (Budianto 2018).

The coercive role played by the state apparatus in the lead-up to 2019 was not limited to the co-option of subnational administrations. Through 2018 and 2019, security service personnel operating at the community level were similarly deployed in service to the administration's re-election campaign. During a series of speeches in 2018, Jokowi demanded that police and military officers disseminate his administration's achievements, while 'hunting down' citizens involved in the spread of loosely defined anti-government 'hoaxes' (Power 2018: 332–3). In the early months of 2019, Jokowi's team grew worried that a decrease in voter turnout—encouraged by voting abstention (*golongan putih; golput*) campaigns initiated by a number of disaffected democracy advocates—was the chief remaining threat to his re-election prospects. In response to this, government officials threatened *golput* advocates with terrorism charges, and instructed local military commands to assist with voter mobilisation (Aspinall and Mietzner 2019: 304). Shortly before election day, a subdistrict police commander in Garut, West Java, alleged that his district chief had instructed officers to mobilise support for the Jokowi–Ma'ruf Amin ticket (Briantika 2019); while this claim was later withdrawn, its plausibility reflected the highly politicised character of law enforcement and security under the Jokowi administration.

The government's efforts through 2018 and 2019 to deploy the law enforcement and security apparatus for electoral advantage were unprecedented in the post-Suharto era. However, Jokowi achieved only moderate gains in 2019. His victory fell short of the overwhelming mandate he had sought, and the electoral map instead showed a sharp increase in ethnoreligious polarisation (see Warburton, this volume). In the presidential vote, at least, declarations of support from regional leaders did not deliver a consistent advantage at the ballot box. This is not to suggest the executive's strategy was ineffectual, however; notably, the AGO's 'recruitment' of local notables helped NasDem secure the biggest legislative swing of any party. In the aftermath of the election, one opposition parliamentarian mused that 'should NasDem hold the AGO for another five years, it will win the 2024 election'.[6] NasDem's coalition partners took a similar view of its manipulation of the AGO. PDI-P bluntly demanded Prasetyo's exclusion from Jokowi's second-term cabinet while working to capture the department for itself. In October 2019, Jokowi assigned the AGO to ST Burhanuddin, brother of PDI-P powerbroker TB Hasanuddin, implying the presidential party would further consolidate its control over law enforcement.

The early months of Jokowi's second term suggested that executive efforts to co-opt subnational leaders may evolve from backchannels of legal coercion and protection to a raft of formal legal changes. Tito Karnavian, whose loyal service as national police chief saw him appointed the new home affairs minister, announced plans to wind back direct election in regions deemed to lack 'democratic maturity', returning to the pre-2005 system of legislative appointment (Jaffrey 2020). This would be an attack on the subnational democratic framework akin to that engineered by Prabowo's neo-authoritarian coalition in 2014—which was widely seen

---

6   Correspondence with Sukamta, May 2019.

as the clearest manifestation of that coalition's anti-democratic intent. It is very plausible that these plans are—at least in part—a response to Jokowi's underwhelming electoral performance in regions where his coalition had secured realignments and endorsements from local executives. Importantly, Tito's proposal would disproportionately affect regions outside Java, including many where Jokowi's electoral support stagnated or dropped in 2019. Given the growing centralisation of party organisations (see Mietzner, this volume) and the even greater expansion of Jokowi's second-term governing coalition, the winding back of *pilkada* would effectively formalise vertical lines of control from national coalition elites to regional executives, accelerating the recentralisation of political power.

THE HOBBLING OF THE KPK

The KPK was established in 2003 as a bastion of independent law enforcement. It was institutionally insulated from executive intervention, its rank-and-file investigators had a mandate to run autonomous investigations and sting operations, and—as a means of reducing malfeasance in the handling of cases—investigations could not be dropped once initiated (Butt 2012: 22–32).[7] Through much of its first decade, the KPK maintained a 100 per cent conviction rate—a testament to the ubiquitous nature of corruption and the agency's dogged pursuit of graft suspects, if somewhat unlikely given the scope for technical and administrative errors during prosecutions (Butt 2012: 2). Importantly, the KPK's record of investigations from 2004 to 2019 does not display the partisan biases so apparent in recent police and AGO cases. From the start of the Yudhoyono presidency to the end of Jokowi's first term, the KPK prosecuted 5 incumbent government ministers, 5 party chiefs, 76 national parliamentarians (including 47 from government parties) and 129 subnational executives from across the party spectrum.[8] During Yudhoyono's tenure, even members of the extended first family were not beyond the agency's grasp (Dick and Mulholland 2016: 48).

Unsurprisingly given its high-profile prosecutions, the KPK has faced sustained obstruction and elite opposition throughout its lifespan. Tensions between the KPK and Polri—which initially erupted at the end of Yudhoyono's first term with a string of criminal indictments against

---

7 Thus, once a suspect had been named, the KPK was required to follow through on prosecution.

8 Author calculations.

top KPK officials (Widojoko 2017: 259)—reached a crescendo following Jokowi's 2014 inauguration. In early 2015, the KPK's charging of Budi Gunawan—Jokowi's nominee for national police chief—drew severe retaliation with criminal counter-charges issued against many top KPK officials (Muhtadi 2015: 360). A controversial pre-trial judgement then invalidated the agency's indictment of Budi, who was ultimately handed the influential post of deputy police chief before being promoted to head the State Intelligence Agency (Badan Intelijen Negara, BIN) in 2016.

While Budi's career flourished, the KPK was severely damaged in the fallout from this confrontation. Police charges forced two KPK leaders to stand down, leading to the appointment of interim officials until the next group of commissioners was selected in December 2015. This new group of commissioners, who held office through the remainder of Jokowi's first term, were seen as more amenable than their predecessors to the interests of leading government powerbrokers, and notably failed to pursue investigations that threatened several senior PDI-P politicians in 2017 and 2018 (Power 2018: 331).[9]

Nevertheless, KPK operations remained sufficiently independent to embarrass and frustrate the administration. This was particularly due to the substantial autonomy afforded to the agency's rank-and-file investigators under the KPK law (see Butt 2012). Despite mounting pressure on the agency, it prosecuted several high-profile government politicians who lacked the protection available to the president's inner circle and his foremost political patrons. Among those charged by the KPK from 2017 to 2019 were the Golkar minister for social affairs, Idrus Marham, and the National Awakening Party (Partai Kebangkitan Bangsa, PKB) minister for youth and sports, Imam Nahrawi; in addition, it investigated and prosecuted both Setya Novanto and Romahurmuziy, the party chairmen who had ushered their compromised organisations into Jokowi's coalition. Meanwhile, Jokowi's first term saw the KPK significantly step up its investigations of subnational executives. As many as 75 subnational executives were charged during Jokowi's first five years in office, compared to a total of 53 through Yudhoyono's decade in office (Figure 14.2). The KPK's increased activity in the regions—an effort, perhaps, to dispel perceptions of its decline—almost compensated for the reduced number of cases formally pursued by the police and AGO (cf. Figure 14.1).

---

9 Among the 20 parliamentarians arrested by the KPK during the 2015–19 term were just two from PDI-P, one from PKB and none from NasDem. Author calculations.

Figure 14.2   Alignment of current and former subnational executives named KPK suspects by presidential term, 2004–19

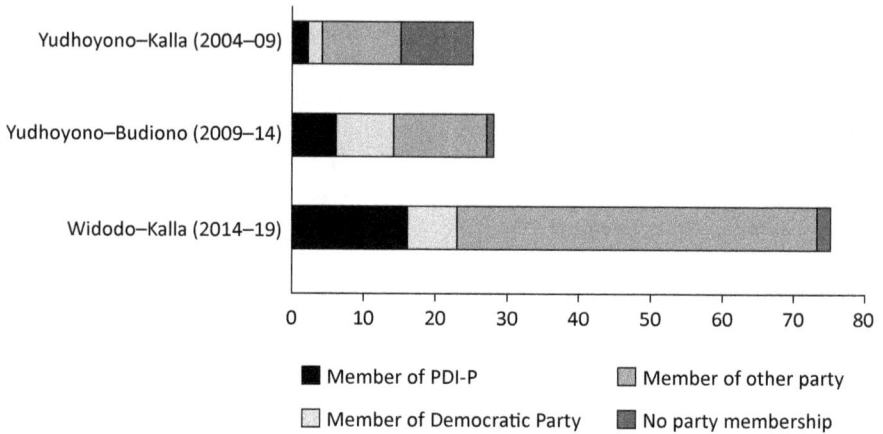

Although the national-level elites from particular government parties appeared beyond the grasp of the KPK, this impunity did not extend to subnational officeholders. The KPK prosecuted 16 PDI-P-aligned subnational executives in 2014–19, in contrast to the single deputy district head from the presidential party to be prosecuted by the larger law enforcement agencies. The KPK also charged eight NasDem-affiliated executives, including several who had switched from other parties while in office. At the subnational level, at least, KPK investigations did not replicate the increasingly partisan biases evident in patterns of police and AGO activity. Thus, the KPK's activities—already deeply unpopular with elites of all political stripes—now additionally posed a problem for the governing coalition's efforts at subnational co-option through legal coercion. Government powerbrokers could not guarantee legal protection to their regional clients while the KPK remained untamed.

It was against this backdrop that the KPK faced its most severe threat to date in the latter half of Jokowi's first term. An executive-sanctioned assault on the agency's independence was manifested through physical violence, through rhetorical delegitimation and, finally, through legislative sabotage. In April 2017, Novel Baswedan—one of the most prominent KPK investigators—was subject to a vicious acid attack, carried out by two police officers, which saw him hospitalised and left him blind in one eye. The assault took place while Novel was investigating a number of high-profile cases, one of which implicated then Polri chief Tito Karnavian

(Indonesia Leaks 2019). After long delays, the two officers who carried out the assault on Novel were convicted and handed light sentences in mid-2020. Nevertheless, many anti-corruption campaigners saw the Novel case as a brutal warning to the KPK's rank-and-file investigators that certain avenues of investigation would no longer be tolerated.[10]

Alongside physical intimidation and violence, the KPK faced executive-led efforts to undermine its reputation for independence. In particular, this entailed the dissemination and amplification of the alleged ideological biases and political agendas of its investigators. From late 2018, pro-government social media 'buzzers' churned out claims that a puritanical Islamist clique—referred to as the 'Taliban faction'—had become pre-eminent among KPK investigators, and was deliberately targeting government-aligned politicians in order to destabilise the Jokowi administration (see also Nuraniyah, this volume). This narrative filtered into mainstream media discourse through 2019, where it was promoted by government politicians and presidential spokespeople. In the words of one leading activist, the radicalisation narrative was 'consciously repeated … [to generate] fear among the public that there is a far more urgent problem within the KPK than the eradication of corruption'.[11] This manufactured alarm, in turn, was leveraged as justification for the government-led 'reforms' to the agency that came in the aftermath of Jokowi's re-election (*Mata Najwa* 2019).

The government's campaign against the KPK reached a head in the weeks before Jokowi's second-term inauguration. In September 2019, the outgoing DPR—actively encouraged by the president—abruptly announced substantial revisions to the KPK law that crippled the agency's independence across multiple dimensions. Having previously operated without direct executive oversight, the KPK was now incorporated into the executive branch and its employees were made civil servants. In addition, approval from a newly established Oversight Board—comprising presidential appointees—was required for a range of key investigative operations, including wire-taps, searches and property seizures. The KPK was also given the freedom to drop ongoing investigations, opening its cases up to the modes of manipulation rife within other law enforcement agencies. Alongside these revisions, the legislature and president approved the appointment of the most deeply compromised board of commissioners to date, headed by an active police officer who had himself been implicated in recent corruption scandals (Trianita 2019).

---

10   Interviews with Indonesia Corruption Watch analysts, 9 August 2018.
11   Anita Wahid, appearing on *Mata Najwa*, 18 September 2019.

These revisions had swift and severe implications for the KPK. While some of the KPK's rank-and-file investigators still sought to initiate independent operations, their efforts were hamstrung by the new regulations and the agency's highly compromised leadership. In early 2020, KPK investigators' attempted arrest of PDI-P secretary-general Hasto Kristiyanto—who had been implicated in the bribery of an Electoral Commission official—provided an insight into this deepening impotence. Following the arrest of two PDI-P staffers, Hasto received backchannel information that he was the target of an impending sting operation. He then allegedly sought refuge at the Police Higher Education Institute (Perguruan Tinggi Ilmu Kepolisian, PTIK) in South Jakarta. When KPK investigators arrived at the institute, they were detained and interrogated by police, with their equipment and phones confiscated (Trianita 2020). KPK staff were also prevented from conducting a search of PDI-P offices, with the party lodging a formal complaint to the Oversight Board on the grounds that the operation had not received board authorisation (CNN Indonesia 2020). In the weeks that followed, KPK executives refused to pursue the investigation against Hasto and curtailed the investigation into PDI-P, forsaking the agency's rank-and-file staff and instead acquiescing to the interests of the governing party.

Prior to 2019, the KPK was for many Indonesians the most important embodiment of post-Suharto law-and-order reform. Popular support for the agency had proved a vital bulwark against attacks from the police and lawmakers during Yudhoyono's tenure and into the early Jokowi era (Lim 2013; Mietzner 2012). This popularity was revealed once again, as the 2019 revisions—tellingly passed by a lame duck parliament and newly re-elected government—prompted an outpouring of public protest spearheaded by the largest student demonstrations in 20 years. These protests were consistent with a trend throughout Jokowi's tenure, whereby the erosion of formal institutional checks on executive power had seen political opposition increasingly concentrated within civil society, and oppositional activity increasingly manifested in street protest and social media discourse. Yet in its interactions with civil society, too, the executive deployed its legal-coercive power to constrict democratic space, shut down extra-institutional avenues for opposition, and tighten its control over the political landscape.

THE SUPPRESSION OF CIVIL SOCIETY DISSENT AND OPPOSITION

The erosion of formal democratic checks and balances through the late 2010s has encouraged an upswing in extra-institutional opposition (Mietzner and Muhtadi 2018). The government's domestication of parliament, co-option of regional executives and manipulation of law enforcement left civil society as the last major arena for democratic dissent and pushback against the executive's agenda of aggrandisement. Thus, the Jokowi era has seen the re-emergence of large-scale popular protest, as well as the increased concentration of critical expression and dissent in social and independent media. Yet the Jokowi administration's responses to civil society–led opposition have been among the most overt expressions of its mounting authoritarian tendencies. Executive interactions with civil society have been increasingly characterised by the weaponisation of law enforcement and the 'criminalisation' of previously tolerated forms of dissent and opposition.

While these trends were apparent even during the final years of the Yudhoyono era—exemplified, for example, by the growing number of Indonesians prosecuted using the draconian Electronic Information and Transactions Law (ITE Law; see Setiawan, this volume)—they greatly intensified amid the unprecedented Islamist mobilisations that swung the Jakarta gubernatorial election of 2017. The scale of the Defence of Islam actions left the government with little alternative to short-term concessions, most notably with the issuing of blasphemy charges against Jakarta governor Basuki Tjahaja Purnama ('Ahok'). However, the broader government response relied heavily on the deployment of coercive tactics. From late 2016, many government critics were investigated, charged and arrested for offences including treason, criminal defamation, hate speech, blasphemy, insulting state symbols and various other speech crimes. While an initial wave of arrests in late 2016 targeted relatively peripheral government critics, a raft of criminal charges was later issued against the movement's figurehead, the Islamic Defenders Front (Front Pembela Islam, FPI) leader Habib Rizieq Shihab, who fled into exile in Saudi Arabia (Sulistiyanto 2018). Executive authority to restrict and police civil society activity was also expanded in response to the 2016–17 demonstrations. In mid-2017, the government issued a decree giving it the authority to unilaterally disband civil society organisations, by abolishing the established requirement of judicial review (Hadiz 2017: 270). This decree was immediately deployed to outlaw the nonviolent Islamist organisation Hizbut Tahrir Indonesia (HTI) following its prominent role in the protests, and—in a potent echo of New Order doctrine—was then used to threaten similar bans on any organisations the executive deemed to contravene Pancasila (Rahadian 2017).

As with the government's response to the KMP, a utilitarian argument could be made that these illiberal measures at least aimed to shield Indonesia's political status quo against the more severe Islamist-populist threat presented by the '212 movement' (Mietzner 2018). However, this interpretation could not be extended to subsequent crackdowns on electorally oriented popular opposition ahead of Jokowi's re-election campaign, nor to the heavy-handed dismantling of pro-democracy student protests in late 2019.

From early 2018, a number of opposition activists and politicians congealed into a movement using the tagline '2019 Change the President' (2019GantiPresiden); this movement represented an attempt to consolidate grassroots opposition and establish rudimentary campaign infrastructure amid uncertainty about the identity of Jokowi's 2019 presidential challenger.[12] Having mounted a viral social media campaign, 2019GantiPresiden activists were by mid-year scheduling a series of mass gatherings to take place in a number of major cities across Indonesia. Though the 2019GantiPresiden movement incorporated elements of the Islamist 212 constituency, its leaders consistently emphasised its purely electoral and constitutional objectives. Nevertheless, government spokespeople accused the movement of harbouring an anti-system and even treasonous agenda, attempting to frame a democratic opposition group as a threat to social cohesion, political stability and existing state institutions. These allegations were accompanied by a nationwide pattern of police suppression, with public gatherings of 2019GantiPresiden supporters either prohibited or forcibly broken up, often with support from pro-government counter-mobilisations (Power 2018: 331–2; see also Nuraniyah, this volume).

Alongside the suppression of physical mobilisation by opposition groups, a number of government critics were investigated, arrested and imprisoned in the lead-up to the 2019 election. Perhaps the most prominent of these was musician and Prabowo ally Ahmad Dhani, who was arrested on questionable charges of hate speech, sentenced to prison in early 2019, and thus removed from the presidential campaign trail (Aspinall and Mietzner 2019: 302). However, numerous other opposition leaders and ordinary citizens were publicly threatened with criminal charges or arrested and imprisoned through 2018 and 2019; in many

---

12   Interview with Mardani Ali Sera, 6 August 2018.

cases, these charges arose from online posts deemed insulting to the president or his political allies. Whereas cases against government critics were routinely followed up and brought to trial, criminal complaints filed against government allies invariably disappeared—indeed, Aspinall and Mietzner (2019: 303) note that 'no online insults against Prabowo were brought to court' ahead of the election. The legal intimidation and criminalisation of opposition activists again revealed close cooperation between government partisans and law enforcement agencies. For instance, at least half a dozen criminal complaints targeting opposition figures—including those against Dhani—were lodged by Jack Boyd Lapian, co-founder of the pro-Jokowi and PDI-P-aligned 'Cyber Pancasila' group,[13] which dedicates itself to the online policing of anti-government content (Mukhtar 2019).

Leading into 2019, it appeared that state repression of dissent was focused on the short-term goal of Jokowi's re-election bid (Power 2018); by implication, these trends would ease once a second presidential term was secure. However, the aftermath of the 2019 election revealed, if anything, an accelerated effort to expand executive control at the expense of democratic rights and norms. In September 2019, thousands of protesters—most of them students—took to the streets of Jakarta to demand an executive order rescinding the newly passed revisions to the KPK law, and calling for the cancellation of proposed revisions to the Criminal Code.[14] These quickly escalated into the largest pro-democracy demonstrations in 20 years, with rallies erupting in almost every major city. Government spokespeople obfuscated the president's central role in initiating the KPK revisions by suggesting he was seriously contemplating such an annulment (Ihsanuddin 2019). Meanwhile, the executive again turned to its coercive toolkit to quash the mobilisations.

Violent confrontations broke out between police and protesters in several cities, exacerbated by the presence of heavily armed riot squads; these clashes saw hundreds of students seriously injured and five killed, including two shot dead in Kendari (CNN Indonesia 2019). Meanwhile, the Ministry for Research, Technology and Higher Education announced that sanctions would be enforced against universities whose students participated in the demonstrations, which in turn resulted in threats of expulsion for those involved (Bustomi 2019). Continuing the longstanding pattern of intimidation and criminalisation of opposition, journalist and pro-democracy activist Dandhy Laksono—a vocal supporter of the

---

13 According to several party sources.
14 These were chief among a set of demands issued by student leaders.

student demonstrations—was arrested and charged with alleged hate speech relating to his comments on the contemporaneous civil rights protests in Papua. Another journalist, Ananda Badudu, was detained by police for fundraising in support of the pro-KPK mobilisations. Dozens of students were also arrested or detained. Through early October the protests dissipated, and while revisions to the Criminal Code were postponed, the democracy movement's battle for the KPK was lost.

The government crackdown on the student protests—carried out through the assertive deployment of security personnel, threats of academic penalties and expulsion, and a number of high-profile arrests—proved extremely effective. The suppression of dissent continued amid the 2020 COVID-19 outbreak, as the police launched a now predictable flurry of arrests targeting citizens who criticised the government's response to the crisis.[15] The early months of Jokowi's second term thus indicated that the incumbent executive, through its partisan manipulation of the state's coercive apparatus, would continue to assail both formal and extra-institutional mechanisms of democratic accountability.

CONCLUSION: DETERIORATING ACCOUNTABILITY AND EXECUTIVE AGGRANDISEMENT

Recent analyses of Indonesian politics have drawn attention to the Jokowi government's adoption of repressive and anti-democratic tactics, characterising these as 'executive illiberalism' (Aspinall and Mietzner 2019) or as part of an 'authoritarian turn' (Power 2018). This chapter has built on these analyses, arguing that one key consequence of this executive-led illiberalism or neo-authoritarianism has been the dismantling and co-option of democratic accountability mechanisms that could otherwise check the exercise of executive power. These patterns are evident in both the realm of formal political institutions—through the hamstringing of party-based opposition, the narrowing of electoral competition, central government encroachment into the subnational arena and the enfeeblement of independent law enforcement—as well as in executive–civil society relations, where opposition mobilisation and critical dissent have become increasingly fraught.

At the heart of these trends is the executive weaponisation of law enforcement, which had, by the outset of Jokowi's second term, reached

---

15 The first three months of 2020 saw 33 new ITE cases initiated—50 per cent more than were lodged over the duration of 2019 (SAFEnet 2020). By 8 April 2020, 77 citizens had been named suspects for spreading online 'hoaxes'.

heights unrivalled since the collapse of the New Order. Taken in sum, these processes reveal a specific and ongoing form of executive aggrandisement, whereby the incumbent government has suppressed perceived 'challenges' to its authority by manipulating its established powers and exploiting the shortcomings of Indonesia's post-1998 political landscape.

Crucially, we have seen a shift in the types of 'challenge' met with the executive's deployment of law enforcement. The Jokowi government's initial moves to consolidate executive power provoked at worst ambivalence among many democratically minded Indonesians, directed as they were against credibly authoritarian opposition in the KMP and the Islamist 212 movement. However, that picture has shifted dramatically. First, through the 2018–19 campaign period, the executive deployed the state's coercive apparatus in service to partisan electoral interests—an effort to co-opt regional powerbrokers and suppress opposition mobilisation in ways that advantaged the incumbent coalition. Then, in the aftermath of Jokowi's re-election, his government oversaw the sabotage of the independent KPK and a crackdown on the pro-democracy demonstrations that sought to defend it. These moves at once extended executive capture of law enforcement and revealed the inability of civil society to arrest the contemporary democratic crisis. As this volume demonstrates, Indonesian democracy is presently beset by an array of pressing threats. An increasingly untrammelled executive, unencumbered by the normative constraints of democratic toleration and forbearance, may be the greatest among them.

REFERENCES

Aidit, D.N. 1964. 'The Indonesian revolution and the immediate tasks of the Communist Party of Indonesia'. Report delivered to the Higher Party School of the Central Committee of the Communist Party of China, 2 September 1963. Peking: Foreign Languages Press.

Aspinall, E. 2010. 'The irony of success'. *Journal of Democracy* 21(2): 20–34.

Aspinall, E. and M. Mietzner. 2014. 'Indonesian politics in 2014: democracy's close call'. *Bulletin of Indonesian Economic Studies* 50(3): 347–69.

Aspinall, E. and M. Mietzner. 2019. 'Indonesia's democratic paradox: competitive elections amidst rising illiberalism'. *Bulletin of Indonesian Economic Studies* 55(3): 295–317.

Bermeo, N. 2016. 'On democratic backsliding'. *Journal of Democracy* 27(1): 5–19.

Briantika, A. 2019. 'Eks kapolsek Pasirwangi: instruksi dukung Jokowi lewat WA dan rapat'. *Tirto*, 31 March. https://tirto.id/eks-kapolsek-pasirwangi-instruksi-dukung-jokowi-lewat-wa-dan-rapat-dkDB

Budianto, E.E. 2018. 'Kades pendukung Sandiaga divonis 2 bulan penjara'. *Detik*, 13 December. https://news.detik.com/berita-jawa-timur/d-4342198/kades-pendukung-sandiaga-divonis-2-bulan-penjara

Bustomi, M.I. 2019. 'Pengakuan mahasiswa, ditawari uang hingga diancam agar tak gelar aksi'. *Kompas*, 18 October. https://megapolitan.kompas.com/read/2019/10/18/08511591/pengakuan-mahasiswa-ditawari-uang-hingga-diancam-agar-tak-gelar-aksi

Butt, S. 2012. *Corruption and Law in Indonesia*. Abingdon, Oxon: Routledge.

CNN Indonesia. 2019. 'Mahasiswa tewas dalam unjuk rasa di Kendari jadi dua orang'. CNN Indonesia, 27 September. https://www.cnnindonesia.com/nasional/20190927073715-20-434506/mahasiswa-tewas-dalam-unjuk-rasa-di-kendari-jadi-dua-orang

CNN Indonesia. 2020. 'PDIP laporkan pegawai KPK ke Dewas: demi rakyat Indonesia'. CNN Indonesia, 16 January. https://www.cnnindonesia.com/nasional/20200116202718-32-466103/pdip-laporkan-pegawai-kpk-ke-dewas-demi-rakyat-indonesia

Cribb, R. 2011. 'A system of exemptions: historicizing state illegality in Indonesia'. In *The State and Illegality in Indonesia*, edited by E. Aspinall and G. van Klinken, 31–44. Leiden, Netherlands: KITLV Press.

Dahl, R.A. 1982. *Dilemmas of Pluralist Democracy: Autonomy vs. Control*. New Haven and London: Yale University Press.

Diamond, L. 2008. *The Spirit of Democracy: The Struggle to Build Free Societies throughout the World*. New York: Times Books.

Dick, H. and J. Mulholland. 2016. 'The politics of corruption in Indonesia'. *Georgetown Journal of International Affairs* 17(1): 43–9.

Dongoran, H.A. 2018. 'Musim deklarasi buat inkumben'. *Tempo*, 28 September. https://majalah.tempo.co/read/nasional/156278/musim-deklarasi-buat-inkumben

Farisa, F.C. 2019. 'Tjahjo Kumolo dilaporkan ke Bawaslu karena meminta ASN tidak netral'. *Kompas*, 8 March. https://nasional.kompas.com/read/2019/03/08/19285781/tjahjo-kumolo-dilaporkan-ke-bawaslu-karena-meminta-asn-tidak-netral

Feith, H. 1962. *The Decline of Constitutional Democracy in Indonesia*. Ithaca, NY: Cornell University Press.

Fionna, U. and D. Tomsa. 2017. 'Parties and factions in Indonesia: the effects of historical legacies and institutional engineering'. *ISEAS Working Paper* No. 1. Singapore: ISEAS – Yusof Ishak Institute.

Gatra. 2018. 'Saat kepala daerah Sulut ramai-ramai merapat ke Nasdem'. *Gatra*, 1 October. https://www.gatra.com/detail/news/350271-Saat-Kepala-Daerah-Sulut-Ramai-Ramai-Merapat-ke-Nasdem

Habermas, J. 1995. 'On the internal relation between the rule of law and democracy'. *European Journal of Philosophy* 3(1): 12–20.

Hadiz, V.R. 2017. 'Indonesia's year of democratic setbacks: towards a new phase of deepening illiberalism?'. *Bulletin of Indonesian Economic Studies* 53(3): 261–78.

Ihsanuddin. 2015. 'Yasonna dianggap "begal" demokrasi, fraksi gabungan parpol di KMP sepakat melawan'. *Kompas*, 13 March. https://nasional.kompas.com/read/2015/03/13/14383861/Yasonna.Dianggap.Begal.Demokrasi.Fraksi.Gabungan.Parpol.di.KMP.Sepakat.Melawan

Ihsanuddin. 2019. 'Melunak, Jokowi kini pertimbangkan terbitkan Perppu KPK'. *Kompas*, 26 September. https://nasional.kompas.com/read/2019/09/26/17010651/melunak-jokowi-kini-pertimbangkan-terbitkan-perppu-kpk

Indonesia Leaks. 2019. 'Teka-teki buku merah: antara novel, KPK dan pertemuan di Pattimura'. *Tirto*, 17 October. https://tirto.id/teka-teki-buku-merah-antara-novel-kpk-dan-pertemuan-di-pattimura-ejUa

Jaffrey, S. 2020. 'Is Indonesia becoming a two-tier democracy?'. Commentary, 23 January. Carnegie Endowment for International Peace. https://carnegieendowment.org/2020/01/23/is-indonesia-becoming-two-tier-democracy-pub-80876

Khaitan, T. 2019. 'Executive aggrandizement in established democracies: a crisis of liberal democratic constitutionalism'. *International Journal of Constitutional Law* 17(1): 342–56.

Lay, C., H. Hanif, Ridwan and N. Rohman. 2017. 'The rise of uncontested elections in Indonesia: case studies of Pati and Jayapura'. *Contemporary Southeast Asia* 39(3): 427–48.

Levitsky, S. and D. Ziblatt. 2018. *How Democracies Die*. New York: Crown.

Liddle, R.W. 1985. 'Soeharto's Indonesia: personal rule and political institutions'. *Pacific Affairs* 58(1): 68–90.

Lim, M. 2013. 'Many clicks but little sticks: social media activism in Indonesia'. *Journal of Contemporary Asia* 43(4): 636–57.

Mata Najwa. 2019. 'KPK: kiamat pemberantasan korupsi'. Trans7, 18 September [Television broadcast]. https://www.youtube.com/watch?v=dkMEju1NMhk

McLeod, R.H. 2008. 'Inadequate budgets and salaries as instruments for institutionalizing public sector corruption in Indonesia'. *South East Asia Research* 16(2): 199–223.

Mietzner, M. 2007. 'Party financing in post-Soeharto Indonesia: between state subsidies and political corruption'. *Contemporary Southeast Asia* 29(2): 238–63.

Mietzner, M. 2012. 'Indonesia's democratic stagnation: anti-reformist elites and resilient civil society'. *Democratization* 19(2): 209–29.

Mietzner, M. 2013. *Money, Power, and Ideology: Political Parties in Post-Authoritarian Indonesia*. Singapore: NUS Press.

Mietzner, M. 2015. 'Dysfunction by design: political finance and corruption in Indonesia'. Critical *Asian Studies* 47(4): 587–610.

Mietzner, M. 2016. 'Coercing loyalty: coalitional presidentialism and party politics in Jokowi's Indonesia'. *Contemporary Southeast Asia* 38(2): 209–32.

Mietzner, M. 2018. 'Fighting illiberalism with illiberalism: Islamist populism and democratic deconsolidation in Indonesia'. *Pacific Affairs* 91(2): 261–82.

Mietzner, M. and B. Muhtadi. 2018. 'Explaining the 2016 Islamist mobilisation in Indonesia: religious intolerance, militant groups and the politics of accommodation'. *Asian Studies Review* 42(3): 479–97.

Muhtadi, B. 2015. 'Jokowi's first year: a weak president caught between reform and oligarchic politics'. *Bulletin of Indonesian Economic Studies* 51(3): 349–68.

Mukhtar, U. 'Sosok Jack Boyd: pelapor Anies, Dhani, hingga Rocky Gerung'. *Republika*, 31 January. https://www.republika.co.id/berita/nasional/politik/19/01/31/pm6elm430-sosok-jack-boyd-pelapor-anies-dhani-hingga-rocky-gerung

Nordholt, H.S. 2005. 'Decentralisation in Indonesia: less state, more democracy?'. In *Politicising Democracy: The New Local Politics of Democratisation*, edited by J. Harriss, K. Stokke and O. Törnquist, 29–50. London: Palgrave Macmillan.

Partai NasDem. 2018. 'Petrus Fatlolon tambahi kepala daerah Nasdem jadi 195'. *Partai Nasional Demokrat*, 7 November. https://partainasdem.id/read/6492/2018/11/07/petrus-fatlolon-tambahi-kepala-daerah-nasdem-jadi-195

Power, T.P. 2018. 'Jokowi's authoritarian turn and Indonesia's democratic decline'. *Bulletin of Indonesian Economic Studies* 54(3): 307–38.

Rahadian, L. 2017. 'Daftar panjang ormas anti-Pancasila dan langkah pemerintah'. CNN Indonesia, 9 August. https://www.cnnindonesia.com/nasional/20170809121706-20-233459/daftar-panjang-ormas-anti-pancasila-dan-langkah-pemerintah

SAFEnet (Southeast Asia Freedom of Expression Network). 2020. 'Daftar kasus netizen yang terjerat UU ITE'. SAFEnet, 10 April. https://id.safenet.or.id/daftarkasus/

Schmitter, P.C. and T.L. Karl. 1991. 'What democracy is ... and is not'. *Journal of Democracy* 2(3): 75–88.

Slater, D. 2004. 'Indonesia's accountability trap: party cartels and presidential power after democratic transition'. *Indonesia* 78(October): 61–92.

Slater, D. 2018. 'Party cartelisation, Indonesian-style: presidential power-sharing and the contingency of democratic opposition'. *Journal of East Asian Studies* 18(1): 23–46.

Sözen, Y. 2019. 'Competition in a populist authoritarian regime: the June 2018 dual elections in Turkey'. *South European Society and Politics* 24(3): 287–315.

Sulistiyanto, P. 2018. 'Indonesia in 2017: Jokowi's supremacy and his next political battles'. *Southeast Asian Affairs* 2018: 153–66.

Tomsa, D. 2015. 'Local politics and corruption in Indonesia's outer islands'. *Bijdragen tot de Taal-, Land- en Volkenkunde* 171(2–3): 196–219.

Trianita, L. 2019. 'Jenderal polisi sarat kontroversi'. *Tempo*, 14 September. https://majalah.tempo.co/read/laporan-utama/158397/jenderal-polisi-sarat-kontroversi

Trianita, L. 2020. 'Di bawah lindungan Tirtayasa'. *Tempo*, 11 January. https://majalah.tempo.co/read/laporan-utama/159436/di-balik-gagalnya-operasi-kpk-menangkap-hasto-kristiyanto

Warburton, E. and E. Aspinall. 2019. 'Explaining Indonesia's democratic regression: structure, agency and popular opinion'. *Contemporary Southeast Asia: A Journal of International and Strategic Affairs* 41(2): 255–85. https://www.muse.jhu.edu/article/732137

Widojoko, J.D. 2017. 'Indonesia's anticorruption campaign: civil society versus the political cartel'. In *The Changing Face of Corruption in the Asia-Pacific: Current Perspectives and Future Challenges*, edited by M. dela Rama and C. Rowley, 253–66. Amsterdam: Elsevier Asian Studies Series.

Ziegenhain, P. 2017. 'Decentralization and its impact on the democratization process'. In *Rethinking Power Relations in Indonesia: Transforming the Margins*, edited by M. Haug, M. Rössler and A.-T. Grumblies, 29–42. Abingdon, Oxon: Routledge.

15 In the state's stead? Vigilantism and policing of religious offence in Indonesia[1]

Sana Jaffrey

It was an awkward encounter. Deputy National Police Chief Nanan Soekarna shifted in his seat as the popular talk-show host Najwa Shihab tried to extract a promise from Muhammad Al Khaththath, the secretary-general of the Forum of the Islamic Community (Forum Umat Islam, FUI), that his organisation would no longer conduct vigilante raids on food stalls in the upcoming fasting month.[2] Al Khaththath remained defiant. 'Raids are only conducted when citizens complain to us. If there is no response from the police [to stop the sale of food when Muslims are fasting], Islamic mass organisations [*ormas*] will be forced to act in their place', he asserted. When reminded of the newly passed *ormas* law,[3] which prohibits such raids, he lamented the limited law enforcement capacity of the police and insisted that citizens had the right to punish wrongdoers: 'Just think about it, even when we catch a thief, don't we beat him up?'

Unlike National Police Chief Timur Pradopo, who was known to be close to hardline Islamist organisations and frequently expressed his gratitude for their support in maintaining public order (*Tempo* 2010), Soekarna had a rocky relationship with these groups. Just a few days earlier, he had issued a stern warning to the *ormas*: 'Unofficial raids are

---

1 Some of the analysis presented in this chapter has been previously published in Jaffrey and Mulyartono (2017).
2 The show, *Mata Najwa*, aired on Metro TV at 9:30 pm, 10 July 2013.
3 Law No. 17/2013 on Mass Organisations.

prohibited, and it is our duty to take action against anyone involved in anarchic activities' (Arnaz 2013).

That evening, however, Soekarna appeared more conciliatory. There was no mention of dire consequences, only gentle attempts to guide vigilantes' demands through the proper channels. He calmly explained that enforcing the law was the job of the police, and if officers were not responsive to citizens' complaints, they could be fired: 'With a policy of swiftly firing non-responsive police officers, the *ormas* really can trust us to get the job done'. This appeal for trust prompted even more indignation from Al Khaththath, who berated the police for not paying attention to issues that offended Muslim sensibilities. 'There would be no need for [our] raids if the police took preventative action', he claimed. 'That is why [we] are now pushing the police to conduct the raids.' On this point, the two men found common ground. Soekarna agreed that the vigilante organisations should work through the police, rather than in their stead. 'From now on, the duty of the *ormas* is to rebuke, rectify and warn [uncooperative] police officers, so that there is no need for violence', he concluded.

Hardline Islamist organisations that once operated on the political margins have emerged as formidable players in mainstream politics during the second decade of democratic rule in Indonesia. Previously notorious for their harassment of religious minorities and moral racketeering, these organisations are now undermining Indonesian democracy by polarising the public along religious lines and enforcing these divisions at the grassroots level through threats of mob violence. The brief encounter from 2013 described above illustrates two enduring factors that explain this transformation. First, hardline organisations are regulating a widening range of moral and religious offences in Indonesia by actively building on an existing template of widespread crime-control vigilantism that has broad social legitimacy. Second, the effectiveness of using vigilante violence as a tactic for enforcing a narrowly defined religious vision of society derives both from these organisations' direct punishment of transgressions, as well as from their ability to compel the state to do their bidding. While they cite lenient laws and low police capacity as motivations for taking the law into their own hands, in reality religious vigilantes draw on the presence and authority of state institutions to cow their victims into submission. This power to deploy the state apparatus in the service of their goals explains why hardline Islamist organisations have gained political influence without ever having to contest popular elections.

The deepening political polarisation in Indonesia involves two ideological camps: one that seeks to maintain the pluralist foundations of Indonesian democracy, and another that demands a fundamental reconstitution of the polity to ensure a privileged position for the Muslim majority, by restricting the democratic rights of minorities. Successive electoral defeats suffered by the majoritarian camp have prevented it from translating its Islamist vision into constitutional change. However, this chapter argues that hardline organisations have adopted vigilantism against religious offence as an alternative mechanism for dismantling basic democratic freedoms from the bottom up.

In the first section of this chapter, I briefly recount how Islamist organisations brought the issue of blasphemy into the political spotlight. I show that while most attention has been paid to hardline groups, mainstream Islamic organisations have also used vigilante tactics to to counter criticism. In the second section I explain the emergence of vigilantism as a tactic for regulating religious offence at the grassroots level, by taking a broader look at patterns of vigilante violence in Indonesia. I argue that Islamist organisations seek legitimacy for their actions by replicating an existing template of collective violence that is routinely used to punish criminal offences. In the third section I demonstrate that, contrary to existing theories that attribute mob violence to state absence, vigilantism in Indonesia has risen in tandem with a rapid expansion of the state's coercive presence. I explain that the perpetrators of vigilante violence leverage increasingly harsh state regulations and use their influence over local officials to intimidate their victims into submission. In the conclusion, I examine the implications of these findings for Indonesia's democracy. Although individual incidents tend to be small in scale, the cumulative impact of widespread vigilantism is rapidly narrowing the range of permissible behaviour for religious, social and sexual minorities. I argue that, far from discouraging mob violence, attempts to appease vigilantes by enacting a harsher legal code will only embolden them.

VIGILANTISM AND THE QUOTIDIAN EFFECTS OF POLITICAL POLARISATION

A contentious election puts religious offence in the spotlight

In 2016, three consecutive Defence of Islam (Aksi Bela Islam) rallies in Jakarta put the issue of religious offence in the political spotlight. Observers were taken aback by the social resonance of blasphemy accusations against Basuki Tjahaja Purnama ('Ahok'), Jakarta's Christian Chinese governor and the candidate favoured by President Joko Widodo in the upcoming gubernatorial election. Following his remarks about a verse of the Qur'an (Al-Maidah 51) that is said to prohibit Muslims from voting for non-Muslim leaders, the notorious but politically marginal hardline mass organisation, the Islamic Defenders Front (Front Pembela Islam, FPI), accused Ahok of blasphemy and called for his immediate arrest.

Given the incumbent governor's popularity with voters and their appreciation of his efforts to improve public service delivery, these charges were initially considered a nuisance. After all, FPI had been campaigning against Ahok for a long time, first claiming that, as a *kafir* (infidel), he was not fit to lead a Muslim-majority province, and then lodging corruption and maladministration charges against him. While these previous efforts had failed to dampen Ahok's electoral prospects, the blasphemy accusations mobilised a sustained popular movement against him that not only changed the expected outcome of Jakarta's election, but also unleashed a new wave of vigilantism in Indonesia.

The movement, led by FPI, was soon endorsed by Indonesia's top Islamic clerical body, the Indonesian Council of Islamic Scholars (Majelis Ulama Indonesia, MUI), which issued a fatwa condemning Ahok as a blasphemer, even before a police investigation had been concluded. Some sections of Indonesia's mainstream Islamic organisations, Nahdlatul Ulama (NU) and Muhammadiyah, joined in the effort. This turned a small movement into a national political coalition (Gerakan Nasional Pembela Fatwa MUI, GNPF MUI) that was able to mobilise the largest mass protest in Indonesia's history (Fealy 2016). Ahok lost the election during a run-off, and within a few weeks a court had found him guilty of blasphemy and sentenced him to two years in prison.

Following this extraordinary show of force in the nation's capital, fears grew that Islamists were gaining ground in Indonesia (IPAC 2018). Local organisations, affiliated with or inspired by FPI, launched a series of mob attacks against religious minorities across Indonesia. In Bandung, such groups prohibited Christian residents from holding Christmas celebrations in public buildings (Halim and Dipa 2016). In the religiously diverse city of Yogyakarta, vigilantes vandalised advertising boards portraying hijab-wearing Muslim students attending a Christian university (Utama 2016). In Surabaya, FPI raided shopping malls to prevent Muslim employees from donning Christmas-themed clothes (Andriansyah 2016). In Medan, FPI copycats lodged blasphemy accusations against a Buddhist Chinese woman who had objected to the volume of the loudspeaker at her local mosque. Vigilantes demanded that the local MUI branch issue a fatwa against her and burned down several Buddhist temples in the process (Mulyartono et al. 2018).

Vigilante mobs hunt for 'offenders' across the ideological spectrum

Vigilante attacks were expected to subside after Ahok's imprisonment. However, when the police charged FPI's firebrand leader, Habib Rizieq Shihab, in a pornography case, the organisation was armed with an excuse to protect the reputation of its leader, and found an opportunity to keep the issue of religious offence alive for the upcoming national elections in 2019. With Rizieq in self-imposed exile in Saudi Arabia, FPI members unleashed a new round of vigilante attacks on his critics. Data compiled by free speech advocacy network SAFEnet show that between January and June 2017, at least 59 people were subjected to intimidation by violent mobs after criticising FPI on social media (Purba 2017). Of the recorded cases, 34 took place in May, after the police named Rizieq a potential suspect. Initially most incidents occurred in Jakarta, but gradually the violence spread to other parts of the country.

Two cases in particular triggered a public outcry due to the blatant nature of the attacks. In the first incident, the victim was a 15-year-old boy from Jakarta, accused of posting offensive material about Rizieq on his Facebook page. A video of the attack, recorded by the perpetrators and shared widely on social media, shows the teenager surrounded by several men claiming affiliation with FPI. As the mob coerces him into reading an apology, the teenager is repeatedly told that other offenders have suffered a much worse fate. 'We at FPI still follow procedure but people can't contain themselves if their leader is insulted', they tell him. As if to demonstrate, two men strike the teenager's face while the crowd breaks into raucous laughter (*BeritaSatu* 2017). Clearly under duress, the victim and his mother sign the apology. Pictures of their ordeal were immediately posted on social media as proof of FPI's success in doling out swift punishment to transgressors, presumably in a bid to deter others from doing the same. The assault of a minor documented in the video triggered outrage from child protection groups and forced the police to temporarily arrest two FPI members. Shortly afterwards, however, the victim's family was evicted by their landlord, who feared there would be further reprisals from FPI (BBC Indonesia 2017).

The second incident involved a doctor in West Sumatra who had berated Rizieq in a Facebook post for fleeing abroad to dodge the legal process (*TribunJabar* 2017). The doctor was attacked by a group of FPI affiliates while she was driving home from work with her two small children. The mob demanded that she immediately post an apology on her social media page; otherwise, FPI members from the entire province would mobilise against her. Despite complying with this demand, she was called to her supervisor's office the following day, where leaders of the local FPI chapter told her to sign another apology—the original retraction was not deemed sufficient. A second note of apology from the doctor, endorsed by the police, was publicised widely, along with a photograph of the doctor with the FPI leaders. Even so, she continued to receive threatening phone calls and visits from the group. Although the local police chief was suspended for mishandling the case, persistent threats from vigilantes eventually forced the victim to flee to Jakarta for safety.

FPI's religious offence charges were not reserved just for ordinary citizens who expressed criticism online; they were also used to coerce major mainstream publications. In May 2018, FPI attacked the Jakarta offices of *Tempo* magazine after accusing it of offending Muslims by publishing a satirical cartoon of Rizieq (Ridhoi 2018). In a televised event, FPI members could be seen inside the building, threatening the staff and demanding an immediate apology, which was eventually issued by the editor-in-chief.

Rightly noting the organisation's political interest in keeping this issue alive, observers have focused on the prominence of FPI in vigilante attacks against alleged instances of religious offence. However, the significance of vigilantism goes beyond the narrow political interests of any single organisation. Instead, it has become an increasingly common tactic for regulating religious offence, used by organisations from across the ideological spectrum. In fact, Indonesia's largest mainstream Islamic organisation, NU, also conducts online monitoring as part of an agreement with the Indonesian National Police (Polri) (Faizal 2016; NU Online 2016). Over the past few years, members of NU's youth militia, Banser, have identified and 'handled' several individuals accused of posting derogatory comments about NU's religious leaders (*kiai*). In November 2016, a housewife from Serpong, on the outskirts of Jakarta, was accused of insulting the revered NU *kiai* Maimun Zoebair (*Indonesia* n.d.). She had used crude words to dismiss his suggestion that Ahok's apology was sufficient to put the blasphemy matter to rest. Following a visit by Banser members, she was driven to Central Java, where she apologised to Maimun in person. A Jakarta resident who ridiculed a tweet by senior NU cleric Mustofa Bisri met with similar treatment (Batubara 2016). In January 2017, NU's cyber team tracked offensive comments about the organisation's leader, Said Aqil Siradj, to a man living in Jember. The man accused of causing the offence issued a public apology at a press conference arranged by the local Banser chapter (Mulyono 2017). Another man living in Jakarta initially refused to retract his allegedly offensive comments about the prominent Sufi cleric Habib Luthfi Yahya, but following a visit from local Banser personnel, he promptly signed a statement of apology and posted it on his social media page (Nafys 2017).

Members of Indonesia's second-largest Islamic organisation, Muhammadiyah, have taken a similar course. In May 2017, the organisation's youth wing in Sidoarjo, East Java, took issue with the online comments of a local man, accusing him of insulting two former leaders, Din Syamsuddin and Amien Rais. Members of the group took the man to a local police station, where he provided 'clarification' of his remarks and signed a written apology before posing for pictures with the group (Pwmu.co 2017).

The vigilante campaigns against religious offence by FPI, Muhammadiyah and NU target individuals with different identities and affiliations, according to the ideological vision of each organisation. The level of violence used or implied by these organisations also varies. There are no reports of NU or Muhammadiyah members punishing alleged offenders by engaging in the kind of physical assault seen in the video of FPI's attack on the Jakarta teenager. The scale of NU's and Muhammadiyah's efforts to regulate their critics is also much smaller than FPI's sustained campaign against its critics.

Despite the differing ideologies and levels of mobilisation of these organisations, however, the template of violence used to respond to religious offence is the same: the person accused of an offence is reported through a dedicated social media account; the offensive post is circulated until the accused is tracked down; and a group claiming affiliation with the offended organisation visits the accused and intimidates them into issuing an apology (Figure 15.1).[4] There is no attempt to conduct these proceedings in secrecy. On the contrary, the organisation's visit and the accused offender's apology are a highly publicised affair, with photographs and videos circulated widely on social media in order to deter others.

BUILDING ON A PREVALENT TEMPLATE OF VIOLENCE

Growing political salience of hardline Islamist organisations

Most existing studies focus on explaining the factors that drive the rise of hardline Islamist organisations in politics, but do not explain why vigilantism is increasingly their preferred mode of action. Some have

---

4 Despite the Islamic organisations' claims that their members are acting spontaneously, human rights groups have provided evidence of the systematic and organised nature of their vigilante campaigns, equating them with the workings of a 'machine' (Andayani 2017).

Figure 15.1   The three stages of vigilantism against religious offence

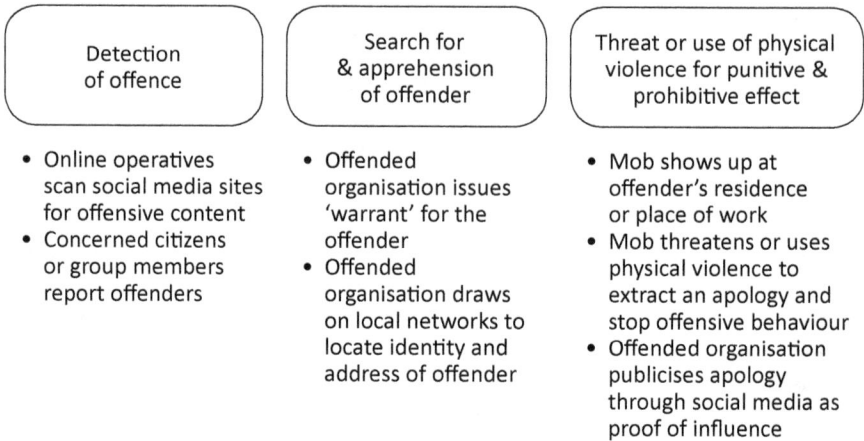

Detection of offence	Search for & apprehension of offender	Threat or use of physical violence for punitive & prohibitive effect
• Online operatives scan social media sites for offensive content • Concerned citizens or group members report offenders	• Offended organisation issues 'warrant' for the offender • Offended organisation draws on local networks to locate identity and address of offender	• Mob shows up at offender's residence or place of work • Mob threatens or uses physical violence to extract an apology and stop offensive behaviour • Offended organisation publicises apology through social media as proof of influence

pointed to longstanding structural factors, claiming that recent trends are a manifestation of deep-seated problems in Indonesia's nationalist narrative. Often erroneously understood as secular, Indonesia's national ideology is actually deeply religious and, consequently, the state recognises citizens' rights based on their religious affiliation, not as individuals (Menchik 2016). Thus, while the state extends formal recognition and protection to several religions, there is little tolerance for deviance from their established doctrines. This suggests that the regulation of religious offence through vigilantism is part of a broader contest between mainstream groups such as NU and Muhammadiyah, and hardline organisations such as FPI, to enforce the boundaries of acceptable religious conduct according to their particular interpretation of Islam. Another structural perspective locates the instrumental use of Islam in a longstanding political contest for wealth and power between oligarchs (Hadiz 2016). According to this view, the actions of groups like FPI are a manifestation of populism, meant to dislodge old, powerful interests and make space for new ones. Thus, vigilante organisations may employ religious messaging as a basis for popular appeal, but their activities are guided by material interests rather than doctrinal conviction.

In contrast, scholars of political behaviour locate the power of hardline Islamist organisations in changing public opinion. Human rights organisations and advocacy groups have long pointed to the increasingly intolerant views of the country's Muslim majority towards religious minorities (Human Rights Watch 2013). New survey data show that the increased level of mobilisation for Islamist causes has less to do with rising levels of intolerance, however, than with the changing socio-economic profiles of people who subscribe to such views (Mietzner and Muhtadi 2018). Specifically, the data show that, on some indicators, the number of people expressing intolerant views about religious minorities actually declined in Indonesia between 2010 and 2016. However, people who express such views are increasingly likely to come from economically better-off backgrounds and do not require monetary incentives to attend large events. This shift in the core constituency of Islamist supporters has enabled more sustained mobilisation for Islamist causes. Although middle-class supporters tend to be peaceful, the need to sustain their engagement incentivises hardline organisations to keep the issue of religious offence alive through small but well-publicised attacks on alleged offenders.

Finally, a third perspective is that the increasing salience of hardline groups is driven by their political evolution (Arifianto 2017; Jones 2015; Mudhoffir 2017; Wilson 2015) and their ability to use social media to amplify their beliefs and mobilise supporters (Hamayotsu 2013). Proponents of this view claim that although ideology is important to FPI, its vigilante violence, mass mobilisation and campaigning are geared more towards improving the political fortunes of the organisation and its leaders. Its selection of allies in civil society and within the state, definition of enemies and use of tactics are based on a calculus about building the organisation's strength. Thus, FPI's activities during the Jakarta election and its acts of violence in the aftermath could be viewed as a dress rehearsal for future elections.

Patterns of everyday vigilantism

While these perspectives on drivers of Islamist mobilisation are crucial for understanding the *motives* behind the recent actions of hardline organisations, they do not explain the choice of vigilantism as their main *tactic*. To grasp the social resonance of recent vigilante campaigns against religious offence, and why this tactic works, we need to examine how these organisations are adapting and replicating a template of coercion that is already widely used in everyday situations by ordinary Indonesians.

The general mode of vigilante action used by FPI, where mobs either demand enforcement of the law to their satisfaction or directly punish alleged transgressions, has long been rampant throughout Indonesia. Between 2005 and 2014, the National Violence Monitoring System (NVMS) recorded 33,627 victims of vigilante violence in 16 provinces that represent

50 per cent of Indonesia's population.[5] This estimate includes 1,659 people who died and many others who sustained serious injuries. To put these numbers in perspective, consider that communal riots and political clashes during the same period resulted in 10,433 victims, including 637 fatalities. This means that victims of vigilante violence are three times higher than casualties from all other forms of collective violence. In terms of trends, the data show a sharp rise in vigilantism since 2007. Between 2007 and 2014, vigilantism-related deaths increased by 56 per cent and incidents rose by 15 per cent (Figure 15.2).

Apart from a quantitative increase, the data indicate a qualitative shift: vigilantism in democratic Indonesia is directed against a much broader range of transgressions. Attacks against sorcerers are relatively few, but petty theft is still the leading trigger for crime control vigilantism. Alleged perpetrators of traffic accidents, rapes and assaults are also frequent targets. Most remarkable, however, is the increased targeting of people for moral and ideological 'offences'. These violations include fornication, adultery, homosexual relationships and raids to restrict the activities of minority religious communities. Overall, the data show that 79 per cent of vigilante attacks carried out between 2005 and 2014 targeted transgressions that were criminal offences, while the remaining 21 per cent of attacks targeted moral and ideological offences.

The NVMS data also show that over 88 per cent of all vigilante attacks are perpetrated by ordinary citizens who do not have a clear affiliation with vigilante organisations. But even though only a small number of incidents involve vigilante organisations, they tend to be high-profile attacks related to controversial issues. In contrast, ordinary residents tend to use vigilantism to deal with local issues that arise in their own neighbourhoods. This difference is reflected in the data: over 80 per cent of incidents of vigilante violence perpetrated by residents in 2005–14 were triggered by criminal offences. During the same period, vigilante organisations stayed away from punishing criminal offences and 80 per cent of their attacks were in response to moral and ideological offences.

Finally, in terms of geographic distribution, the data show that vigilantism is widespread but that it is unevenly distributed across Indonesia (Figure 15.3). All 245 districts covered in the NVMS dataset registered at least one incident of vigilante violence between 2005 and 2014, and 80 per cent of the districts recorded at least one lynching. However, the magnitude of the violence was highly skewed: 75 per cent

---

5   I led the team compiling the NVMS dataset between 2008 and 2013, in collaboration with Patrick Barron and Ashutosh Varshney. See Barron et al. (2016) for details of the collection process and methodology.

Figure 15.2   The rise of vigilante violence in democratic Indonesia, 2007–2014

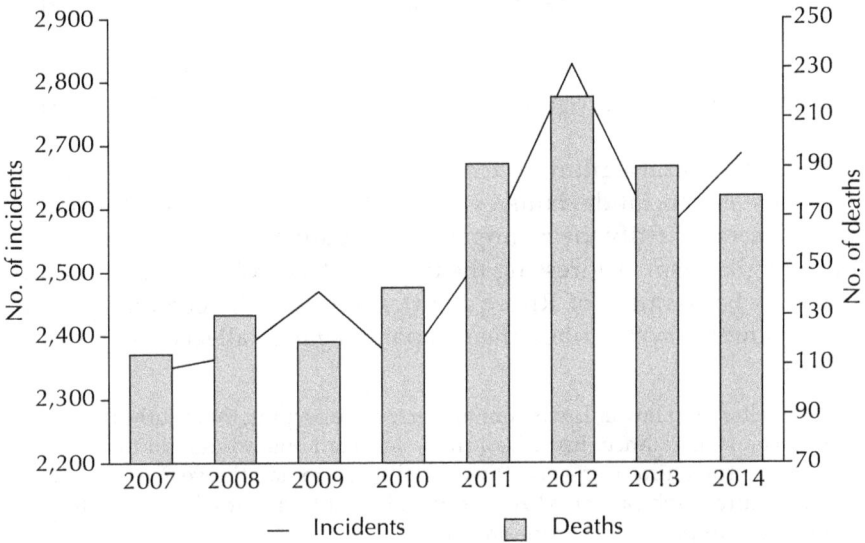

— Incidents   ▨ Deaths

Source: NVMS dataset.

Figure 15.3   Victims of vigilantism in districts by province, 2005–2014 (number per 100,000 people)

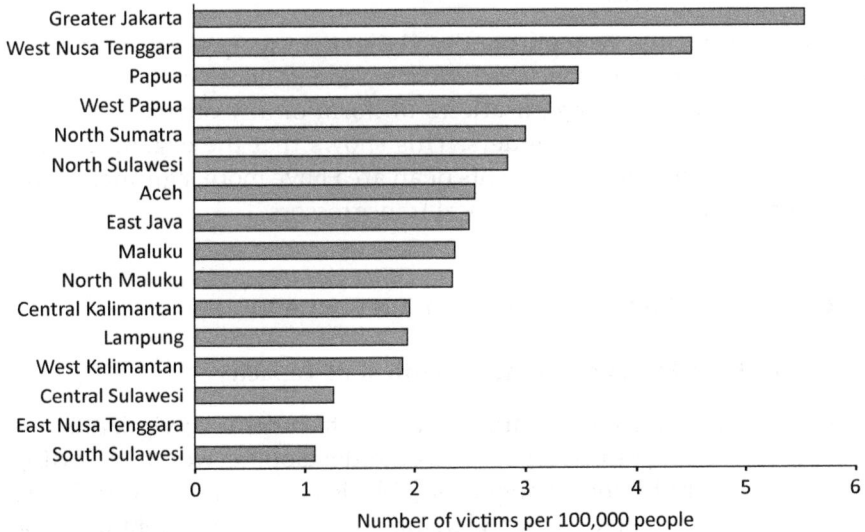

Number of victims per 100,000 people

Source: NVMS dataset.

of all incidents and deaths related to vigilantism were concentrated in just 20 per cent of the districts. In the past, vigilante violence was mainly associated with the countryside, but it has gradually spread to Indonesia's modern urban centres. Even after controlling for the vast population disparity between urban and rural areas, the data show that, today, vigilantism is three times more likely to occur in urban districts than in rural districts.

Given the social legitimacy accorded to violent punishment of alleged criminals and social deviants by ordinary citizens, it is not surprising that FPI leaders justify their campaign by equating it with these everyday acts of vigilantism. Addressing the public outcry over his organisation's relentless harassment of Rizieq's critics, former FPI secretary-general Novel Bamukmin described the campaign against alleged offenders as follows:

> We are helping law enforcement officers, not usurping their authority, so this is just assistance. Just like a thief, we catch one, we detain him and then we turn him over—aren't we all allowed to nab thieves? Aren't we allowed to catch pinchers? Aren't we allowed to arrest corrupters? It is just that simple. (BBC Indonesia 2017)

The next day, FPI's head of public relations, Slamet Maarif, used the same analogy to justify the organisation's persecution of alleged wrongdoers:

> Let me give you an illustration, let's say that a motorbike thief is found by some residents. Do you want the residents to just let him go and then report him to the police? Can't we even detain him with the evidence? (CNN Indonesia 2017)

In a further attempt to replicate the vigilantism template during these campaigns, FPI made a concerted effort to send its 'local' members—who were not wearing the organisation's uniform or any other identifying markers—to deal with offenders. This shows that the organisation is aware of the fact that the residents of an area have more legitimacy than outsiders to accuse and punish local transgressors.

DRAWING STRENGTH FROM THE STATE

The rise of vigilantism in tandem with state capacity

The trends described above are not unique to Indonesia; vigilantism is taking centre stage in politics across the developing world, including in India, the Philippines, Bangladesh, Mexico and South Africa. There are two main explanations for vigilantism in the global literature. The dominant one is the state substitution hypothesis, which claims that citizens adopt vigilantism as a means of managing their own security in order to cope with the inadequate provision of order by the state. This may be due to uneven reach of the state (Abrahams 1998; O'Donnell 1993), low coercive capacity of the state (Bates 2008; Kaldor 2007), discriminatory policing (Arias and Goldstein 2010; Auyero 2007) or a security shock that overwhelms the formal law enforcement apparatus (Bateson 2013; Higazi 2008). The second explanation is the critical citizenship hypothesis, which claims that vigilante violence is motivated by popular rejection of the law itself (Smith 2019). The rise of a liberal rights regime, often brought about by a democratic transition, results in greater restrictions being placed on the state's use of repressive measures. This may create a perception that the state is treating offenders too leniently, leading citizens to engage in vigilantism as a way of correcting the perceived liberal bias of the formal legal system.

In Indonesia, these two explanations of vigilantism are found both in the vernacular understanding of the issue and in scholarly analysis. Particularly brutal or contentious incidents of vigilantism that catch public attention are often lamented as having occurred because 'the state is absent' (*negara tidak hadir*). Vigilantes themselves are the first to blame biased and corrupt policing practices, claiming that they compel otherwise upstanding citizens to take the law into their own hands. A conversation about law enforcement with residents of a middle-class neighbourhood is unlikely to conclude without someone reciting the popular phrase, '*Hukum di Indonesia tumpul ke atas dan tajam ke bawah*': 'In Indonesia, the law is a sword that is blunt [accommodating] when striking upward [towards the wealthy] but sharp [harsh] when striking downward [towards the poor]'.

Scholars of Indonesian politics have explicitly linked vigilantism to ineffective state institutions and a lack of security. Studies have shown that in the parts of Indonesia where state security forces were absent during the New Order, citizens adopted vigilantism as their own means of regulating local order (Tajima 2014). Polri's own reports blame vigilantism on low levels of public trust in law enforcement agencies (Dermawan 2013). Some scholars have shown that vigilante justice is particularly prevalent in the Indonesian borderlands that lie beyond the state's reach (Eilenberg 2011), while others explain lynching in densely populated regions of Java as a 'dangerous and highly undesirable side effect of the withdrawing state' (Bakker 2017: 29).

The rise of vigilantism in Indonesia has also been described as a reaction to the heightened insecurity and institutional uncertainty accompanying the early years of democratic transition (Colombijn 2002; Djalal 2000; Welsh 2008). Several scholars have noted that communities responded to conflicts by forming militias tasked with maintaining order during the crisis (Ryter 2002; Schulte Nordholt 2002; van Dijk 2001; Wilson 2006). Others show that the mass anxiety created by Suharto's sudden exit from power led to the lynching of hundreds of suspected sorcerers in East Java (known as 'ninja' killings), and subsequent reprisals (Herriman 2013, 2016).[6] Even in places that did not experience widespread chaos, such as Lombok, private crime-fighting militias (*pam swakarsa*) were formed with the explicit backing of local police and military (Telle 2014; Tyson 2013).

While state substitution theories may explain the spike in vigilantism during Indonesia's early transition years, they do not explain why vigilantism continues to flourish despite significant improvements in the country's overall security environment and a massive expansion of the national police force. The insecurity of the transition subsided after a combination of security interventions and peace deals brought Indonesia's ethno-communal conflicts and civil wars to an end. In the provinces worst affected by the violence, this led to a remarkable 79 per cent drop in the average number of violent deaths per annum, from 1,738 in the conflict period (1998–2003) to 365 in the post-conflict period (2004–2012) (Barron et al. 2016: 201). Today, Indonesia has one of the lowest homicide rates in the world, while levels of other types of violent crime have remained more or less constant.[7]

Most importantly, the formal separation of the roles of the military and the police in 1999 has resulted in a rapid expansion of the national police, in terms of both budget and personnel. Polri's budget increased fivefold between 2005 and 2015, from $831 million to almost $4.5 billion (Figure 15.4). More than two-thirds of the budget has been allocated to personnel expenses (salaries), leading to a dramatic increase in the strength of the police force. The number of police personnel rose from around 297,000 in 2004 (Siregar et al. 2015: 121) to more than 430,000 in 2015 (Jaya 2016), reducing the police-to-civilian ratio from 1:700 to 1:597. The main focus of reform efforts has been to expand the ground-level presence of the Community Guidance Unit (Satuan Pembinaan Masyarakat, Sat

---

6 In 1999, mobs of attackers wearing ninja masks lynched hundreds of alleged sorcerers in Banyuwangi district and surrounding areas. This triggered reprisals from the country's largest Muslim organisation, NU, whose members were disproportionately targeted in these attacks. Roaming mobs of NU supporters apprehended and killed scores of individuals accused of being 'ninjas' before the police arrested the perpetrators and the chaos finally subsided.

7 According to the United Nations Office on Drugs and Crime, Indonesia recorded 0.5 homicides per 100,0000 people in 2016, which was lower than the rate for Norway (0.51).

Figure 15.4   *Budget of the Indonesian National Police (Polri), 2005–2015 ($ million)*

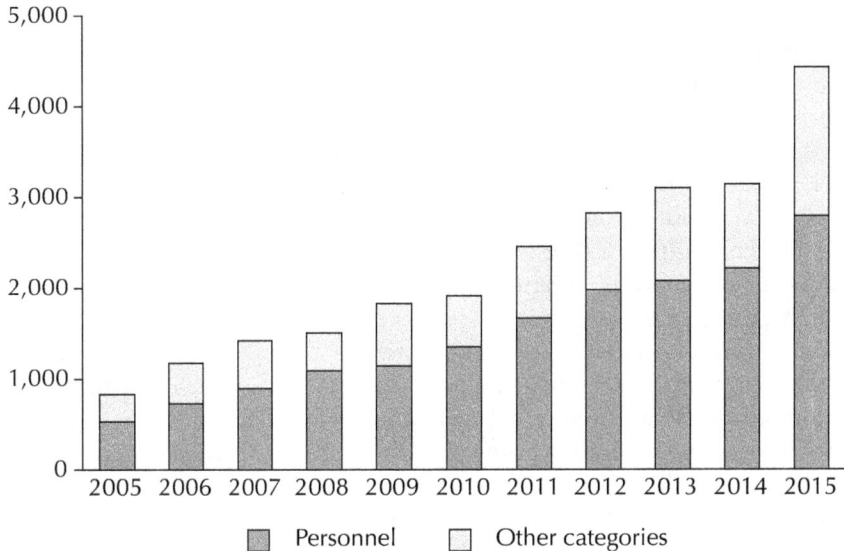

    Personnel   Other categories

Source: Extracted from the central government's annual financial reports (Laporan Keuangan Pemerintah Pusat, LKPP) prepared by the National Audit Agency (Badan Pemeriksa Keuangan, BPK).

Binmas), which has received the largest share of new recruits (*Bangka-pos* 2018). Apart from these organisational improvements, public trust in law enforcement institutions is surprisingly high in Indonesia. In 2006, citizens reported a relatively high rate of trust in the police (65 per cent) and the judiciary (56 per cent). In 2011, the numbers remained stable at 65 per cent and 55 per cent, respectively.[8]

The 'leniency' of the law is routinely cited as a driving force for vigilantes. Lawmakers are quick to refer to the threat of vigilante violence when stipulating new criminal offences or prescribing harsher penalties for existing ones. For example, during the debate on revisions to the Criminal Code, the attorney general called for sorcery to be classified as a criminal offence in order to prevent vigilantism (Triyoga 2015). His deputy emphasised the need for stricter punishments for adultery, because 'this problem results in public anxiety that makes people take the law into their own hands, as the law does not regulate it' (Taufiqurrohman 2015).

---

8 Calculations by the author, based on Asian Barometer Survey, waves 2 and 3.

Apart from lawmakers, law enforcement officers also criticise what they call the law's 'new' preoccupation with human rights.[9]

Contrary to perceptions of excessive liberalisation of law enforcement in Indonesia, the legal system has in fact become harsher since the democratic transition. Civilian oversight has curbed the use of arbitrary detention, but torture and police shootings of criminals remain rife (Hernawan 2015; Pohlman 2008). Indonesia's democratically elected lawmakers have prescribed harsher penalties for existing criminal offences and substantially increased the number of legally punishable acts—from about 885 at the end of the New Order to more than 1,600 today (Akbari 2018). Using the powers invested in them by Indonesia's decentralisation laws, provincial and district governments have passed their own regional regulations (*peraturan daerah*, perda) criminalising a host of moral and social offences (Buehler 2016; Bush 2008). The most extreme case can be seen in Aceh province, where a dedicated unit of the municipal police enforces a set of Islamic regulations (Qanun Syariah) that stipulate stringent corporal punishments for fornication, adultery and homosexuality. Has the harsher regulation of morality by the state mollified Aceh's vigilantes? Far from it: NVMS data show that despite the enforcement of harsh punishments, the incidence of vigilantism against moral transgressions in Aceh is three times higher than the national average.

Victims trapped between prosecution and persecution

What explains the rise of vigilantism in Indonesia alongside a significant expansion in the state's coercive presence and enactment of harsher laws? Contrary to the popular perception that the state is perennially 'absent' in Indonesia, local officials are not only present in cases of vigilantism, but also play a critical role in ensuring victims' compliance with vigilantes' demands. Consider the case of the Jakarta teenager described earlier: FPI gave the local neighbourhood head advance notice of its intentions and the entire encounter took place in his office (Qodar 2017). In the case of the doctor from West Sumatra, law enforcement authorities were also involved: an intelligence officer first warned the doctor about the impending visit from FPI; the subdistrict police chief facilitated and acted as a witness to her apology; and the district police chief, who was eventually removed from her post for her role in the case, met with the

---

9   For a detailed discussion of how the focus on human rights is perceived to affect police officers' ability to maintain order, see Tajima (2014).

doctor several times to convince her that compliance with FPI's demands was necessary to guarantee her security (*NET.Z* 2017).

What explains this response to vigilantism? Two mutually reinforcing dynamics are at play. First, there are strong institutional incentives for law enforcement officers to push for semi-formal mediation of social disputes. The police are generally under pressure to de-clog the already overwhelmed criminal justice system. When faced with a mob, these bureaucratic concerns are compounded by the need to avoid a potentially embarrassing violent confrontation through negotiation. As a result, junior police officers are required to engage in 'problem solving' with communities to resolve disputes amicably (*secara kekeluargaan*) through dialogue (*musyawarah*) (Polri 2017). Typically, this involves holding a mediation session between the person accused of wrongdoing and the complainants, in the presence of other government officials. The accused signs a letter admitting guilt and promising not to repeat the offence, while the complainant signs a letter accepting any compensation that has been negotiated and promising not to press legal charges. All officials co-sign the stamped letters and the case is considered resolved.

This form of arbitration is mostly used to resolve disputes between individuals, such as petty theft, adultery, assault and traffic accidents. However, it is also becoming the routine method for settling religious disputes in which one party is either an individual or a religious minority with considerably less leverage than the other party (Panggabean and Ali-Fauzi 2015). In cases where one side is backed by a mob with a propensity to use violence, state officials explicitly cite the threat of violence as a reason to initiate mediation (Sasongko and Rahadian 2015). In dealing with recent cases of intimidation by FPI, the local police seem broadly to have followed this procedure.

Second, issuance of strict legislation to control online defamation (Postill and Saputro 2017), and harsher enforcement of existing blasphemy laws (Crouch 2012), have created strong incentives for people who have been accused of offences to agree to semi-formal mediations. Consider the alternative. Even if an individual is prepared to risk mob violence and refuses mediation, that person would face a lengthy legal investigation that is highly likely to result in an arraignment. According to data gathered by SAFEnet, 71 cases of defamation, filed with the police between 2008 and 2014, resulted in accused individuals being formally charged (SAFEnet 2014). To make matters worse for individuals accused of defaming religion, the same mob that demands an apology also mobilises to 'guard' (*kawal*) the legal process and ensure that a satisfactorily hefty sentence is doled out (Ramadhan 2017). Given widespread concerns about the susceptibility of the courts to this kind of pressure, the odds of a conviction are high

(Sihombing et al. 2012). At the same time, the offended organisation is likely to lean on employers and neighbours to impose social sanctions on the accused. Given these options, it is not difficult to see why accused individuals would rather resign themselves to the outcome of an unfair mediation than risk prosecution by the state.

CONCLUSION: DISMANTLING DEMOCRACY FROM THE BOTTOM UP

Islamist campaigns to regulate religious offence through mob violence in Indonesia are deeply rooted in broader patterns of everyday vigilantism and the collusive relationships between local state agents and vigilantes. Although individual acts of vigilantism tend to be small in scale, cumulatively they pose two significant challenges to democratic institutions and practices in Indonesia. First, the selective nature of vigilantism and the use of spectacular acts of violence have proven to be an effective strategy for dismantling liberal rights from the bottom up. By punishing individual offenders through highly publicised use of violence, vigilantes demonstrate the cost of transgressing their mandated social order, inducing compliance from others in the community. Over time, these small but frequent acts of violence force citizens to conform to an increasingly narrow range of socially acceptable behaviour, gradually eroding their constitutionally guaranteed rights.

Second, the moral claims advanced by vigilantes to support their cause make their actions an effective form of violent lobbying. Unlike anarchists, who dispute the state's authority, or insurgents, who seek to usurp it, vigilantes pursue their goals by bending the state to their will, either by demanding harsher enforcement of existing laws or by seeking the enactment of new ones. In Indonesia, this is seen in the increasingly harsh enforcement of previously dormant blasphemy laws and in the rapid enactment of local laws regulating intrareligious doctrinal disputes, women's access to economic opportunities and citizens' sexual behaviour. However, these attempts by successive governments to appease vigilantes have only emboldened them further. If planned revisions to the Criminal Code that include stringent punishments for a range of moral and social offences are enacted, they are bound to prompt more violence from vigilantes seeking a 'satisfactory' interpretation of the law. Any efforts to curb religious and moral vigilantism in Indonesia must therefore address everyday forms of crime control vigilantism, by identifying and eliminating the factors that encourage collusive interactions between vigilantes and the state.

REFERENCES

Abrahams, R. 1998. *Vigilant Citizens: Vigilantism and the State.* Cambridge: Polity Press. http://www.lavoisier.fr/livre/notice.asp?ouvrage=1536006

Akbari, A.R. 2018. 'Talking Indonesia: a new criminal code'. *Indonesia at Melbourne,* 15 March. http://indonesiaatmelbourne.unimelb.edu.au/talking-indonesia-a-new-criminal-code/

Andayani, D. 2017. 'Atasi persekusi, pemerintah diminta tak cuma pakai pendekatan hukum'. *DetikNews,* 4 June. https://news.detik.com/berita/3519924/atasi-persekusi-pemerintah-diminta-tak-cuma-pakai-pendekatan-hukum

Andriansyah, M. 2016. 'Kawal fatwa MUI soal atribut Natal, FPI datangi mal di Surabaya'. *Merdeka,* 18 December. https://www.merdeka.com/peristiwa/kawal-fatwa-mui-soal-atribut-natal-fpi-datangi-mal-di-surabaya.html

Arias, E.D. and D.M. Goldstein, eds. 2010. *Violent Democracies in Latin America,* The Cultures and Practices of Violence Series. Durham: Duke University Press.

Arifianto, A.R. 2017. 'Islamic Defenders Front: an ideological evolution?'. *RSIS Commentary* No. 228. Singapore: Nanyang Technological University. December. https://www.rsis.edu.sg/wp-content/uploads/2017/12/CO17228.pdf

Arnaz, F. 2013. 'Polri tegaskan akan tindak ormas yang gelar razia'. *BeritaSatu,* 3 July. https://www.beritasatu.com/megapolitan/123425/polri-tegaskan-akan-tindak-ormas-yang-gelar-razia

Auyero, J. 2007. *Routine Politics and Violence in Argentina: The Gray Zone of State Power.* New York: Cambridge University Press.

Bakker, L. 2017. 'Lynching, public violence and the internet in Indonesia'. In *Global Lynching and Collective Violence. Volume 1: Asia, Africa, and the Middle East,* edited by M.J. Pfeifer, 10–33. Urbana, IL: University of Illinois Press.

Bangkapos. 2018. 'Pasukan terbanyak Polri adalah Bhabinkamtibmas'. *Bangkapos,* 6 December. http://bangka.tribunnews.com/2018/12/06/pasukan-terbanyak-polri-adalah-bhabinkamtibmas

Barron, P., S. Jaffrey and A. Varshney. 2016. 'When large conflicts subside: the ebbs and flows of violence in post-Suharto Indonesia'. *Journal of East Asian Studies* 16(2): 191–217.

Bates, R.H. 2008. 'State failure'. *Annual Review of Political Science* 11: 1–12.

Bateson, R.A. 2013. 'Order and violence in postwar Guatemala'. PhD thesis. New Haven, CT: Yale University.

Batubara, H. 2016. 'Ditemani ibu, Pandu Wijaya temui Gus Mus dan minta maaf telah menghina'. *DetikNews,* 25 November. https://news.detik.com/berita/d-3355030/ditemani-ibu-pandu-wijaya-temui-gus-mus-dan-minta-maaf-telah-menghina

BBC Indonesia. 2017. ' "Tampar anak" dan persekusi orang, "perilaku FPI yang harus dilawan" '. BBC Indonesia, 1 June. https://www.bbc.com/indonesia/trensosial-40121705

BeritaSatu. 2017. 'Remaja 15 tahun menjadi korban persekusi ormas di Cipinang'. *BeritaSatu,* 1 June. https://www.youtube.com/watch?v=S5zwgogd5EM

Buehler, M. 2016. *The Politics of Shari'a Law: Islamist Activists and the State in Democratizing Indonesia.* Cambridge: Cambridge University Press.

Bush, R. 2008. 'Regional sharia regulations in Indonesia: anomaly or symptom?' In *Expressing Islam: Religious Life and Politics in Indonesia*, edited by G. Fealy and S. White, 174–91. Singapore: Institute of Southeast Asian Studies (ISEAS).

CNN Indonesia. 2017. 'Rizieq Shihab dicaci, FPI bergerak—kasus persekusi Solok dan Cipinang Muara'. CNN Indonesia, 2 June. https://www.youtube.com/watch?v=F2L5774B_-4

Colombijn, F. 2002. 'Maling, maling! The lynching of petty criminals'. In *Roots of Violence in Indonesia*, edited by F. Colombijn and J.T. Lindblad, 299–329. Leiden: KITLV Press and Singapore: Institute of Southeast Asian Studies (ISEAS).

Crouch, M.A. 2012. 'Law and religion in Indonesia: the Constitutional Court and the Blasphemy Law'. *Asian Journal of Comparative Law* 7(1): 1–46. https://doi.org/10.1515/1932-0205.1391

Dermawan, M.K. 2013. *Polisi dan Tindakan Main Hakim Sendiri*. Jakarta: Komisi Kepolisian Nasional (Kompolnas).

Djalal, D. 2000. 'The new face of Indonesian justice'. *Far Eastern Economic Review* 163(28): 68–70.

Eilenberg, M. 2011. 'Flouting the law: vigilante justice and regional autonomy on the Indonesian border'. *Austrian Journal of South-East Asian Studies* 4(2): 237–53. https://pure.au.dk/portal/files/41998905/ASEAS_4_2_A3.pdf

Faizal, A. 2016. 'Polri dan PBNU teken MoU penanganan kerawanan sosial'. *Kompas*, 1 September. https://regional.kompas.com/read/2016/09/01/19502271/polri.dan.pbnu.teken.mou.penanganan.kerawanan.sosial

Fealy, G. 2016. 'Bigger than Ahok: explaining the 2 December mass rally'. *Indonesia at Melbourne*, 7 December. https://indonesiaatmelbourne.unimelb.edu.au/bigger-than-ahok-explaining-jakartas-2-december-mass-rally/

Hadiz, V.R. 2016. *Islamic Populism in Indonesia and the Middle East*. Cambridge: Cambridge University Press.

Halim, H. and A. Dipa. 2016. 'Muslims lambast Christmas service raid in Bandung'. *Jakarta Post*, 8 December. https://www.thejakartapost.com/news/2016/12/08/muslims-lambast-mob-attack-in-bandung.html

Hamayotsu, K. 2013. 'The limits of civil society in democratic Indonesia: media freedom and religious intolerance'. *Journal of Contemporary Asia* 43(4): 658–77. https://doi.org/10.1080/00472336.2013.780471

Hernawan, B. 2015. 'Torture as a mode of governance: reflections on the phenomenon of torture in Papua, Indonesia'. In *From 'Stone Age' to 'Real-Time': Exploring Papuan Temporalities, Mobilities, and Religiosities*, edited by M. Slama and J. Munro, 195–220. Canberra: ANU Press.

Herriman, N. 2013. 'Sorcery, law, and state: governing the black arts in Indonesia'. *Australian Journal of Asian Law* 13(2) Article 5: 1–14.

Herriman, N. 2016. *Witch-hunt and Conspiracy: The 'Ninja Case' in East Java*. Clayton: Monash University Publishing.

Higazi, A. 2008. 'Social mobilization and collective violence: vigilantes and militias in the lowlands of Plateau state, central Nigeria'. *Africa: Journal of the International African Institute* 78(1): 107–35.

Human Rights Watch. 2013. 'In religion's name: abuses against religious minorities in Indonesia'. New York: Human Rights Watch. 28 February. https://www.hrw.org/report/2013/02/28/religions-name/abuses-against-religious-minorities-indonesia

Indonesia. n.d. 'Heboh! Menghina Mbah Maimoen sesat dan Goblok, wanita ini dijemput Banser NU untuk meminta maaf—Harian Rakyat'. *Indonesia* (anonymous blog post), accessed 24 March 2019. http://portalgkr.blogspot.com/2016/11/heboh-menghina-mbah-maimoen-sesat-dan.html

IPAC (Institute for Policy Analysis of Conflict). 2018. 'After Ahok: the Islamist agenda in Indonesia'. *IPAC Report* No. 44. Jakarta: IPAC. 6 April.

Jaffrey, S. and S. Mulyartono. 2017. 'Between persecution and prosecution: vigilantes, the state and the politics of offence'. *Indonesia at Melbourne*, 21 June. http://indonesiaatmelbourne.unimelb.edu.au/between-persecution-and-prosecution-vigilantes-the-state-and-the-politics-of-offence/

Jaya, G.N. 2016. 'Kapolri sebut personel polisi di RI terbanyak nomor 2 di dunia'. *Merdeka*, 16 September. https://www.merdeka.com/peristiwa/kapolri-sebut-personel-polisi-di-ri-terbanyak-nomor-2-di-dunia.html

Jones, S. 2015. 'Sisi gelap reformasi di Indonesia: munculnya kelompok masyarakat madani intoleran'. In *Sisi Gelap Demokrasi: Kekerasan Masyarakat Madani di Indonesia*, edited by H. Mubarok and I. Rafsadi, 3–29. Jakarta: PUSAD Paramadina. https://www.paramadina-pusad.or.id/buku/sisi-gelap-demokrasi-kekerasan-masyarakat-madani-di-indonesia/

Kaldor, M. 2007. *New and Old Wars: Organized Violence in a Global Era*. Stanford, CA: Stanford University Press.

Menchik, J. 2016. *Islam and Democracy in Indonesia: Tolerance without Liberalism*. Cambridge and New York: Cambridge University Press.

Mietzner, M. and B. Muhtadi. 2018. 'Explaining the 2016 Islamist mobilisation in Indonesia: religious intolerance, militant groups and the politics of accommodation'. *Asian Studies Review* 42(3): 479–97.

Mudhoffir, A.M. 2017. 'Islamic militias and capitalist development in post-authoritarian Indonesia'. *Journal of Contemporary Asia* 47(4): 495–514.

Mulyartono, O.S., I. Rafsadi and A. Nursahid. 2018. 'Rekayasa kebencian dalam kasus Meiliana di Tanjung Balai'. Jakarta: PUSAD Paramadina. https://tirto.id/rekayasa-kebencian-dalam-kasus-meiliana-di-tanjung-balai-cUEe

Mulyono, Y. 2017. 'Pria di Jember minta maaf hina ketum PBNU di grup medsos'. *DetikNews*, 3 January. https://news.detik.com/berita/d-3387010/pria-di-jember-minta-maaf-hina-ketum-pbnu-di-grup-medsos

Nafys. 2017. 'Media sosial penghina Habib Luthfi pucat didatangi Banser NU'. *Seword*, 19 May. https://seword.com/politik/ketika-preman-media-sosial-penghina-habib-luthfi-pucat-didatangi-banser-nu

NET.Z. 2017. 'Curhat Dokter Fiera, korban intimidasi karena status Facebook'. *NET.Z*, 1 June. https://www.youtube.com/watch?v=a6RPaZLXTis

NU Online. 2016. 'Prihatin konten dunia maya, NU Jatim bentuk cyber force'. *NU Online*, 2 September. http://www.nu.or.id/post/read/70918/prihatin-konten-dunia-maya-nu-jatim-bentuk-cyber-force

O'Donnell, G. 1993. 'On the state, democratization and some conceptual problems: a Latin American view with glances at some postcommunist countries'. *World Development* 21(8): 1,355–69.

Panggabean, R. and I. Ali-Fauzi. 2015. *Policing Religious Conflicts in Indonesia*. Jakarta: PUSAD Paramadina. https://www.paramadina-pusad.or.id/buku/policing-religious-conflicts-in-indonesia/

Pohlman, A. 2008. '*Testimonio* and telling women's narratives of genocide, torture and political imprisonment in post-Suharto Indonesia'. *Life Writing* 5(1): 47–60.

Polri (Polisi Republik Indonesia). 2017. 'Problem solving: kemampuan yang wajib dimiliki oleh Bhabinkamtibmas'. *TribrataNews*, 10 January. http://tribratanews.polri.go.id/?p=22926

Postill, J. and K. Saputro. 2017. 'Digital activism in contemporary Indonesia: victims, volunteers and voices'. In *Digital Indonesia: Connectivity and Divergence*, edited by E. Jurriens and R. Tapsell, 127–45. Singapore: ISEAS – Yusof Ishak Institute.

Purba, D.O. 2017. 'Peneliti SAFE Net: ada tren peningkatan korban persekusi'. *Kompas*, 6 April. https://nasional.kompas.com/read/2017/06/04/18080011/peneliti.safe.net.ada.tren.peningkatan.korban.persekusi

Pwmu.co. 2017. 'Diklarifikasi Pemuda Muhammadiyah, Iyyas Subiakto minta maaf telah fitnah Amien Rais dan Din Syamsuddin'. Pwmu.co, 18 May. https://pwmu.co/30290/05/18/diklarifikasi-pemuda-muhammadiyah-iyyas-subiakto-minta-maaf-telah-fitnah-amien-rais-dan-din-syamsuddin/

Qodar, N. 2017. 'Remaja korban persekusi Cipinang sempat dipukuli di rumahnya'. *Liputan6*, 2 June. https://www.liputan6.com/news/read/2975424/remaja-korban-persekusi-cipinang-sempat-dipukuli-di-rumahnya

Ramadhan, D.I. 2017. 'FPI Jabar kawal kasus guru SMA yang diduga hina Habib Rizieq'. *DetikNews*, 29 May. https://news.detik.com/berita-jawa-barat/d-3514259/fpi-jabar-kawal-kasus-guru-sma-yang-diduga-hina-habib-rizieq?_ga=2.106862275.153658556.1496375740-1949263078.1474447746

Ridhoi, M.A. 2018. 'Anggap karikatur hina Rizieq Shihab, FPI demo kantor Tempo'. *Tirto*, 16 March. https://tirto.id/anggap-karikatur-hina-rizieq-shihab-fpi-demo-kantor-tempo-cGhy

Ryter, L.S. 2002. 'Youth, gangs, and the state in Indonesia'. PhD thesis. Seattle, WA: University of Washington.

SAFEnet (Southeast Asia Freedom of Expression Network). 2014. 'Daftar kasus netizen yang terjerat UU ITE'. SAFEnet. https://id.safenet.or.id/daftarkasus/

Sasongko, J.P. and L. Rahadian. 2015. 'FPI Kepung markas Ahmadiyah, kepolisian gelar mediasi'. CNN Indonesia, 15 June. https://www.cnnindonesia.com/nasional/20150615145454-20-60084/fpi-kepung-markas-ahmadiyah-kepolisian-gelar-mediasi

Schulte Nordholt, N. 2002. 'Violence and the anarchy of the modern Indonesia state'. In *Violence and Vengeance: Discontent and Conflict in New Order Indonesia*, edited by F. Hüsken and H. de Jonge, 52–70. Saarbrücken: Verlag für Entwicklungspolitik Saarbrücken.

Sihombing, U.P., Pultoni, S. Aminah and M.K. Roziqin. 2012. *Injustice in Belief: Monitoring the Results of Cases on Blasphemy of Religion and Religious Hate Speech in Indonesia*. Jakarta: Indonesian Legal Resource Center.

Siregar, S.N., I.N. Bhakti, I. Samego, S. Yanuarti and M. Haripin. 2015. *Reformasi Struktural Polri: Tahun 1999–2010*. Yogyakarta: Penerbit Andi and Jakarta: P2P–LIPI.

Smith, N.R. 2019. *Contradictions of Democracy: Vigilantism and Rights in Post-Apartheid South Africa*. New York: Oxford University Press.

Tajima, Y. 2014. *The Institutional Origins of Communal Violence: Indonesia's Transition from Authoritarian Rule*. New York: Cambridge University Press.
Taufiqurrohman. 2015. 'Kejagung usul aturan perzinaan termuat di RUU KUHP'. *Liputan6*, 8 September. https://www.liputan6.com/news/read/2312037/kejagung-usul-aturan-perzinaan-termuat-di-ruu-kuhp
Telle, K. 2014. 'Policing and the politics of protection on Lombok, Indonesia'. In *Policing and the Politics of Order-Making*, edited by P. Albrecht and H.M. Kyed, 40–56. Routledge.
Tempo. 2010. 'Timur Pradopo: FPI bisa bantu keamanan'. *Tempo*, 7 October. https://nasional.tempo.co/read/283067/timur-pradopo-fpi-bisa-bantu-keamanan
TribunJabar 2017. 'Kronologi persekusi ormas di Solok kepada Dr Fiera Lovita'. *TribunJabar*, 2 June. https://jabar.tribunnews.com/2017/06/02/kronologi-persekusi-ormas-di-solok-kepada-dr-fiera-lovita?page=all
Triyoga, H. 2015. 'Timbulkan keresahan, pasal santet diperlukan'. *DetikNews*, 7 September. https://news.detik.com/berita/d-3012163/timbulkan-keresahan-pasal-santet-diperlukan
Tyson, A. 2013. 'Vigilantism and violence in decentralized Indonesia: the case of Lombok'. *Critical Asian Studies* 45(2): 201–30.
Utama, A. 2016. 'FUI Yogyakarta desak UKDW copot baliho mahasiswi berjilbab'. CNN Indonesia, 7 December. https://www.cnnindonesia.com/nasional/20161207194544-20-178075/fui-yogyakarta-desak-ukdw-copot-baliho-mahasiswi-berjilbab
van Dijk, K. 2001. 'The privatization of public order: relying on the *satgas*'. In *Violence in Indonesia*, edited by I. Wessel and G. Wimhöfer, 152–67. Hamburg: Abera Verlag.
Welsh, B. 2008. 'Local and national: *keroyokan* mobbing in Indonesia'. *Journal of East Asian Studies* 8(3): 473–504.
Wilson, I.D. 2006. 'Continuity and change: the changing contours of organized violence in post–New Order Indonesia'. *Critical Asian Studies* 38(2): 265–97.
Wilson, I.D. 2015. *The Politics of Protection Rackets in Post–New Order Indonesia: Coercive Capital, Authority and Street Politics*. Abingdon: Routledge.

16 Rumour, identity and violence in contemporary Indonesia: evidence from elections in West Kalimantan[1]

Irsyad Rafsadie, Dyah Ayu Kartika, Siswo Mulyartono

The rapid expansion of internet services in Indonesia and in many other developing countries over the past decade has bolstered the circulation of online information. Today Indonesia boasts one of the largest and most active communities of social media users in the world (*Jakarta Post* 2018). While improvements to telecommunications technology have provided many social, economic and educational benefits, the global digital revolution is widely seen as something of a double-edged sword. In particular, scholars have identified the expansion of social media technology as allowing for the far more rampant and widespread manipulation and falsification of information (Bradshaw and Howard 2019).

Over the past decade, increasing analytical attention has been paid to the propagation through social media of rumours, misinformation and disinformation, and the profound effects this can have on public

---

1 This chapter is based on part of a larger research project on misinformation and mob violence in Indonesia, funded by WhatsApp Misinformation and Social Science Research Awards. We thank Ihsan Ali-Fauzi, Sana Jaffrey and Titik Firawati, who provided insight and expertise that greatly assisted this study. We are also grateful to Eve Warburton and Thomas Power, the convenors of the 2019 Indonesia Update, for their thoughtful comments and thorough revisions that significantly improved this chapter.

opinion and political polarisation. Rumours are unverified stories and uncertain accounts of people, events and occurrences. They may or may not be constructed and deployed with a political agenda, and can take on a life of their own, spreading and evolving in sometimes organic ways. Misinformation is, similarly, unintentionally misleading or unverified content. On the other hand, disinformation—often also described as fake news—is systematically designed and maliciously deployed with an intention to mislead. It is often deployed in service to specific political objectives, such as attempts to influence a voting public.

Rumours and disinformation are longstanding features of electoral politics in Indonesia. However, research on the ways in which these patterns have been affected by the digital revolution—particularly the spread of smartphones, growing use of social media and expansion of internet connectivity—remains in its relative infancy. A burgeoning body of evidence suggests that evolving communications technology has facilitated rapid, cost-effective dissemination of rumour and disinformation, producing serious and unpredictable consequences. In recent Indonesian elections, we have seen the emergence of 'cyber troops' and political social media campaigners, known locally as 'buzzers', who produce disinformation to orchestrate smear campaigns against political opponents, generate and manipulate communal anxieties, and even challenge the legitimacy of democratic processes in a systematic and organised manner (CIPG 2019; Lamb 2018; Potkin and Da Costa 2019).

More broadly, disinformation and rumour—facilitated by the anonymous and unfiltered nature of social media communication—has been linked to a number of recent cases of political violence around the world. For instance, the Indian government associated a surge in political violence with the social media application WhatsApp, and demanded that the company introduce features to limit the spread of unverified and provocative information (Arun 2019). In Indonesia, during the post-election protests in May 2019, the government decided to limit internet access to inhibit the distribution of inflammatory photos and videos, which it claimed would help prevent the spread of false information, and in turn the spread of violence (Idris 2019a). In early September 2019, during a wave of protests in Papua, the government took further action by entirely shutting down internet access in affected regions (Idris 2019b). In these cases, policymakers explicitly tied outbreaks of political violence to the spread of rumours through social media.

By extension, these government policies imply that restricting social media access is an effective and appropriate prophylactic against rumour-inspired political violence. Such an approach is problematic on multiple fronts. First, it may be used to justify policies that curtail online organisation and freedom of expression. Second, this approach tends to overlook the underlying factors that render some communities more vulnerable to the spread of rumours and disinformation than others. Third, there are a range of factors beyond social media use that determine whether misleading political information is liable to provoke violent conflict. Research into the WhatsApp-linked lynchings in India, for example, emphasises that histories of conflict, the timing of elections, the composition of electoral tickets and many other factors all coalesce to determine whether malicious online content produces offline violence (Arun 2019; Banaji et al. 2019).

In this chapter, we examine the spread and impact of political rumours and disinformation in one province in Indonesia—West Kalimantan. Unlike Jakarta, West Kalimantan is a region at the periphery of the digital revolution. Its large geographic area and relatively underdeveloped infrastructure serve to limit internet penetration, producing disparities in access to online information. In the lead-up to West Kalimantan's 2018 gubernatorial election, analysts expressed concern about the potential for violence, citing a history of ethnic conflict and the potential use of identity politics as a campaign tool (IPAC 2018a). Disinformation and identity politics emerged as major features of the electoral campaign, making it one of the most polarising local elections in recent history. Either side of the election, rumours and disinformation were spread through online platforms in a manner that exacerbated long-established ethnic and religious cleavages. This spread of rumour was accompanied by outbreaks of electoral violence and intimidation. However, violence was relatively geographically limited, taking place in just a few areas in Landak and Mempawah. In this chapter, we investigate what factors may account for this variation. We ask under what conditions do rumours and disinformation lead to violent mobilisation and, conversely, when does peace prevail?

To answer these questions, we leverage both qualitative and quantitative data. The qualitative data is based on interviews with 52 informants including police officers, ethnic and religious leaders, election organisers, campaign team members, journalists, non-government organisation activists, neighbourhood heads and ordinary residents. In addition, we utilise quantitative data on elections, demographics and violence from the National Violence Monitoring System.

While social media did play a role in the spread of disinformation and rumours during the 2018 election, we find that violence was most likely to arise in those places with recent histories of conflict. Although almost two decades had passed between the last deadly wave of ethnic conflict and the 2018 election, those historical moments of immense violence continue to have implications. We argue that the combination of growing social media use, new forms of disinformation and the increasingly polarised nature of the national-level political landscape can have a profound effect in post-conflict regions like West Kalimantan. Our findings suggest that such regions continue to require focused and well-resourced peace-building efforts to ensure that the new challenges facing Indonesia's democracy do not lead to further and more serious outbreaks of communal conflict.

The rest of the chapter is structured as follows: in the first section, we explain the case and context of West Kalimantan. We then look at rumour and disinformation in the lead-up to election day in 2018. The third section outlines the incidents of rumour and violence on and following election day in Landak and Mempawah. In section four we examine variation between villages. We conclude with reflections on what the nexus between rumour, historical legacies of violence and contemporary political conflict means for Indonesia's democratic quality.

THE CASE AND ITS CONTEXT

West Kalimantan is a province rich in natural resources and ethnoreligious diversity. The largest ethnic groups are the Dayaks (35 per cent of the population) and Malays (34 per cent). The remaining 31 per cent of the population comprises Javanese, Madurese, Chinese and other ethnicities (Ananta et al. 2015). Dayaks in West Kalimantan are often assumed to be Christian, even though one-third of Indonesia's Dayak population is Muslim. The Malay population, on the other hand, is almost entirely Muslim.

Historically, this province has experienced multiple outbreaks of extreme ethnic violence. Indeed, West Kalimantan's communal conflicts have been identified as among the world's most intractable cases of interethnic hostility (Davidson 2008; Horowitz 2001; Peluso 2008). The post-independence period has seen two particularly deadly outbreaks of mass violence. The first occurred in late 1967 and was directed against the ethnic Chinese community. This was a perpetuation of the anti-communist purges that swept across the country from late 1965.[2] The second major outbreak was the pogroms directed against Madurese transmigrants at the end of the 1990s. The mass killing of ethnic Madurese

---

2   The military provoked Dayaks to take revenge against the Chinese, who were arbitrarily associated with the communist party. Davidson (2008) estimated that the Chinese death toll ranged from 2,000 to 5,000, and thousands of others were displaced.

was carried out by Dayaks in 1997 and by Malays in 1999. The latter incidents caused a significant reduction in the number of Madurese living in West Kalimantan, and sharpened ethnic segregation in the province.

In the late 1990s, the spread of polarising, ethnically and religiously charged rumours was a major factor in the incitement of communal violence (Human Rights Watch 2001; International Crisis Group 2001). These rumours often focused on challenges to the existing distribution of land and resources; threats to social, cultural and religious rights; or particular incidents of violence or injustice perpetrated by members of one ethnic group against members of another. In some cases, these rumours were grounded in real events and phenomena; in others, they reflected deep-seated communal fears and prejudices.

The ethnic rivalries that erupted into violence during the collapse of the New Order were not erased with the transition to democracy. Instead, ethnoreligious identity became a central feature of electoral campaigns and coalitions in the post-authoritarian era. Moreover, interethnic competition for state patronage—in the form of bureaucratic and political positions—became more overt with the introduction of regional autonomy and the proliferation of new administrative units (Tanasaldy 2007).[3] West Kalimantan's first direct gubernatorial election, in 2007, saw the Christian Dayak politician Cornelis emerge victorious, having relied heavily on the support of the Dayak, Madurese and Chinese communities. Cornelis had wooed these constituencies with promises of security,[4] and his tenure saw many advantages directed to Dayak constituents at the expense of ethnic Malays. For instance, Dayak civil servants were disproportionately promoted, whereas non-Dayak bureaucrats were coerced into supporting the incumbent governor through threats of reassignment to remote areas.[5] These divisive and coercive tactics proved effective in consolidating Cornelis's grip on provincial politics, and he won re-election in 2012.

---

3 Before 1999, West Kalimantan had only one city (Pontianak) and six regencies (Kabupaten Pontianak, Kapuas Hulu, Ketapang, Sambas, Sanggau and Sintang). After *reformasi*, West Kalimantan was divided into twelve regencies (Bengkayang, Kapuas Hulu, Kayong Utara, Ketapang, Kubu Raya, Landak, Melawi, Mempawah, Sambas, Sanggau, Sekadau and Sintang) and a second city was established (Singkawang) (Figure 16.1). This proliferation provided opportunities for minority ethnic groups to administer regions in which their populations are concentrated (Hartriani and Wardani 2014).

4 Interview with Madurese informant, Pontianak, 18 June 2019.

5 Interview with local civil servant, Mempawah, 25 June 2019. The threat that an uncooperative or disloyal civil servant will be 'cast out' (*dibuang*) to a remote area is commonly used by subnational executive officeholders across Indonesia.

However, the 2018 gubernatorial election took place in a very different political environment that provided opportunities for a rebalancing of power relations between the Dayak and Malay ethnic groups. There were two major reasons for this. First, Cornelis had served his maximum two terms in office and was barred from contesting the 2018 race. Second, the simultaneous elections of 2018 were taking place in the shadow of the highly successful Islamist campaign that swung the 2017 Jakarta election against the Christian Chinese incumbent Basuki Tjahaja Purnama ('Ahok'). Malay elites saw this as an opportunity to emphasise a religious rather than racial cleavage, and sought to offset the demographic disadvantages of the ethnic Malay community by replicating the Islamist campaign that had swung the 2017 Jakarta gubernatorial election. Against this backdrop, the election was far more polarising, which in turn raised the stakes of electoral competition and increased the chances of conflict.

The three candidate pairs nominated for the 2018 race—and the results of the election—reflected this more religiously polarised dynamic. The first pair was Milton Crosby and Boyman Harun, who were nominated by Gerindra (Gerakan Indonesia Raya, Greater Indonesia Movement) and the National Mandate Party (Partai Amanat Nasional, PAN). The pairing of Milton (a Dayak Christian) and Boyman (a Malay Muslim) conformed to a common strategy for *pilkada* nominations in ethnically and religiously heterogenous regions, whereby a diverse ticket allows for cross-cutting ethnic and religious appeals that prevent the alienation of any significant constituency (see, for example, Aspinall et al. 2011). However, this centrist strategy proved ineffective, and the Milton–Boyman pairing received only 6.65 per cent of the vote.

The main axis of competition was instead between two religiously and ethnically homogenous tickets. The second candidate pair, sponsored by the outgoing governor Cornelis, comprised two Christian Dayak politicians. Cornelis chose his daughter Karolin Margret Natasa, a former national parliamentarian and the newly elected Landak regent, as his preferred successor. Her running mate was the Bengkayang regent, Suryadman Gidot. They received support from three nationalist parties: the Indonesian Democratic Party of Struggle (Partai Demokrasi Indonesia-Perjuangan, PDI-P), the Democratic Party (Partai Demokrat, PD) and the Indonesian Justice and Unity Party (Partai Keadilan dan Persatuan Indonesia, PKPI). Our interviews with local community leaders indicated that many Dayaks doubted Karolin's ability and thought of her only as a puppet of her father. With the help of her husband, a prominent ethnic Javanese, Karolin sought to supplement her Dayak base with support from the Javanese community.

The third pair of nominees—Pontianak mayor Sutarmidji and Mempawah regent Ria Norsan—were both Muslim Malays. Sutarmidji had patronised a number of Islamist figures and organisations during his tenure in Pontianak, and many of the province's most influential Islamic groups supported his gubernatorial ticket. Sutarmidji–Norsan received support from the Pontianak Sultanate, the Islamic Defenders Front (Front Pembela Islam, FPI) and five political parties: Golkar, the National Democratic Party (Partai Nasional Demokrat, NasDem), the People's Conscience Party (Partai Hati Nurani Rakyat, Hanura), the National Awakening Party (Partai Kebangkitan Bangsa, PKB) and the Prosperous Justice Party (Partai Keadilan Sejahtera, PKS). Notably, groups like FPI and PKS had played a major role in the Islamist mobilisations that shaped the 2017 Jakarta election.

The 2018 West Kalimantan election therefore saw a stark religious and ethnic division between the two strongest candidate pairs, both of which worked to exacerbate polarisation in an attempt to consolidate their respective support bases. Ultimately, the Malay Muslim pair of Sutarmidji and Ria Norsan prevailed, winning 51.55 per cent of votes to Karolin–Gidot's 41.79 per cent. Importantly, the distribution of votes for each pair closely reflected the ethnoreligious composition of each region. Figure 16.1 illustrates the strong association between the votes gained by each candidate pair and the religious make-up of each regency in West Kalimantan. It shows that Sutarmidji–Norsan won Malay Muslim–majority areas while Karolin–Gidot won Dayak Christian–majority areas.

RUMOURS AND DISINFORMATION LEADING UP TO ELECTION DAY

The use of rumours and disinformation in political mobilisation is not a new phenomenon in Indonesia. Scholars observed the pervasive use of rumour in the North Maluku conflict (Bubandt 2008) and in West Kalimantan during the late 1990s (Human Rights Watch 2001; International Crisis Group 2001). In the pre–social media era, rumours were disseminated by word of mouth or through the distribution of written texts (pamphlets, posters, etc.). Printed materials helped shape 'a conspiratorial political imagination and [mobilized] emotions and people to communal violence … [written texts were] able to appeal to and help confirm different political imaginaries simultaneously' (Bubandt 2008: 812). The growth of internet access and communications technology has allowed for rumours and disinformation to be spread online. This enables the transmission of

Figure 16.1 *Distribution of gubernatorial vote share and religious population by city and regency, West Kalimantan, 2018*

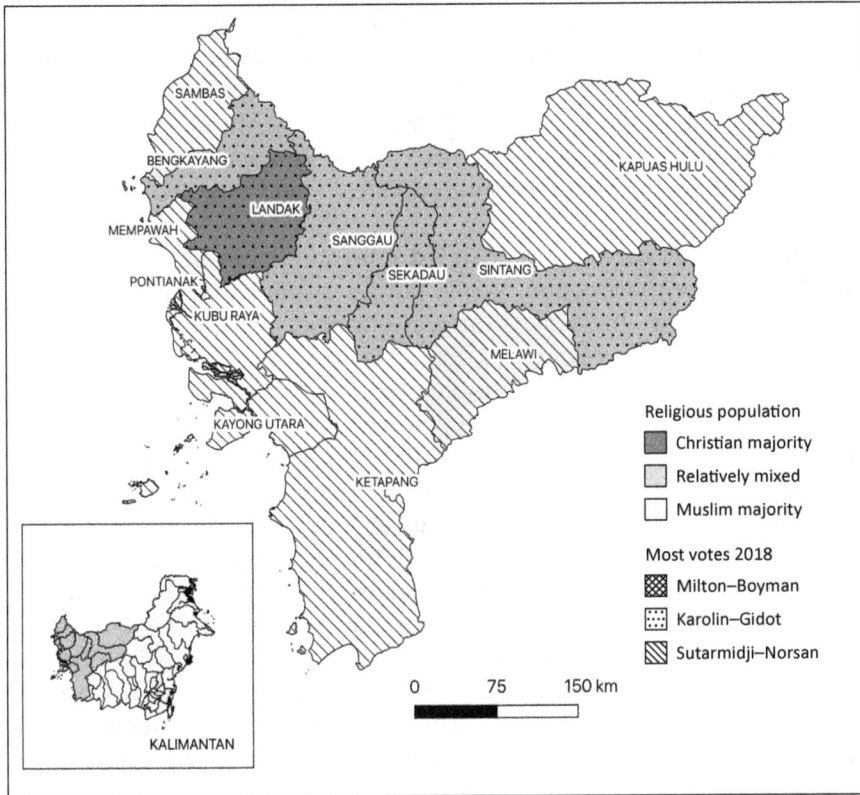

rumours in a faster and more convincing way, as they are frequently accompanied by photos and videos.

In the lead-up to the election, a mix of smear tactics, exaggeration and disinformation was widely used by both sides, serving to inflame deep-seated ethnic and religious tensions. These tactics were designed to mobilise support from within their own ethnoreligious constituency. For example, throughout the campaign period, Islamic groups that sided with Sutarmidji used narratives similar to those used in the Ahok case as an appeal for Muslims to support their candidate. They said that Muslims should vote Muslim, and those who are not following the call should be seen as 'having left Islam; therefore, other Muslims are no longer obliged to pray over their bodies when they die' (IPAC 2018b: 4). On Karolin's side, too, political support was closely tied to ethnic Dayak and non-Muslim identity.

Against this already tense backdrop, rumours and disinformation circulated widely. For example, a man was arrested and charged under Law No. 11/2008 on Electronic Information and Transactions for calling Karolin a 'porn queen' in reference to her alleged appearance in a sex tape leaked in 2012 (*Delik Kalbar* 2018). Complaints were lodged against Karolin's supporters for sharing an image portraying a prominent Christian Dayak as an Islamic fundamentalist after he declared support for Sutarmidji (*Tribun Pontianak* 2018a). A Muslim activist was reported after he claimed on social media that Dayaks had targeted and signed Muslim homes with pig's blood.

One video in particular escalated tensions between the two sides just days before the election. While not an example of misinformation or disinformation—the video was real—its wide circulation created an atmosphere in which rumours spread during and after the election campaign would have greater resonance. The clip leaked on 5 June 2018 showed Cornelis making a speech in an internal Dayak meeting, where he asserted that non–Dayak Muslims were 'colonisers' in West Kalimantan: 'We Dayaks have too long been colonized by [outside] kingdoms, starting with the kings of Majapahit, the kings of Sriwijaya. The worst was the Malay and Islamic kingdoms, along with the Dutch, they colonized us for centuries. So, our mentality is that of slaves' (IPAC 2018b: 5). The Islamic community was furious and framed his statement as an attack on Islam. On 26 June 2018, a Muslim activist under the United Muslims Forum (Forum Umat Islam Bersatu, FUIB) filed a formal report against Cornelis for blasphemy and hate speech. FPI brought the case to a national protest on 6 July 2018 in Jakarta, urging police to arrest Cornelis and other figures who were perceived to defame Islam.

The circulation of rumours, disinformation and inflammatory materials in West Kalimantan can be seen as a microcosm for the massive and systematic campaigns that have increasingly coloured national-level politics in Indonesia. It is possible that the 'cyber armies' active in West Kalimantan may have collaborated with—or been part of—national-level teams; this is credible given that the sources and types of narratives circulated here look remarkably similar to those spread during the 2014 presidential campaign and the 2017 Jakarta election.[6] Nonetheless, it is apparent that rumours and narratives were also produced and spread by individual actors and local community groups.

---

6   Interview with Edo Sinaga, Hoax Crisis Centre, Pontianak, 18 June 2019.

VIOLENCE BREAKS OUT IN LANDAK AND MEMPAWAH

The polarised nature of the gubernatorial campaign ratcheted up communal tensions and exacerbated deep-seated ethnic and religious anxieties. Against this backdrop, the rapid transmission of rumours—facilitated by social media—contributed to a number of violent incidents in the immediate aftermath of the election.

The first reported outbreak of violence occurred on voting day—Wednesday, 27 June 2018. Once voting had closed, public vote counting at local polling stations started to show who had prevailed at each ballot box. In the Javanese Muslim–majority village of Sambora, in the Landak regency, Sutarmidji–Norsan led with 1,055 votes to Karolin–Gidot's 597 votes. A group of Dayak residents from another village, outraged that the Javanese community had overwhelmingly voted for Sutarmidji despite a prior commitment to support Karolin, responded angrily to the vote tally. They flipped over ballot boxes and knocked down motorcycles, rapidly escalating communal tensions within the village.[7] Calm was restored only after a prominent Dayak resident of Sambora talked with Karolin's supporters and asked them to leave.

However, the days after the election saw further escalation. On Thursday 28 June—the day after the election—a group of Dayaks from the neighbouring villages of Salatiga and Mandor rode into Sambora on motorbikes, shouting threats and obscenities at the local residents. They yelled at Javanese houses: 'Kill the Javanese! Damn them!'[8] Local police and military officers responded by taking up positions in Sambora, which prompted the provocateurs to leave.

These events also prompted the rapid circulation of inflammatory rumours, through WhatsApp and by word of mouth. Rumours spread among the Javanese and Muslim communities that Dayaks had launched attacks on Javanese in Sambora, and that they planned to attack and expel Javanese residents in other parts of the regency. Meanwhile, rumours circulated among the Dayak community suggesting that the Javanese in Sambora were riding in convoy to celebrate the Muslim candidates' victory, and were publicly mocking the Dayaks for their political defeat. These rumours spread through neighbouring villages, such as Kepayang and Anjongan, leading to a dramatic escalation of ethnic and religious tensions. Anticipating an attack by the Dayaks, some Javanese residents even fled with their families. Police and army personnel were

---

7   Interview with Daniel, police officer in Toho, 20 June 2019, and interview with Mustafa, Sambora resident, Sambora, 24 July 2019.

8   Interview with Mustafa, Sambora resident, Sambora, 24 July 2019.

now deployed more widely to keep the peace, while local heavies set up roadblocks to guard entrances and exits to the villages.

Still, inflammatory rumours continued to spread and escalate. On the afternoon of Friday 29 June, a group of young Dayaks assembled in the Ngabang terminal in the administrative centre of Landak regency, 98 kilometres from Sambora. These youths were disappointed by Karolin's loss in the gubernatorial contest and had heard the rumours of Javanese triumphalism coming out of Sambora. In addition, some claimed they were offended by online memes that humiliated Cornelis.[9] Stoked by this collective animus, the initially casual gathering descended into a rampage as the crowd slaughtered pigs, burned rubber tyres on the streets and wrecked Javanese food stalls in the nearby Bardan soccer field (*ProKalbar* 2018). Photos and videos of the incident were shared on Facebook and WhatsApp groups, and attracted local and national media attention. Ngabang police were forced to call on Cornelis to calm the masses down. Cornelis eventually agreed to talk with the masses by mobile phone, with his messages passed on to the crowd via a policeman using a loudspeaker.[10] The mob later dispersed, but most Javanese stayed indoors through the night, anxious at the prospect of a large-scale attack.

On the same afternoon, a similar outbreak of violence took place at Karangan, a village on the border between the Mempawah and Landak regencies with a mixed ethnic composition including Dayaks, Malays and Javanese. Again, Sutarmidji's victory in the local polling stations aroused the ire of the Dayaks towards their Muslim neighbours. A group of Dayaks gathered at the Karangan market, burned rubber tyres in the streets and made intimidatory shouts and jeers. These events exacerbated the fears of Muslim residents who had been exposed to pre-election rumours that the Dayaks were planning to kill all Muslims and Malays on the grounds that they were 'colonisers'.[11] On 29 and 30 June, most of the Malay residents of Karangan fled their homes, with more than 200 seeking refuge at a nearby army base.

In this manner, over a period of several days, tensions continued to escalate despite some attempts at intervention by police and political elites who sought to calm the situation with calls for patience and reconciliation. The head of the West Kalimantan police, Didi Haryono, initiated communication with Karolin and Cornelis, asking them to

---

9   Interview with Baron, Cornelis loyalist, 20 June 2019.

10   Interview with Bowo Gede, head of Landak Police, 21 June 2019.

11   Interview with Sjarif, Malay resident, Karangan, 20 June 2019.

control their supporters.[12] Didi also assured Cornelis that Sutarmidji's supporters would not contribute to further escalation by rallying against the Dayaks. On 30 June, Cornelis finally agreed to issue a press release calling for the cessation to ethnic mobilisation (*Tribun Pontianak* 2018b), and Didi was able to have Karolin and Cornelis flown into Landak on a police helicopter to hold a peace ceremony with Karolin's supporters. Social media messages shared on Facebook and WhatsApp certainly played an important role in spreading instructions from Cornelis and Karolin to ease tensions, but the decision to bring Karolin and Cornelis to the scene of the strife showed that the physical presence of the leader remained an important means of containing anger and preventing violence. The combination of these direct, in-person activities and the rapid communication possible through social media seem to have played a crucial role in preventing even more severe violence. Notably, recordings of the peace ceremony—which showed Cornelis and Karolin's involvement—at Landak were disseminated through social media, and Karolin's decision to acknowledge Sutarmidji's victory afterwards helped to ease tensions elsewhere in the province.

During the first week of July, a degree of calm had returned to Karangan. Residents returned to their homes after receiving assurances of their security from the local police and the major Dayak community group, Dewan Adat Dayak (*Tribun Pontianak* 2018c). A Dayak peace ceremony (*pamabakng*) was conducted jointly by police officials, community leaders and traditional ethnic leaders. Once again, physical ceremonies with significant cultural connotations played an important role in defusing intercommunal friction, but social media helped ensure that messages of calm, peace and restraint were widely conveyed.

WHEN DO RUMOURS AND DISINFORMATION LEAD TO VIOLENCE?

Why did violence break out in Landak and Mempawah, and not in other parts of West Kalimantan? The correlation between polarising rumours and outbreaks of violence was clear from our research: in every village that experienced violence following the 2018 election, residents reported having heard rumours of attacks on Javanese people or insults against the Dayak community. These rumours were spread through both digital and analogue modes of communication: social media no doubt played a

---

12 Interview with Didi Haryono, head of West Kalimantan Police, 19 June 2019.

part, but rumours were also spread by word of mouth as people travelled between villages or spoke to their neighbours. We can therefore say with some certainty that social media facilitated the spread of polarising rumours, but we also saw how it facilitated the dissemination of messages calling for the cessation of violence.

It is more useful to look elsewhere when exploring the limits of social media in promoting political violence. Notably, we found that polarising rumours were spread far more widely than in just those regions where tensions escalated into violence and large-scale intimidation. In other words, not all villages that were exposed to rumours witnessed an outbreak of communal violence. It is therefore apparent that exposure to rumours alone was not sufficient to generate communal conflict: rather, a range of factors were at play that served to diminish or exacerbate the impact of rumours.

Rumour and disinformation was far more likely to provoke violent responses under the following conditions: when such information was targeted at electoral losers; where a neighbourhood is politically divided; where residents have good internet access; and, most importantly, where an area has been exposed to ethnic and religious violence in the recent past. These findings suggest that post-conflict areas are especially vulnerable to new outbreaks of violence when faced with inflammatory political rumours and disinformation. In other words, the role of social media in provoking violence proved secondary: it may have facilitated the spread of rumours, disinformation and misinformation, but the degree to which this process produced conflict was heavily dependent upon legacies of communal violence. Social media did not lead to the 'spread' of violence, but—potentially—increased the likelihood that conflict would arise within specific geographic areas defined by their past exposure to violence. In Landak and Mempawah, histories of communal violence are often associated with ethnically and religiously diverse communities where economic, social and political grievances may be more easily layered onto these indicators of identity.

To illustrate our findings, we mapped the locations of villages in Landak and Mempawah that were exposed to rumours in the 2018 election and geocoded them according to several dimensions (Figure 16.2). First, the proportion of Muslims and Christians within the population of each village is indicated by grayscale gradation. Second, each village is coded according to the winning candidate of the 2018 election, indicated by the line and dot fill. Third, we distinguish between villages that were affected by violence in the aftermath of the 2018 election, identified using black labels, and those that remained peaceful, which are assigned white

*Figure 16.2   Distribution of gubernatorial vote share, religious population
and violence, Landak and Mempawah, 2018*

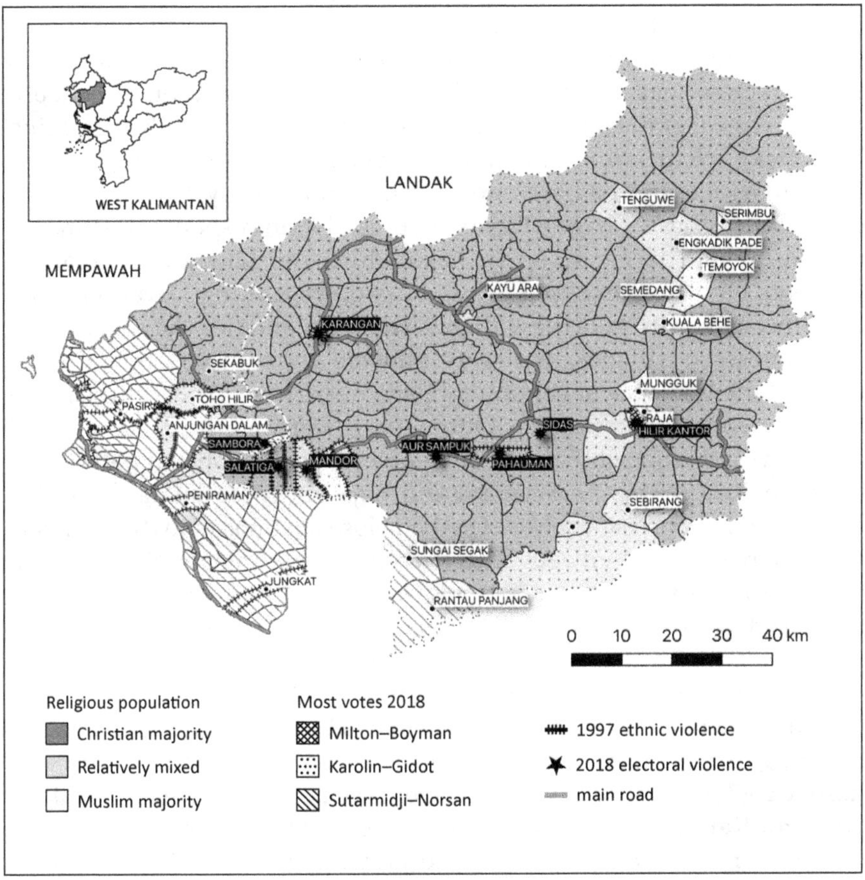

labels. Lastly, we highlight the borders of villages that experienced ethnic
violence in the late 1990s.

The first point to note is that this geocoded map reveals a fairly
consistent pattern of ethnoreligious voting. Landak (on the right) is a
Christian Dayak–majority area won by Karolin, but within it are some
Muslim Malay– and Javanese-dominated villages won by Sutarmidji.
Meanwhile, Mempawah (on the left) is majority Muslim Malay, but
contains two heterogeneous, Dayak-majority subdistricts near the
border with Landak. Within these subdistricts, we see a pattern whereby
predominantly Dayak Christian villages supported Karolin, whereas
predominantly Muslim Javanese villages voted for Sutarmidji.

The second, more noteworthy, point arising from this map is that the villages that were most affected by violence in the aftermath of the 2018 election were ethnically and religiously mixed villages with past exposure to violent conflict, such as Karangan and several villages in Ngabang subdistrict (e.g. Hilir Kantor and Hilir Tengah). These are concentrated in border regions, near the main road, or at the subdistrict centres. Notably, these areas generally have good internet coverage, potentially increasing their exposure to online rumours; however, in many cases they are also more accessible by road and are therefore more likely to be visited by outsiders. In these villages, Dayak mobilisation in response to rumours was faster and larger in scale. Meanwhile, the Malay and Javanese residents who were exposed to rumours of impending Dayak violence were more likely to take these threats seriously and flee their homes.

Conversely, villages that were affected by rumours but did not descend into violence or communal panic were in many cases relatively homogeneous communities. Often, they were equipped to defend themselves or enjoyed the protection of a powerful political patron. For instance, Karolin lost in Serimbu and Raja but these villages avoided violent retaliation, ostensibly due to their close relations with the Sultanate of Pontianak. Mixed villages with friendly interethnic relations—which were not racked by the legacy of violent conflict in the late 1990s—also remained relatively secure. In those villages, Dayak residents even protected their Javanese and Malay neighbours from outside threats.

Interestingly, Karolin won in many areas that are predominantly Muslim, such as Mungguk, Temoyok, Sebirang and Kayu Ara. In Sebirang, for example, Sutarmidji received only 7 per cent of the vote despite a 47 per cent Muslim population. We believe that many Muslims voted for Karolin because they were concerned that her defeat may lead to violent retribution. Madurese and Javanese residents in one remote village reported they would have preferred to vote for Sutarmidji, but were afraid that doing so may have resulted in their forced expulsion from their homes and land. Ultimately, they voted for Karolin in order to avoid violent repercussions. This implies that the rumours and threats disseminated ahead of the election may have played a significant role in the pre-emptive shaping of voting behaviour in vulnerable communities. However, we believe additional research into this phenomenon is required before concrete conclusions are drawn.

A finding we particularly want to emphasise is that patterns of violence in West Kalimantan following the 2018 election show that neither exposure to rumours, nor particular electoral outcomes, were sufficient to cause outbreaks of violence. Rather, the villages that were vulnerable to political violence were those with a legacy of past ethnic conflict and previous exposure to polarising identity politics. Indeed, many of the regions in which rumours provoked violence were also hotspots of mass violence in the late 1990s, such as Mandor,[13] Ngabang and Pahauman.[14]

On a similar note, places such as Karangan[15] have seen frequent recurrences of these old conflicts, and seem trapped in a cycle of identity-based polarisation, rumour and communal conflict. A year before the election, at the end of Ramadan 2017, communal tensions erupted in Karangan after a Dayak woman was murdered by her Muslim husband. Rumours circulated that the victim had been mutilated and put in a sack, and some members of the Dayak community agitated for retribution against their Malay Muslim neighbours. Most Malays in Karangan fled their homes, and local security forces were placed on high alert to respond to a likely eruption of violence. Once again, local elites played a central role in resolving this conflict, with local powerbrokers—including Karolin, who was then serving as Regent of Landak; the Landak police chief; the local military commander; as well as other prominent Dayak figures—coming to Karangan to calm the masses.

Following the 2018 election, the intervention of local leaders and authorities, and participation in symbolic and customary arbitration ceremonies, seemed a particularly effective means of resolving outbreaks of communal violence sparked by the dissemination of rumours. In order to ease tensions, local leaders and villagers in several places performed *pamabakng*, a Dayak ritual to resolve conflict that imposes severe customary sanctions upon those who subsequently breach the peace. One such ritual was performed near Sambora village, and encouraged the rapid de-escalation of communal tensions. Conversely, in Karangan—which saw the most severe communal violence—elites did not initiate rituals of this sort. The absence of elite-led reconciliation may have contributed

---

13 Mandor remained Cornelis and Karolin's stronghold. In 1997, mass violence involving Dayak and Madura broke out in Salatiga and several other villages in this subdistrict, killing around 250 people and burning 579 Madurese homes (National Violence Monitoring System, NVMS).

14 Ngabang is located about 90 kilometres from Mandor. On the main road that connects the two villages, Aur Sampuk, Pahauman and Sidas also experienced tensions. Violence against Madurese also occurred in Pahauman and several villages in Sengah Temila in 1997. Around 155 Madurese were killed, hundreds injured and 180 Madurese homes burned down. Similar violence occurred in Ngabang. Approximately 49 Madurese died and 33 Madurese houses were burned to the ground (NVMS).

15 Karangan is in Landak regency, located on the border with Mempawah. In 1997, thousands of Dayaks from Karangan attacked Madurese in Mempawah Hulu, Toho and several other areas.

to the more extreme and prolonged quality of communal tension in this village.

A final notable finding of our study relates to the relationship between rumours and conflict at the local and national levels. Despite the particular demographic, historical and social contexts that shaped the nature and impact of rumours in the 2018 West Kalimantan election, this case cannot be wholly separated from the national political landscape in 2018. Studies have shown how intolerance was mobilised through social media in the 2017 Jakarta election by both the incumbent coalition and its Islamist-backed challengers (Lim 2017), as well as the impact of this election on increasing polarisation among Indonesians outside the capital (Mietzner and Muhtadi 2019). We saw similar patterns at work in West Kalimantan. Following the model used by the anti-Ahok coalition in Jakarta, Sutarmidji's camp promoted anti-Cornelis campaigns and called for his arrest and imprisonment on blasphemy charges. On the other side, Cornelis and Karolin's campaign team raised fears of an Islamist intrusion among non-Muslims, and even flirted with Islamophobic sentiment as a means of mobilising and maintaining a strong ethnoreligious coalition.

In summary, the effects of online rumours were filtered through the lens of old problems and exacerbated pre-existing cleavages. While two decades have passed since the devastating communal violence of the late 1990s and early 2000s, the 2018 elections in West Kalimantan provided a clear reminder that historical conflicts continue to have residual effects upon the functioning of democracy. New and more effective channels for spreading rumours and disinformation have pernicious consequences in these post-conflict communities, and therefore require special attention and de-escalation efforts from community leaders, government and non-government organisations. But government policies that curtail internet access or close down social media overemphasise the role of digital media in outbreaks of violence, and risk mistaking the symptoms of identity-based conflict for its causes.

CONCLUSION

The use of polarising political rumours is an old strategy in Indonesian electoral politics, but technological advances have functioned as a catalyst for their more rapid and efficient dissemination. At both the national and regional levels, it has become increasingly routine for political candidates to spread rumours and disinformation in an effort to secure narrow electoral advantages. Moreover, these practices often continue in the aftermath of elections. With the rise of social media, it is increasingly easy to spread rumours that obfuscate election results, threaten political opponents, secure leverage in bargaining processes and win concessions from electoral victors. Meanwhile, incumbents and winning candidates use propaganda and social media 'buzzers' to divert public attention from pressing policy issues, suppress criticism and otherwise manipulate popular opinion.

However, the effectiveness of social media–based rumours, and particularly the degree to which they can provoke outbreaks of violence, seems to depend on the presence of a variety of other factors. Our study of the 2018 West Kalimantan election reveals additional challenges to Indonesia's broader democratic quality and stability. In particular, the intermixing of polarising national-level discourses (which defined the 2017 Jakarta election) and longstanding local ethnoreligious tensions produced a volatile security environment during the 2018 West Kalimantan election. The intrusion of religiously exclusivist militant groups like FPI into a highly polarised electoral environment served to ratchet up tensions and encouraged similarly chauvinistic and aggressive tactics from the Christian Dayak constituency. In regions with a history of political violence, the spread of ethnically and religiously charged rumours—through both online and offline channels—contributed to the resurrection of longstanding patterns of conflict, intimidation and social polarisation.

As identity-based polarisation becomes more extreme, inflammatory scaremongering becomes more credible; this, in turn, exacerbates the potential for communal violence. The impact of polarised, identity-based national-level campaigns—and the clouds of provocative misinformation and rumour that accompany them—are likely to be especially acute in post-conflict regions such as West Kalimantan. Should this mode of campaigning continue to be normalised, the prospect of election-related violence seems sure to increase. However, it is important not to overstate the role of emerging communications technology in *causing* political violence, and to instead appreciate the complex of factors that contribute to outbreaks of political conflict such as that seen in West Kalimantan.

REFERENCES

Ananta, A., E.N. Arifin, M.S. Hasbullah, N.B. Handayani and A. Pramono. 2015. *Demography of Indonesia's Ethnicity*. Singapore: Institute of Southeast Asian Studies (ISEAS).

Arun, C. 2019. 'On WhatsApp, rumours, and lynchings'. *Economic & Political Weekly* 54(6): 30–5.

Aspinall, E., S. Dettman and E. Warburton. 2011. 'When religion trumps ethnicity: a regional election case study from Indonesia'. *South East Asia Research* 19(1): 27–58.

Banaji S., R. Bhat, A. Agarwal, N. Passanha and M.S. Pravin. 2019. *WhatsApp Vigilantes: An Exploration of Citizen Reception and Circulation of WhatsApp Misinformation Linked to Mob Violence in India*. London: London School of Economics and Political Science.

Bradshaw, S. and P.N. Howard. 2019. 'The global disinformation order: 2019 global inventory of organised social media manipulation'. Working Paper 3. Oxford: Computational Propaganda Research Project. https://comprop.oii.ox.ac.uk/wp-content/uploads/sites/93/2019/09/CyberTroop-Report19.pdf

Bubandt, N. 2008. 'Rumors, pamphlets, and the politics of paranoia in Indonesia'. *Journal of Asian Studies* 67(3): 789–817.

CIPG (Centre for Innovation Policy and Governance). 2019. 'Di balik fenomena buzzer: memahami lanskap industri dan pengaruh buzzer di Indonesia'. Jakarta: CIPG.

Davidson, J.S. 2008. *From Rebellion to Riots: Collective Violence on Indonesian Borneo*. Madison, WI: University of Wisconsin Press.

Delik Kalbar. 2018. 'Diduga menistakan agama, akun Facebook GR dipolisikan'. *Delik Kalbar*, 19 June. https://delikkalbar.com/2018/06/19/diduga-menistakan-agama-akun-facebook-gr-dipolisikan/

Hartriani, J. and S.B.E. Wardani. 2014. 'Politik etnis pada masa pemerintahan gubernur Cornelis di Kalimantan Barat tahun 2007 hingga 2013'. Depok City: FISIP UI. http://lontar.ui.ac.id/naskahringkas/2016-06/S55870-Jeany%20Hartriani

Horowitz, D.L. 2001. *The Deadly Ethnic Riot*. Berkeley, CA: University of California Press.

Human Rights Watch. 2001. 'Indonesia: the violence in Central Kalimantan (Borneo)'. HRW World Report, 28 February. https://www.hrw.org/legacy/backgrounder/asia/borneo0228.htm

Idris, I.K. 2019a. 'More responsive journalism—not social media ban—is needed to fight disinformation in Indonesia'. *The Conversation*, 24 May. https://theconversation.com/more-responsive-journalism-not-social-media-ban-is-needed-to-fight-disinformation-in-indonesia-117604

Idris, I.K. 2019b. 'The internet shutdown in Papua threatens Indonesia's democracy and its people's right to free speech'. *Jakarta Post*, 2 September. https://www.thejakartapost.com/academia/2019/09/02/the-internet-shutdown-in-papua-threatens-indonesias-democracy-and-its-peoples-right-to-free-speech.html

International Crisis Group. 2001. 'Communal violence in Indonesia: lessons from Kalimantan'. *ICG Asia Report* No. 18, 27 June. Jakarta and Brussels: International Crisis Group.

IPAC (Institute for Policy Analysis and Conflict). 2018a. 'The West Kalimantan election and the impact of the anti-Ahok campaign'. *IPAC Report* No. 43, 21 February. Jakarta: IPAC.

IPAC (Institute for Policy Analysis and Conflict). 2018b. 'Update on local election results in West Kalimantan and Papua'. *IPAC Report* No. 50, 16 August. Jakarta: IPAC.

Jakarta Post. 2018. 'Indonesia, fourth highest number of Facebook users in the world'. *Jakarta Post*, 4 March. https://www.thejakartapost.com/life/2018/03/04/indonesia-fourth-highest-number-of-facebook-users-in-the-world.html

Lamb, K. 2018. 'Muslim cyber army: a "fake news" operation designed to derail Indonesia's leader'. *The Guardian*, 13 March. https://www.theguardian.com/world/2018/mar/13/muslim-cyber-army-a-fake-news-operation-designed-to-bring-down-indonesias-leader

Lim, M. 2017. 'Freedom to hate: social media, algorithmic enclaves, and the rise of tribal nationalism in Indonesia'. *Critical Asian Studies* 49(3): 411–27.

Mietzner, M. and B. Muhtadi. 2019. 'The mobilisation of intolerance and its trajectories: Indonesian Muslims' views of religious minorities and ethnic Chinese'. In *Contentious Belonging: The Place of Minorities in Indonesia*, edited by G. Fealy and R. Ricci, 155–74. Singapore: ISEAS – Yusof Ishak Institute.

Peluso, N.L. 2008. 'A political ecology of violence and territory in West Kalimantan'. *Asia Pacific Viewpoint* 49(1): 48–67.

Potkin, F. and A.B. Da Costa. 2019. 'In Indonesia, Facebook and Twitter are "buzzer" battlegrounds as elections loom'. Reuters, 13 March. https://www.reuters.com/article/us-indonesia-election-socialmedia-insigh/in-indonesia-facebook-and-twitter-are-buzzer-battlegrounds-as-elections-loom-idUSKBN1QU0AS

ProKalbar. 2018. 'Sempat mencekam, Ngabang aman'. *ProKalbar*, 30 June. https://kalbar.prokal.co/read/news/2131-sempat-mencekam-ngabang-aman.html

Tanasaldy, T. 2007. 'Politik identitas etnis di Kalimantan Barat'. In *Politik Lokal di Indonesia*, edited by H.S. Nordholt and G. van Klinken, 461–90. Jakarta: Yayasan Obor Indonesia – KITLV.

Tribun Pontianak. 2018a. 'Mantan bupati Landak maafkan Yonas, adat "buat tangah" redam perselisihan'. *Tribun Pontianak*, 24 May. https://pontianak.tribunnews.com/2018/05/24/mantan-bupati-landak-maafkan-yonas-adat-buat-tangah-redam-perselisihan

Tribun Pontianak. 2018b. 'Karolin minta masyarakat dan pendukungnya taat hukum serta menghormati proses demokrasi'. *Tribun Pontianak*, 30 June. https://pontianak.tribunnews.com/2018/06/30/karolin-minta-masyarakatdan-pendukungnnya-taat-hukum-serta-menghormati-proses-demokrasi?page=all

Tribun Pontianak. 2018c. 'Dapat jaminan keamanan 226 warga Karangan pulang kerumah, ini penjelasan kapolres Landak'. *Tribun Pontianak*, 2 July. https://pontianak.tribunnews.com/2018/07/02/dapat-jaminan-keamanan-226-warga-karangan-pulang-kerumah-ini-penjelasan-kapolres-landak

17 Electoral violence in Indonesia 20 years after *reformasi*

Risa J. Toha and S.P. Harish

Over the past two decades, Indonesia has been acknowledged as the world's third-largest democracy and largest Muslim-majority democracy. By 2019, the country had smoothly run four direct presidential elections, five parliamentary elections and hundreds of direct local elections (*pilkada*). Voter participation rates in national elections have hovered around 70 per cent over the years, with greater variation in local executive elections. Following Suharto's resignation in 1998, Indonesia shifted to a multiparty system in which hundreds of thousands of candidates compete across a multitude of legislative and executive races. On 17 April 2019, Indonesia held its most complicated election in history. Billed as one of the world's largest simultaneous elections, the 2019 election saw over 80 per cent of 190 million registered voters cast their vote simultaneously for their local council representatives, parliament members and president in more than 800,000 polling stations across the archipelago. Despite the complicated logistical undertaking, the election proceeded without major incidents of violence.

These successes notwithstanding, many Indonesia specialists have expressed concerns over the quality of democracy in recent years (e.g. Aspinall 2018; Hadiz 2017; Lindsey 2018). An increase in government crackdowns on critics and the politicisation of identities around elections (Warburton and Aspinall 2017), among other indicators, have been identified as worrying symptoms of democratic deterioration. While the 2019 national election went smoothly, the announcement of its results a few weeks later spurred protests by Prabowo Subianto's supporters and a two-day riot that claimed ten lives and injured at least 200 people (BBC 2019; Halim 2019). The authorities deployed more than 40,000 troops, arrested hundreds of rioters and shut down access to social media for several days to prevent the spread of what it termed 'hoaxes' and 'fake news' (*Straits Times* 2019). While order was restored within a few days, authorities claimed that the outburst was purposefully planned to discredit election results, and promised to thoroughly investigate the provocateurs involved (Chan 2019).

This outburst of post-election violence raises a few important questions: To what extent is electoral violence a common occurrence in Indonesia? What can patterns of electoral violence tell us about the country's quality of democracy? Did the May 2019 riots mark a shift to more violence around elections in Indonesia?

In this chapter, we utilise the World Bank's National Violence Monitoring System (NVMS) dataset, a newly available event-level dataset of incidents of violence reported in local papers, as well as our original data covering *pilkada* from 2005 to 2013, to examine patterns of electoral violence. We make three main claims. First, electoral violence in Indonesia is relatively infrequent. Election violence comprises a small fraction of all the incidents that the NVMS reported. Relative to other new democracies, Indonesia also looks much better in terms of its levels of violence around elections. Second, while electoral violence in general is infrequent in Indonesia, some elections have a higher propensity for electoral violence than others. Our data indicate that election violence is (1) more common around local executive elections, while legislative and presidential elections tend to suffer relatively few incidents; (2) more common in post-conflict areas; (3) more likely when elections are particularly competitive; and (4) more likely when identity is especially politicised.

Third, in the high-conflict provinces for which we have consistent data (1998–2014), we found there has been an increase in levels of election violence since 2008. In low-conflict provinces (2005–2014), on the other hand, the levels of election violence have been relatively stable over time, with a slight jump around 2014. A closer look at mass mobilisations around the presidential elections since 2014 suggests that identity politicisation has become more common in national politics. Overall, we find that election violence has increased in recent years, particularly around elections wherein identity was politicised.

The fact that electoral violence is infrequent in Indonesia may be interpreted as a hopeful sign for the overall health of democracy. In most elections in Indonesia, contenders and voters alike accept the legitimacy of elections as a procedure for working out their political preferences. Nonetheless, the incidents of election violence that have occurred, around both local and national races, suggest that voters are susceptible to the politicisation of identity, and, especially in recent years, strategic actors view violent mobilisation as a useful tool for articulating demands and for pressing the government to accommodate them.

WHAT WE KNOW SO FAR ABOUT ELECTION VIOLENCE

In healthy electoral democracies, elections are supposed to be the primary platform for aggregating voters' political preferences in a peaceful manner. However, in many parts of the world, elections can also be violent.

Many scholars of election violence adopt an instrumentalist framework and treat violence as one of the tools that strategic political actors use to secure their political interests. The strategic deployment of electoral violence—broadly defined as 'acts or threats of coercion, intimidation, or physical harm to affect an electoral process or that arises in the context of electoral competition' (Sisk 2008)—may occur before or after elections. In the run-up to a competitive election, strategic actors stir electoral violence to shape voters' preferences and political participation in their favour. When election results are considered disappointing or fraudulent, embittered political actors can mobilise violence to protest against the election results and to leverage their demands (Beaulieu 2014).

There is much empirical evidence supporting the notion that violence is used strategically to shape electoral outcomes by shaping voters' political engagement. In their cross-national study, Hafner-Burton et al. (2014) demonstrate that incumbent candidates are more likely to resort to violence to intimidate opposition supporters when the outcome of the election is less certain. A study of sub-Saharan African countries found that informed voters, who are less easily persuaded by politicians' campaign appeals than uninformed voters, report a greater level of fear of violence around elections, and are less likely to participate in elections (Borzyskowski and Kuhn 2014). Across municipal elections in Mexico, voter turnout tends to be lower in municipalities that have had greater exposure to violence (Trelles and Carreras 2012).

Using a similar logic, Fjelde and Höglund (2016) have argued that elections in countries with majoritarian electoral systems tend to have higher levels of electoral violence because elections carry much higher stakes in these contexts than in settings with proportional systems. In majoritarian elections, losers do not get any representation in the winning government. In proportional systems, losers can still be represented in a coalition government (Lijphart 1977). One direct implication that can be derived from these studies is that competitive, high-stakes elections would be more prone to violent mobilisation.

In addition to shaping voters' participation and political preferences in elections, violence is also effective in shaping and solidifying a winning coalition. In explaining the patterns of Hindu–Muslim riots in India, Wilkinson (2004) contends that strategic politicians allow violence to unfold in certain places to prime voters to vote along ethnic lines and to help them secure victory. In other words, by activating voters' loyalties to their identity-based communities, violence acts as a mobilising tool that pushes voters to vote for their co-ethnic candidates. Beyond the deliberate engineering of violence to prime voters to think along ethnic lines in their voting decisions, politicians in ethnically diverse contexts sometimes rely on ethnic appeals to mobilise voters along ethnic lines (Reilly 2002). Given this body of research, one would expect that elections in ethnically diverse settings can be prone to violence.

Beyond strategic incentives, scholars have also traced violence around elections to structural factors such as the effects of prior conflict. Conflict scholars, for example, have argued that demobilised fighters who are not integrated in the labour market in post-conflict settings become conflict specialists for hire, who can engineer violence for their patrons (Colombo et al. 2019). In a study of countries that have undergone civil wars, Brancati and Snyder (2011) show that rushing to elections increases the probability that elections are vulnerable to violence. These studies show that elections in post-conflict settings are more likely to experience election violence.

This body of comparative work suggests ethnically diverse, post-conflict countries with competitive elections and weak institutions would be prone to outbursts of electoral violence. Indonesia checks many of these boxes: elections are often highly competitive, many areas of the country have high levels of ethnic and religious diversity and some pockets experienced violent conflicts during the democratic transition years. There has also been more ethnoreligious identity mobilisation in major local and national elections in recent years. In the next section, we will discuss our data and analytical approach to examine whether the case of Indonesia conforms to the expectations that have been outlined in the literature.

DATA DESCRIPTION

To examine the patterns of election violence, we rely on the NVMS, a dataset of communal violence in Indonesia from 1997 to 2014. The dataset was compiled by a team of World Bank researchers who read more than one hundred local news sources and coded reported incidents of communal violence. The dataset reports the location, timing, description, injuries, casualties, actors and a number of other variables related to communal violence and categorises these incidents into various types of communal violence. The dataset initially only tracked incidents reported in local newspapers in eight 'high-conflict' provinces (Aceh, Papua, West Papua, Maluku, North Maluku, Central Kalimantan, West Kalimantan and Central Sulawesi) before it expanded its coverage in 2005 to include eight 'low-conflict' provinces (North Sumatra, Lampung, Greater Jakarta, East Java, West Nusa Tenggara, East Nusa Tenggara, South Sulawesi and North Sulawesi) (Barron et al. 2016). In 2014, NVMS coverage expanded again, this time to include local newspapers throughout the whole country (NVMS 2014).

The categories of communal violence in the NVMS are conflicts related to resources, governance, elections and appointments, separatism, identity-based clashes, popular justice conflict, law enforcement, violent crime, domestic violence and other kinds of violence. Each incident in the dataset comes with a narrative of the event that NVMS coders included based on the articles they read in the sampled local newspapers. In total, the NVMS reports 148,541 incidents of all kinds of communal violence from 1997 to 2014.

To the best of our knowledge, this dataset remains to this day the best data on communal violence available, and is the only one that would allow us to examine election violence patterns over such a large period of time and across a broad section of the Indonesian archipelago. Nonetheless, it is worth noting that the dataset stops at 2014, and as such our analysis based on the NVMS dataset excludes the bouts of election violence since 2014. In the final section of this chapter we supplement our findings derived from the NVMS dataset with qualitative insights into post-2014 developments in electoral violence; in particular, we emphasise the ways in which street mobilisations—both peaceful and violent—have emerged as a means by which to influence voters' electoral preferences.

BROAD PATTERNS OF VIOLENCE AROUND ELECTIONS IN INDONESIA

To examine election violence in Indonesia since *reformasi*, we use the incidents that the NVMS categorises as election violence.[1] The dataset

---

1   We use all events coded under 88883 for 'elections and appointment conflict', 3302 for 'other election and public office conflicts', 3303 for 'national election/ appointment', 3304 for 'provincial election/appointment', 3305 for 'district/ municipality election appointment', 3306 for 'subdistrict appointment', 3307

reports 2,220 violent incidents related to elections from 1997 to 2014. Relative to the total number of violent incidents in Indonesia (148,541), election violence comprises approximately 1.5 per cent of all incidents reported in the dataset.

The NVMS category of election violence includes a broad range of incidents, from a stone throwing at *pilkada* candidates, campaign team members and supporters during a rally; to the destruction of campaign posters; to grenade attacks on candidates' homes; to clashes between supporters of rival candidates. While some incidents led to casualties, the majority of incidents recorded as electoral violence did not lead to deaths and involved acts of vandalism, arson, physical intimidation and other less severe attempts to inflict physical harm. To illustrate, we include descriptions of some of the incidents in the NVMS dataset:[2]

> On 27 June 2012, the team, supporters and sympathisers of the Aceh Barat Daya *bupati* hopeful FD were subject to stone throwing when they were attending an event in Alue Sungai Pinang village, Jeumpa subdistrict, Aceh Barat Daya district. There is reason to believe that the attackers were FD's rivals in the *pilkada* race, and that their motive was related to the Aceh Barat Daya *pilkada* race.

> Supporters of the late John Mailoa ran amok and set fire to the PDI-P [Partai Demokrasi Indonesia-Perjuangan, Indonesian Democratic Party of Struggle] flag in the PDI-P branch office on Jl. Ahmad Yani, Maluku Tengah, 13 April 2007. This incident is related to the candidate submitted by the PDI-P Central Board to the Maluku Tengah Electoral Commission to replace Mailoa [as the party's *bupati* candidate].

> A number of unidentified individuals attacked the KPU [Komisi Pemilihan Umum; Elections Commission] office in Ketapang, allegedly because they were dissatisfied with the temporary election results that the KPU office announced. One announcement board was destroyed (19 June 2010).

> Along the road from Menggala to Banjar Agung subdistrict, Tulang Bawang, Lampung, an unidentified person has destroyed 500 campaign posters that contain the image of one of the contenders and his running mate in the *pilkada* race in the district. The motive behind the destruction is believed to be linked to the imminent *pilkada* race in Tulang Bawang (5 September 2012).

---

for 'village/*kelurahan* elections appointment', 3308 for 'other government office' and 3309 for 'office/influence/power in political parties'.

2   The descriptions of the incidents in the NVMS data are written in Bahasa Indonesia. To include the given examples, one of the authors translated the descriptions from the original language into English.

These narratives highlight the broad range of manifestations of election violence, from clashes between rival candidates' supporters to vandalism of campaign materials, to physical assault on candidates. Earlier accounts of election violence in Indonesia indicate that murders of political candidates are rare in Indonesia (Buehler 2009).

To get a broader picture of the pattern of election violence in Indonesia, we plotted the number of incidents of election violence in a given day in the eight high-conflict provinces from 1997 to 2014, and in the high-conflict and low-conflict provinces from 2005 to 2014. In both the high-conflict and low-conflict provinces, election violence appears to increase in more recent years, though the number of incidents in a given day never exceeded 15 (Figure 17.1).

Although election violence in Indonesia appears to have become more common in recent years, relative to other countries in Southeast Asia, Indonesia's electoral violence is considerably less frequent and less deadly. Take, for example, electoral violence in the Philippines. Most recently, mayoral candidate Rodel Batocabe died three days before Christmas in 2018 from eight gunshot wounds, after two unidentified men shot him at an event for senior citizens in Burgos, Daraga (Cepeda 2018). Such incidents are not uncommon around elections in the Philippines. In six elections from 1986 to 2001, an average of 274 violent incidents occurred per election cycle (Patino and Velasco 2004). According to the Philippine Election Commission, 40 candidates were murdered and 18 were injured in the country's 2004 election (Buehler 2009). In 2016, the Philippine National Police reported 106 incidents that involved 192 victims during the elections (Caliwan 2019). Thailand has a long history of election violence (Anderson 1990). After 1997, the mode of election violence there shifted towards more intimidation and crackdown on protesters as attempted assassinations of canvassers and politicians declined (Prajak 2016).

By comparison, the NVMS recorded 347 incidents around the 2014 legislative election in Indonesia, involving 8 fatalities and 304 injuries. The previous legislative election in 2009 had a total of 246 incidents and led to 12 deaths and 115 injuries.

In Figure 17.2, we plot the count of deaths and injuries incurred by incidents of election violence across the 16 provinces in Indonesia from 2005 to 2014, as well as the count of incidents that led to no injuries or deaths. Overall, most incidents incurred very few deaths. Throughout the ten-year period from 2005 to 2014, election violence in the 16 provinces led to a total of 84 deaths and 1,489 injuries. Most incidents involved injuries, although a number of incidents had neither deaths nor injuries.

In Figure 17.3, we show the proportion of elections that involved civilian deaths in several Southeast Asian countries from 1945 to 2012,

Figure 17.1   Incidents of electoral violence, 1998–2014

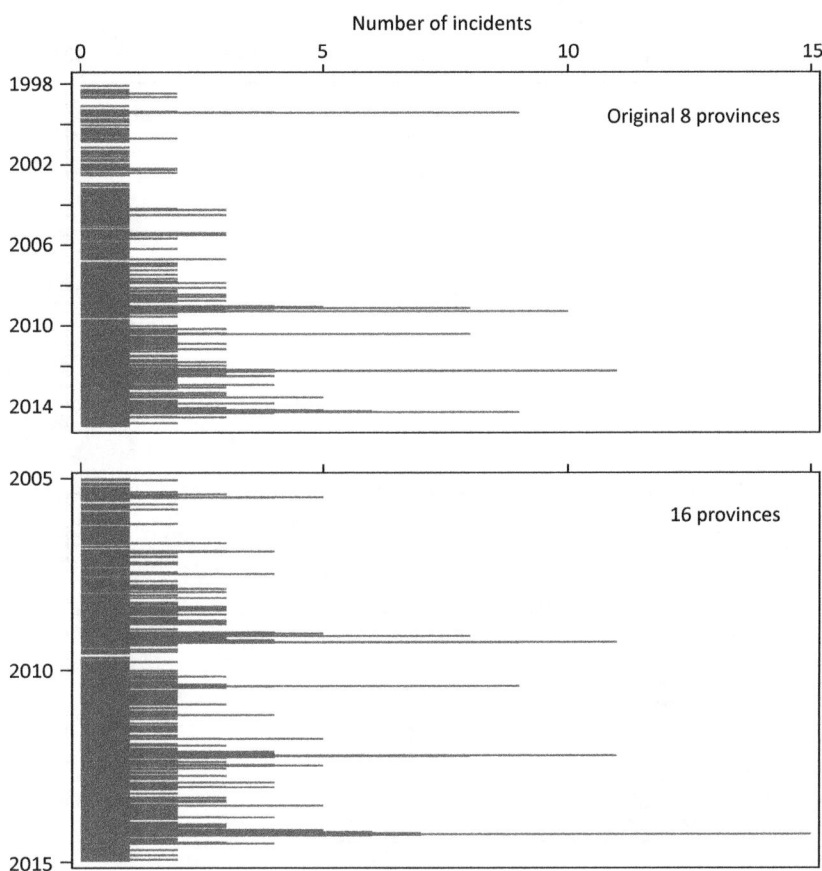

using cross-national data.[3] There are, of course, significant variations in terms of these countries' regime types and in the number and type of elections they have held over this period. However, these data are intended simply as an indicative, aggregated picture of violence around elections in the region, and the results show that Indonesia is indeed a country with less electoral violence.

---

3 We use data from the National Elections across Democracy and Autocracy dataset (https://nelda.co) to identify violent elections in different countries of Southeast Asia. The specific question we use is an indicator variable coded for 'Was there significant violence involving civilian deaths immediately before, during, or after the election?'

Figure 17.2   *Election violence by intensity in 16 provinces, 2005–2014*

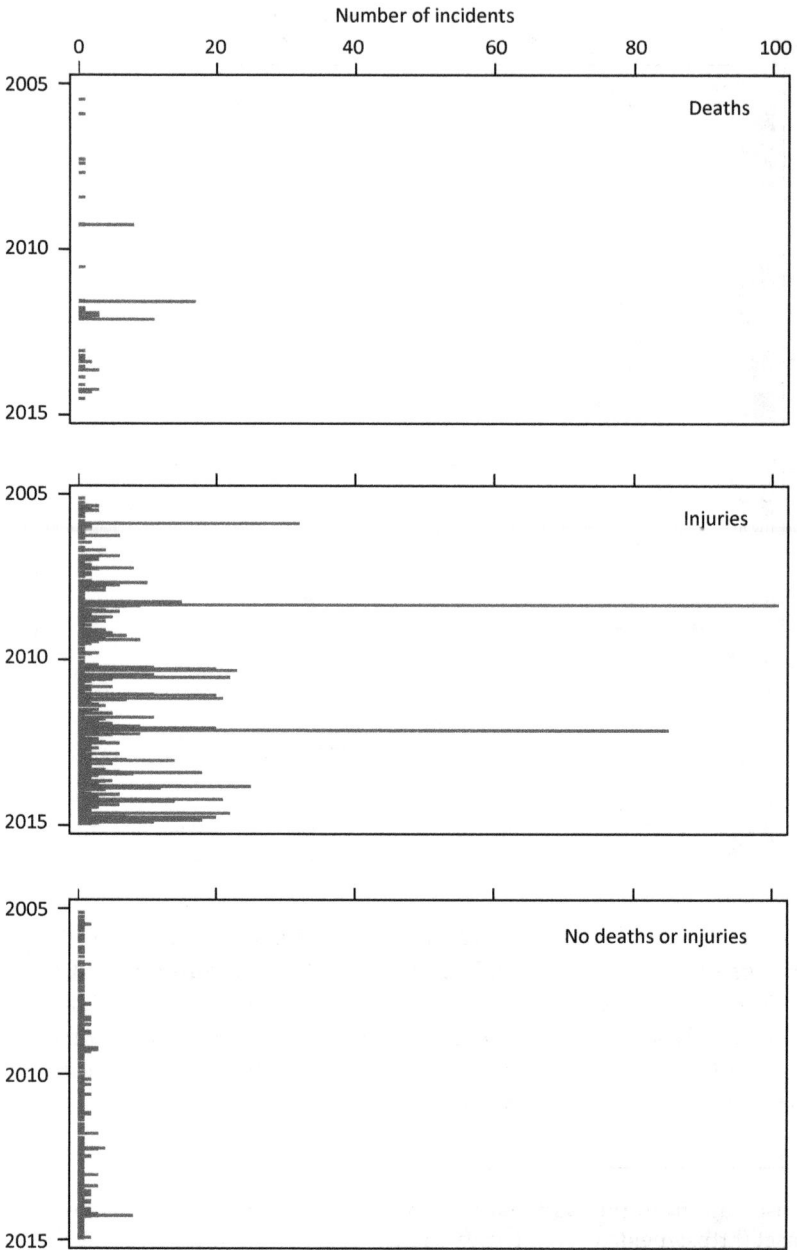

Figure 17.3   *Proportions of elections with civilian deaths in Southeast Asia, 1945–2012*

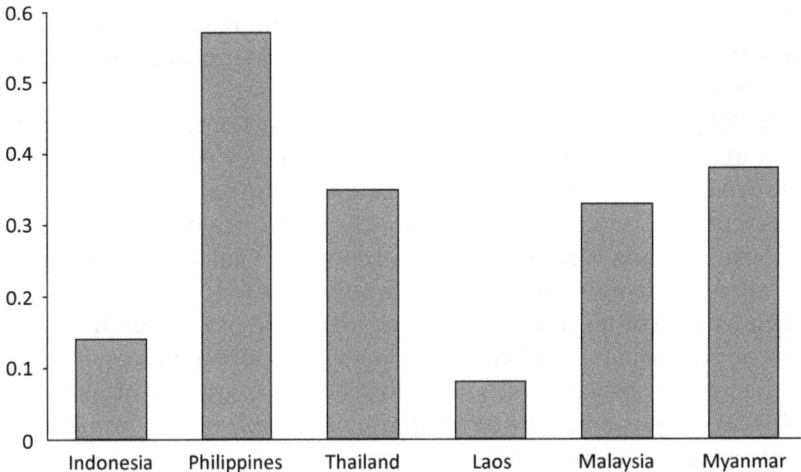

Source: National Elections across Democracy and Autocracy dataset (https://nelda.co).

Indonesia's election violence also pales in comparison to emerging democracies outside Southeast Asia. For example, Nigeria, which transitioned from military rule to a civilian government in 1999, has witnessed many incidents of elections-related violence (Onubogu and Hassan 2018). In Colombia, where politicians have regularly been targeted with violence around local elections, 52 community leaders died as a result of violent attacks five months before local elections in October 2019 (Alsema 2019).

VIOLENCE RELATED TO DIFFERENT TYPES OF ELECTIONS IN INDONESIA

To further understand violence around different types of elections in Indonesia, we read through the narratives of incidents of election violence and developed a set of keywords that we used to identify whether an incident was related to the national presidential or legislative elections. With this approach, we found the NVMS reported 281 incidents of violence related to legislative elections and 245 incidents related to presidential elections across two election cycles (2009, 2014). The remaining 1,458 incidents of violence around elections in the NVMS are related to local elections.[4]

When we disaggregate violence related to presidential, legislative and local elections, we find that most incidents of electoral violence revolved around local elections, and that legislative and presidential elections have generally been peaceful.

Figure 17.4 plots violence related to all kinds of elections, and legislative, presidential and local elections in the 16 provinces for which the NVMS has data from 2005 to 2014. The graph of all election violence includes incidents reported as related to legislative elections, presidential elections and local elections. As Figure 17.4 demonstrates, the total levels of violence around all three categories of election are relatively low, especially in light of violence in other countries outlined earlier. We can infer that local elections appear to have higher total counts of incidents in a given day within the period observed, although this relative frequency of violence around local races can also be attributed to the much higher number of *pilkada* races within a single year.

Geographically, the districts with the highest counts of election violence (of all types) in the period covered in the dataset are Ternate (North Maluku), Aceh Utara (Aceh), Kota Lhokseumawe (Aceh), Maluku Tengah (Maluku), Bireuen (Aceh), Kota Bima and Bima district (West Nusa Tenggara), Pidie (Aceh), Kota Jayapura (Papua) and Kota Ambon (Maluku). From this list of top-ten districts with the highest counts of election violence, one can see that administrative units in Aceh and Maluku appear frequently. In fact, 20 per cent of all election violence in the 16 provinces in the dataset from 2005 to 2014 were reported in Aceh.

In Figure 17.5, we graph the count of electoral violence incidents that the NVMS reported six months before and six months after the 2009 and 2014 legislative elections, in the 16 provinces in the NVMS dataset. The 2009 election had 246 incidents of violence, and the 2014 legislative election had 347 incidents of violence, an increase of more than 40 per cent. Within that total number of incidents, there was a decrease in the number of deaths but an increase in the number of injuries. In 2014, the total count of legislative election violence in a day never surpassed nine incidents. Most incidents occurred between January and voting day in April. While skirmishes after the election occurred as well, they were much fewer in number compared to the pre-electoral violence.

---

4   The category of local election includes both *pilkada* elections at the provincial and district/municipal level, as well as other kinds of local elections/ appointments such as the appointment of subdistrict heads, village chiefs and local party leaders.

Figure 17.4   Patterns of violence in 16 provinces, 2005–2014

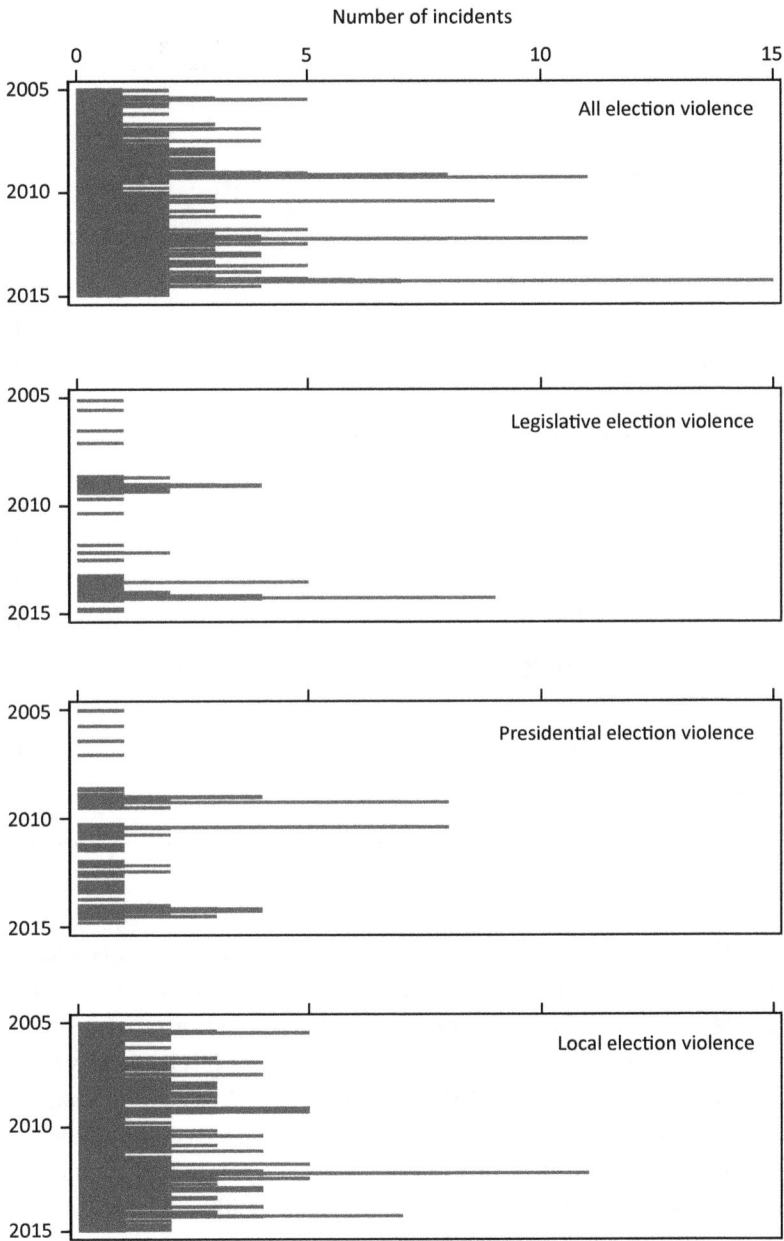

Figure 17.5   Electoral violence around legislative elections, 2009 and 2014

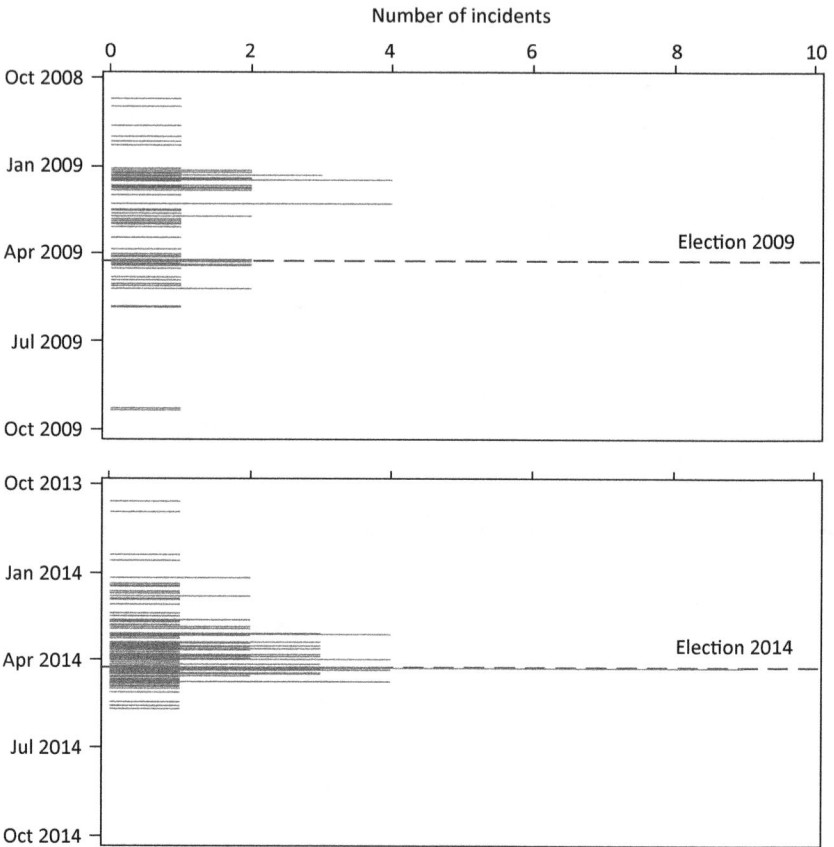

A similar pattern holds for election violence around presidential elections (Figure 17.6). In 2009 and 2014, presidential elections occurred in July, a few months after the national legislative elections. In both waves of presidential elections, there were few incidents of electoral violence within a six-month time frame before and after voting day. Clashes were few and mostly concentrated before the election. Between the 2009 and 2014 elections, the number of violent incidents related to presidential elections in the 16 provinces increased from 43 to 100 (133 per cent). The number of deaths decreased from 12 to 7 (42 per cent) but the number of injuries increased from 107 to 273 (155 per cent). That is, while incidents have increased over time, they have not necessarily increased in severity.

Figure 17.6   Electoral violence around presidential elections, 2009 and 2014

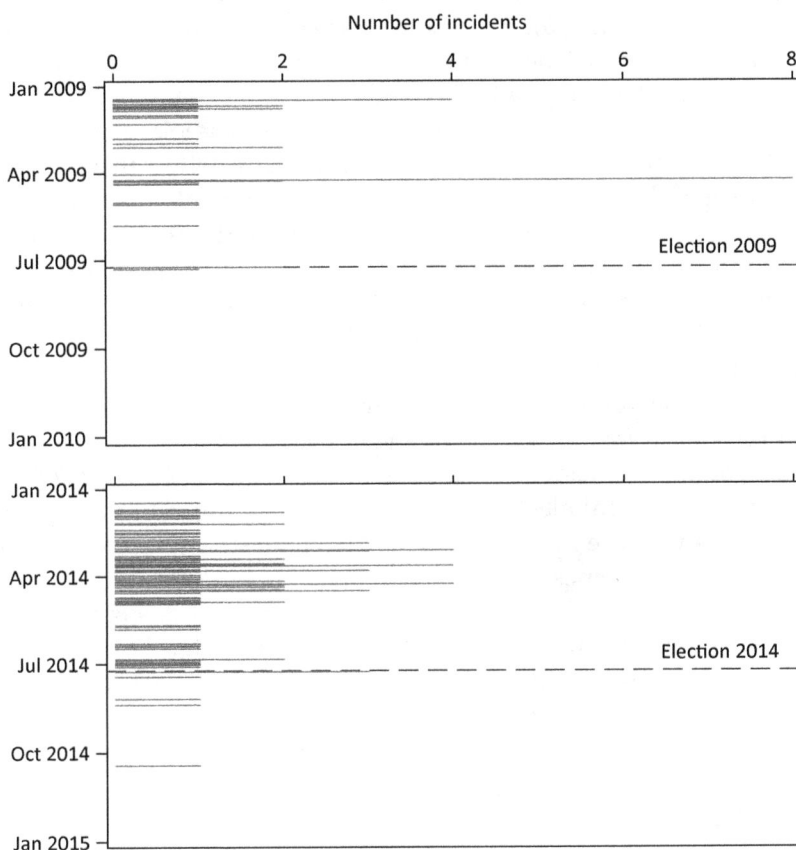

While the numbers remain small overall, we again find a rise of incidents of violence in this set of provinces. This is an important and worrying finding, since it suggests that despite the increasing age of Indonesia's democracy, electoral violence has become more common.

VIOLENCE AROUND LOCAL ELECTIONS

Almost 75 per cent of the incidents of election violence in the NVMS dataset were related to local elections. In an earlier study, Harish and Toha (2019) showed that more than 1,000 incidents of election violence occurred around *pilkada*. The violence around *pilkada* in our data was also relatively evenly distributed across the years 2004 to 2012, with each year having about 10–20 per cent of total incidents in the dataset. No single year stood out as particularly violent (Harish and Toha 2019). In other words, the rates of violence around *pilkada* in the 8 years from 2004 to 2012 remained relatively stable.

About 20 per cent of *pilkada* in our dataset had no violence recorded. Using the average levels of violence around *pilkada*, we show that districts and municipalities in Aceh, Maluku, Papua, Central Sulawesi and West Kalimantan witnessed much more violence around *pilkada* than other areas of Indonesia (Harish and Toha 2019). This finding on *pilkada*-specific violence is consistent with the ranking of districts with the highest counts of election violence that we discussed earlier.

In that study we found that, overwhelmingly, clashes that occurred around local elections in Indonesia happened just before the election or immediately afterwards (Harish and Toha 2019). While post-election violence did occur, incidents were considerably fewer. That most of the violence around local elections occurred in the run-up to voting day suggests that violence may be partially driven by strategic incentives to shape electoral outcomes.

This broad pattern of election violence around *pilkada* suggests that election violence remained relatively constant at a low level from 2005 to 2012, indicating that while violence has not debilitated local elections, it has not dissipated either. Even as Indonesia's democracy advanced in age, democratic reforms implemented thus far have not sufficiently addressed the deeper problems in local politics to prevent these limited but steady incidents of violence.

THE PICTURE SINCE 2014: MASS MOBILISATIONS AROUND ELECTIONS

Since full coverage of NVMS data ends in 2014, we turn to qualitative evidence to analyse more recent trends in electoral violence. Strikingly, the years since 2014 have seen multiple waves of mass rallies related to elections taking over the streets of major cities in Indonesia. While many of the rallies were relatively peaceful, some led to small clashes and skirmishes, and several resulted in widespread violence, injuries and fatalities. In the following paragraphs we discuss a few noteworthy examples, reflect on their implications for contemporary trends in election-related violence, and discuss their broader ramifications for the quality of Indonesia's democracy.

Some of the largest protests around elections in recent years were the Defence of Islam movement (Aksi Bela Islam) rallies against Basuki Tjahaja Purnama ('Ahok'), the former Christian Chinese governor of Jakarta, during his campaign for the Jakarta governor race in 2017. The circumstances that led to these protests are discussed in greater detail elsewhere in this volume. In Table 17.1 we list some examples of prominent mass mobilisations that have occurred since 2014.

As Table 17.1 indicates, waves of protests unfolded in the months between the circulation of Ahok's Al Maidah video on social media in September 2016 and Ahok's sentencing in May 2017. Protesters consistently demanded that Ahok be legally investigated, arrested and removed from his seat. Habib Rizieq Shihab, leader of the Islamic Defenders Front (Front Pembela Islam, FPI), who initiated the first of many protests, said: 'If Ahok is not arrested, we will [protest] again' (CNN Indonesia 2019). Mass mobilisations continued well into the 2019 election cycle. An incident of a burning of a Tauhid flag in Garut prompted many protesters to take to the streets, demanding that the perpetrators be punished and for President Joko Widodo to resign. In the second half of 2018, #2019GantiPresiden rallies appeared in numerous cities, demanding that the president be replaced. Mass rallies again descended onto the streets of Jakarta after the presidential election results in May 2019, this time with outbursts of violence.

Mass rallies around election issues have not only become more frequent in recent years, they have also adopted a religious framing that is very effective in mobilising turnout. With crowds as large as millions occupying prominent squares of Jakarta, the Aksi Bela Islam protesters dressed in white religious outfits, sported religious symbols, listened to sermons and prayed together (Fealy 2016). The protesters' justification for their demands was that Ahok offended Islam. The participants and coordinators of the protests identified themselves religiously: the FPI, the Forum of the Islamic Community (Forum Umat Islam, FUI), the National Movement to Guard the Fatwa of Ulama (Gerakan Nasional Pengawal Fatwa Ulama, GNPFU) and the Indonesian Council of Islamic Scholars (Majelis Ulama Indonesia, MUI). The MUI statement lent credibility to the protesters' demands (MUI 2016).

This religious framing was effective; protesters came out in thousands, some crowds amounting to millions. Many protest participants travelled from outside Jakarta, some as far afield as outside Java (Fealy 2016). The shift in popular opinion was reflected in the polls as well. Although he enjoyed high approval ratings (over 50 per cent) before the video went viral, by November 2016, Ahok's approval rating had dropped to less than 25 per cent (Setijadi 2017).

Table 17.1   Mass mobilisations during Jokowi's first presidential term

Date	Rally name	Size (estimated)	Location
4 November 2016	Aksi 411	150,000–250,000	Istana Merdeka
2 December 2016	Aksi 212	500,000–750,000, to 3 million	Monas, Bundaran HI, Tugu Tani
11 February 2017	Aksi 112	thousands	Masjid Istiqlal
21 February 2017	Aksi 212 – jilid 2	thousands	DPR-RI complex
31 March 2017	Aksi 313	thousands	Patung Kuda
5 May 2017	Aksi 55		
26 August 2018	#2019GantiPresiden	hundreds	Solo, Tangerang, Gorontalo, Banyuwangi, Pekanbaru, Surabaya
October 2018	Aksi Bela Tauhid		Garut
21–22 May 2019	May riots		Jakarta

Sources: BBC (2018), *Kumparan* (2017), *Republika* (2017), Tristiawati (2018).

While many of these recent rallies were peaceful, the government clearly recognised their mobilising capacity and risks for violent escalation, and adopted a more accommodative approach. As the 411 rally protesters demonstrated and insisted on an audience with the president at the palace in Jakarta, the president was out of the palace for a site visit at the airport and did not return to the palace until much later in the evening. Instead, representatives of the protesters met with Vice President Jusuf Kalla and several other government officials to deliver their demands. Disappointed by not receiving an audience with the president, protesters clashed with security officers, burning a mobile brigade (brimob) truck and a security barrier car (Amelia 2016). Shortly after midnight, the president gave a 5-minute televised press conference, promising Ahok's investigation.

Table 17.1   (continued)

Demands	State response
An audience with President Joko Widodo to demand investigation into Ahok's alleged blasphemy	Protesters met with Vice President Jusuf Kalla and Coordinating Minister for Political, Legal and Security Affairs Wiranto; protesters clashed with security personnel. President Joko Widodo's press conference stated there will be a 'rapid and transparent' legal investigation of Ahok's alleged blasphemy. Ahok was named 'suspect' on 15 November.
A joint prayer	President Joko Widodo attended the gathering and participated in the Friday prayer
A joint prayer, with Ahok's election rivals in attendance	
Removal of Ahok from his post as governor	Wiranto again met with representatives of the protesters
A fair sentence in Ahok's trial	7 May 2017: Ahok was found guilty and sentenced to 2 years' prison
Removal of Jokowi as president in the upcoming 2019 elections	Clashes between anti- and pro-Jokowi protesters; protests were banned; key figures detained and barred from attending protests
Justice for the Tauhid flag burning perpetrators; removal of Jokowi	Government-initiated dialogue between key Muslim leaders
Protest against election results	Riots police fired tear gas at protesters, arrests, hundreds injured and 10 people killed

Ahok was named suspect within 24 hours of the press conference. At the December 2016 protest, President Joko Widodo made a surprise appearance to attend the joint prayer with protesters. Although Ahok was poised to win the Jakarta governor race, the religious framing of the protests effectively shifted the central issue of the election away from his performance to his offence against Muslims (Power 2018), and put pressure on the government to accommodate protesters' demands.

Subsequent rallies followed the same formula of religious framing, large crowds and a threat of violence. In October 2018, a video showing the burning of a Tauhid flag associated with the banned transnational Islamist group Hizbut Tahrir Indonesia (HTI) went viral on social media. Within days, protesters took the streets to 'defend Tauhid' (Aksi Bela Tauhid) against the flag-burning incident, which they claimed was an 'act of defaming Islam' (Burhani 2018). Although the primary demand was for justice for the perpetrators, speakers in the rallies also demanded for Joko Widodo to be removed (BBC 2018). In much the same way the anti-Ahok 'defend Islam' rallies weakened Ahok in the Jakarta governor race, these mobilisations against the flag-burning incident in 2018 were directed towards weakening Jokowi in the 2019 presidential race. In response, Vice President Jusuf Kalla invited key representatives of Islamic mass organisations, and Wiranto met with representatives of the GNPFU MUI and 212 rally.

In the second half of 2018, the #2019GantiPresiden campaign emerged in various cities (for example, Solo, Surabaya, Pekanbaru, Tangerang) around Indonesia, explicitly demanding that Joko Widodo be removed. Initially started as a hashtag in a Twitter tweet by a Prosperous Justice Party (Partai Keadilan Sejahtera, PKS) politician, Mardani Ali Sera, the #2019GantiPresiden campaign gained momentum and prompted Jokowi's supporters to launch counter campaigns on social media (#2019TetapJokowi, #Jokowi2Periode, #DiaSibukKerja) and stage counter protests in cities around the country. In several cities, clashes unfolded. In Surabaya in August 2018, for example, Nahdlatul Ulama (NU) and Banser activists clashed with the #2019GantiPresiden protesters and conducted sweeping raids to ensure that the #2019GantiPresiden protesters would not wear their campaign T-shirts around town (*Merdeka* 2018). Following this clash in Surabaya, the authorities banned a subsequent #2019GantiPresiden protest in Pekanbaru and detained one of the campaign's key donors and leaders, Neno Warisman, for several hours and sent her back on the plane to Jakarta on grounds of fear of further violence (*Kompas* 2018).

The protests following the announcement of the 2019 presidential election results indicate that some political players in Indonesia perceive mass mobilisation and threats of violence as a powerful means to articulate their demands and pressure the government. Despite the early quick count results that established Joko Widodo as the winner of the 2019 presidential election, Prabowo Subianto's camp claimed that the election had suffered 'massive fraud' (Aditya and Salna 2019a). In the weeks leading up to the official election results announcements, prominent party politicians and supporters of Prabowo called on supporters to hold a 'people power' rally (Chan 2019). Representatives of the 212 movement claimed that the group would stage a protest in front of the General Elections Commission (Komisi Pemilihan Umum, KPU) headquarters in Jakarta on 22 May, the day scheduled for the announcement of the official election results (Anugerah 2019).

When the KPU announced on 21 May that Joko Widodo was the winner of the presidential election with more than 55 per cent of valid votes,

Prabowo rejected the official results. Within hours of the announcement, around one thousand Prabowo supporters gathered in front of the KPU headquarters. Although the protest was initially peaceful, as night fell, the police began firing tear gas, rubber bullets and water cannon at protesters who had hurled fireworks and rocks at the police and burned police vehicles. Three riots occurred in west and central Jakarta, prompting the authorities to shut down major roads and government buildings and block access to social media to prevent the spread of misinformation (Kapoor and Ardiansyah 2019). Forty thousand police and army personnel were deployed across the capital. Ten people died and more than 700 were wounded during the two-day riot. Jakarta governor Anies Baswedan reported that the majority of the wounded protesters were aged in their twenties.

National police spokesperson Muhammad Iqbal stated in a press conference that the riot 'is not a spontaneous incident, this is something by design. There are indications that the mobs are paid and bent on causing chaos' (Kapoor and Ardiansyah 2019). Police seized an ambulance bearing Prabowo's Gerindra party logo; the ambulance was carrying rocks, tools and envelopes stuffed with Rp 250,000 to 500,000 in cash, which the police believe was to be distributed to rioters (Human Rights Watch 2019). Beyond the hundreds of rioters that were detained, the police also arrested a former marine officer who had carried a sniper rifle with a silencer near the protest site and five of his accomplices, 31 terrorism suspects, and politicians who had posted false and incendiary posts on social media (Human Rights Watch 2019). The Constitutional Court hearing declared in June 2019 it had not found any evidence of fraud, as Prabowo had claimed in his petition. While disappointed, the losing candidate stated he respected the court's decision and urged his supporters to do the same (Aditya and Salna 2019b).

Finally, while not directly related to the elections, other sorts of political protests were remarkably violent in 2019. Protests against human rights abuses and discrimination in Papua led to 32 deaths in September. That same month, hundreds of thousands of students took to the streets in major cities around the country to protest the recently re-elected Jokowi government's passing of a controversial law that would weaken the Corruption Eradication Commission (Komisi Pemberantasan Korupsi, KPK). Clashes with police resulted in hundreds of injuries and five fatalities.

So, whereas elections violence before 2014 remained at a low level and focused around local issues related to specific *pilkada* races (Aspinall 2011), the Jokowi era has been marked by increasing mass mobilisations and elections-related violence, and more protests and violence in relation to general political grievances too. Many of these protests and clashes around elections have elevated the status and political utility of previously fringe groups such as FPI and other hardline Islamist groups, as coordinators, participants and narrative-framers of mass mobilisation around elections.

Mass protests around elections have unlocked a potent formula—religious framing, large crowds and a looming threat for violence—that effectively moved many voters and prompted government intervention. Although Ahok enjoyed high favourability ratings before his blasphemy scandal, he lost decisively after months of anti-Ahok rallies. The president conceded to protesters' requests for Ahok's legal investigation; members of the government met with protest leaders; the president attended the 212 rally in December 2019; and Ma'ruf Amin, who had issued the MUI statement against blasphemy, became the president's running mate in 2019. While protests and the politicisation of identity are nothing new in elections in Indonesia, the mobilisation of large rallies advocating grievances around Islam to shape electoral politics has become particularly pronounced in recent years.

Despite Indonesia's successful transition to a competitive electoral democracy, we suggest that trends in recent years highlight new democratic vulnerabilities: local races have become a source of information about future issues in national politics and raised the stakes of local competition; Islamist groups have become more salient political players and mobilisers; and the return of mass political rallies and street protests have led to more violent clashes between citizens, and between citizens and security apparatus.

CONCLUSION

This chapter set out to understand the patterns and dynamics of violence around elections in Indonesia. We used NVMS data that covers reported incidents of various kinds of communal violence in Indonesia from 2005 to 2014 to examine the patterns of election violence. We found that election violence makes up a very small fraction of the total communal violence in Indonesia. When election violence did occur, it generally incurred few deaths but many injuries. We also found that violence around local elections (*pilkada*) is concentrated in areas with high exposure to prior violence, such as Aceh, Maluku and North Maluku. Although the overall count of incidents and intensity of violence is low relative to that of other countries in Southeast Asia and other emerging democracies, across the period observed in this chapter we found that election violence has become more common.

As NVMS data stop in 2014, we supplemented our analysis with a discussion of cases of violence around elections since 2014. The Islamist rallies around Ahok's blasphemy case in the run-up to the 2017 Jakarta elections, the 'defend Tauhid' rallies in response to a Tauhid flag-burning incident in 2018, and the May 2019 riots following the presidential election results all suggest the increasing political importance of Islamist groups, mobilisation of large crowds, and the effectiveness of Islam-based grievances in mobilising voters and shaping electoral politics. Increasing polarisation between Islamist groups and pluralist constituencies produced a tense electoral atmosphere in 2019, and no doubt contributed to what were the most violent presidential elections in Indonesia's post-Suharto history.

What do these findings imply about the challenges of democracy in Indonesia? While more data and in-depth research are necessary, the broad patterns we have unearthed here suggest that for much of the past two decades, elections in Indonesia have functioned relatively well as a vehicle for citizens to work out their differences. Election violence has been infrequent, and when cases of violence did occur, there were generally few fatalities. Yet as Indonesia's democracy has consolidated, the number of violent incidents recorded at legislative and presidential elections has increased, and 2019 was a strikingly violent year in comparison to earlier elections. This uptick in violence has taken place against the backdrop of the increasing politicisation of identity and deepening polarisation, which have arguably raised the stakes of electoral competition and contributed to these violent outbreaks.

REFERENCES

Aditya, A. and K. Salna. 2019a. 'Indonesia says there was no fraud in presidential vote'. *Bloomberg*, 24 April. https://www.bloomberg.com/news/articles/2019-04-24/indonesia-says-no-fraud-in-presidential-vote-as-count-disputed

Aditya, A. and K. Salna. 2019b. 'Indonesia court rejects appeal against Jokowi's re-election'. *Bloomberg*, 27 June. https://www.bloomberg.com/news/articles/2019-06-26/indonesia-on-edge-as-court-set-to-rule-on-jokowi-s-re-election

Alsema, A. 2019. 'Five months ahead of Colombia's local elections, political violence already surpassed that of 2015 vote'. *Colombia Reports*, 9 May. https://colombiareports.com/five-months-ahead-of-colombias-local-elections-political-violence-already-surpassed-that-of-2015-vote/

Amelia, M. 2016. 'Kronologi demo 4 November: dari damai hingga berakhir ricuh'. *DetikNews*, 7 November. https://news.detik.com/berita/d-3339694/kronologi-demo-4-november-dari-damai-hingga-berakhir-ricuh

Anderson, B. 1990. 'Murder and progress in modern Siam'. *New Left Review* 181: 33–48.

Anugerah, P. 2019. 'Pengumuman hasil pilpres 22 Mei dibayangi rencana aksi massa dan ancaman serangan teror'. BBC, 20 May. https://www.bbc.com/indonesia/indonesia-48329778

Aspinall, E. 2011. 'Democratization and ethnic politics in Indonesia: nine theses'. *Journal of East Asian Studies* 11(2): 289–319.

Aspinall, E. 2018. 'Twenty years of Indonesian democracy—how many more?' *New Mandala*, 24 May. https://www.newmandala.org/20-years-reformasi/

Barron, P., S. Jaffrey and A. Varshney. 2016. 'When large conflicts subside: the ebbs and flows of violence in post-Suharto Indonesia'. *Journal of East Asian Studies* 16(2): 191–217.

BBC. 2018. 'Aksi "Bela Tauhid" di Jakarta dengan teriakan "ganti presiden" '. BBC, 26 October. https://www.bbc.com/indonesia/indonesia-45990053

BBC. 2019. 'Indonesia post-election protests leave six dead in Jakarta'. BBC, 22 May. https://www.bbc.com/news/world-asia-48361782

Beaulieu, E. 2014. *Electoral Protest and Democracy in the Developing World*. New York: Cambridge University Press.

Borzyskowski, I. and P.M. Kuhn. 2014. 'Dangerously informed: Protestant missions, information, and pre-electoral violence in sub-Saharan Africa'. Empirical Studies of Conflict Working Paper.

Brancati, D. and J. Snyder. 2011. 'Rushing to the polls: the causes of premature postconflict elections'. *Journal of Conflict Resolution* 55(3): 469–92.

Buehler, M. 2009. 'Suicide and progress in modern Nusantara'. *Inside Indonesia* 97(July–September): 1–8.

Burhani, N. 2018. 'Aksi Bela Tauhid: manufacturing religious cleavages for the 2019 presidential election?'. *Commentaries*, 8 November. ISEAS – Yusof Ishak Institute. https://www.iseas.edu.sg/medias/commentaries/item/8521-aksi-bela-tauhid-manufacturing-religious-cleavages-for-the-2019-presidential-election-by-ahmad-najib-burhani

Caliwan, C.L. 2019. 'Election-related violence down by 60%: PNP'. Philippine News Agency, 14 May. https://www.pna.gov.ph/articles/1069778

Cepeda, M. 2018. 'Who is Rodel Batocabe?'. *Rappler*, 22 December. https://www.rappler.com/nation/219476-rodel-batocabe-profile

Chan, F. 2019. 'Jakarta remains under heavy guard after May unrest'. *Straits Times*, 3 June. https://www.straitstimes.com/asia/se-asia/jakarta-remains-under-heavy-guard-after-may-unrest

CNN Indonesia. 2019. 'Ahok sang pemicu rentetan aksi bela Islam dan nama besar 212'. CNN Indonesia, 22 January. https://www.cnnindonesia.com/nasional/20190115135955-32-360979/ahok-sang-pemicu-rentetan-aksi-bela-islam-dan-nama-besar-212

Colombo, A., O. D'Aoust and O. Sterck. 2019. 'From rebellion to electoral violence: evidence from Burundi'. *Economic Development and Cultural Change* 67(2): 333–68.

Fealy, G. 2016. 'Bigger than Ahok: explaining the 2 December mass rally'. *Indonesia at Melbourne*, 7 December. https://indonesiaatmelbourne.unimelb.edu.au/bigger-than-ahok-explaining-jakartas-2-december-mass-rally/

Fjelde, H. and K. Höglund. 2016. 'Electoral institutions and electoral violence in sub-Saharan Africa'. *British Journal of Political Science* 46(2): 297–320.

Hadiz, V. 2017. 'Behind Indonesia's illiberal turn'. *New Mandala*, 20 October. https://www.newmandala.org/indonesia-illiberal/

Hafner-Burton, E., S. Hyde and R. Jablonski. 2014. 'When do governments resort to election violence?'. *British Journal of Political Science* 44(1): 149–79.

Halim, D. 2019. 'Polri: 9 korban meninggal dunia rusuh 21–22 Mei 2019 kami duga perusuh'. *Kompas*, 11 June. https://nasional.kompas.com/read/2019/06/11/20190081/polri-9-korban-meninggal-dunia-rusuh-21-22-mei-2019-kami-duga-perusuh

Harish, S.P. and R. Toha. 2019. 'A new typology of election violence: insights from Indonesia'. *Terrorism and Political Violence* 31(4): 687–711.

Human Rights Watch. 2019. 'Indonesia: set independent inquiry into Jakarta riots: 8 protesters fatally shot'. Human Rights Watch, 31 May. https://www.hrw.org/news/2019/05/31/indonesia-set-independent-inquiry-jakarta-riots

Kapoor, K. and T. Ardiansyah. 2019. 'Protesters, police clash in second night of post-election protests in Indonesia'. Reuters, 22 May. https://www.reuters.com/article/us-indonesia-election-casualties/protesters-police-clash-in-second-night-of-post-election-protests-in-indonesia-idUSKCN1SS0AS

Kompas. 2018. 'Menurut BIN, jika Neno Warisman tetap di Pekanbaru, kericuhan akan meluas'. *Kompas*, 27 August. https://nasional.kompas.com/read/2018/08/27/22130021/menurut-bin-jika-neno-warisman-tetap-di-pekanbaru-kericuhan-akan-meluas

Kumparan. 2017. 'Rangkuman aksi massa Islam, dari 1410 hingga 112'. *Kumparan*, 11 February. https://kumparan.com/@kumparannews/rangkuman-aksi-massa-islam-dari-1410-hingga-112-879590969

Lijphart, A. 1977. *Democracy in Plural Societies: A Comparative Exploration.* New Haven, CT: Yale University Press.

Lindsey, T. 2018. 'Is Indonesia retreating from democracy?'. *The Conversation*, 9 July. https://theconversation.com/is-indonesia-retreating-from-democracy-99211

Merdeka. 2018. 'Tolak dibubarkan, massa pro #2019GantiPresiden di Surabaya diusir Banser'. *Merdeka*, 26 August. https://www.merdeka.com/peristiwa/tolak-dibubarkan-massa-pro-2019gantipresiden-di-surabaya-diusir-banser.html

MUI (Majelis Ulama Indonesia). 2016. 'Pendapat dan sikap keagamaan MUI terhadap Ahok bukan fatwa, benarkah surat Al Maidah ayat 51 tentang pemilihan pemimpin?'. *Kompasiana*, 12 November. https://www.kompasiana.com/blackdiamond/5826d1a54423bd79346e4821/pendapat-dan-sikap-keagamaan-mui-terhadap-ahok-bukan-fatwa-benarkah-surat-al-maidah-ayat-51-tentang-pemilihan-pemimpin?page=all

NVMS (National Violence Monitoring System). 2014. 'NVMS expands its national coverage to cover all of Indonesia's 34 provinces'. NVMS, 17 December. http://snpk.kemenkopmk.go.id/About/Activity?lang=en&randdo=35b62408-8265-4978-b736-17f83db1135b&userid=13642505&id=6&page=1

Onubogu, O. and I. Hassan. 2018. 'The risk of election violence in Nigeria is not where you think'. United States Institute of Peace, 5 December. https://www.usip.org/publications/2018/12/risk-election-violence-nigeria-not-where-you-think

Patino, P. and D. Velasco. 2004. 'Election violence in the Philippines'. Friedrich Ebert Stiftung Philippine Office. https://library.fes.de/pdf-files/bueros/philippinen/50071.pdf

Power, T.P. 2018. 'Jokowi's authoritarian turn and Indonesia's democratic decline'. *Bulletin of Indonesian Economic Studies* 54(3): 307–38.

Prajak, K. 2016. 'Thailand's failed 2014 election: the anti-election movement, violence, and democratic breakdown'. *Journal of Contemporary Asia* 46(3): 467–85.

Reilly, B. 2002. 'Electoral systems in divided societies'. *Journal of Democracy* 13(2): 156–70.

Republika. 2017. 'Ini 7 rangkaian aksi bela Islam sebelum Ahok divonis 2 tahun penjara'. *Republika,* 10 May. https://nasional.republika.co.id/berita/opp5r4330/ini-7-rangkaian-aksi-bela-islam-sebelum-ahok-divonis-2-tahun-penjara-part2

Setijadi, C. 2017. 'The Jakarta election continues: what next for embattled governor Ahok?' *Perspective* No. 18, 21 March. Singapore: ISEAS – Yusof Ishak Institute.

Sisk, T. 2008. 'Elections in fragile states: between voice and violence'. Paper presented to the International Studies Association Annual Meeting, 24–28 March. San Francisco.

Straits Times. 2019. 'Indonesia police arrest "people power" rally instigator for alleged treason'. *Straits Times,* 15 May. https://www.straitstimes.com/asia/se-asia/indonesia-police-arrest-people-power-rally-instigator-for-alleged-treason

Trelles, A. and M. Carreras. 2012. 'Bullets and votes: violence and electoral participation in Mexico'. *Journal of Politics in Latin America* 4(2): 89–123.

Tristiawati, P. 2018. 'Ratusan warga aksi damai 2019 ganti presiden di Tangsel'. *Liputan6,* 23 September. https://www.liputan6.com/pilpres/read/3650403/ratusan-warga-aksi-damai-2019-ganti-presiden-di-tangsel

Warburton, E. and E. Aspinall. 2017. 'Indonesian democracy: from stagnation to regression?'. *The Strategist,* 17 August. Australian Strategic Policy Institute. https://www.aspistrategist.org.au/indonesian-democracy-stagnation-regression/

Wilkinson, S. 2004. *Votes and Violence: Electoral Competition and Ethnic Riots in India.* New York: Cambridge University Press.

Index

371

INDONESIA UPDATE SERIES

1989
Indonesia Assessment 1988 (Regional Development)
Edited by Hal Hill and Jamie Mackie

1990
Indonesia Assessment 1990 (Ownership)
Edited by Hal Hill and Terry Hull

1991
Indonesia Assessment 1991 (Education)
Edited by Hal Hill

1992
Indonesia Assessment 1992: Political Perspectives on the 1990s
Edited by Harold A. Crouch and Hal Hill

1993
Indonesia Assessment 1993: Labour: Sharing in the Benefits of Growth?
Edited by Chris Manning and Joan Hardjono

1994
Indonesia Assessment 1994: Finance as a Key Sector in Indonesia's Development
Edited by Ross McLeod

1996
Indonesia Assessment 1995: Development in Eastern Indonesia
Edited by Colin Barlow and Joan Hardjono

1997
Indonesia Assessment: Population and Human Resources
Edited by Gavin W. Jones and Terence H. Hull

1998
Indonesia's Technological Challenge
Edited by Hal Hill and Thee Kian Wie

1999
Post-Soeharto Indonesia: Renewal or Chaos?
Edited by Geoff Forrester

2000
Indonesia in Transition: Social Aspects of Reformasi and Crisis
Edited by Chris Manning and Peter van Diermen

2001
Indonesia Today: Challenges of History
Edited by Grayson J. Lloyd and Shannon L. Smith

2002
Women in Indonesia: Gender, Equity and Development
Edited by Kathryn Robinson and Sharon Bessell

2003
Local Power and Politics in Indonesia: Decentralisation and Democratisation
Edited by Edward Aspinall and Greg Fealy

2004
Business in Indonesia: New Challenges, Old Problems
Edited by M. Chatib Basri and Pierre van der Eng

2005
The Politics and Economics of Indonesia's Natural Resources
Edited by Budy P. Resosudarmo

2006
Different Societies, Shared Futures: Australia, Indonesia and the Region
Edited by John Monfries

2007
Indonesia: Democracy and the Promise of Good Governance
Edited by Ross H. McLeod and Andrew MacIntyre

2008
Expressing Islam: Religious Life and Politics in Indonesia
Edited by Greg Fealy and Sally White

2009
Indonesia beyond the Water's Edge: Managing an Archipelagic State
Edited by Robert Cribb and Michele Ford

2010
Problems of Democratisation in Indonesia: Elections, Institutions and Society
Edited by Edward Aspinall and Marcus Mietzner

2011
Employment, Living Standards and Poverty in Contemporary Indonesia
Edited by Chris Manning and Sudarno Sumarto

2012
Indonesia Rising: The Repositioning of Asia's Third Giant
Edited by Anthony Reid

2013
Education in Indonesia
Edited by Daniel Suryadarma and Gavin W. Jones

2014
Regional Dynamics in a Decentralized Indonesia
Edited by Hal Hill

2015
The Yudhoyono Presidency: Indonesia's Decade of Stability and Stagnation
Edited by Edward Aspinall, Marcus Mietzner and Dirk Tomsa

2016
Land and Development in Indonesia: Searching for the People's Sovereignty
Edited by John F. McCarthy and Kathryn Robinson